Law and Order in Virtual Worlds:
Exploring Avatars, Their Ownership and Rights

Angela Adrian
*Attorney at Law, Louisiana, USA &
Solicitor, England and Wales, UK*

 **INFORMATION SCIENCE REFERENCE**

Hershey · New York

Director of Editorial Content:	Kristin Klinger
Director of Book Publications:	Julia Mosemann
Acquisitions Editor:	Lindsay Johnston
Development Editor:	Christine Bufton
Publishing Assistant:	Myla Harty
Typesetter:	Brittany Metzel
Production Editor:	Jamie Snavely
Cover Design:	Lisa Tosheff
Printed at:	Yurchak Printing Inc.

Published in the United States of America by
Information Science Reference (an imprint of IGI Global)
701 E. Chocolate Avenue
Hershey PA 17033
Tel: 717-533-8845
Fax: 717-533-8661
E-mail: cust@igi-global.com
Web site: http://www.igi-global.com/reference

Library of Congress Cataloging-in-Publication Data

Adrian, Angela, 1968-
  Law and order in virtual worlds : exploring avatars, their ownership and
rights / By Angela Adrian.
       p. cm.
  Includes bibliographical references and index.
  Summary: "This book examines the legal realities which are emerging from
Massively Multiplayer Online Role-playing Games (MMORPGs) or virtual worlds
that demonstrate many of the traits we associate with the Earth world:
interpersonal relationships, economic transactions, and organic political
institutions"--Provided by publisher.
   ISBN 978-1-61520-795-4 (hardcover) -- ISBN 978-1-61520-796-1 (ebook) 1.
Shared virtual environments--Law and legislation. 2. Avatars (Computer
graphics)--Law and legislation. I. Title

K564.C6A75 2010
 343.09'944--dc22

2009041384

British Cataloguing in Publication Data
A Cataloguing in Publication record for this book is available from the British Library.

All work contributed to this book is new, previously-unpublished material. The views expressed in this book are those of the authors, but not necessarily of the publisher.

Table of Contents

Foreword

The world of tomorrow is virtual.

Cyberspace has many dimensions which cross the boundary between virtual and physical realities. Virtual worlds are rapidly emerging as an alternative means to the real world for communicating, collaborating, and organizing economic activity. In these three-dimensional worlds, individuals relate to one another through avatars, human-like digital depictions that represent real people in a simulated world. It is no longer designed as a fantasy world where inhabitants escape from the real world. Rather, the user is placed in a real social or business context, where people maintain their own identities, rather than assume new ones. In addition to setting online games and entertainment applications, virtual worlds offer a safe haven for those dealing with real-world problems. They have become an interface many companies use in various fields, including retail, client services, B2B and advertising – similar to the interface behind Google Earth that has been put to real world use. There is genuine content being generated in these virtual worlds, true interaction with actual business, life, creativity, social networking, etc. Virtual worlds are treated not as a game but as an extension of the real world. It is art imitating life.

Because virtual worlds replicate the real world, they raise new and compelling legal questions about such issues as owning virtual assets, intellectual property right infringements and liabilities. They reflect what is really going on in our own world.

Law and Order in Virtual Worlds is timely for several reasons. Whether we like it or not, virtual worlds have created a complex system of property management and serious, daunting legal challenges. The issues of rights and obligations that emanate out of the relationship between the owner and creator of a virtual world and its resident customers are growing in complexity. They pose increasingly serious challenges to our notions about the nature of property, the legal rights of players in virtual worlds and even the presumed boundary between the real and the imagined worlds: should laws from our "real" lives influence, or even be enforced in, virtual world?

This book aspires to provide understanding of the interface between the laws of the real world and the laws of the virtual worlds. The strength of this book is the depth and breadth of the information. It is a valuable guide to navigating the complex - but transcending - world where virtual laws meet real life laws.

Virtually Yours,

Sylvia Kierkegaard
President, International Association of IT Lawyers

Sylvia Mercado Kierkegaard *(AB Mass Comm, M. Eco, LLB,MSC,MA,LLM,PHD,PG Dip. Private Law; PG Dip.EU Law, DTheo) is a Professor of Law. She is currently Visiting Professor at several universities, including Southampton University and Renmin University. She is also an International Associate of i-Laws and a PHD Supervisor-Professor at the Communications University of China. Sylvia finished her education in the US, UK, the Netherlands, Denmark and the Philippines with distinction. She is the editor- in- chief of the International Journal of Private Law, the Journal of International Commercial Law and Technology, International Journal of Liability and Scientific Enquiry; managing editor of the Journal of Legal Technology Risk Management; associate editor of International Journal of Intercultural Information Management; Associate Editor of the International Journal of Innovation in the Digital Economy; and member of the editorial board of over 20 international journals. She is also the President of the International Association of IT Lawyers and member of the Scientific Board of the European Privacy Association and EICAR. Sylvia is the Conference Organiser and Chairman of the Legal, Security and Privacy Issues Conference (LSPI), International Business Law &Technology Conference (IBLT) and the International Law and Trade Conference (ILTC). She is also an expert for the EU (e-practice, e-content & Safer Internet, e-participation, e-government and the EU-China Info Society Project on Info Security) and a regulatory expert for the Council of Europe. She is the Principal Investigator for the co-Reach project, which will conduct a comparative analysis of the copyright law between China and selected EU member states. She has published over 2000 articles and books and has won 2 journalism awards. She is also advisor to several international associations, government bodies and companies. Her main area of expertise is cyberlaw, contract law and public administration law.*

Preface

This book examines the legal realities which are emerging from Massively Multiplayer Online Role-playing Games (MMORPGs) or virtual worlds. These virtual worlds demonstrate many of the traits we associate with the Earth world: interpersonal relationships, economic transactions, organic political institutions, and so on. These virtual worlds are continuing to evolve daily into virtual communities with separate rules and expectations. They operate under their own system of private laws which often deviate abruptly from those of the physical world. Because they exist only online, they seek to 'legally link' the online world and the physical world through the agreements that create private rules in the absence of effective jurisdiction by real world governments and the potential development of "self-regulatory structures on the net." Most citizens of these communities are unaware of these contractual restrictions until they unknowingly breach one of the provisions. As a general rule, courts are reluctant to intrude into the rules of a game, but they will do so if the court believes that it is necessary. Some scholars have called for separate treatment of virtual worlds because they believe that these worlds are separate and distinct from the real world and thus entitled to their own courts and laws. However, as individuals invest their time, personality, and finances into these environments, the legal rules that apply to all other aspects of their lives are sure to follow.

Virtual world designers have a duty to appreciate and comprehend the laws that apply to their creations. More importantly, the people who make and interpret laws, in turn, have a duty to recognize, or at the very least be aware of, virtual worlds. If they do not understand what they are regulating, how can they how to regulate it? This book aspires to provide understanding of the interface between the laws of the real world and the laws of the virtual worlds.

AIM

This book is designed for anyone who has ventured into a virtual reality space and wondered what the real world consequences were for their actions. There are many people whose children, spouses, friends, or acquaintances spend a phenomenal time in these worlds. Virtual worlds are more than just games. Some games are more than just a way to waste time. This book endeavours to explain this phenomenon and its potential legal consequences.

As such, chapter one will begin by looking at the three qualities of man as defined by Frederic Bastiat. In order to investigate this concept further, chapter two will provide a foundation regarding the nature of games and virtual worlds. An examination of what is real versus what is virtual will be made. Ideas regarding interactivity, physicality and persistence will be analysed. Chapter three will explain how one explores these virtual worlds through avatars. Concepts such as immersion and presence will clarify why these virtual worlds are so popular. Bastiat's second quality, personality, will be surveyed in chapter four via an examination of the personhood of avatars because identity is a key notion in virtual reality. It substantiates the notions of property, especially intellectual property. The first of Frederic Bastiat's qualities, property or in this case virtual property, will be delved into in chapter five including a study of the difference between crafting and creating.

These virtual spaces rely on a distinct culture of shared norms and common values. In virtual worlds, any division between "rights" and "property" is an artificial and false dichotomy. "Property" is information, and "power" is the ability to control information. Property rights are not absolute. Unlike physical property which can physically possessed, property rights in information are intangible. Numerous individuals can possess the same information. Once the secret is out, property interests in information can only be protected through statutory or contractual rights. Chapter six explores the more specific ideas of intellectual property rights, in particular copyright. A legal analysis will follow regarding the means of protecting authorship rights and other copyrights which are possibly generated by these virtual worlds.

Finally, Bastiat's third quality, liberty: some virtual world creators try to limit the liberties the players try to acquire. Others, on the other hand, have embraced the idea of granting intellectual property rights of all kind to their participants. To this end, end user license agreements will be thoroughly discussed. As many of these MMORPGs are based in the United States, the focus shall be on the laws of the United States with comparisons to other jurisdictions when helpful. Because virtual worlds are beginning to impinge upon the real world more and more, tort law and criminal law will be examined in relation to actions which cross over between the two. A conclusion suggesting an interface between the real and virtual shall be offered.

Angela Adrian, Bournemouth University, UK

Chapter 1
Why Virtual Worlds?

Innovation makes enemies of all who prospered under the old regime, and only lukewarm support is forthcoming from those who would prosper under the new. Their support is indifferent partly from fear and partly because they are genuinely incredulous, never really trusting new things unless they have tested them by experience. — Machiavelli

INTRODUCTION

The internet has produced an increasing number of shared virtual reality spaces, with a combined population well into the millions. The term "virtual reality (VR)" is used to describe an environment that is simulated by a computer. Most virtual reality environments use visual experiences predominantly which are displayed either on a computer screen or through special stereoscopic goggles. In addition, some simulations include additional sensory information, such as sound through speakers. The space allows users to manipulate the VR environ-ment, either through standard input devices like a keyboard, or through specially designed devices like a cyberglove. The simulated interactive environment may range from real world simulations (i.e., pilot or combat training) to purely imagined worlds of aliens or elves, as in VR games. In practice, the better the technology and processing power, the more convincing the virtual reality experience becomes. Immersive VR have developed a number of unique characteristics which can be summarized as follows:

- Head-referenced viewing provides a natural interface for the navigation in three-dimensional space and allows for look-around, walk-around, and fly-through capabilities in virtual environments.
- Stereoscopic viewing enhances the perception of depth and the sense of space.
- The virtual world is presented in full scale and relates properly to the human size.
- Realistic interactions with virtual objects via data glove and similar devices allow for manipulation, operation, and control of virtual worlds.

DOI: 10.4018/978-1-61520-795-4.ch001

- The convincing illusion of being fully immersed in an artificial world can be enhanced by auditory, haptic, and other non-visual technologies.
- Networked applications allow for shared virtual environments. (Beier)

This book will examine the legal realities which are emerging from Massively Multiplayer Online Role-Playing Games (MMORPGs). MMORPGs are any computer network-mediated games in which at least 1,000 players are role-playing simultaneously in a graphical environment. They are also known as virtual worlds. The term virtual reality was coined by Jaron Lanier in 1989. Lanier is one of the pioneers of the field, founding the company VPL Research (from Virtual Programming Languages) which built some of the first systems in the 1980s. The related term artificial reality has been in use since the 1970s and cyberspace dates to 1984.

These virtual worlds demonstrate many of the traits we associate with the Earth world: interpersonal relationships, economic transactions, organic political institutions, and so on. These virtual worlds are continuing to evolve daily into virtual communities with separate rules and expectations. They operate under their own system of private laws which often deviate abruptly from those of the physical world. Because they exist only online, they seek to 'legally link' the online world and the physical world through the agreements that create private rules in the absence of effective jurisdiction by real world governments and the potential development of "self-regulatory structures on the net" (Johnson & Post, 1996). Most citizens of these communities are unaware of these contractual restrictions until they unknowingly breach one of the provisions.

"[A] virtual world is a place you co-habit with hundreds of thousands of other people simultaneously. It's persistent in that the world exists independent of your presence, and in that your actions can permanently shape the world. The fact that you exist with other real people from around the globe adds a level of immersion that just has to be experienced to be believed" (*Ultima Online*). Welcome to a virtual paradise. A place where a blacksmith can live in the castle of his dreams, if he does not mind working eighty hours a week hoarding digital dung and double-clicking pig iron. The economy is distinguished by extreme inequality. Yet the life there is still very attractive to those who come to visit and then remain. The population swells every day with hundreds of immigrants from different places around the world, but especially the United States and China. There are an estimated 12.5 million people subscribing to 32 major virtual worlds (Woodcock, 2008).

An interesting thing about the new world is its location. For example, Norrath is the virtual world of *EverQuest* that exists entirely on forty computers in San Diego, California (Marks, 2003). Unlike many internet ventures, virtual worlds are making money - - with annual revenues expected to be US$7.3 billion by 2005 (Entertainment Software Association, Press Release, 2005). This translates to commerce within these worlds generating in excess of US$2 billion. The total value of transactions within one of the more popular worlds exceeds US$20 million in one month alone (Sipress, 2006).

Considering, if network effects are comparable with other internet innovations, then virtual worlds could become the centre point for most online activity. In 2001, the estimated gross national product of Norrath was equal to that of Bulgaria (Castronova, 2002). Since then, the value of virtual economies has continued to grow, with estimates claiming a $200 million market for virtual items (Leupold, 2005; Ondrejka, 2005). In fact, the information technology industry's largest group of professional research analysts, Gartner, Inc., has predicted that by 2011, 80% of active internet users will soon join the growing body of participants in virtual worlds.

This rapid increase in popularity and economic value has resulted in a conflict with respect to virtual world object ownership. As such, virtual world designers have a duty to appreciate and comprehend the laws that apply to their creations. More importantly, the people who make and interpret laws, in turn, have a duty to recognize, or at the very least be aware of, virtual worlds. If they do not understand what they are regulating, how can they know how to regulate it? This book aspires to provide understanding of the interface between the laws of the real world and the laws of the virtual worlds. First, the need for a right of personality will be argued. Second, the case for property rights will be made. Finally, this book will use the three qualities of man as defined by Frederic Bastiat to examine these propositions.

A. INTERFACE & FREDERIC BASTIAT

Existence, faculties, assimilation - in other words, personality, liberty, property - that is what man is. Of these three things one may say, without any demagogic quibbling, that they are anterior and superior to all human legislation. It is not because men have passed laws that personality, liberty, and property exist. On the contrary, it is because personality, liberty, and property already exist that men make laws. (Frederic Bastiat)

The French philosopher, Frederic Bastiat, succinctly summed up what defines a person: 'Existence, faculties and assimilation' or 'personality, liberty and property'. Avatars are the reflection of people in virtual worlds. People, now, can and do explore these concepts in greater detail via massively multi-player online role playing games via their avatars. As these spaces become increasingly lifelike, powerful and significant, they will come to be used for more than storytelling and entertainment. They will be used for research.

Hunter Hoffman in *Scientific American* (2004) described treatment advances in the use of virtual reality technology where patients gets relief from pain or overcome phobias through immersion in a virtual world. Education: The virtual world, *Second Life*, created by Linden Lab, reports that six university classes in disciplines ranging from urban planning to theatre use the gamespace to conduct class (Delwiche, 2004). At the end of the day, the people who gather in these virtual worlds want to participate in the building of a new world, not just shooting space invaders. These people do not act alone. They collaborate in this pursuit, and what they are pursuing is a civil society.

So although it would be easy to write off virtual worlds as sophisticated virtual reality systems or just games, the fact remains that these worlds are part of everyday life for many people globally. They are becoming important means of commerce and communications. Another emerging technology similar to virtual worlds is ubiquitous computing. It shares the same technological characteristics of virtual worlds such that it would make a displacement of property rights in real world objects possible in the same way that virtual world technology makes such a displacement possible for potential property rights in virtual world objects (Boone, 2008)

As a general rule, courts are reluctant to intrude into the rules of a game, but they will do so if the court believes that it is necessary (Chein, 2006). Some scholars have called for separate treatment of virtual worlds because they believe that these worlds are separate and distinct from the real world and thus entitled to their own courts and laws (Lastowka & Hunter, 2004). However, as individuals invest their time, personality, and finances into these environments, the legal rules that apply to all other aspects of their lives are sure to follow (Kennedy, 2009).

In order to investigate this concept further a foundation regarding the nature of games and virtual worlds will be explored including an examination of what is real versus what is virtual.

Ideas regarding interactivity, physicality and persistence will be analysed. The first of Frederic Bastiat's qualities, property or in this case virtual property, will be delved into including a study of the difference between crafting and creating. Bastiat's second quality, personality, will be surveyed via an examination of the personhood of avatars because identity is a key notion in virtual reality. It substantiates the notions of property, especially intellectual property.

These virtual spaces rely on a distinct culture of shared norms and common values (McMurdo, 1995). In virtual worlds, any division between "rights" and "property" is an artificial and false dichotomy. "Property" is information, and "power" is the ability to control information (Gibbons, 1997). Property rights are not absolute. Unlike physical property which can physically possessed, property rights in information are intangible. Numerous individuals can possess the same information. Economists describe this as 'public goods'. A "public good" is a good for which "it is possible at no cost for additional persons to enjoy the same unit" (Demsetz, 1970). Rivalrousness needs to be considered. Once the secret is out, property interests in information can only be protected through statutory or contractual rights. A legal analysis will follow regarding the means of protecting authorship rights and other copyrights which are possibly generated by these virtual worlds.

Finally, Bastiat's third quality, liberty; some virtual world creators try to limit the liberties the players try to acquire. Others, on the other hand, have embraced the idea of granting intellectual property rights of all kind to their participants. To this end, end user license agreements will be thoroughly discussed. As many of these MMORPGs are based in the United States, the focus shall be on the laws of the United States with comparisons to other jurisdictions when helpful. Because virtual worlds are beginning to impinge upon the real world more and more, tort law and criminal law will be examined in relation to actions which cross over between the two. A conclusion suggesting an interface between the real and virtual shall be offered. But first, a digression shall be taken into how virtual worlds came into being in the first place.

B. FROM GUTENBERG TO DIGITISATION

Imagine that you find yourself in the fifteenth century, when Johannes Gutenberg wanders into town with one of his first printing presses. He describes it in great, passionate detail and offers three options. First, purchase a book. Second, buy a printing press to make your own book. Third, buy shares in his company, Gutenberg Press. Considering what is now known and everything that can be reasonably traced to the invention of the printing press - immense changes in politics and religion, development of capitalism, universal literacy, and the creation of communities across geographic boundaries - what choice do you make? (Kennedy, 2001). Johannes then looked into the future with GutenbergPress.com and that future appears to be digital. Digital technologies have been producing the some of the greatest changes in the way information is distributed since Gutenberg first set up shop.

Nicholas Negroponte (1996) summed up the future nicely. "The information superhighway is about the global movement of weightless bits at the speed of light. As one industry after another looks at itself in the mirror and asks about its future in a digital world, that future is driven almost 100 percent by the ability of that company's product or services to be rendered in digital form." "The rise of an electronic medium that disregards geographical boundaries throws the law into disarray by creating entirely new phenomena that need to become the subject of clear legal rules but that cannot be governed, satisfactorily, by any current territorially based sovereign" (Johnson and Post, 1996). As is usual, technological innovation outpaces legal innovation. This advancement is taking place in two parallel ways. First is digitisation which is exploited further via the second advancement of the internet.

Digitisation is an enabling technology which breaks down complex information into a series of simple instructions which a microprocessor can understand. It is the translation of information (including text, speech, paintings, photographs, animation, film, video, music and other sounds) into a common 'language' consisting of simple binary codes which can be recorded, stored and manipulated by computers. The combination of these various elements is the essence of multimedia. Once digitised, such copyrightable creations as films, sound recordings, books, plays, and works of art can be stored, manipulated, and transferred swiftly to sites around the world. Digitisation of the familiar types of creative works is stretching the existing categories of copyright as multimedia becomes the norm for new creative works. The development of increasingly more technically sophisticated personal computers is facilitating the one-to-many broadcasting of electronic media to be united with the one-to-one interaction of the telephone. People are now beginning to be able to take part within many-to-many forms of cultural and social communications.

Most people know of the internet without being able to properly define it. Commentators generally agree that the internet can be described as an international public network of networks. "A network is a group of computers that are physically linked together and which run the same particular software that allows them to recognise that they are all part of the same group" (Terrett and Monaghan, 2000). The internet is a very large version of this. There are numerous services available on the internet. The one that concerns this book is The Web.

The Web can be depicted as a wide-area hypermedia information retrieval initiative aim-ing to give universal access to a large universe of documents. The hypermedia being created behaves like a database which may be retrieved on demand by individuals as well as a repository for users' own material. The development process begins with the creation of digital versions of pre-existing types of cultural expression, i.e., text, audio, visual, and graphics. Following this is the emergence of another type of hypermedia which leads to the invention of completely new cultural genres.

Hypermedia is the term used for the new cultural and social forms emerging from the convergence of the media, computing and tele-communications. This convergence is driven by the adoption of digital technologies across these three sectors. The word is a logical extension of the term hypertext, in which audio, video, plain text, and non-linear hyperlinks intertwine to create a generally non-linear medium of information. This contrasts with multimedia, which, although often capable of random access in terms of the physical medium, is essentially linear in nature. The World Wide Web is a classic example of hypermedia, whereas a movie on a DVD is an example of standard multimedia. Of course, the lines between the two can (and often do) blur depending on how a particular technological medium is implemented. In other words, it is a system of linking together hundreds of millions of electronic documents (web pages) on millions of computers (web sites) together across the internet, each of which are reachable via a unique but changeable name or Universal Resource Locator (URL). Information and business is now being conducted internationally in a digital format.

Massively Multiplayer Online Games (MMOGs) are the epitome of this. "MMOGs function as communication networks in at least three different ways:

- As one-to-many networks (developer to community). Virtual worlds, in other words, are created by a team of developers and include assumptions, values and beliefs in the structure, design, and art of the game.

- As many-to-many networks. Virtual worlds are networked communication systems, which allow for interactive chat, internal email, and private and public messaging. Communication can occur among and between any of the online participants in a multitude of configurations.

- As one-to-many networks (player to community). Virtual worlds also offer individual players increasing access to a new form of 'broadcast' from things as basic as avatar appearance and selection to the ability to create and display objects or messages in public forums or virtual space. Digital technologies are producing huge changes in the way information is distributed" (Fouts, 2005).

C. CYBERSPACE: FROM FICTION TO REALITY

William Gibson's novel *Neuromancer* (1984) gave us the term 'cyberspace'. William S. Byassee (1995) summarized the term cyberspace as: "In Gibson's vision, cyberspace is a 'consensual hallucination that felt and looked like a physical space but actually was a computer-generated construct representing abstract data.' As commonly used today, cyberspace is the conceptual 'location' of the electronic interactivity available using one's computer. Cyberspace is a place 'without physical walls or even physical dimensions' in which interaction occurs as if it happened in the real world and in real time, but constitutes only a 'virtual reality'. Cyberspace is the manifestation of the words, human relationships, data wealth, and power. ... by people using [computer-mediated communications]" (Byassee, 1995).

This fantasy of 'meatless' subjects incorporated into a computer resonates with the hopes and anxieties stemming from the internet as a new medium shaping the public sphere. Gibson, however, did not have the internet in mind when he coined the term cyberspace. He found his inspiration in video games:

[In arcades] I could see in the physical intensity of their postures how rapt these kids were. It was like one of those closed systems out of a Pynchon novel: you had this feedback loop, with photons coming off the screen into the kids' eyes, the neurons moving through their bodies, electrons moving through the computer. And these kids clearly believed in the space these games projected. Everyone who works with computers seems to develop an intuitive faith that there's some kind of actual space behind the screen (Turkle, 1995).

Gibson sees the player as already being subsumed by computer, already as a cyborg, a hybrid of machine and organism, a creature of social reality as well as a creature of fiction. Video games epitomize a new cyborgian relationship with entertainment technologies, linking our everyday social space and computer technologies to virtual spaces and futuristic technologies (Lahti, 2003). They "represent the most complete symbiosis generally available between human and computer – a fusion of spaces, goals, options, and perspectives." (Bukatman, 1993). Others claim that humans will functionally fuse with technology but will never fully merge with them. In other words, we will never be cyborgs, half humans-half machines, but rather fryborgs, that is, functionally using technology even if it is within the body without losing our physical boundaries; this is the kind of world we already live in where we rely on tools, devices, and gadgets to orient ourselves (Stock, 2002).

Already many current computing devices have had this effect. The most ubiquitous device is the mobile phone and the characteristics of the services associated with it (Giradin & Nova, 2006). This ubiquitous computing has been described as the "colonization of everyday life" (Greenfield, 2006) by computers and information technology. In a ubiquitous computing premise, computing functionality is embedded and mobile in an environment of universal connectivity that produces a high level of automation.

An illustration of this comes from another author, Philip K. Dick (1969). The following conversation takes place between the protagonist and his front door in the short story, *Ubik*:

The door refused to open. It said, "Five cents, please."

He searched his pockets. No more coins; nothing. "I'll pay you tomorrow," he told the door. Again he tried the knob. Again it remained locked tight. "What I pay you," he informed it, "is in the nature of a gratuity; I don't have to pay you."

"I think otherwise," the door said. "Look in the purchase contract you signed when you bought this [condominium]."

In his desk drawer, he found the contract. ... . Sure enough; payment to his door for opening and shutting constituted a mandatory fee. Not a tip.

"You discover I'm right," the door said. It sounded smug.

From the drawer beside the sink [he] got a stainless steel knife; with it he began systematically to unscrew the bolt assembly of his [condominium's] money gulping door.

"I'll sue you," the door said as the first screw fell out.

[He] said, "I've never been sued by a door before. But I guess I can live through it." (Id.).

Ubiquitous computing and virtual worlds both involve the application of computing technology to environments, whether physical or virtual. Because the characteristics of both environments flow from their computer-mediated nature, a ubiquitous computing world can serve as useful source of information about virtual worlds.

D. ONCE UPON A TIME...

A John Dugger, 43 year-old Wonder Bread delivery man, logged on to eBay and bought himself a large beautiful house. This three storied home had nine rooms, a rooftop patio, and walls of solid stonework. Mr. Dugger's modest redbrick ranch house in Stillwater, Oklahoma could not compare. His new home had an excellent location, situated at the foot of a quiet coastal hill. The house was a pleasant walk from a quaint seaside village and a short commute from two lively cosmopolitan cities. His new home was perfect, except for one small detail. The house was imaginary, as were its grounds and gardens, the ocean view, the neighbouring cities, and just about everything else associated with it. Only Dugger himself, the man he bought it from, and the money he paid were real. Dugger's winning bid of $750 for this property set him back more than a week's wages. This may seem an incredible amount of money for what he actually purchased: one very small piece of Britannia, the fantasy world in which the networked role-playing game *Ultima Online* unfolds (Dibbell, 2003).

This traffic in virtual goods has been perceived by economists to be not merely a new market, but a whole new species of economy (Castronova, 2002). Virtual worlds use electronically-simulated physical context as means of conveying large amounts of information quickly to computer users. Humans do not process things in lists, but via context. For example, if you are shopping for a sofa on the internet, you cannot know whether it will fit your living room or whether it will match your other furniture. If you were shopping for a sofa through the medium of a virtual world, you could arrange the furniture in a virtual simulacrum of your home, before buying it. Ikea offers a basic version of this service, but only for its products and not for different manufacturers.

The world's economy has moved from the tangible to the intangible. Industry gave way to services which in turn has yielded to post-industry. The selling of actual products has progressed to the selling of the brand of those products. Gold bricks in steel vaults have evolved into financial derivatives half a dozen levels of abstraction removed from physical reality. Knowledge is the key to any successful business. Knowledge content is becoming more important even in traditional agricultural or industrial products. Farmers today know how to produce five times more corn per acre than they could in 1920. Four-fifths of the costs spent on manufacturing a pair of Levi jeans goes to information and marketing i.e., the branding, not to actual production (Stewart, 1997). This is developing into products that in essence are pure knowledge, without any physical shape, or at least without any significant shape. The intention was to develop a so-called virtual economy - a realm of atomless digital products traded by cyborgian consumers in frictionless digital environments for paperless digital cash (Negroponte, 1996). Perhaps it has. However, did anyone guess that this would so literally consist of the buying and selling of castles in the air?

Now that a background to this phenomenon has been provided, the next chapter explores how and why these virtual universes are so engaging and so important. How did the unreal become as significant as the real? The ideas of interactivity, physicality and persistence will be explained in relation to MMORPGs. An in-depth review of what defines a virtual world will be made with an emphasis as to its rivalrous or non-rivalrous nature. After all, is it not all just a game?

REFERENCES

Bastiat, F. (1993). *The Law* (Russell, D., Trans.). New York: The Foundation for Economic Education.

Beier, K. P. (n.d.). *Virtual Reality: A Short Introduction*. Retrieved from http://www-vrl.umich.edu/intro/index.html.

Boone, M.S. (2008). *Ubiquitous Computing, Virtual Worlds, and the Displacement of Property Rights*. 4 I/S: J. L., & Pol'y for Info. Soc'y 91.

Bukatman, S. (1993). *Terminal Identity: The Virtual Subject in Post-Modern Science Fiction*. Durham, NC: Duke University Press.

Byassee, W.S. (1995). *Jurisdiction of Cyberspace: Applying Real World Precedent to the Virtual Community*. 30 Wake Forest L. Rev. 197.

Castronova, E. (2002). *On Virtual Economies*. The Gruter Institute of Working Papers on Law, CESifo Working Paper No. 752.

Chein, A. (2006) *A Practical Look at Virtual Property*. 80 St. John's L. Rev. 1059.

Delwiche, A. (2004). *Massively Multiplayer Online Games in the College Classroom*, N.Y. L. Sch. L. Rev. (online publication) at http://www.nyls.edu/lawreview

Demsetz, H. (1970). *The Private Production of Public Goods*. 13 J.L., &. De Economía, 293.

Dibbell, J. (2003). *The Unreal Estate Boom: 79th Richest Nation on Earth Doesn't Exist*. Wired Magazine.

Dick, P. (1969). *Ubik*.

Entertainment Software Association Press Release. (2005, January 26). *Computer and Video Game Software Sales Reach Record $7.3 Billion in2004*. Retrieved from http://wwwtheesa.com/archives/2005/02/computer_and _vi.php

Fouts, J. (2005, June). *Internationalism: Worlds at Play.* Paper presented at the International DiGRA Conference, Vancouver, British Columbia, Canada.

Gartner, Inc. (2007). *Gartner Says 80% of Active Internet Users will have a Second Life in the Virtual World by the End of 2011.* Gartner Symposium/ITXpo. Retrieved from http://www.gartner.com/it/page.jsp?id=503861

Gibbons, L.J. (1997). *No Regulation, Government Regulation, or Self-Regulation: Social Enforcement or Social Contracting for Governance in Cyberspace.* 6 Cornell J.L., & Pub. Pol'y 475.

Gibson, W. (1984). *Neuromancer.* London: HaperCollins Publishers.

Giradin, F., & Nova, N. (2006). Getting Real with Ubiquitous Computing: The Impact of Discrepancies on Collaboration. *eMinds: Int'l J. on Human-Computer Interaction, 60.*

Greenfield, A. (2006). *Everyware: The Dawn of Ubiquitous Computing.*

Hoffman, H. (2004). Virtual Reality Therapy. *Scientific American, 291,* 58–65.doi:10.1038/scientificamerican0804-58

Johnson, D.R., & Post, D. (1996). *Law and Borders – The Rise of Law in Cyberspace.* 48 Stan L. Rev. 1367.

Kennedy, D. (2001). *Key Legal Concerns in E-commerce: The Law comes to the New Frontier.* 18 T.M. Cooley L. Rev. 17.

Kennedy, R. (2009). *Law in Virtual Worlds.* 12 No. 10 J. *Internet, L,* 2.

Lahti, M. (2003). As We Become Machines – Corporealized Pleasures in Video Games. In Wolf, M. J. P., & Perron, B. (Eds.), *The Video Game Theory Reader.* London: Routledge.

Lastowka, G., & Hunter, D. (2004). *The Laws of the Virtual World.* 92 Calif. L. Rev. 1.

Leupold, T. (2005, May 6). Virtual Economies Break Out of Cyberspace. *Gamespot.* Retrieved from http://www.gamespot.com/news/2005/05/06/news_6123701.html

Machiavelli, N. (1992). *The Prince* (2nd ed.). London: W.W. Norton.

Marks, R. B. (2003). *EverQuest Companion: The Inside Lore of a Gameworld.* Berkeley, CA: New Riders Publishing.

McMurdo, G. (1995). *Netiquette for Networkers.* 21 J. Info. Science 305.

Negroponte, N. (1996). *Being Digital.* London: Hodder and Stoughton.

Ondrejka, C. (2005, May 7). A $200 Million Market? *Terra Nova.* Retrieved from http://terranova.blogs.com/terra_nova/2005/05/a_200m_market.html

Sipress, A. (2006, December 26). Where Real Money Meets Virtual Reality, the Jury is Still Out. *The Washington Post.* Retrieved from http://www.washingtonpost.com/wp-dyn/content/article/2006/23/25/AR2006122500635.html

Stewart, T. A. (1997). *Intellectual Capital: The New Wealth of Organizations.* New York: Currency.

Stock, G. (2002). *Redesigning Humans: Our Inevitable Genetic Future.*

Terrett, A., & Monaghan, I. (2000). The Internet – An Introduction for Lawyers. In Edwards, L., & Waelde, C. (Eds.), *Law & the Internet: a framework for electronic commerce.* Oxford, UK: Hart Publishing.

Turkle, S. (1995). *Life on the Screen: Identity in the Age of the Internet.* New York: Simon & Schuster.

Ultima Online Visitor's Center. *What is a Virtual World?* (n.d.). Retrieved from http://www.uo.com/visitor/whatisvw.html

Woodcock, B. S. (2008). *An Analysis of MMOG Subscription Growth.* Retrieved from http://www.mmogchart/com

Chapter 2
It is Only a Game

"The human imagination is an amazing thing. As children, we spend much of our time in imaginary worlds, substituting toys and make-believe for the real surroundings that we are just beginning to explore and understand. As we play, we learn. And as we grow, our play gets more complicated. We add rules and goals. The result is something we call games.

Games cultivate – and exploit – possibility space better than any other medium. In linear storytelling, we can only imagine the possibility space that surrounds the narrative: What if Luke had joined the Dark Side? What if Neo isn't the One? In interactive media, we can explore it." (Wright, 2006)

"We live in a complex world, filled with myriad objects, tools, toys, and people. Our lives are spent in diverse interaction with this environment. Yet, for the most part, our computing takes place sitting in front of, and staring at, a single glowing screen attached to an array of buttons and a mouse. Our different tasks are assigned to homogeneous

overlapping windows. From the isolation of our workstations we try to interact with our surrounding environment, but the two worlds have little in common. How can we escape from the computer screen and bring these two worlds together?" (Wellner, Mackay & Gold, 1993)

INTRODUCTION

Ubiquitous computing foresees computers that are embedded throughout the physical environment, that can communicate with each other, and that can monitor their surroundings and respond in dynamic, "intelligent" ways. (Boone, 2008) The power of computing will be utilized beyond the traditional box and be applied to almost every aspect of our lives. While this may seem a distant proposition, a different type of technology-produced world is already here: the virtual world.

In many ways, ubiquitous computing is viewed as the opposite of virtual reality. The earliest writings on ubiquitous computing recognized this fundamental difference. "Perhaps most diametrically opposed to our vision [of ubiquitous computing]

DOI: 10.4018/978-1-61520-795-4.ch002

is the notion of 'virtual reality,' which attempts to make a world inside the computer . . . . Virtual reality focuses an enormous apparatus on simulating the world rather than on invisibly enhancing the one that already exists. Indeed, the opposition between the notion of virtual reality and ubiquitous, invisible computing is so strong that some of us use the term 'embodied virtuality' to refer to the process of drawing computers out of their electronic shells." (Weiser, 1991) Yet, the two share an important common trait: both are mediated by computing ability.

The previous chapter introduced "MMORPGs" which are also sometimes referred to as game worlds or virtual worlds. Some of the most popular American MMORPGs are World of Warcraft, Everquest, Ultima Online, Dark Age of Camelot, Star Wars Galaxies, and City of Heroes. Legend of Mir, Final Fantasy XI, Lineage II, MU Online, Ragnarok Online, Lineage, and Kingdom of the Winds are some popular Asian MMORPGs. Dubit, Runescape, Playdo, and Habbo Hotel are popular in Europe. (Terra Nova, 2008)

Another type of popular virtual world is the social virtual world, also sometimes referred to as "unstructured." Some popular social virtual worlds are Second Life, Sims Online, Project Entropia, and There. (Virtual Worlds Review, 2008) Categorization as "social" does not fully comprehend these virtual worlds. Each world relies to an extent on user-created content. For example, Second Life started as a largely blank slate with most in-world objects being designed and created in-world by individual players. (Second Life, Create Anything, 2008) Social worlds can also have some game-like incentive aspects. The entire concept embodies far more than traditional video games.

A. WHAT IS A GAME?

Frasca (2001) defines a videogame as "any forms of computer-based entertainment software, either textual or image-based, using any electronic platform such as personal computers or consoles and involving one or multiple players in a physical or networked environment." They tend to have the elements shown in Table 1.

Following Caillois (2001) videogames offer combinations of chance, competition, role-play and kinaesthetic pleases. They can offer both paidea and ludus rules thereby allowing players to engage in goal-oriented or 'free play' activity. In this manner, videogames are not to be viewed as restrictive rule systems. Recognition must be given to the necessity of exploration and deduction as well as the player's ability to ignore or even subvert a designer's intention. A player can develop tactics and strategy, perhaps exploiting weaknesses or flaws in the game, or they may even define their own games within the world made available, thus imposing their own ludus rules. Furthermore, the definition of a video games employed here recognises that certain games – or certain sequences or modes within games – are designed as non-goal-oriented 'playgrounds'. (Newman, 2004)

In a best games review for gaming platforms, Berens and Howard (2001) demonstrate the relevance of industry-derived genres, as 'they are useful pointers and reflect the industry's current view of how they operate.' Integrating some similar categories, they present seven game types: (1) action and adventure, (2) driving and racing, (3) first-person shooter, (4) platform and puzzle, (5) role-playing, (6) strategy and simulation, and (7) sports and beat-'em ups. (Id.)

On the other hand, what is not a videogame? Rollings and Morris (2000) state "a game is not: a bunch of cool features, a lot of fancy graphics, a series of challenging puzzles, nor an intriguing setting and story." They do not preclude these characteristics; rather these qualities do not, in themselves, make a videogame nor help to describe the uniqueness of the form.

So, what do players want in a videogame? Rouse (2001) identifies a range of player moti-

Table 1. (source: adapted from Howland 1998)

Graphics	Any images that are displayed and any effects performed on them. This includes 3D objects, 2D tiles, 2D full-screen shots, full motion video (FMV), statistics, informational overlays and anything else the player will see.
Sound	Any music or sound effects that are played during the game. This includes starting music, CD music, MIDI, MOD tracks, Foley effects, environmental sound.
Interface	The interface is anything that the player has to use or have direct contact with in order to play the game... it goes beyond simply the mouse/keyboard/joystick [and] includes graphics that the player must click on, menu systems such as how to steer or control pieces in the game.
Gameplay	Gameplay is a fuzzy term. It encompasses how much fun a fame is, how immersive it is and the length of playability.
Story	The game's story includes any background before the game starts, all information the player gains during the story or when they win and any information they learn about characters in the game.

vations and expectations. Among them, three are most important: (1) challenge, (2) immersion, and (3) players expect to do, not to watch. Livingstone (2002) found similar expectations. "In interviews with children regarding their experience of screen entertainment culture, what is most notable when children talk about computer games, the words that appear over and over are 'control', 'challenge', and 'freedom'." All of these point to the importance of player activity. A videogame must provide novel or exciting situations to experience, stimulating puzzles to engage with, and interesting environments to explore. Moreover, it must offer the player not merely suitable or appropriate capabilities, but capabilities that can be earned, honed, and perfected. (Sherry, 2001) Virtual worlds foster the sense of first-hand participation in a game world generated by the computer and as such can be understood as a form of 'embodied experience'. (Newman, 2002)

B. THE REAL AND THE VIRTUAL

Virtual worlds are just that, virtual. They are not real, but rather unreal. Unreal means artificial, fictitious, imaginary, intangible, and invented. (Ryan, 1999) However, to say that virtual worlds are purely unreal is not quite accurate. They are also real in the sense that all things that are artificial or invented do not fall entirely outside reality. If they did, many actions and creations of mankind

would need to be removed from reality such as economics, language, and most importantly, laws. "[It may seem that] socio-political reality is not that different, finally, from the virtual kind, and that a human being never inhabits a physical landscape without also inhabiting its ghostly, abstract counterpart - the geography of language, law, and fantasy we overlay, collectively, on everything we look at." (Dibbell, 1998) Laws are 'invented' and 'intangible', but hardly insignificant. "Law creates truth - it makes things true as a matter of law. It makes things true in the eyes of the law. And when law makes things true in its own eyes, this has important consequences in the world." (Balkin, 2003) Laws regulate action within a social system. (Lastowka and Hunter, 2004)

Our culture is awash in such unreal realities, which take the form of deceptions, myths, fantasies, neuroses, and daydreams. Indeed, mythologies and shared illusions may provide an important basis for cultural cohesion. For example, in the classic Hans Christian Andersen story, "The Emperor's New Suit", an innocent child ultimately reveals that the Emperor's new suit, which no one has ever seen, does not exist. The greater moral of the story, however, and the reason for its popularity, is that it is common to encounter social conventions which require participants to embrace a shared illusion. This story, and the stories in other cultures that resemble it, merely highlight extreme examples of this phenomenon. (Andersen, 1984) There are many senses of the words 'real' and 'unreal.' Ontologically speaking, virtual worlds have much in common with Disneyland. (Dibbell, 1998) Mark Poster (1999) notes, post-modern cynics like Jean Baudrillard have gone so far as to claim that Disneyland is reality, and America is the simulation. Tomorrowland, Fantasyland, and Main Street are physically real, but that physical reality is largely a faux representation of (unreal) environments from science fiction, fantasy, and American history - the real and the represented are blended together. (Doctorow, 2006) Common cultural spaces like cinemas share a similar status. They provide a setting where we may be scared, saddened, and frustrated by things that are significantly unreal. In fact, video games (especial MMORPGs) have been called a 'new frontier of cinema'. (Wolf and Perron, 2003, citing, Le Diberder, 1996)

Christian Metz (1982), writing of the psychodynamic effects at work in cinema reception, observes that film is like the 'primordial mirror' – the original instance in which subjects are constituted through identification with their own image – in every way but one. Although on the cinema screen "everything may come to be projected, there is one thing and one thing only that is never reflected in it: the spectator's own body." This will be discussed later in greater detail with regard to copyrights and the concept that interpretation is an act of creation. A theory put forward by Pierre Bourdieu which complements the theories of immediacy, immersion and presence also discussed later. The process of identification is clearly involved in film viewing, and yet the cinema screen fails to offer the spectator its own body with which to identify as an object. For example, in *Last Action Hero:* "Young Danny Madigan is a big fan of Jack Slater, a larger-than-life action hero played by Arnold Schwarzenegger. When his best friend, Nick the projectionist, gives him a magic ticket to the new Jack Slater film, Danny is transported into Slater's world, where the good guys always win. One of Slater's enemies, Benedict the hit man, gets hold of the ticket and ends up in Danny's world, where he realizes that if he can kill Schwarzenegger, Slater will be no more. Slater and Danny must travel back and stop him." (http://www.imdb.com/title/tt0107362/plotsummary). What seems a silly plot for a movie is actually what game player seeks when they play MMORPGs.

Metz (1982) is forced to distinguish between primary (ongoing) and secondary (intermittent) identifications with the camera that records a given scene and the human actors that appear within the field of vision. But the application of psychoanalytical theory to technological mediations of identity is both simplified and complicated when it comes to figures that appear on screen as direct extensions of the spectator: sites of continuous identification within a diegesis. *Diegesis*, from the Greek term for 'recounted story', is conventionally employed in film theory to refer to the 'total world of the story action.' (Bordwell and Thompson, 2001). It is used here to designate the narrative-strategic space of any given video game – a virtual environment determined by unique rules, limits, goals, and 'history', and additionally designed for the staging and display of agency and identity. The video game avatar, presented as a human's double, merges spectatorship and participation in ways that fundamentally transform both activities. (Rehak, 2003)

Virtual worlds have not always been necessary to create these shared illusions. Game-playing allows many to share an illusion and have been around for a long time. Elements of play have been intrinsic to interactive impromptu dramas long before the advent of modern war games. Children's games, such as 'playing house' or 'Cowboys and Indians,' are the quintessence of very simple role-playing games. These games are a type of scenario where players take on the roles and personas of fictional characters via role-playing.

Essentially, these games are a form of interactive and collaborative storytelling. While novels, television shows, and cinema, are passive, role-playing games actively engage the participants. This allows them to be simultaneously the audience, an actor, and an author. A classic example of this would be in a thriller when an unlucky character ventures alone down the wrong alleyway. The audience experiences dramatic irony and says "Don't go down there!" because they know the serial killer is patiently waiting for his next victim. This is called Reader-Response Theory. It was developed as a response to the New Criticism idea of the autonomy of text. (Iser, 1978; Iser, 1989; Todorov, 1980) Two strands of reader-response theory take a different approach to the question of reader authorship. Closer to the argument here, Wolfgang Iser (1978) sees readers as co- creators. Georges Poulet (1980), on the other hand, suggests a greater distance between reader and text. He sees the interaction as largely one of two consciousnesses. Further, David Bleich (1978) argues that the first step in reader-response is fictionalization, the making of an aesthetic object no longer real. This response theory has also been applied to images such as art. (Freedberg, 1989) In a role-playing game, the player may experience a sixth sense which tells him to choose an alternative route. (Pagliassotti)

In many role-playing games, players take the roles of characters in an imaginary world that is organized, adjudicated, and sometimes created by a game master. Each gaming system has its own name for the role of the game master, such as 'judge', 'narrator', 'referee' or 'storyteller', and these terms not only describe the role of the game master in general but also help define how the game is intended to be run. For example, the Storyteller System used in White Wolf Game Studio's storytelling games calls its GM the 'storyteller', while the rules- and setting-focused Marvel Super Heroes Role-Playing Game calls its GM the 'judge'. A few games apply system- or setting-specific flavourful names to the GM, such as the 'Dungeon Master' (or 'DM') in Dungeons & Dragons. The games master's role is twofold.

First, he provides an imaginary world with a cast of characters for the players to interact with (and adjudicates how these interactions proceed). Second, he is likely to be responsible for advancing some kind of storyline or plot, albeit one which is subject to the somewhat unpredictable behaviour of the players. (Pagliassotti)

The collaborative feature of role-playing games comes in two forms. The first feature is very different to other games such as most sports, board games and card games which place players in opposition, with the goal of coming out the winner. In role-playing games, the players are generally not competing against each other. It is not a zero-sum game. "Zero-sum describes a situation in which a participant's gain (or loss) is exactly balanced by the losses (or gains) of the other participant(s). It is so named because when you add up the total gains of the participants and subtract the total losses then they will sum to zero. Cutting a cake is zero-sum because taking a larger piece for yourself reduces the amount of cake available for others. Situations where participants can all gain or suffer together, such as a country with an excess of bananas trading with an other country for their excess of apples where both benefit from the transaction, are referred to as non-zero-sum." (Wright, 2001) Hence, when playing most of these games, the only way to lose in fact is not to enjoy the game. The second form of collaboration is highly creative in that all of the players are writing the story together, as a team. At the end of the session the events that transpired could be written into a book that would tell a story written by all of its participants. This is an important point to note, especially in MMORPGs, if one were asserting copyrights.

Traditionally, role-playing games developed from war gaming. However, they are generally simpler, more fantastic, and less realistic or historically exacting. They also usually require far less space and equipment than the older and more traditional hobby of recreating battles. The term 'role-playing game' is used for certain distinct methods of play. One is the traditional method where a pen-and-paper or tabletop game is played with dice by several people. This frequently involves several types of polyhedral dice. Another method of these games incorporates the use figurines on a grid (usually a square or hexagonal one) to illustrate strategic and tactical scenarios for play. These are used particularly during combat which is often a major feature of such games. When figurines are used, position, terrain, and other elements can affect the probabilities. For example, a character making an attack from an opponent's rear or flank may gain a significant bonus on their chances 'to hit' and may also gain advantages on any damage they inflict. On the other hand, figurines may not be used at all. Instead a whiteboard, chalkboard or similar drawing surface is used in the place of any figures or tokens. Nonetheless, many gamers are also collectors of the figurines and engage in the related hobby of painting and customizing them. (Appelcline)

A further style of play is live action role-playing (LARP). Here, the players physically act out their characters' actions. "When it comes to immersive game play, some people just have to get off the couch. They are LARPs, a catch all term for the battle re-enactments, medieval militiamen, and anime imitators. This type of game play is usually more focused on characterization and improvisational theatrics and less focused on combat and the fantastic, if only because of the physical limitations of the players themselves. Live action gamers often dress up as their characters and use appropriate props in the game. The related style of freeform role-playing is less physically oriented, and is often played at conventions." (Zjawinski, 2006) Chislehurst Caves, Kent play host to these games regularly.

'Role-playing' is also the term used as a name for a genre of video games that lack the 'role-playing' element of pen-and-paper games but borrows game play elements from these games.

These games are called CRPGs which stands for 'computer role-playing games' or 'console role-playing games' depending on whether the game is played on a personal computer or on a video game console. These computerized simulations have become increasingly popular. The most recent computer role-playing games have endeavoured to incorporate social interaction via networking. They began in the realm of text based chat rooms, and soon moved to static persistent worlds represented in the text MUD. "In computer gaming, a MUD (multi-user dungeon, dimension, or sometimes domain) is a multi-player computer role-playing game typically running on a bulletin board system or Internet server. Players assume the role of a character, and see textual descriptions of rooms, objects, other characters, and computer-controlled creatures or non-player characters (NPCs) in a virtual world. They may interact with each other and the surroundings by typing commands that resemble plain English. Traditional MUDs implement a fantasy world populated by elves, goblins, and other mythical beings with players being knights, sorcerers, and the like. The object of the game is to slay monsters, explore a rich world and complete quests. Other MUDs have a science fiction setting." (Bartle, 1990) Now, they have advanced to incorporate graphical representations of tokens (characters, equipment, monsters, etc.), as well as physical simulations obscuring much of the underlying rules of the games from users. Online role-playing games of today are defined by massively multiplayer online games such as *EverQuest, Ultima Online* and *World of Warcraft.*

In technical terms, games have spiralled into a realm previously reserved for special effects (SPFX) driven action movies. (Negroponte, 1996) Special effects (SPFX) are used in the film, television, and entertainment industry to create effects that cannot be achieved by normal means, such as depicting travel to other star systems. They are also used when creating the effect by normal means is prohibitively expensive, such as an enormous explosion. They are also used to enhance previously filmed elements, by adding, removing or enhancing objects within the scene. Many different visual special effects techniques exist, ranging from traditional theatre effects, through classic film techniques invented in the early 20th century, to modern computer graphics techniques (CGI). Often several different techniques are used together in a single scene or shot to achieve the desired effect. Special effects are often 'invisible.' That is to say that the audience is unaware that what they are seeing is a special effect. This is often the case in historical movies, where the architecture and other surroundings of previous eras are created using special effects. (Information Slurp)

These new games remediate cinema; that is, they demonstrate the propensity of emerging media forms to pattern themselves on the characteristic behaviours and tendencies of their predecessors. In introducing the concept of re-mediation, Bolter and Grusin (2000) emphasize the hybrid, dialectical nature of media appropria-tion: "The new medium can remediate by trying to absorb the older medium entirely, so that the discontinuities between the two are minimized. The very act of remediation, however, ensures that the older medium cannot be entirely effaced; the new medium remains dependent on the older one in acknowledged or unacknowledged ways." The non-networked computer games resemble the mental world of a two-year old: everything evolves around you and nothing happens when you are not present. (Lastowka and Hunter, 2004) Virtual worlds are different. Computer games of this nature subtly reflect our way of thinking about the real world. (Bolter, 1984) They are created by computer code designed to act like real world property. (Fairfield, 2005)

C. INTERACTIVITY, PHYSICALITY, AND PERSISTENCE

Virtual world is a term used by the creators of the game *Ultima Online*, though they seem to prefer 'persistent state world' instead (www.uo.com). Neither is a universally accepted term. Perhaps the most frequently used term is 'MMORPG,' which means 'massively multi-player on-line role-playing game,' apt since virtual worlds were born and have grown primarily as game environ-ments. However, virtual worlds probably have a future that extends beyond this role. Moreover, MMORPG is impossible to pronounce. Other terms include 'MM persistent universe,' with 'MM' meaning 'massively-multiplayer;' also, there is Holmsten's term, 'persistent online world.' 'Virtual worlds' captures the essence of these terms in fewer words, with fewer syllables and a shorter acronym; by Occam's Razor, it is the better choice. These virtual worlds are computer programs with three defining features:

- **Interactivity:** it exists on one computer but can be accessed remotely (i.e. by an internet connection) and simultaneously by a large number of people, with the command inputs of one person affecting the command results of other people.

- **Physicality:** people access the program through an interface that simulates a first-person physical environment on their computer screen; the environment is generally ruled by the natural laws of Earth and is characterized by scarcity of resources.

- **Persistence:** the program continues to run whether anyone is using it or not; it remembers the location of people and things, as well as the ownership of ob-jects." Castronova, 2002) Joshua Fairfield (2005) uses a similar description to explain rivalrous code which he, in turn, defines as virtual property.

Interactivity is a key value of multimedia. As noted earlier, traditional media gives the user a passive role of watching or listening as a linear work unfolds. The benefit of digitisation is that it allows users to select precisely the information or experience they want. (Williams, et al, 1996) MMORPGs are the first persistent (24 hours a day/ 7 days a week) virtual worlds, and the first instance of individualized mediated experiences within a mass audience (each player's experience is unique despite the large number of simultaneous participants). (Wolf and Perron, 2003) Another definition of MMORPGs is any computer network-mediated games in which at least 1,000 players are role-playing simultaneously in a graphical environment. (http://www.mmorpg.com) They are also the first interactive mass medium to unite entertainment and communication in one phenomenon. (Filiciak, 2003)

A virtual world is the consequence of blending the graphical three dimensional environments of games like Tomb Raider and DOOM with the chat-based social interaction systems developed in the world of MUDs. Ironically, both games have now been turned into big screen movies. Traditional first-person shooter games organize its user interface around a software-simulated 'camera' that, in the game's representational system, serves double duty as a body situated in the diegesis. For example, in Tomb Raider, you manoeuvre Lara Croft around on your screen and do things. In a virtual world, other people are running around in the same virtual space as you are, and they can talk to you. "J.R.R. Tolkien, perhaps the cultural and intellectual father of these worlds, used the term 'Secondary World' to describe his fantasy universe. It would amaze Tolkien how completely un-secondary his fantasy worlds have become. Virtual worlds are neither fantasy (constructions of the mind) nor reality (impositions of nature). They are Artistry: mental constructs expressed by their creators in whatever media the physical world allows. At the 20th annual Arts Electronica Festival, a Golden Nica was given to

Team chman for their development of the game Banja. The award horrified purists of electronic arts. Yet anyone who has wandered in worlds like Norrath has experienced the art of other people at an unprecedented deep psychological and social level. You are not looking at a painting. You are *in it.* And it is not a painting at all, but immersive scenery that induces you and thousands of other people to play parts in what becomes an evolving and unending collective drama." (Grau, 2003)

The avatar's navigation of 'contested spaces' and interaction with others generates the narrative. Arguing that video games are as much about architectural, sculptural, and other 'spatial' properties as they are about narrative or cinematic pleasures, Jenkins and Squire (2002) remind us that, "If games tell stories, they do so by organizing spatial features. If games stage combat, then players learn to scan their environments for competitive advantages. Game designers create immersive worlds and relationships among objects that enable dynamic experiences." The hot digital cinematography alone does not make a digital story immersive.

Unlike single-player games, these virtual environments do not go into cryogenic suspension in your absence. Events transpire. Battles are fought. Rivalries flare. Alliances are formed. What makes the game immersive is a world where no territory is off-limit, anything you see is fair game. This virtual world cannot be turned on and off. Actions have lasting consequences, both narratively and socially. (Herz, 1997) As players construct their characters (avatars), accruing strength and skill with experience, they also rely on other characters. Despite this generally non-competitive nature, role playing games usually have rules, which enable the players to determine the success or failure of their characters in their endeavours. Normally this will involve assigning certain abilities to each character - from something as mundane as being quite strong to having x-ray vision. (http://www.clubsandguilds.com/Role-playing_game/encyclopedia.htm) Success relies more on social interaction and less upon combat skill. Avatars enter the mythology; and their actions accrete to the continuity of the galaxies. (Herz, 1997)

As such, the MMORPGs bring another type of code into existence; one which is designed to act more like land or chattel than like ideas. A type of code more prevalent on the internet than the first type of code and which uses most of the internet's resources. In fact, it makes up the structural components of the internet itself. The chattel-like code creates virtual property akin to real life property. This type of code is rivalrous, if one person owns and controls it, others do not. Fairfield (2005) points out that rivalrousness of consumption - the fact that one actor's use of a resource bars others from use as a consequence - is different than exclusivity. Exclusivity is a function of rivalrousness. Many resources, including purely non-rivalrous resources, can be protected by exclusionary rules. For example, the Recording Industry Association of America has attempted to use exclusionary rules to protect its non-rivalrous music.

Cyberspace is a (virtual) reality within the world's computers and computer networks. While cyberspace should not be confused with the real Internet, the term is often used simply to refer to objects and identities that exist largely within the computing network itself, so that a web site, for example, might be metaphorically said to 'exist in cyberspace.' According to this interpretation, events taking place on the Internet are not therefore happening in the countries where the participants or the servers are physically located, but 'in cyberspace'. This becomes a reasonable viewpoint once distributed services (e.g. Freenet) become widespread, and the physical identity and location of the participants become impossible to determine due to anonymous or pseudonymous communication. The laws of any particular nation state would therefore not apply. (Heylighen, 1994) This 'space' in cyberspace refers to something in particular: the rivalrousness, or 'spatial' nature, of certain internet resources, like URLs, domain names, email ac-

counts, virtual worlds, and more. Many oppose the analogy that the internet is a space; however, many online resources mimic physical properties. (cf. Goldsmith, 1998; Sommer, 2000; O'Rourke, 2001; Wu, 2000) For example, a chat room is just like a conference room; a URL is similar to real estate in the real world. This type of code is ubiquitous and consequential as well as sharing three legally relevant characteristics with real world property: rivalrousness, persistence, and interconnectivity. To the extent academics have approved of place language describing online resources, they have done so out of a sense of psychological utility, not a sense that the language is descriptively accurate. (Yen, 2002) "Of the many metaphors that have been applied to the Internet, the most prominent and influential has been the imagination of the Internet as a separate, new physical space known as 'cyberspace,' and its comparison to America's Western Frontier." (Id.)

Rivalrousness, in the physical world, lets the owner exclude other people from using owned objects. For an analysis of the right to exclude in physical property, see Thomas W. Merrill, (1998) who stated that "the right to exclude others is... the sine qua non" of property rights. The desire for the power to exclude in cyberspace is strong too. So this power has been designed into code. By design, code can be made so that it can only be possessed by one person. Thus, rivalrousness exists also in code. If one person controls rivalrous code, nobody else does. (Fairfield, 2005) For example, if one person has a given email address, nobody else can receive mail at that same address. If John Smith owns a given internet address, Paul Walker cannot put his website up at that address. No one but John Smith (or those he permits) can post content to that address.

There are other characteristics drawn from the physical world that are incorporated into code as well. Objects and places in the physical world are persistent. For example, a painting need only be painted once. After that, it remains in existence for as long as someone wants it. Similarly, code is often made persistent - that is, it does not fade after each use, and it does not run on one single computer. For example, an email account can be accessed from a laptop, a desktop, or the local library. When an email account owner turns her laptop off, the information in that account does not cease to exist. It persists on the server of her Internet Service Provider. The trait of persistence is linked to a technological phenomenon that will have greater importance in the discussion that follows. The trait of persistence is achieved through distributed computing - that is, the code runs on multiple computers simultaneously. A common form is that code is split between a client program that runs locally, and a server that manages coordination between other interconnected accounts. Thus, for example, your email client may run on your local laptop, and receive its information from your Internet Service Provider's server, where the information is stored. As will be demonstrated in the next chapter, this is an important feature in virtual worlds.

Objects in the real world are also naturally interconnected and affect each other. Two people in the same room experience exactly the same objects. Likewise, code can be made interconnected, so that although one person may control it, others may experience it. The value of a URL or an email address is not solely that the owner can control it; the value is that other people can connect to it, and can experience it. They may not be able to control it without the owner's permission, but - as with real estate in the real world - with the owner's invitation they may interact with it. This becomes a very important argument for the owner's of virtual worlds. They want to control the world and those who are allowed to experience.

In summary, the traits - rivalrousness, persistence, and interconnectivity - mimic real world properties. If I wield a sword, I have it and you do not: Rivalrousness. If I put the sword down and leave the room, it is still there: Persistence. Anyone can interact with my sword - with my permission, you can experience it: Interconnectivity.

Rivalrousness gives one the ability to invest in property without fear that other people may take what one has built. Additionally, rivalrousness lowers monitoring and detection costs for protecting property. Whereas in commons property misuse is quite hard to police (because the misuser is entitled to be on the property and make some use of it), interference with rivalrous private property is very easy to detect. For example, if you take my pen from me, I will detect the loss fairly quickly. (Ellickson, 1993) Persistence protects that investment by ensuring that it endures. Interconnectivity increases the value of the property due to network effects - not least of which is the fact that other people's experience of this resource may be such that it becomes desirable, and hence marketable, to them.

The audience does not just watch the story or play a game. The audience is the story. The participants are as interconnected virtually as they would be in reality. They are creating as much as they are consuming. This is a quantum leap from conventional first person shooter technology. (Fitch, 2004)

D. STAR WARS

Virtual worlds, populated by thousands of people, are giving rise to new kinds of stories that demand a world-builder's creative aspirations and attention to dramatic potential. (King) This is a new concept in games. Based in San Rafael, California, LucasArts has grown from its roots in 1982 as a small research group funded by Atari into a full-fledged software developer that employs 350 people. Their ambition is concentrated on *Galaxies,* which was under construction for two years in partnership with an Austin-based team from Sony Online Entertainment. The architects of *Star Wars Galaxies* are welding together an interactive galaxy whose size and complexity will make the Death Star look like a moon globe. The epic saga that fans have consumed on the Empire's terms will become an interactive galaxy of their own adventures as smugglers, mercenaries, canteen keepers, and aspiring Jedi Knights. (LucasArts Press Release, 2006)

Some games are based on novels and comic books, such as *Star Wars*. The films and video games established legions of characters and locations to avid fans, yet these digital thrill rides revealed very little of the tightly controlled *Star Wars* universe. One could be the top gun of the Rebel Alliance in *Shadow of the Empire* for Nintendo 64, but one could not get drunk and sing "You've Lost That Loving Feeling" in the Mos Eisley canteen afterward and have the locals remember you. Your adventure was not a permanent event. The player had less influence than a minor comic book character because the fantasy vanished as soon as the game was over, and with it, any of the player's exploits. Their stories were lost. Massive multi-player online game changes these experiences into a new type of game in which layer upon layer of experiences are melded together in a persistent virtual environment. Although this would pose the possible questions, whether a Rebel Alliance star pilot known as Maverick Starkiller singing this song in an effort to attract the attention of some lovely female alien in the style of Maverick the U.S. Navy Fighter Pilot from *Top Gun* (Paramount, 1986) would be a copyright violation of 1) the film *Top Gun* and its associated rights, or 2) the song "You've Lost That Loving Feeling", The Righteous Brothers (performers) written by Phil Spector, Barry Mann, and Cynthia Weil; produced by Phil Spector and released December 1964 on Philles; and its associated rights; or the trademark in the name and/or representation of Maverick.

Twenty-five years ago George Lucas conjured up a galaxy for the original *Star Wars* movie. LucasArts is now expanding that galaxy so that others may interact in it. Nevertheless in one fundamental way this galaxy is drastically different. Everything is not under the game-maker's control. This multimedia product combines both computer-generated displays and digitized pre-existing information to form its images, which are far more diverse than the images which appeared in the film. (Turner, 1995) The individual elements of the product are all protected by copyright in their digital format. (17 U.S.C.A. §102(a) (1996); CDPA 1988, ss 1-8) The software which enables the action is also protected. (17 U.S.C.A. §102(a) (1996); CDPA 1988, ss 1-8)

However, the characters in *Galaxies* will not be actors, or drawings in a comic book, or passages in a novel. They will be autonomous human beings, each with a mind, ego, and agenda of their own. (Grodal, 2003) Crucial to this evolution is the avatar's gradual but relentless acquisition of 'liveliness'. In appearance, movement, and disposition, avatars have ever more clearly come to mimic their player, developing personality, individuality and an ability to act within the virtual world. (Id.) Players exist with their avatars in an unstable balancing act. Players experience games through the exclusive intermediary of another – the avatar – the 'eyes', 'ears', and 'body' of which are components of a complex technological and psychological apparatus. Just as one would not equate a glove with the hand inside it, one should not presume the subjectivity produced by video games to transparently correspond to, and thus substitute for the player; although, it is precisely this presumption which appears necessary to secure and maintain a sense of immersion in 'cyberspace'. (Rehak, 2003)

Spacewar! established a set of elements vital to avatarial operations in most video games which followed it:

1. Player identification with an onscreen avatar.
2. Player control of avatar through a physical interface.
3. Player-avatar's engagement with narrative-strategic constraints organizing the on-screen diegesis in terms of its (simulated) physical and semiotic content – the 'meaning' of the game's sounds and imagery – that constitute

rules or conditions of possibility governing play.

4. Imposition of extra-diegetic constraints further shaping play (for example, timer, music, scorekeeping and other elements perceptible to the player but presumably not by the entity represented by the avatar; an instance of this in the relatively austere *Spacewar!* would be the software function that ended a game when one player 'died').

5. Frequent breakdown and reestablishment of avatarial identification through the destruction of avatar, starting or ending of individual games and tournaments, and ultimately the act of leaving or returning to the physical apparatus of the computer. (Jenkins and Squire, 2002)

'Liveliness' comes from the increasing *subjectivization* of video games: a move from the god's-eye perspective utilized in early games to perspective rendering that simulates three-dimensionality, first as static scenery, then as fluidly navigable space. Avatarial operations flow from two elements that inter-depend in various ways. First is the foregrounding of an onscreen body, visible in whole or in part. Second is the conceit of an off-screen but assumed body constituted through the gaze of a mobile, player-controlled camera. Differing articulations between camera-body and avatar-body lead to different, though related, modes of play and subject effects. In every case, the intent – to produce a sense of embodiment – announces itself from the dawn of video game history. (Levy, 1984)

Concurrently, characters and material from the games have been overlaid onto the movies. When the original *Star Wars* trilogy was re-released onto video and DVD, it had new scenes and overhauled special effects. For example, the ship invented for Dash Rendar in *Shadows of the Empire* had a cameo appearance in the *Special Edition,* which came out in 1997. There's a scene as Luke Skywalker and Obi-Wan are coming into Mos Eisley to look for a pilot who will take them off the planet. You see the ship flying over the town. (Dibbell, 2003) In *Episode I,* the names broadcasted for the pod race were originally conceived for *Episode I Racer,* a game that sent players slaloming through the desert canyons on Nintendo 64s. The superimposition is subtle. And subtlety is the most important feature of credible fiction. Making sure these superimpositions take is a tricky business. There is a religious dedication to the integrity of the fictional environment.

Most Hollywood studios use McDonalds' Happy Meals, video games and other tie-ins to stoke the box office. "Some video game companies are offering product placement in their games. Virtual ads are viewed by real eyeballs. In game advertising industry generates more than $60 million which is predicted to grow to half a billion dollars by 2009. One of the biggest players, Massive, Inc., has inserted ads in almost 50 titles." (Gaudiosi, 2006) In contrast, the people who run *Star Wars* do not consider novels, toys, comic books, and video games to be promotional vehicles that exist merely to pad the bottom line. (Herz, 2002) These products are considered to be shards of an alternate reality. Each one must be scrupulously verified against all the others, for fear that it may break continuity. (Id.; Star Wars Galaxies FAQ) Accordingly, the licensing division of Lucasfilm has developed into a type of secular clergy, whose primary function is to illuminate the *Star Wars* oeuvre. George Lucas is very particular about maintaining control over his work. In order to do this, he originally contracted with 20th Century Fox to make only one movie, but retained the rights over any sequels. He also insisted on maintaining all rights in merchandising and licensing. It is remarkable that he was able to do so; but back in the 1970s, movie studios were not interested in nor understood the power of merchandising and licensing. Charles Lippincott, LucasArts Marketing Director, changed all of that. (*Empire of Dreams: The Story of Star Wars* on Bonus Materials from *Star Wars* Trilogy

DVD set (2004)).

Licensing maintains a FileMaker Pro database with, at last count, twenty-five thousand entries, gleaned from every scrap of media the company has produced, in addition to an extensive archive of imagery. All of this is accessible to employees and licensees on a corporate intranet. For all intents and purposes, this database is the *Star Wars* bible. All functional, aesthetic, and metaphysical queries are referred to it assiduously. The entire *Star Wars* oeuvre is maintained in a database commonly called 'the canon' by Lucas employees, without a trace of irony as they really do see themselves as a secular clergy. A smaller version of this database can be found at http://www.starwars.com/databank/. Every time a player creates a new character, that character is put into a database. That character is forever maintained in the continuity that is the epic *Star Wars*. Every character must be fixed for this alternate reality to maintain continuity and game play.

The *Star Wars* 'canon' is subject to theological debate just like any other religious touchstone. As *Galaxies* will transport the universe into the future after the films, an enormous degree of scrutiny is focused on every detail of the interactive experience. (Herz, 2002) For example, how should a character be brought back after they have been killed? Cloning was deemed to be the answer. So, players can go to a facility and create a replica of their character/avatar. A chain of 'cloning facilities' are situated throughout the universe. Each cloning facility is effectively a place where a player gets to reconstruct a partial 'save game'. "The cloning facility 'saves' your character's current physical attributes (including customisations) and knowledge (represented by skills and XP values)." (http://swg.crgaming.com/faq/default.asp?Category+17&Page=4) When a character dies, he or she will re-spawn at the last cloning facility they visited, with their attributes, skills, and XP reset to whatever they were the last time the character was cloned. So each character has a replica maintained in a cloning vat in the character database maintained by LucasArts. (Herz, 2002)

Notwithstanding that the new *Star Wars* testament continuously checks itself against the old, *Galaxies* feeds new information into 'the canon'. For example, the films provide you with only a glimpse of small sections of any given planet. However, all of the planet must be traversable in the game realm. All of the known areas must be connected. Thus, the builders must generate new terrain. The maps are then uploaded to the Ranch and become permanent planetary surveys. "That will happen with everything," says Blackman, "Every time we create a new character, a new creature, a new location, every time we include an event, those become part of continuity. Already, we have created several hundred creatures, and they are all now established in the continuity as native to whatever planet they are on." (Strickler, 2002) Skywalker Ranch is a cross between Disneyland and Yellowstone Park. Home to George Lucas' production company, the 2,600-acre ranch is a reflection of its owner: high-tech and low-key. Although he has become famous for pushing the envelope of special-effects technology, Lucas still writes his scripts in longhand. While technicians fiddle with a physics lab full of paraphernalia, he takes quiet walks in the solitude. (Id.)

A game's success is contingent upon players' willingness to invest themselves (financially and emotionally) in their characters. (King) They must want to become citizens of this virtual world, if it is going to prosper. (Id.; Herz, 2002) The very development of a massive multi-player game mirrors this change. Game designers are no longer authors. They must now act more like urban planners, or local politicians. (Bartle, 2004)

E. SECOND LIFE

Second Life is a privately owned three dimensional virtual world, just like *Galaxies,* but is only partly subscription-based. (Parker, 2003) It was originally made publicly available in 2003 by

San Francisco-based Linden Lab, and founded by former RealNetworks CTO Philip Rosedale. Philip Rosedale (Philip Linden within *Second Life*) has stated that his goal with *Second Life* is to demonstrate a viable model for a virtual economy or virtual society. In his own words, "I'm not building a game. I'm building a new country." (Terdiman, 2004) Players visit this virtual world, as if it were a real place. They are more like travellers than game players. They explore, meet new people, and participate in individual and group activities. If they decide to visit frequently, they learn new skills and mature socially. In a sense, they are learning the culture of the virtual world. (Id.)

The *Second Life* world is generated by a large assortment of servers known cooperatively as 'the grid' which run sims that are owned, operated and maintained by Linden Lab. There are currently two grids available for public use, Agni is referred to as the Main Grid, and Siva, the Preview Grid for public beta testing. There are possibly other grids for Linden Lab's use as well. *Teen Second Life* is often thought to be on a separate grid as well, but in fact it exists on Agni. The origin of use of 'grid' could come from the fact that sims are arranged in a grid-like matrix pattern or it could come from the real-life use of 'grid' to refer to a collection of networked servers (which *Second Life* is).

A *Second Life* client program provides its Residents or users with programming tools to view and modify the *Second Life* universe. The term, Resident, is used by Linden Lab and may be meant to give users a feeling of 'belonging' and ownership of the virtual world. It is also used throughout most of *Second Life*'s user interface in place of 'user'. The Residents may also participate in its virtual economy, which simultaneously has begun to operate as a 'real' market. As of December, 2006, between about ten and twenty thousand users are in *Second Life* at any one time. At precisely 8:05:45 AM PDT, October 18, 2006, the number of registered accounts in *Second Life* hit 1 million Residents. (Pathfinder, 2006) Eight weeks later, on December 14, 2006, this number

doubled to 2 million Residents. (Terdiman, 2006)

When Linden Lab released *Second Life* in 2003, it had crafted a reflection of the architecture of modern societies, complete with contemporary clothing, buildings, vehicles, and opportunities for starting online businesses. (Yi, 2003; Totilo, 2004) *Second Life* accurately simulates the laws of physics in virtual space: flags move in the wind, objects fall to the floor if a character drops them. Linden Lab also gave its users a scripting language and an integrated development environment for building new objects. Users could assemble prefabricated shapes into composite objects and give those objects behaviours. All objects in *Second Life* are composed of one or more geometric building blocks called 'primitives,' or (more colloquially) 'prims'. Each prim can be sized, shaped, coloured and textured. Additionally, through the use of the Linden Scripting Language, programmers can insert event-based actions into a prim, so that it can interact with avatars or with other prims inside of an object. For example, by coding an 'onTouch' function, a developer could make a 'button' prim in a phone respond to the touch of an avatar, enabling someone to retrieve voicemails from a 'voicemail' prim. (*Linden Scripting Language Wiki*, http://secondlife.com/badgeo/wakka.php?wakka=prim) By combining verisimilitude with the power of malleability, residents gained the freedom to craft ingenious objects, and they put that ability to use. According to Linden Lab's Cory Ondrejka (2005), residents have inserted over 100 million such objects into the world. Over 380,000 distinct objects changed hands in the month of July 2006 in ten million user-to-user transactions, which (given the exchange rate of 300 Linden Dollars (L$) to one U.S. dollar) yielded an internal economy of US $10 million for that month. Linden Dollars can be freely exchanged to U.S. dollars through Linden Lab's LindeX Currency Exchange. (Id.)

The story of *Second Life* is an interesting story of information economics. The legal implications are intriguing. By granting its participants intellectual property rights, *Second Life* has given its residents a significant stake in the virtual world. Individually, the residents now 'own' a part of *Second Life;* and, as a collective body, *Second Life* residents thereby 'own' most of the content of the virtual world. As a result, residents retain significant control over their world and, by extension, power.

Constitutional theorists will be quick to point out that the source of this power is still maintained by *Second Life*'s provider, Linden Lab. (Lastowka and Hunter, 2004; Balkin, 2004; Balkin, 2005) Theoretically, Linden Lab could -- if it wanted to -- reverse its policy. After such a change, any participants who create new content would once again have to consent to transferring their intellectual property rights to Linden Lab. The theoretical potential reversibility of the decision to grant participants of virtual worlds 'rights' means that Linden Lab's decision is not formally akin to signing a virtual Magna Carta. With or without 'rights' granted to its participants, Linden Lab's relations to *Second Life*'s content creators remain contractual on an individual, rather than societal, level. John Perry Barlow in *A Declaration of the Independence of Cyberspace*, proclaimed, "Governments of the Industrial World, you weary giants of flesh and steel, I come from Cyberspace, the new home of Mind. On behalf of the future, I ask you of the past to leave us alone. You are not welcome among us. You have no sovereignty where we gather." (http://homes.eff.org/~barlow/Declaration-Final.html)

Given this situation, supposing Linden Lab was to grant its participants a 'right' to decide -- perhaps through referenda -- what changes they want in the world. Such a delegation of governance to the people of *Second Life* might be viewed as a social contract. The legal ramification would be different. At best, only the contractual relationship between Linden Lab and each of its customers would change. Should Linden Lab violate this right, users would have no recourse other than leaving *Second Life*. *Second Life*'s Terms of Service stipulate that "Linden may amend this Agreement

... and/or modify the Community Standards at any time in its sole discretion by posting the amended Agreement or modified Community Standards at http://www.lindenlab.com, http://www.secondlife.com, another current website designated by Linden or by communicating these changes through the primary contact methods you have established with us." (See *Second Life* Terms of Service, § 1.2) The Resident's only choice may seem to be to exit.

However, this has not happened. Instead, they mutiny. For example, the Resident's of *Second Life* had a virtual equivalent to the Boston Tea Party when an early idea to tax residents on the objects they made was overturned. It is a tax-free free-trade area with minimal regulations which has more in common with a kind of spirited frontier capitalism than it does with the collaborative, everything-for-free ethic of sites like Wikipedia. (Harkin, 2006) Another example was when the participants of *Second Life* also held demonstrations at the entry points of the world. They would light their avatars on fire and wander around telling new players of all the terrible problems with the place until Linden Lab was forced to fix them. (Ondrejka, 2005)

There is a difference between Linden Lab granting such participation 'rights' and the 'rights' it granted its players in November 2003. Linden Lab granted - intellectual property rights - that are rights guaranteed by real-world intellectual property laws. Granting intellectual property rights in virtual world objects injects real-world guarantees into the virtual world. This, in turn, creates a relationship between the two realms that is described as permeability. (*Second Life* Wiki, GJSL) Linden Lab is not simply bound to a contract with its customers, but to the social contract of Linden Lab's real-world jurisdiction. Any content created thereafter by *Second Life*'s participants is their intellectual property, not Linden Lab's. Should Linden Lab decide to change its policy again, content created before that change would remain the participants' property. This concession to participants of real-world intellectual property rights in their creations inserts real-world "legal DNA into *Second Life*'s genetic makeup," and subjects Linden Lab to an external authority. (Mayer-Schönberger and Crowley, 2006) Bruce Ackerman (1989) argued that a "distinctive aspect of the American constitutional tradition" is its "evolving commitment to dualistic democracy: its recurring emphasis on the special importance of those rare moments when political movements succeed in hammering out new principles of constitutional identity that gain the considered support of a majority of American citizens after prolonged institutional testing, debate, decision." In a similar manner to this type of constitutional moment, Linden Lab limited its future behaviour through its own decision.

Economic forces may prompt more virtual world providers to follow *Second Life*'s lead. However, this process of constitutionalization, i.e., voluntary constraining norms in virtual spaces through norms of a real-world jurisdiction, while restricting what virtual world providers can do in relation to virtual world participants, is not synonymous with a movement towards democratic governance within virtual worlds. Linden Lab provided a constitutional moment, not a democratic one.

The constitutionalization of virtual worlds has been made possible by the confluence of two factors: property rights and the permeability between the virtual world and the real world. Judge Easterbrook (1996) suggested that virtual spaces need stable property rights. Linden Lab did not act because a real-world government command forced it to act, nor because of aggressive popular demand among its participants. More precisely, Linden Lab introduced intellectual property rights because of second-order market forces. The need to compete - and thus retain and enhance its power in relation to other virtual worlds - impelled it to sacrifice power within its own jurisdiction.

Business acumen is only half the story. Without a real-world legal system and a real-world guarantee of intellectual property rights that can be exercised out with the virtual worlds and their own internal rules, Linden Lab's property rights guarantee lack a 'constitutional' nature. Real-world law functions merely as a catalyst for the advancement of virtual world governance. Even if virtual world creators grant intellectual property rights to their participants, market forces will continue to fuel an intense regulatory dynamic. "[E]conomic globalization intensifies competition among nation-states." (Kapstein, 1994)

In other words, jurisdictions may be forced to surrender power within their realms in order to gain competitive advantage among their competitors, enabling a capital mobility that reinforces the jurisdiction's need to compete ferociously with others for this capital. Manuel Castells, in *The Rise of the Network Society* (1996) pointed to the importance of the "political capacity of national and supranational institutions to steer the growth strategy of those countries or areas under their jurisdiction" for staying competitive in a global economy. Jagdish Bhagwati, *In Defense of Globalization* (2004) summarized some of the main arguments of globalization critics: "corporations would ... be able to seek profits by searching for the most likely locations to exploit workers and nations, thereby putting intolerable pressure on their home states to abandon their gains in social legislation." As such, Linden Lab may have brought the forces of globalization into the sphere of virtual worlds.

F. PAIDEA VS. LUDUS

Working out the rules of a game constitutes a large part of the fascination and challenge of playing the game, and is the prime motivation for play. Once the rules have deduced and overcome, the games may lose their appeal. The demands made by videogames on the player's imagination have been overlooked frequently in accounts of play. (Newman, 2004) Deducing, collating, and working within or around a game's rule sets represents a large part of the pleasure of videogame play and highlights the active, participatory role of the player. Two computer programs facilitate a virtual world - one program runs on the player's personal computer, and the other program runs on a game server accessed by the player using the Internet. (Fitch, 2004) These online role-playing games generate revenue from a player's purchase of the computer program that runs on his personal computer and from a monthly subscriber fee that allows the player to access the game server.

The market is very competitive. Since virtual worlds are human networks, one could forecast that only a few virtual worlds will eventually dominate the market. (Woodcock, 2008; Castronova, 2002) The inclination to network monopoly is improved by the partiality most players to 'live' in one fantasy world at a time. Add to that the fact that switching is expensive because it can take weeks to become familiar with a new world. "To someone raised in an historical worldview – one valuing linearity, genealogies, traditions, *rules* – explanations of the game sound haphazard, unplanned and immature. But to someone familiar with global information spaces such as the world wide web, games such these provide environments for learning postmodernist approaches to communication and knowledge: navigation, constructive problem-solving, dynamic goal-construction." (Johnson-Eilola, 1998)

Moreover, the growth in the number of virtual worlds has been spurred by a growth in user base and revenues. Games are big business. According to the Games Developer's Conference (www.gdconf.com/aboutus.html), game industry revenues have exceeded box office revenues since 1999. One recent survey estimated the market for online electronic games in 2003 was $ 1.9 billion, predicted to grow to $ 5.2 billion in 2006, and $ 9.8 billion by 2009. In parts of Asia, online games have become ubiquitous; an estimated one in four teenagers in South Korea play NCsoft's Lineage. (Associated Press, 2003) Virtual worlds

are notable as one area of internet commerce that seems to be profitable. (Dibbell, 2003; Terdiman, 2004) Most software game titles require the player to pay a one-time fee to purchase the game. Virtual world-based games require the player to purchase the game software and then pay additional monthly fees (from $10 to $20) to access the virtual world on an ongoing basis. This revenue stream seems to be stable and growing. (Sellers, 2006; Castronova, 2002)

Millions of individuals are embracing the unreality of virtual worlds by paying substantial sums of money to exist in them. Hundreds of millions of dollars in revenue are flowing into the coffers of Sony, Electronic Arts, and the other companies that own virtual worlds. (Snider, 2003) "Massive, Inc. has inserted the Coca-Cola logo into *SWAT 4* and put Diet Sprite Zero vending machines in *Tom Clancy's Splinter Cell Chaos Theory*. Massive can also place updatable graphics on billboards – each rented to the highest bidder – in networked games like *Anarchy Online*. CEO Mitch Davis says gamers will soon be able to, say, test-drive the latest Porsche in a racing game or outfit their characters in Rocawear's new fall line. 'Imagine if a certain brand of sneakers increased your avatar's dexterity,' Davis muses." (Gaudiosi, 2006) Intel and McDonald's have reportedly paid millions of dollars to place their products in front of the eyes of avatars. (Edwards, 2003; Richtel, 2002) One might predict that where large amounts of real money flow, legal consequences follow. Hard cash alone, however, does not establish the legal significance of virtual worlds. (Lastowka and Hunter, 2004)

Hard cash does inspire currency speculation though. Jamie Hale of Gaming Open Market (GOM) has seen a way to make some real cash from unreal currencies. Gaming Open Market (GOM) is an exchange site designed specifically for trading online game currencies. The trades are *cheaper* than the auction and dealer sites, and the trades are *instant* and *secure*. They traffic in the currencies of virtual worlds, trading game money for U.S. dollars or, soon, even allowing players to trade across games. The GOM Currency Exchange (GCX) makes buying and selling game currency incredibly easy. It offers market overview and historical charting. It has a complete view of where the market has been, and a better idea of where it's going. All in real-time. The online games it serves include *Ultima Online, Star Wars Galaxies, Second Life, The Sims Online, There* and others. (http://www.gamingopenmarket.com/index.php) Hale and his colleagues have avatar accounts in each of the games whose currencies trade on GOM and will personally deliver the funds to the buyer in the virtual world. Currently, GOM only facilitates dollar-to-game-currency trades. (Id.) In the future, once traffic in the various currencies increases, Hale intends the exchange to allow players to make trades directly between, for example, Lindenbucks, *Second Life* currency, and Simoleans, the currency of *The Sims Online,* using variable exchange rates. (Terdiman, 2004)

Some game developers find that such behaviour is an anathema. For example, game companies, like Origin, which produces *Ultima Online,* say they do not mind if players buy and sell the virtual goods in secondary markets because, ultimately, it increases interest in the game. Linden Lab, which produces the metaverse *Second Life,* actively encourages secondary-market trading, because it sees such activity as part of a larger social and economic experiment, with its game at the center. And still others, like *EverQuest* publisher Sony Online Entertainment, see such trafficking as nothing but a headache. "The official line is that the selling of characters, items or equipment in *EverQuest* goes against our end-user licensing agreement," says Sony Online Director of Public Relations Chris Kramer. "It's currently not something the company supports and causes us more customer-service and game-balancing problems than probably anything else that happens within the game." (Terdiman, 2004) At the moment, Hale is hoping that they can either fly beneath the radar long enough to establish a reputation

for protecting players or, alternatively, that they can convince the developers to let them continue unheeded. But Philip Rosedale, CEO of Linden Lab makers of *Second Life,* believes there is nothing at all wrong with what Hale is attempting to achieve. "It's so great. It's hyper-liquid," said Rosedale. "When you reduce trade borders you get faster development.... If you're a casual player of an online game, say, *Star Wars Galaxies*, you're not going to go on eBay and make a bid. I mean, that's lame. You go on Gaming Open Market, and it's done." (Terdiman, 2004*)*

The skill of attracting customers who are prepared to pay an ongoing fee to visit their virtual world is the key to business success of these virtual worlds. That in itself requires virtual world builders to offer a form of entertainment that is unceasingly more attractive than the competition. As it happens, virtual worlds appear capable of offering entertainment that is appealing enough to people that they sacrifice large amounts of their time to it. (Alter, 2007) They offer an alternative reality. They can live their life in a different country if they so choose. In reality, life in a virtual world is exceedingly desirable to many people. A competition has arisen between Earth and the virtual worlds, and for many, Earth is the lesser option.

REFERENCES

Ackerman, B. (1989). Constitutional Politics/Constitutional Law. *Yale L.J., 99(453).*

Alter, A. (2007, August 10). Is This Man Cheating on His Wife? *The Wall Street Journal.*

Andersen, H. C. (1984). *The Complete Hans Christian Andersen Fairy Tales.* London: Landoll.

Appelcline, S. (n.d.). *A Brief History of Role Playing.* Retrieved from http://www.skotos.net/articles/TTnT_134.phtml

Balkin, J. (2003). The Proliferation of Legal Truth. *Harv. J. L. & Pub. Pol'y, 26*(5).

Balkin, J. (2004). Virtual Liberty: Freedom to Design and Freedom to Play in Virtual Worlds. *Va. L. Rev., 90*(2043).

Balkin, J. (2005). Law and Liberty in Virtual Worlds. *N.Y.L. Sch. L. Rev., 49*(63).

Bartle, R. (1990, November 15). *Early MUD History*. Retrieved from http://www.mud.co.uk/richard/mudhist.htm

Bartle, R. (2004). *Designing Virtual Worlds*. Berkeley, CA: New Riders Publishing.

Beren, K., & Howard, G. (2001). *The Rough Guide to Videogaming*. London: Rough Guides.

Bhagwati, J. (2004). *In Defense of Globalization*. Oxford: Oxford University Press.

Bleich, D. (1978). Subjective Criticism. [National Council of Teachers.]. *Urbana (Caracas, Venezuela)*, IL.

Bolter, J. D. (1984). *Turing's Man: Western Culture in the Computer Age*. Chapel Hill, NC: University of North Carolina Press.

Bolter, J. D., & Grusin, R. (2000). *Remediation: Understanding New Media*. Cambridge, MA: MIT Press.

Boone, M.S. (2008). Ubiquitous Computing, Virtual Worlds, and the Displacement of Property Rights. *I/S: J. L. & Pol'y for Info. Soc'y, 4*(91).

Bordwell, D., & Thompson, K. (2001). *Film Art* (6th ed.). New York: McGraw-Hill.

Caillois, R. (2001). *Man, Play, and Games* (Barash, M., Trans.). Urbana, IL: University of Illinois Press.

Castells, M. (1996). *The Rise of the Network Society*. London: Blackwell Publishing Professional.

Castronova, E. (2002). *On Virtual Economies*. The Gruter Institute of Working Papers on Law, CESifo Working Paper No. 752.

(1999). Cyberspace, Virtuality, and the Text . InRyan, M.-L. (Ed.), *Cyberspace Textuality: Computer Technology and Literary Theory*. Southbend, IN: Indiana University Press.

Dibbell, J. (1998). *My Tiny Life*. New York: Henry Holt & Co.

Dibbell, J. (2003 March). Your Next Customer is Virtual, But his Money is Real. *Business 2.0*. Retrieved from http://www.business2.com.articles/mag/0,1640,47157,00.html

Doctorow, C. (2006 April). The Massively Multiplayer Magic Kingdom: Theme Park Imagineer Danny Hillis on the Wonderful Virtual World of Disney. *Wired Magazine*.

Easterbrook, F.H. (1996). Cyberspace and the Law of the Horse. *U. Chi. Legal F., 207*.

Edwards, E. (2003). Plug (the Product) and Play; Advertisers Use Online Games to Entice Customers. *Washington Post*, A1.

Elins, M. (2006 April). Dream Machines: Will Wright Explains How Games Are Unleashing the Human Imagination. *Wired*.

Ellickson, R.C. (1993). Property in Land. *Yale L.J., 102*(1315).

Fairfield, J. (2005). *Virtual Property*. Indiana University School of Law – Bloomington, Legal Studies Research Paper Series, Research Paper Number 35.

Filiciak, M. (2003). Hyperidentities – Post-modern Identity Patterns in Massively Multiplayer Online Role-Playing Games . In Wolf, M. J. P., & Perron, B. (Eds.), *The Video Game Theory Reader*. London: Routledge.

Fitch, C. (2004). *Cyberspace in the 21ˢᵗ Century: Mapping the Future of Massive Multiplayer Games*. Retrieved from http://www.gamasutra.com/features/20000120/fitch_04.htm

Frasca, G. (2001). *Videogames of the Oppressed: Videogames as a Means for Critical Thinking and Debate.* Georgia Institute of Technology Masters Thesis. Retrieved from http://www.jacaranda.org/frasca/thesis

Freedberg, D. (1989). *The Power of Images: Studies in the History and Theory of Response.* Chicago, IL: University of Chicago Press.

Gaudiosi, J. (2006 April). Product Placement to Die For: The Rise of In-game Advertising. *Wired Magazine.*

Goldsmith, J.L. (1998). Against Cyberanarchy. *U. Chi. L. Rev., 65*(1199).

Grau, O. (2003). *Virtual Art: From Illusion to Immersion.* Cambridge, MA: The MIT Press.

Grodal, T. (2003). Stories for Eye, Ear, and Muscles: Video Games, Media, and Embodied Experiences . In Wolf, M. J. P., & Perron, B. (Eds.), *The Video Game Theory Reader.* London: Routledge.

Harkin, J. (2006, November 17). Get a (second) life. *Financial Times.*

Herz, J. C. (1997). *Joystick Nation: How Video Games Ate Our Quarters, Won Our Hearts and Rewired Our Minds.* Boston, MA: Little, Brown, and Company.

Herz, J.C. (June 2002). 50,000,000 Star Warriors Can't Be Wrong, *Wired Magazine*

Heylighen, F. (1994, October 17). *Cyberspace.* Retrieved from http://pespmc1.vub.ac.be/CYB-SPACE.html

Howland, G. (1998). *Game Design: the Essence of Computer Games.* Retrieved from http://www.lupinegames.com/articles/essgames.htm

Information Slurp. (n.d.). Retrieved from http://www.informationslurp.com/Film/Special_effect.html

Iser, W. (1978). *The Act of Reading: A Theory of Aesthetic Response.* Baltimore, MD: John Hopkins University Press.

Iser, W. (1989). *Prospecting: From Reader Response to Literary Anthropology.* Baltimore, MD: John Hopkins University Press.

Jenkins, H., & Squire, K. (2002). The Art of Contested Spaces . In King, L. (Ed.), *Game On: The History and Culture of Video Games.* New York: Universe.

Johnson-Eilola, J. (1998). Living on the surface: learning in the age of global communications networks . In Snyder, I. (Ed.), *Page to Screen: Taking Literacy into the Electronic Era.* London: Routledge. doi:10.4324/9780203201220_chapter_9

Kapstein, E. B. (1994). *Governing the Global Economy: International Finance and the State.* New York: McGraw Hill.

King, B. (n.d.). *World Creators: We Got Game.* Retrieved from http://www.wired.com/news/culture/0,1284,42381,00.html

King, B. (n.d.). *Star Wars Fans Strike Back.* Retrieved from http://www.wired.com/news/digiwood/0,1412,52561,00.html

Lastowka, F.G. & Hunter, D. (2004). The Laws of the Virtual World. *Calif. L. Rev., 92*(1).

Levy, S. (1984). *Hackers: Heroes of the Computer Revolution.* New York: Anchor.

Life, S. *Create Anything.* (2008). Retrieved from http://secondlife.com/whatis/create.php.

Linden, P. (n.d.). *Second Life Official Blog.* Retrieved from http://blog.secondlife.com/2006/10/18/when-precisely-did-we-hit-1-million-residents/

Linden Scripting Language Wiki. (n.d.). Retrieved from http://secondlife.com/badgeo/wakka.php?wakka=prim

Livingstone, S. (2002). *Young People and New Media: Childhood and the Changing Media Environment*. London: Sage.

Mayer-Schönberger, V. & Crowley, J. (2006). Napster's Second Life? The Regulatory Challenges of Virtual Worlds. *Nw. U. L. Rev., 100*(1775).

Merrill, T.W. (1998). Property and the Right to Exclude. *Neb. L. Rev., 77*(730).

Metz, C. (1982). *The Imaginary Signifier: Psychoanalysis and the Cinema* (Britton, C., Trans.). Bloomington, IN: Indiana University Press.

Negroponte, N. (1996). *Being Digital*. London: Hodder and Stoughton.

Newman, J. (2004). *Videogames*. Abingdon, UK: Routledge.

O'Rourke, M. A. (2001). Property Rights and Competition on the Internet: In Search of an Appropriate Analogy. *Berkeley Tech. L.J., 16*(561).

Ondrejka, C. (2005). *Changing Realities: User Creation, Communication, and Innovation in Digital Worlds*. Retrieved from http://www.themisgroup.com/uploads/Changing% 20Realities.pdf

Ondrejka, C. (2005, November 27). *CTO, Linden Lab, Remarks at the Berkman Center Luncheon Series*.

Ondrejka, C. (2005, May 7). A $200 Million Market? *Terra Nova*. Retrieved from http://terranova.blogs.com/terra_nova/2005/05/a_200m_market.html

Pagliassotti, D. (n.d.). What is Role-playing? *The Harrow: The RPG Collection*. Retrieved from http://www.theharrow.com/rpg/whatisroleplaying.html

Parker, S. (2003, June 23). Second Life goes live. *Yahoo! Games*. Retrieved from http://videogames.yahoo.com/newsarticle?eid=434909&page=0

Poster, M. (1999). Theorizing Virtual Reality . In Ryan, M.-L. (Ed.), *Cyberspace Textuality: Computer Technology and Literary Theory*. Southbend, IN: Indiana University Press.

Poulet, G. (1980). Criticism and the Experience of Interioricity . In Tompkins, J. P. (Ed.), *Reader Response Criticism: From Formalism to Post-Structuralism*. Baltimore, MD: John Hopkins University Press.

Rehak, B. (2003). Playing at Being: Psychoanalysis and the Avatar . In Wolf, M. J. P., & Perron, B. (Eds.), *The Video Game Theory Reader*. London: Routledge.

Richtel, M. (Nov. 28, 2002). *Big Mac Is Virtual, But Critics Are Real*, N.Y. Times, at G8.

Rollings, A., & Morris, D. (2000). *Game Architecture and Design*. Scottsdale, AZ: Coriolis.

Rouse, R. (2001). *Game Design Theory and Practice*. Plano, TX: Wordware Publishing.

Second Life Wiki. *GJSL*. (n.d.). Retrieved from http://secondlife.com/tiki/tiki-index.php?page=GJSL.

Sellers, M. (2006, January 9). *The Numbers Game*. Retrieved from http://terranova.blogs.com/terra_nova/2006/01/index.html

Sherry, J., Lucas, K., Rechtsteiner, S., Brooks, C., & Wilson, B. (2001). *Videogame Uses and Gratifications as Predictors of Use and Game Preference*. ICA Convention Video Game Research Agenda Theme Session Panel. Retrieved from http://www.icdweb/cc/purdue.edu/~sherry/videogames/VGUG.pdf

Smed (John Smedley, President, Sony Online Entertainment). (2005, April 19). Message posted to EverQuest II Official Forums. Retrieved from http://eqiiforums.station.sony.com/eq2/board/message?board.id=stcx&message.id=76&view=by_date_ascending&page=1

Snider, M. (2003, June 24). When Multiplayer Worlds Collide. *USA Today*,1D.

Sommer, J.H. (2000). Against Cyberlaw. *Berkeley Tech. L.J., 15*(1145).

Star Wars Galaxies. (n.d.). Retrieved from http://starwarsgalaxies.station.sony.com/features/faq_pages/faq_2.jsp#201

Strickler, J. (2002, May 19). Skywalker Ranch: George Lucas creates a magic world in real life found. *Star Tribune*. Retrieved from http://www.startribune.com/stories/411/2839700.html

TechTarget. (n.d.). *MP3*. Whatis.com definition. Retrieved from http://whatis.techtarget.com/definition/0,sid9_gci212600,00.html

Terdiman, D. (May 8, 2004). *Fun in Following the Money*, Wired Magazine.

Terdiman, D. (2004, January 23). Virtual Cash turns into Real Greed. *Wired Magazine*.

Terdiman, D. (2004 February). When Play Money becomes Real. *Wired Magazine*.

Terdiman, D. (2006, December 14). 'Second Life' hits second million in eight weeks. *Cnet News*. Retrieved from http://news.com.com/2061-10797_3-6143909.html?part=rss&tag=2547-1_3-0-5&subj=news

Terra Nova Blogs. (2008). Retrieved from http://www.terranova.blogs.com.

Todorov, T. (1980). Reading as Construction . In Suleiman, S. R., & Crosman, I. (Eds.), *The Reader in The Text*. Princeton, NJ: Princeton University Press.

Totilo, S. (2004, November 11). Do-It-Yourselfers Buy Into This Virtual World. *N.Y. Times*, G5.

Turner, M. (1995). Do the Old Legal Categories Fit the New Multimedia Products? A Multimedia CD-Rom as a Film. *E.I.P.R., 3*(107).

United States Copyright Office. (2001a). *DMCA Section 104 Report*. Retrieved from http://www.copyright.gov/reports/studies/dmca/sec-104-report-vol-1.pdf

United States Copyright Office. (2001b). *Executive Summary Digital Millennium Copyright Act, Section 104 Report*. Retrieved from http://www.copyright.gov/reports/studies/dmca/dmca_executive.html

Virtual Words Review. (2008). *Index*. Retrieved from http://www.virtualworldsreview.com/index.shtml

Weiser, M. (1991, Sept.). The Computer for the 21st Century. *Scientific American*, 94. doi:10.1038/scientificamerican0991-94

Wellner, P. Mackay, W. & Gold, R. (1993). Computer-Augmented Environments: Back to the Real World. *Commc'ns of the ACM, 36*(24).

Williams, A., Callow, D., & Lee, A. (1996). *Multimedia: Contracts, Rights, and Licensing*. London: FT Tax & Law.

Wolf, M. J. P., & Perron, B. (Eds.). (2003). *The Video Game Theory Reader*. London: Routledge.

Woodcock, B. S. (2008). *An Analysis of MMOG Subscription Growth*. Retrieved from http://www.mmogchart/com

Wright, R. (2001). *Nonzero: The Logic of Human Destiny*. New York: Vintage.

Wu, T. (2000). When Law & the Internet First Met. *Green Bag, 3*(171).

Yen, A. C. (2002). Western Frontier or Feudal Society?: Metaphors and Perceptions of Cyberspace. *Berkeley Tech. L.J., 17*(1207).

Yi, M. (2003, June 23). Online Game Bets on Self-Expression: Linden Lab's Second Life Premieres Today. *S.F. The Chronicle*, E1.

Zjawinski, S. (2006 April). The Players. *Wired Magazine*.

Chapter 3
Avatars

"The inner life of video games is bound up with the inner life of the player whose response is aesthetic." *(Poole, 2000)*

INTRODUCTION

Virtual worlds may be the future of e-commerce. The game designers who fashioned these flourishing virtual worlds have invented a much more appealing way to use the internet: through an avatar. This usage of the term was coined in 1985 by Chip Morningstar, a user of the first avatar environment created by LucasFilm called Habitat. Habitat lacked many of the features we have in today's games such as quests and puzzles. It was more similar to a social MUD in which the interactivity between avatars was the ultimate goal. According to Encarta: "*Avatar* [Sanskrit]: 1. incarnation of Hindu deity: an incarnation of a Hindu deity in human or animal form, especially one of the incarnations of Vishnu such as Rama and Krishna. 2. embodiment of something: somebody who embodies, personifies, or is the manifestation of an idea or concept. 3. image of person in virtual reality: a movable three-dimensional image that can be used to represent somebody in cyberspace, for example, an Internet user."

Unlike previous video game alter-egos, these avatars can be completely customized and are designed mainly for social interaction (Lastowka and Hunter, 2004). The average player dedicates hundreds of hours (and hundreds of dollars, in some cases). To cultivate his avatar. A survey suggested that approximately 20 percent of Norrath's citizens deem it their place of residence; they just commute to Earth and back. To a large and growing number of people, virtual worlds are an important source of material and emotional well-being. (Yee). Ordinary people, who are bored and frustrated by regular web commerce, participate vigorously and passionately in avatar-based on-line markets.

DOI: 10.4018/978-1-61520-795-4.ch003

A. WHAT IS AN AVATAR, AND HOW DO I CREATE ONE?

Economists have asked, "What features of the virtual worlds give them this competitive edge?" (Castronova, 2001; Simpson, 1999; Barzel, 1997; Lehdonvirta). A synopsis of the conditions for existence in virtual worlds will provide some interesting answers. To enter a virtual world, the player must first connect to the server via the internet. Once the connection is established, the player enters a program that allows him to choose an avatar for himself. In all of the major virtual worlds, one can spend a surprisingly lengthy time at this first stage, choosing the appearance of the avatar as well as its abilities. Avatars, like their human counter-parts, express themselves through appearance and body language. "*Ultima Online* gives you the option to choose your character from a set of templates of traditional professions. You are certainly not required to build your character from a template, but we highly recommend it for the first-time player. You may create multiple characters on each shard (except the Siege shards), so do not worry about creating a character you may not like. Using a template for your first character is an excellent way to get a feel for *Ultima Online*.

To create a character from a template, choose the 'Samurai', 'Ninja', 'Paladin', 'Necromancer', 'Warrior', 'Mage', or 'Blacksmith' option. The 'Advanced' option is for those comfortable enough with the UO skill system to build a character from scratch.

Once you have chosen a starting profession, you will need to customize the 'look' of your character. The image you create will be visible to other players in the game whenever they double-click on you. This image is also known as your 'paperdoll.' You can specify gender, skin colour, hair style and colour, shirt colour, pants/skirt colour and, if you've chosen to play a male character, facial hair style and colour.

Your first character will show up with defaults for all of these options, to change them, simply click on the corresponding part on your character. If you click on an item of clothing, you will then be able to select a colour by clicking anywhere in the palette box to the right of your character. If the selected item is a hair-style, you will see a drop-down menu appear to the left of your character listing all of the style options. Clicking on one will apply it to your character. When you are satisfied with your appearance, click the small green arrow to continue." (http://www.uo.com/newplayer/newplay_0.html).

Depending on the game universe, the player can freely, within the confines of the world's 'realities', select sex, appearance, profession, and physical features (Damer, 1998). Always wondered what it is like to be a dwarf? Choose a very short avatar. Want to be one of the geniuses amongst your peers? Make your avatar a brilliant wizard. Need to work on your anger management skills or just get out your aggressions? Give your avatar immense strength and a high skill in wielding a mace. The player then divides the residual pool of ability points between Strength, Stamina, Agility, Dexterity, Intelligence, and Charisma. Most role-playing games have a system for the selection of the numbers mentioned above with intricate rules and many choices. Attributes represented can range from fundamental (endurance, social skill), to the trivial (favourite colour, height), depending on the nature of the game and the degree of detail the players want to go into. These attributes describe the way in which that character will typically act and what the character is capable of doing (See for example, *Ultima Online, supra.* at http://www.uo.com/newplayer/newplay_0.html).

The initial choice of character occurs under a budget constraint of these attributes so that equality of opportunity in the world occurs. Your mace-wielding troll will be stupid, and your clever wizard will have a glass jaw. Simultaneously, the budget constraint guarantees equality among avatars along dimensions that most people think should not matter for social achievement. In particular, male and female avatars have the same initial budget of skills and attributes. Avatars whose physical characteristics (i.e. skin tone, size). are associated with any benefit in the game must accept some compensating disadvantage. Any inequality in the virtual world can only be due to one of two things: a) a person's choices when creating the avatar, or b) their subsequent actions in the virtual world (Filiack, 2003; Castronova, 2003).

Once the avatar is created, she needs a name. So the player must choose one. If they cannot think of one which matches the game's universe, an automatic name generator can be used. This name will become your identifier; your identity, in fact. Your name will be on what you build your reputation. This will become your trade mark. (Walsh, 2004). For example, in *Marvel Enterprises, Inc. and Marvel Characters, Inc. v NCSoft Corporation, NC Interactive, Inc. and Cryptic Studios, Inc.*, Case No. CV 04-9253-RGK in US District Court for the Central District of California, Marvel claimed that NCSoft's computer game 'City of Heroes' infringed their trademarks with their character creation system which allows and encourages players to create heroes that are similar to, or identical in appearance to Marvel's well-known comic book characters. In the United Kingdom, the courts have found these types of characters ineligible for copyright protection, but have not been presented with the trademark question (See e.g., *King Features Syndicate Inc v O&M Kleeman Ltd.*, [1941] A.C. 417, [1941] 2 All E.R. 403 regarding the character of Popeye).

Now it is time to deposit the avatar at some place in the virtual world. As many of the laws of earth science apply, much of the time, it is relatively simple to 'become' the avatar as you observe this new world through its eyes, seeing only where you are looking. If you are at Point A and want to get to point B, you will have to walk or fly your avatar in that direction. You cannot walk through walls. If you jump off a cliff, you will fall and hurt yourself, possibly die. When the sun sets, it gets darker and you will need a light. If you do something repeatedly, you will get better at it. If you hold things, you might drop them; if you drop them, someone else may pick them up. You can give things to another avatar if you wish. You can hit other avatars and biots. Biots are characters controlled by the game and not by another player. You may kill them if you can. And they may kill you.

As defined above, the avatar is the representation of the self in a given physical environment. This environment creates an idealized situation in which a player may freely shape her own 'self'. She has full control over her own image. The majority of players create avatars which resemble themselves to simplify identification. Nonetheless, they tend to take advantage of the game's possibilities to improve their representations, making themselves prettier, stronger, and smarter. It is also significant to note that people talking about their activities while in the game world use the pronoun 'I', each identifying his or her 'self' with their avatar they have created (Filiciak, 2003).

As virtual worlds support diverse social interaction, many who have chosen to visit virtual worlds remain residents of them. For example, the average *EverQuest* player (Norrath avatar), spends about twenty hours a week within the virtual world (Yee). Virtual world citizens design clothes, create furniture, and build houses for their avatars. They also sell their creations to others (Dibbell, 2003; Damer, 1998). They buy and barter virtual chattels on eBay. They form clubs and organizations devoted to mutual aid and protection. Notwithstanding substantial investments of time and creativity, and in light of the emergence of new virtual social orders, the activities within virtual worlds are viewed still by some as games and diversions, not worthy of serious attention. The standard argument is that, at a fundamental level, these social environments are not real and, therefore, not worthy of serious consideration. This argument is mistaken (Lastowka and Hunter, 2004).

The Earth is a natural physical world, with certain natural physical laws of motion, gravity, force, and so on. Events which occur on Earth are seen, heard, and felt by us, through our physical senses. Thus, when our minds experience the Earth, they do so through our physical bodies. These physical bodies must react to the forces imposed on them by the Earth's atmosphere. When we sense an occasion to achieve a goal, we must focus our bodies to act in the Earth's atmosphere to achieve the goal. In that regard, our real bodies are our Earth avatars. Whilst we are in Earth, our selves are embodied in and symbolized by a body that exists in Earth, and only there (Castronova, 2003; Damer, 1998).

When we travel in a virtual world, we do so by engaging with a body that exists there, and only there. The virtual body, like the Earth body, is an avatar. When travelling in a virtual world, one uses the avatar in that world like a means of transport of the self. It is like a vehicle that your mind is driving. You 'get in,' look out the window of your virtual eyes, and then travel around by making your virtual body move. The avatar mediates our self in the virtual world: we inhabit it; we operate it; we collect all of our sensory information about the world from its viewpoint (Id.). I find that I sometimes suffer from a sense of vertigo if I move too quickly or too fast in a virtual world.

B. PRESENCE AND IMMERSION

". . . Video games allow the viewers to engage actively in the scenarios presented. . . . [Players] are temporarily transported from life's problems by their playing, they experience a sense of personal involvement in the action when they work the controls, and they perceive the video games as not only a source of companionship, but possibly as a substitute for it." (Provenzo, 1991). Avatars create 'presence'. This is a technical term used for the scientific application of virtual reality and is the basis for developing a set of aesthetic criteria for analyzing three dimensional video game designs. 'Presence' means the successful feeling of 'being there'.

"Presence is closely related to the phenomenon of distal attribution or externalization, which refer to the referencing of our perceptions to an external space beyond the limits of the sensory organs themselves. In unmediated perception, presence is taken for granted. What could one experience other than one's immediate physical surroundings? However, when perception is mediated by a communication technology, one is forced to perceive two separate environments simultaneously: the physical environment in which one is actually present, and the environment presented via the medium.... Telepresence is the extent to which one feels present in the mediated environment, rather than in the immediate physical environment.... Telepresence is defined as the experience of presence in an environment by means of a communication medium.... In other words, 'presence' refers to the natural perception of an environment, and 'telepresence' refers to the mediated perception of an environment. This environment can be either a temporally or spatially distant 'real' environment (for instance, a distant space viewed through a video camera)., or an animated but non-existent virtual world synthesized by a computer (for instance, the animated 'world' created in a video game).." (Steuer, 1992).

"Presence: the artificial sense that a player has in a virtual environment that the environment is unmediated." (Bolter and Grusin, 2000). "*Immediacy* (or *transparent immediacy*).: A style of visual representation whose goal is to make the viewer forget the presence of the medium (canvas, photographic film, cinema, and so on). and believe that he is in the presence of the object of representation. One of the two strategies of remediation; its opposite is *hypermediacy*, 'A style of representation whose goal is to remind the viewer of the medium.'" (Id.).

The terms immersion and presence are seen together, although both have been so loosely defined as to be interchangeable. Immersion means the player is caught up in the world of the game's story (the diegetic level), but it also refers to the player's love of the game and the strategy that goes into it (the nondiegetic level). It seems clear that if we are talking about immersion in video games at the diegetic level and immersion at the nondiegetic level, then we are talking about two different things, with possibly conflicting sets of aesthetic conventions. No specific terminology has yet been proposed to clarify those issues. In addition, humanities scholars have started to pick up, from scientific literature on virtual reality, the term presence, defined loosely as 'the feeling of being there.' (McMahan, 2003).

A rousing narrative in any medium can be experienced as a virtual reality. "In short, he so buried himself in his books that he spent nights reading from twilight till daybreak and the days from dawn until dark; as so from little sleep and much reading his brain dried up and he lost his wits. He filled his mind with all that he read in them, with enchantments, quarrels, battles, challenges, wounds, wooings, loves, torments, and other impossible nonsense; and so deeply did he steep his imagination in the belief that all the fanciful stuff he read was true, that . . . [h]e decided . . . to turn knight errant and travel through the world with horse and armour in search of adventures." (Miguel de Cervantes, *Don Quixote de la Mancha* (1605), Walter Starkie trans., 1957).

Our brains are designed to tune into stories with a concentration that can eliminate the world around us. The experience of being carried away to an elaborately imagined place is pleasurable in itself, regardless of the fantasy content. This experience is referred to as immersion. This is the gaming world's corresponding theory to the Reader-response Theory discussed early. Immersion is a metaphorical term derived from the physical experience of being submerged in water. "The same feeling is sought from a psychologi-cally immersive experience as that from a plunge in the ocean or swimming pool: the sensation of being surrounded by a completely other reality, as different as water is from air, that takes over all of our attention, our whole perceptual apparatus... in a participatory medium, immersion implies learning to swim, to do the things that the new environment makes possible... the enjoyment of immersion as a participatory activity." (Murray, 1997).

Today's technology does not allow complete immersion in a computer-mediated reality. "Actually, current technology allows a person participating in an internet-based shared virtual reality environment to receive sensory input from two sources at once. To see things in the virtual reality space, one looks at the computer screen. The screen displays an image of the virtual reality space as it would appear to the eyes of the avatar. At the same time, peripheral vision and momentary sideward glances also deliver images from Earth reality to the mind. Similarly, the mind receives sound from both cyberspace and Earth; it receives tactile sensation exclusively from the Earth. Thus, given current technology, "inhabiting an avatar" actually involves nothing more that receiving significant sensory input from a shared virtual reality space. As technology advances, the degree to which signals from cyberspace can dominate total sensory reception will increase." (Kline, Dyer-Witheford, and de Peuter, 2003).

However, players in virtual worlds appear to experience these worlds fully. They fully 'immerse' their minds in the virtual place. The extent of immersion is such that the player is in effect oblivious of his Earth surroundings. After 'jacking in', (term by Gibson, 1984). The player gives his core mental attention to indicators from virtual reality, with only minor input from Earth. They no longer give the impression of being 'here,' but rather 'there.' This is true even to the point that events 'there' have more emotional meaning than something the person experiences on Earth. For example, Ric Hoogestraat (aka Dutch Hoorenbeek). is married to Sue Hoogestraat in Phoenix,

Arizona and to Tenaj Jackalope (the avatar of Janet Spielman).. Ric has never met Janet nor spoken to her on the phone. "But their relationship has taken on curiously real dimensions. They own two dogs, pay a mortgage together and spend hours shopping at the mall and taking long motorcycle rides. This May when Ric needed real-life surgery, [Tenaj] cheered him up with a private island that cost her $120,000 in virtual world's currency, or about $480 in real world dollars. Their bond is so strong that three months ago, Ric asked Janet to be his virtual wife." Needless to say, his real life wife is not amused (Alter, 2007).

When sensor impulses or signals are being received from cyberspace, they received by the mind through the eyes and ears (and, in the future, nose, skin, and tongue), of the avatar. More concretely, a computer program registers a sensory input to the avatar in cyberspace, and that input is delivered via internet, and then interface devices (monitors, speakers, force-feedback gloves, etc.), to the sensory receptors of the mind. (Kline, et al, 2003). Most agree that total photo- and audio- realism is not necessary for a virtual reality environment to produce in the viewer a sense of immersion, a sense that the world they are in is real and complete, although this awareness has not stopped virtual reality producers from aiming for photo- and audio-realism. Also taken for granted is that the more surrounding the virtual reality exhibition technology is (the bigger the screen, the better the surround-sound), the more immersive it will be. However, it is quite possible to become nearly wholly immersed in a desktop virtual reality, for immersion is not totally dependent on the physical dimensions of the technology.

McMahan (2003). identified three conditions which create a sense of immersion in a virtual reality: (1) the user's expectations of the game or environment must match the environment's conventions fairly closely; (2) the user's actions must have a non-trivial impact on the environment; and (3) the conventions of the world must be consistent, even if they don't match those of 'meatspace' (term by Gibson, 1984).

Narrative and narrative genres are often used as a way of defining the conventions of a world and to help the user align their expectations with the logic of the world. It is no accident that role-playing and adventure games, the video game genres that have the most in common with more linear time-based narrative forms such as the cinema, were among the first to go three dimensional. However, narrative is not necessarily a key component of most video games. Instead, many players value games at a nondiegetic level - at the level of gaining points. They try to formulate a winning (or at least an extravagant). Strategy, and want to show off their expertise to other players during the game and afterward, during replay. To be so engaged with a game that a player reaches a level of near-obsessiveness is sometimes referred to as *deep play*. The term originated with Jeremy Bentham, in his *The Theory of Legislation* (Amsterdam: Thoemmes Cortinuum, 1931 reprinted 2005). Bentham was referring to a state of mind in which users would enter into games almost irrationally, even though the stakes were so high it was pointless for them to engage in them at all. "The example given was: a man whose fortune is a thousand pounds; if he wagers five hundred of it on an even bet, the marginal utility of the pound tie stands to win is clearly less than the marginal disutility of the one he stands to lose. 'Having come together in search of pleasure [both participants] have entered into a relationship which will bring the participants, considered collectively, net pain rather than net pleasures.'" (Id.).

According to users, the term *deep play*, as used in gaming magazines, refers to "a player accessing/accumulating layers of meaning that have strategic value... like 'deep play' in a Dungeons and Dragons [board game] context would mean knowing all the monsters and the different schools of magic, for example, whereas 'shallow' play would mean more 'up and running hack and slash' style of play." (Herz, 1997). The term *deep play*, when referring to video games, then, is a measure of a player's level of engagement.

Seeing how much time is devoted to virtual worlds, it seems that a significant portion of the population finds a life mediated through one's Earth avatar less fulfilling than life mediated through an Earth avatar and one or more virtual others as was seen, for example, with Dutch and Tenaj (Alter, 2007). Digital media, including video games, enable them to manipulate their 'selves' and to multiply them indefinitely (Filiciack, 2003). Many appear to enjoy these different identities each of which enjoys its own reputation.

The notion of identity is one of the most important questions posed by Western culture; 'self' is the measure of reality (Bolter, 1984). We match our 'selves' to social relations and in specific situations we present a different 'version' of ourselves. To be conscious is to be engaged in a world that embeds and defines the subject (Davies, 2002). Carl Jung wrote about *personas*, the mask being an integral part of our personality and shaped according to the need to match it with cultural requirements (Campbell, 1972 citing Jung, 1959). Today individuals are encouraged to create their personas according to standards presented by mass media. One creates a persona for oneself in a manner similar to the celebrities who are creating trade marks for not only their products but also for themselves (Walsh, 2004; see also, *Pickett v Prince*, 207 F.3d 402, 403 (7th Cir. 2000).).

A random sample of the moniker changes of celebrities shows a rather predictable fact that when authors and celebrities adopt new symbols to identify themselves, they pick better trademarks: shorter, more memorable names with more appealing connotations. Fabricated monikers include Woody Allen (Allen Konigsberg)., Alan Alda (Alphonso D'Abruzzo)., Anne Bancroft (Anna Maria Italiano)., Pat Benatar (Patricia Andrejewski)., Jack Benny (Benjamin Kubelsky)., Mel Brooks (Melvin Kaminsky)., George Burns (Nathan Birn-baum)., Tom Cruise (Thomas Mapother IV)., Tony Curtis (Bernard Schwartz)., Kirk Douglas (Issur Danielovitch)., Bob Dylan (Robert Zimmerman)., Cary Grant (Archibald Leach)., Elton John (Reg Dwight)., Karl Malden (Mladen Sekulovich)., Barry Manilow (Barry Alan Pincus), Ricky Martin (Enrique Martin Morales), Walter Matthau (Walter Matuschanskayasky), Chuck Norris (Carlos Ray), George Orwell (Eric Blair)., Jack Palance (Walter Palanuik), Martin Sheen (Ramon Estevez), Ringo Starr (Richard Starkey)., Sting (Gordon Sumner), and Mark Twain (Samuel Clemens). For more examples, see Nom de Guerre, http://go.to/real-names. Such monikers are not always voluntarily adopted. Some performers have been pressured to use stage names. This was allegedly the case with John Mellencamp (ne John Mellencamp, but previously called Johnny Cougar, John Cougar, and John Cougar Mellencamp).. Not all celebrities take or are forced to take this course - for instance, Madonna and Britney Spears are well known for the hyper-fabrication of their popular images, but have retained their birth names: Madonna Louise Ciccone and Britney Jean Spears, respectively. Another example, Prince Rogers Nelson (who was formerly known as "Prince"). changed his name to a symbol defying conventional articulation. Though the symbol defies articulation, it has the benefit of being registered as a trademark and also subject to copyright protection, unlike the vast majority of personal names. Judge Posner explained: "The defendant, identified only as "Prince" in the caption of the various pleadings, is a well-known popular singer whose name at birth was Prince Rogers Nelson, but who for many years performed under the name Prince and since 1992 has referred to himself by an unpronounceable symbol reproduced as Figure 1 at the end of this opinion. The symbol is his trademark but it is also a copyrighted work of visual art that licensees of Prince have embodied in various forms, including jewellery, clothing, and musical instruments." *Pickett v Prince*, 207 F.3d 402, 403 (7th Cir. 2000).

C. IDENTITY AND REPUTATION

In a place that offers numerous different virtual worlds, the virtual body becomes the vehicle of choice. The thinking part of humanity – the Self – will find it expedient to don and remove avatars as economic, social, and political circumstances dictate (Huhtamo, 1995). Avatars "are much more than a few bytes of computer data – they are cyborgs, a manifestation of the Self beyond the realms of the physical, existing in a space where identity is self-defined rather than preordained." (Reid). Some have taken this idea all the way to court. In *Tyler v Carter*, 151 F.R.D. 537 (S.D.N.Y. 1993)., the plaintiff claimed she was a cyborg who received her information through 'proteus'. Among other things, the plaintiff alleged that former President Jimmy Carter was the secret head of the Ku Klux Klan and that he, former President Bill Clinton, and Ross Perot were responsible for the murder of at least ten million black women in concentration camps. Needless to say, the case was dismissed sua sponte for being fantastic and delusional under United States Federal Rule of Procedure 12(b).(6).. Virtual environments are the domain of liquid identity. This identity question causes all kinds of insecurities. Just who is the puppeteer hidden behind this little mass of bits and bytes displayed on my computer screen? Can I trust this person? Are they who they say they are? Are they really representing what they say they represent? Can I do business with someone I can not see?

In any medium, social cooperation relies on trust. "The very possibility of achieving stable mutual cooperation depends upon there being a good chance of a continuing interaction" because it is through repeat play that trust is developed (Axelrod, 1984). Signals of commitment are needed to support cooperative behaviour. We usually rely on face-to-face mechanisms for creating these signals and trust (Moringiello, 2005). Cyberspace by its nature facilitates interaction which is independent of geography, physical space or even physical place. It changes how we engage in social relations (Noveck, 2005). As soon as something is valuable and persistent, we seek to associate rights and duties with it. What will those rights be? And what will be the law of online identity to which those rights apply? Raph Koster (2000). has drawn up a Declaration of the Rights of Avatar. "Foremost among these rights is the right to be treated as people and not as disembodied, meaningless, soulless puppets. Inherent in this right are therefore the natural and inalienable rights of man. These rights are liberty, property, security, and resistance to oppression."

At first blush, this may seem to pose a marked challenge for legal theory. Law is built on the concept that the self is a unitary, rational actor. Nevertheless, psychologist, Sherry Turkle, has contended that "the ability of the agent to represent herself as a different person in different online communities, without anyone being able to trace one identity to another, effectively creates multiple ways of knowing, which can be thought of as multiple selves." (Turkle, 1995). This may be a semantic issue. In such an argument, what are referred to as 'multiple selves' are not the same as the 'unitary, rational, choosing self'. To be more precise, the 'multiple selves' exist purely because a unitary higher-order actor, deciding rationally, chose to generate and then occupy them. This higher order actor is the "Self" (Id.). At any given moment, one can actively create himself. One's 'self' arises just to be revoked a moment later and replaced by another 'self' – equally as real as the previous one. Michel Foucault (1980). stressed that "there is no inside 'self', no essence making me who I am." For Foucault, people do not have a 'real' identity within themselves; that's just a way of talking about the self -- a discourse. An 'identity' is communicated to others in your interactions with them, but this is not a fixed thing within a person. It is a shifting, temporary construction.

Post-modern identity is a self-aware identity. The mechanisms running and ruling today's world are complex social relations which require maximum flexibility. Therefore, we relinquish the attempts to maintain a single constant "Self" (Id.). Identity is merely a set of facts: name, location, employment, position, age, gender, or merely certain online behaviours. Identity in the real world is carried with an individual from context to context – the office meeting, the cocktail party or the football field. He 'is' those set of facts. On the other hand, reputation is contextual. On the football pitch, one may be the great coach. But in the office meeting, one might always be the late comer. The fact that one is a winning sports coach is unlikely to automatically earn respect as an expert at a wine tasting. People do not carry a "good" reputation into all the different areas of their lives. Reputations are earned within particular contexts (Zimmer, 2000).

Conceivably the emergence of avatars will expose behaviours that seem contradictory under present theories about the nature of tastes. This flexibility would have been condemned in the old paradigm as inconstancy which is associated with insincerity, hypocrisy, or mental illness. Nowadays, it is a positive attribute. A new, more useful model replaces the non-functional monolithic self. Everybody is a player, and must do everything to the 'Self' to the conditions of the game in order to play better. Anthony Giddens describes this as the "narrative of the self". He believes our everyday activities consist in strengthening and reproducing a set of expectations (theory of structuration).. (as cited by Gauntlett, 2002). This leads to hyper-identity which is related to identity as a hypertext is to a text (Filiciak, 2003; Foucault, 1980). It is more of a process than a finished formation, a complex structure that is updated incessantly by choosing from the multitude of solutions. The argument could be made that the emergence of anonymity on the internet changes nothing essential about the nature of human behaviour. "There will be times and places where it may be alright or even desirable for people to be anonymous, perhaps in areas where confidential feedback is sought or

where knowing specifically who someone is just is not important. Alongside such anonymity, there will be occasions and locations where any kind of dissimulation about identity is not only wrong, it is a felony." said Irving Wladawsky-Berger, chairman emeritus of the IBM Academy of Technology, "For instance, an adult pretending to be a child so that they can enter a virtual world that's meant to be only for kids." (reported by Martens, 2007). Throughout history, technological advancements have allowed the "Self" to act in assorted ways in diverse communities, without anyone being the wiser. The internet only exaggerates this ability.

Hence, it can be suggested that what is changing is not the "Self", which remains unitary, but the effortlessness with which the "Self" can manipulate its appearances in different physical spaces. It exists in the state of continuous construction and reconstruction (Giddens as cited by Gauntlett, 2002). But again, this is nothing new. People have lived double lives since time began. Liquid identity is not in conflict with constancy if the object that integrates the individual's activities. The significance in which these lives are 'double' is wholly a social construct. But it is the individual mind that decides what style coheres. The history of video games indicates that there is no perfectly 'reflective' avatar; i.e., one that resembles the player visually (like in a mirror). and seems to gaze back on her. If the avatar is a reflection, its correspondence to embodied reality consists of mapping not of appearances but of control. One way to consider this 'reflective relationship' in third-person games such as the *Tomb Raider* series (1996 – present)., in which a 'chase camera' follows the avatar but rarely reveals her face, is by analogy a two-mirror system. Positioning a hand mirror so that its reflection is visible in a larger mirror, I can, for example, glimpse the back of my own head: the image is still recognizably me, yet I do not return my own gaze.

From the point of view of theory, no incongruity occurs when someone appears in *Second Life* as both a young man and an old woman. If variety is really the spice of life, theorists would *predict* that the unitary actor will opt for a number of different physical appearances by which to materialize. The development of avatars, and the shifting of the "Self" between them, has no real consequence for the applicability of rational choice theories (Castronova, 2003; Turkle, 1995; Rehak, 2003). In conventional terms of reasoning, post-modern identity can be considered schizophrenic; however, it should not be looked upon as pathology but as a virtue.

However, these changes have consequences for the communities that humans form. Rational choice theories of social effects stress the importance of information for the preservation of social norms. The enforcement of norms is effective only if it is possible to impose some kind of penalty on the violators. Resolving problems is less likely to involve law enforcement and more likely to centre around the contracts entered into when becoming a member of a particular virtual world, according to Beth Simone Noveck, a professor of law at the New York Law School. "We'll see the emergence of more sophisticated contract services," she said, "so that the residents in a virtual community set the rules on which their world is based and take all the major decisions on the criteria for the entry contract." (Martens, 2007).

As such, past reputational data should be preserved, transparent, and widely shared in order to produce reliable and persistent online identities. "Our conception of identity is dependent on the technology that mediates between social interaction." (David, 2005). In a virtual community, the 'real' "Self" is hidden behind the avatar generally. Consequently, any punishments the community may dictate can only be imposed on the avatar, not the "Self". The "Self" is free to simply exit the avatar and escape unscathed (Mnookin, 1996; Lessig, 1999). Although, identity online is more easily created, abandoned or shielded than in real life, virtuosity is making that both easier yet more difficult. Tools such as OpenID and ClaimID are the beginnings of managing virtuosity across

online spaces. OpenID allows people to carry their identity from one virtual place to another for convenience, while ClaimID gives them a tool to pool and manage their various reputations. OpenID is a solution for the log-in problem of having multiple identities online. With OpenID, a person creates one master identity online at a site that he uses a lot and tends to remain logged in to--for instance, a social network site or a personal blog. When that person needs to identify himself to another new site, he points that site toward his main identity-providing site where he is already logged in. His main site sends the new site his log-in credentials, so the new site now knows who he is. In theory, if OpenID was adopted on every Web site around the Web, you'd need only one universal log-in and could forgo the often tedious practice of remembering user names and passwords (http://www.openid.org/news.aspx ; http://www.virtuosity.com/).

Technology, thus, defines the scope of social relationships and our online social interaction has different characteristics. The most important characteristic being that identity is becoming enriched with more persistent forms of reputation. Reputation is of course tied to an identity. They are two sides of the same coin. Reputation, however, is earned over time. As such, identity without reputation is nearly meaningless. It is a measure of reputation allowing us an assessment of risk in doing business with someone. In business at the moment of "transaction" (however it is defined). what is needed is to know and determine is reputation. So, reputation devices like credit scores or a domain name system or eBay ratings have been created (Resnick, Zeckhauser, Swanson, and Lockwood, 2006).

A reputation is the "estimation in which a person or thing is commonly held." (Oxford Dictionary, 1975). Reputation is a fundamental part of your virtual self. Conversations in virtual worlds can be stored, and who you are becomes more a function of the community's view of you, your behaviour and your contributions to a particular piece of a virtual world. In this social software environment of collaborative creativity and interaction, representation becomes malleable and reputation becomes community-created. As such, online reputation needs to recognize the interests of the collective as well as of the individual in the manner in which identity is constructed online.

In a pay-for-play game like *World of Warcraft* for example, reputation is key. Listed below are the different reputation levels. Generally speaking, you start out as neutral with most factions; gaining friendly takes some effort, but it's not excessive. Honored is a bit more challenging; revered and exalted are monumental accomplishments requiring tremendous effort.

Unfair play is punished by banning a player from the game. The player's account is terminated, and all his avatars effectively eliminated, permanently. Unfortunately, nothing can stop the banished player from opening a new account, with a different credit card, and starting new avatars (Mnookin, 1996; Lessig, 1999). Hence, it appears that nothing thwarts anyone from violating any and all social norms, without consequence. This may cause one to think that the future of a stable community in such an environment seem hopeless. The instability of online communities has been studied by sociologists for a long time (Id.; Damer, 1998; Turkle, 1995; Yee). However, economists suggest that people/players will sort themselves into discrete units based upon how interested they are in living in a community regulated by particular social norms (Samuelson, 1994; Johnson, 1997).

Such arrangements are apparent in existing virtual worlds. Virtual worlds with built-in systems for maintaining player reputations seem immeasurably more popular than worlds where reputations cannot be known.

For example, *AlphaWorld* bestows upon all avatars the same capabilities at all times. *AlphaWorld* is the oldest collaborative virtual world on the Internet, and home to millions of people from all over the world. Since its birth in 1995, *AlphaWorld* attempted to do for 3D virtual worlds what web browsers did for the 2D Web: it created a tool for exploring and building three-dimensional spaces. The programmers at Active Worlds created a library of objects that users could assemble like Lego blocks into buildings, cars, and other composite structures. By 1998, they had released a software development kit that enabled users to build their own custom objects, called blocks. See *The Active Worlds SDK*, http://www.activeworlds.com/sdk, and particularly the timeline of changes to the SDK, at *What's New in the Active Worlds SDK*, http://www.activeworlds.com/sdk/whatsnew.htm. With these tools, *AlphaWorld* users have not only replicated Rome's Coliseum, but have created entire parallel worlds. For all this construction and creativity, Active Worlds has never been a commercial success: it only instituted a monthly-fee model in September 1997, and to date has only registered a total of 70,000 users, see *The Activeworlds Corporation: Company Information*, http://www.activeworlds.com/info/index.asp, partially because the world has no te-

Exalted	The highest level of reputation attainable with any faction.
Revered	Special reputation level reserved for heroes.
Honored	10% discount on bought items from vendors.
Friendly	Standard reputation level which gives access to certain vendor items.
Neutral	Standard reputation level for factions that are not on a players list and are not KOS (Kill on Sight)..
Unfriendly	Cannot buy, sell or interact, but are not KOS either. Isn't that a real peach?
Hostile	KOS, there's no coming back from this one folks.
Hated	KOS (all opposing team factions are set on this level)..

(Reputation Guide at http://www.worldofwar.net/guides/reputation/).

leology. That said, *AlphaWorld* set the stage for a new generation of virtual worlds, like Linden Lab's *Second Life*, that not only offer malleability to their users, but also economic freedom to sell their creations in both virtual markets and real-world exchanges. *AlphaWorld* has rapidly grown in size and is roughly as large as the state of California, and now exceeds 60 million virtual objects (Id.). Consequently, a player who defies a social norm in *AlphaWorld*, if banished, can generate a new avatar immediately, using a different name, which will have all of the same capabilities and skills as previously. The community can have no effect on behaviour.

This is in direct contrast with a game like *EverQuest*. In *EverQuest*, a player's ability to be a nuisance to others depends on his level of skills. These skills and talents can only be acquired by dedicating hours to an avatar, in team-based operations with other avatars. As a result, advancement in the game necessitates that a player become recognized for good play, so as to be invited into teams or guilds. A player who breaches the unwritten rules will not advance very far, purely on grounds of reputation. Indeed, there is little or nothing a player can achieve in *EverQuest* without the help of others. A player may weigh up starting again to obtain a new reputation by simply creating a new avatar; however, the new avatars are so weak and poor that they can be of very little use to anyone.

The incorporation of team effort and level-based advancement seems ample to support very strong social norms in the games. Consequently, such norms appear to be present. The wider implication is that the diversity of avatar characteristics is of practical use not only as an end in itself, but also as a means to force players to develop and maintain good reputations for their avatars. In *World of Warcraft*, the players are encouraged to go on quests and adventures for certain factions. What the player gains on the successful completion of the quests is a reputation. Gaining reputation with some factions allows you to purchase items that are unavailable to other players. Building reputation also opens up some unique quests, usually with impressive item rewards, that are similarly unavailable to others (Reputation Guide at http://www.worldofwar.net/guides/reputation/). Specialized traits allow coordination of joint efforts, which can have the derivative consequence of inducing conformity to social norms. Avatars tend to mimic their players as they develop personality, individuality, and an ability to act within the virtual world – as any person on their way to maturity (Rehak, 2003).

At the same time, no hierarchy of norms in virtual worlds can be really oppressive. Anyone wanting to participate according to a certain set of rules, or without any rules at all is free to occupy avatars in their chosen virtual worlds. A noteworthy point is that the systems that encourage norm formation also tend to slow down the shifting of populations which, in turn, leads to equality of opportunity. Equality of opportunity becomes apparent as dissatisfied players can develop capital in different kinds of avatars. It becomes more obvious more quickly if the substitution of one powerful avatar for another can be accomplished swiftly. Reputation is a fundamental part of your virtual self. Conversations in virtual worlds can be stored, and who you are becomes more a function of the community's view of you, your behaviour and your contributions to a particular piece of a virtual world.

In spite of that, a system that promotes reputations will need to require that it is *not* simple to develop capital rapidly in another avatar. If it were, players could ruin their reputation with one avatar, terminate that avatar, and then merely re-emerge with another avatar of comparable powers. Harriet Pearson, IBM's vice president of regulatory policy and the vendor's chief privacy officer, wonders about the concept of reputation bankruptcy. Might an individual who has fallen from grace in the virtual world and acknowledged their shortcomings then be able to effectively hit a "reset button" deleting their previous bad reputation and start over? In the same way that in the real world juvenile offender records are sealed so they can not be widely accessed, in the virtual world a former bad reputation could perhaps be expunged. "You don't want to be bugged by what you did," she said. "Avatars, our stand-ins in virtual environments like Second Life, Active Worlds and There.com, give little away about who's pulling their strings in the real world." (Martens, 2007).

The credibility of social norm enforcement relies on the degree to which a player has a vested interest in the fate of the avatar. If players are deeply invested in their avatars, and are reluctant to create new ones, it will take more time for the levelling process of population shifting to occur. A big problem in *Second Life* is that it takes a long time to figure out how to do things. Once this is solved, *Second Life* could become a smoother road than the web itself. "So taking that average of the four hours it takes now for people to understand *Second Life* down to 40 minutes will move us from 10% retention of users to more than 50% and then the 3D web will rapidly be the dominant thing and everyone will have an avatar." (Bulkley, 2007). There is a trade-off between equal opportunity and social order. Players will choose virtual worlds based on their relative desires for both (Johnson, 1997; Castronova, 2003).

Of course the natural laws of earth do not necessarily apply in a virtual world that exists entirely as software. As such, much of what characterizes an avatar's uniqueness is its ability to bend or break some of these laws and not others. Contingent on the skills selected, an avatar may be able to see for miles, cast spells, hypnotize, heal wounds, teleport themselves, or shoot great flaming fireballs at other avatar's heads. However, there are budget constraints. Those who can heal or hypnotize often have difficulty summoning a fireball worthy of mention. Accordingly, avatars come to view themselves as specialized agents, much as workers in a developed economy do. The avatar's skills will establish whether the avatar

will be a demander or supplier of various goods and services in the virtual world (Damer, 1998). Each avatar cultivates a social role.

While the undertaking of designing enjoyable avatars and virtual worlds may be complex and somewhat byzantine, the fact remains that these virtual worlds are in demand which, consequently, suggests that they will have the net effect of increasing cumulative well-being. IBM believes that virtual worlds and other 3D Internet environments offer significant opportunity to our company, our clients and the world at large, as they evolve, grow in use and popularity, and become more integrated into many aspects of business and society. As an innovation-based company, IBM encourages employees to explore responsibly and to further the development of such new spaces of relationship-building, learning and collaboration. As we engage in these new environments, IBMers should follow and be guided first and foremost by our values and our Business Conduct Guidelines (*IBM Virtual World Guidelines*).

All told, the readiness to pay for participation in a shared virtual reality environment is conditional upon the emotional experiences that the environment provides which, in turn, is a function of the attributes a player is permitted to have, as well as the player's inherent non-physical attributes and the attributes of the environment itself. The virtual world builders control the coding authority, and the coding authority can make the virtual world into absolutely anything that the mind can imagine. Philip Rosedale CEO of Linden Lab told the Guardian that they are building the technology to allow a *Second Life* avatar identity to wander out across the web. The founder of the virtual world Second Life believes that his company, Linden Lab, is at the forefront of the internet's next big revolution - the 3D web. "We are building the backend to support that. We believe the concept of identity through your avatar will span the web. We are going to seek to enable that. Technology-wise, it's only about 18 months away. I do think we will see some interconnected virtual worlds… But reputation must come right along with identity." (Bulkley, 2007).

Therefore, anything that the players can do to influence the virtual world creators, in some manner outside the game, can be used to change the very nature of the virtual world within the game (Lessig, 1999). As we delve deeper and wider into virtual spaces, both our identities and reputations are scattered across them. The rise of these types of difficult problems of choice in cyberspace has nothing to do with the fact that human beings are interacting via avatars in virtual reality; it has everything to do with the fact that they are human beings, interacting. The next chapter explores whether identity gives rise to personhood which, in turn, could create a property right.

REFERENCES

Alter, A. (2007). Is This Man Cheating on His Wife? *The Wall Street Journal. Allakhazam's Magical Realm (*n.d.). Retrieved from http://links. allakhazam.com/EverQuest/Guilds

Axelrod, R (1984). *The Evolution of Cooperation.*

Barzel, Y. (1997). *Economic Analysis of Property Rights* (2nd ed.). Cambridge, UK: Cambridge University Press. doi:10.1017/CBO9780511609398

Bentham, J. (1931). *The Theory of Legislation.* Amsterdam: Thoemmes Cortinuum.

Bolter, J. D. (1984). *Turing's Man: Western Culture in the Computer Age.* Chapel Hill, NC: University of North Carolina Press.

Bolter, J. D., & Grusin, R. (2000). *Remediation: Understanding New Media.* Cambridge, MA: MIT Press.

Bulkley, K. (2007). Today Second Life, tomorrow the world. *The Guardian.*

Campbell, J. (1972). *The Hero with a Thousand Faces.* Princeton, NJ: Princeton University Press.

Castronova, E. (2001). *Virtual Worlds: A First-Hand Account of Market and Society on the Cyberian Frontier.* CESifo Working Paper Series No. 618.

Castronova, E. (2003). *Theory of the Avatar.* CESifo Working Paper Series No. 863.

Cervantes, M. (1605). *Don Quixote de la Mancha (W. Starkie, trans.).* London: MacMillan & Co.

Damer, B. (1998). *Avatars!* Berkeley, CA: Peachpit Press.

David, P. A. (20005). From Keeping 'Nature's Secrets' to the Institutionalization of 'Open Science . In Ghosh, R. A. (Ed.), *CODE: Collaborative Ownership and the Digital Economy.*

Davies, E. (2002). Synthetic Mediations: Cogito in the Matrix . In Toffts, D., Jonson, A. M., & Cavallaro, A. (Eds.), *Prefiguring Cyberculture: An Intellectual History.* Cambridge, MA: MIT Press.

Dibbell, J. (2003). The Unreal Estate Boom: 79th Richest Nation on Earth Doesn't Exist. *Wired Magazine.* eBay (n.d.). *Listings, Internet Games.* Retrieved from http://listings.ebay.com/pool2/ listings/list/all/category4596/index.html

Filiciak, M. (2003). Hyperidentities – Post-modern Identity Patterns in Massively Multiplayer Online Role-Playing Games . In Wolf, M. J. P., & Perron, B. (Eds.), *The Video Game Theory Reader.* London: Routledge.

Foucault, M. (1980). *Power/Knowledge: Selected Interviews and Other Writings 1972-1977* (Gordon, C., Ed.). London: Harvester.

Gauntlett, D. (2002). Anthony Giddens: The Theory of Structuration . In *Media, Gender, and Identity: An Introduction.* London, New York: Routledge. doi:10.4324/9780203360798

Gibson, W. (1984). *Neuromancer*. London: Haper-Collins Publishers.

Herz, J. C. (1997). *Joystick Nation: How Video Games Ate Our Quarters, Won Our Hearts and Rewired Our Minds*. Boston, MA: Little, Brown, and Company.

Huhtamo, E. (1995). Encapsulated Bodies in Motion: Simulators and the Quest for Total Immersion . In Penny, S. (Ed.), *Critical Issues in Electronic Media*. Albany, NY: State University of New York Press.

IBM Virtual World Guidelines (n.d.). Retrieved from http://domino.research.ibm.com/comm/research_projects.nsf/pages/virtualworlds.IBM-VirtualWorldGuidelines.html

Johnson, S. (1997). *Interface Culture: How New Technology Transforms the Way We Create and Communicate*. San Francisco, CA: Harper Edge.

Jung, C. (1959). *The Undiscovered Self*. New York: Signet Books.

Kline, S., Dyer-Witheford, N., & de Peuter, G. (2003). *Digital Play: The Interaction of Technology, Culture, and Marketing*. Montreal, Canada: McGill-Queen's University Press.

Koster, R. (2000). *A Declaration of the Rights of Avatars*. Retrieved from http://raphkoster.com/gaming/playerrights.shtml

Lastowka, G. & Hunter, D (2004). The Laws of the Virtual World. *Calif. L. Rev., 92*(1).

Lehdonvirta, V. (n.d.). *Real Money Trade of Virtual Assets: New Strategies for Virtual World Operators*. Helsinki Institute for Information Technology (HIIT). Retrieved from http://www.hiit.fi/u/vlehdonvirta

Lessig, L. (1999). *Code and Other Laws of Cyberspace*. New York: Basic Books.

Martens, C. (2007). WORLDBEAT: ID malleability creates virtual-world issues. *IDG News Service*. Retrieved from http://www.itworld.com/Net/2614/070627id/

Massive Multiplayer Online: Clans and Guilds, Open Directory Project. Retrieved from http://dmoz.org/Games/Video_Games/Roleplaying/Massive_Multiplayer_Online/Clans_and_Guilds

McMahan, A. (2003). Immersion, Engagement, and Presence: A Method for Analyzing 3-D Video Games . In Wolf, M. J. P., & Perron, B. (Eds.), *The Video Game Theory Reader*. London: Routledge.

Mnookin, J. (1996). Virtual(ly) Law: The Emergence of Law in LambdaMOO. *Journal of Computer-Mediated Communication, 2*(1).

Moringiello, J.M (2005). Signals, Assent, and Internet Contracting. *Rutgers L. Rev., 57*(1307).

Morningstar, C., & Farmer, F. R. (1991). *The Lessons of LucasFilm's Habitat, in Cyberspace: First Steps*. Retrieved from http://www.fudco.com/chip/lessons.html

Murray, J. (1997). *Hamlet on the Holodeck: The Future of Narrative in Cyberspace*. Cambridge, MA: The MIT Press.

Noveck, B. S. (2005). Trademark Law and The Social Construction of Trust: Creating The Legal Framework for Online Identity. Wash. U. L. Q., 83(1733).

The Pocket Oxford Dictionary. (1975). Oxford: Clarendon Press.

Poole, S. (2000). *Trigger Happy: The Inner Life of Videogames*. London: Arcade.

Provenzo, E. (1991). *Video Kids: Making Sense of Nintendo*. Boston, MA: Harvard University Press.

Rehak, B. (2003). Playing. Retrieved from Being: Psychoanalysis and the Avatar . In Wolf, M. J. P., & Perron, B. (Eds.), *The Video Game Theory Reader*. London: Routledge.

Reid, E. (n.d.). *Text-based Virtual Realities: Identity and the Cyborg Body*. Retrieved from http://www.rochester.edu/College/FS/Publications/ReidIdentity.html

Reputation Guide (n.d.). Retrieved from http://www.worldofwar.net/guides/reputation/

Resnick, P., Zeckhauser, R., Swanson, J., & Lockwood, K. (2006). The Value of Reputation on eBay: A Controlled Experiment. *Experimental Economics, 9*(2). doi:10.1007/s10683-006-4309-2

Samuelson, P. (1994). A Manifesto Concerning the Legal Protection of Computer Programs. *Columbia Law Review, 94*(2308).

Simpson, Z. B. (1999). *The In-game Economics of Ultima Online*. Retrieved from http://www.mine-control.com/zack/uoecon/uoecon.html

Steuer, J. (1992). Defining Virtual Reality: Dimensions Determining Telepresence. *The Journal of Communication, 42*(4). doi:10.1111/j.1460-2466.1992.tb00812.x

Turkle, S. (1995). *Life on the Screen: Identity in the Age of the Internet*. New York: Simon & Schuster.

Ultima Online. (n.d.). *New Player Guide*. Retrieved from http://www.uo.com/newplayer/newplay_0.html

Walsh, M. (2004). *I, Product*. Wired Magazine.

Yee, N. (n.d.). *The Norrathian Scrolls: Real-Life Demographics*. Retrieved from http://nickyee.com/eqt/demographics.html

Zimmer, L. (2000). *Identity versus Reputation: Wandering and Wondering in Virtual Spaces*. Retrieved from http://freshtakes.typepad.com/sl_communicators/2007/05/identity_versus.html

Chapter 4
Philosophy, Personality and Property

Property and law are born together, and die together. Before laws were made there was no property; take away laws, and property ceases. —Jeremy Bentham

[T]o be a full individual in liberal society, one must be an appropriator, defined by what one owns, including oneself as a possession, not depending on others, free. — O'Donovan, 1997

INTRODUCTION

What is a body, a matter of law? (Rao, 2007; Scott, 1981). Where is the body? Is it integral or severable from the legal person? Is it a commodity? Have our bodies, our selves, and our labour become commodities with a market exchange value? (Radin, 1996). The bioscientific conversion of the body into information has become labelled postmodern. Jean Baudrillard described this postmodernity as 'hyperreality'. (Poster, 1999). This means that only the viewer only acknowledges the real in its

image – reality, as the hyperreal, is "always already reproduced". (Id.). The process of conversion of the body, the human organism, into genetic information is just such a reproduction. Just as the process of conversion of the personality into reputational information is also such a reproduction. This means that the body need no longer exist only as a corporeal reality, but also as the 'mirroring' body, quite literally 'a body of information.' (Halewood, 2008)

This represents a further stage of 'de-physicalization' of property begun with Hohfeld's (1917) seminal recognition of property as a bundle of rights. The body is now cast as genetic 'information' representing property de-physicalized twice over with intellectual property in bodies, not only is there a bundle of rights in things, but also rights to information about things, or rights to things as information. What has happened to the body reflects what has happened to the economy. Society has moved from one of production to one of information, from manufacturing to information processing. Avatars and their accessories epitomize this shift.

DOI: 10.4018/978-1-61520-795-4.ch004

A. OWNERSHIP OF PERSONS

Similar to most social institutions, property rights are justified by the benefits they bring to individuals in society. The overriding understanding of this justification for all types of property has been an economic formula. Property rights are the most effective method to produce social wealth. (Hughes, 1998). This same general justification has given rise to theories regarding the non-economic benefits of property. Add to this idea that persons are now all free and equal is supposed to be fundamental to modern liberal legal systems - the free person is not only the basic legal unit but also the very *raison d'etre* of our law. (Davies & Naffine, 2001). We do not recognise slavery; one person cannot own another. It is regarded as an abomination to commodify another human being in this manner. This was seen most clearly in the case of *Moore v Regents of the University of California* 793 P2d 479 (Cal. S. Ct. 1990).

The Western democracies outlawed slavery in the nineteenth century, though as Russell Scott (1981) has observed, it has "not all disappeared from the Eastern world or from the African and South American continents." Although English law never openly tolerated slavery, England was home to a number of slavers who derived immense wealth from the traffic in persons. English slavers, however, wisely conducted their trade in other parts of the world. (Baker, 1990). In the famous *Sommersett's Case* of 1772, English law decided against slavery, proclaiming its allegiance to the Enlightenment person and promising a protection for freedom. It was concluded that there was no "positive, or legislative, authorisation of slavery in England." This point of view accords with the views of two of the leading philosophers of political and legal liberty, Immanuel Kant and John Locke, who, in different ways, both condemned the idea of treating other persons as property. Hegel (1952, trans. by Knox) went on to develop a theory of property linked to self-ownership.

According to Kant (1930, trans. by Infield) "a person cannot be property and so cannot be a thing which can be owned, for it is impossible to be a person and a thing, the proprietor and the property." Locke, too, was adamant about the importance of freedom from possession by others. In *The Second Treatise on Government*, Locke (1690, repub. 1967) begins his discourse on slavery by saying that: "The Natural Liberty of Man is to be free from any Superior Power on Earth, and not to be under the Will... of Man ... not to be subject to the inconstant, uncertain, unknown, Arbitrary Will of another man." Further: "This Freedom from Absolute, Arbitrary Power, is so necessary to, and closely joyned with a Man's Preservation, which he cannot part with it, but by what forfeits his Preservation and Life together. For a Man, not having the Power of his own Life, cannot, by Compact or his own Consent, *enslave himself* to anyone ... No body can give more Power than he has himself; and he that cannot take away his Life, cannot give another power over it." (Id.).

Thus, according to modern legal orthodoxy, the categories of person and property are now meant to be utterly separate and distinct. To be a person, it is said, is precisely not to be property. It might then be argued that the one concept negatively defines the other. (Davies & Naffine, 2001). I believe that this idea is susceptible of at least one other analysis especially in light of the concept of avatars as extensions of one's person. The issue is not about slavery, i.e., whether one person can own another, but rather about whether we are in some way our own property. Can a person be property in the sense that he is somehow the proprietor of himself? Can property rights be perceived as a means to protect a personality interest or 'personhood' of an individual?

Persons are not property: to be a person is not to be reduced to the property of another. Yet, I would suggest that we own ourselves. If this is so, then to be a person is to be imbued with the idea of property. To be a person is be a proprietor and also to be property – the property of oneself. It can be said that this idea is legal shorthand to help describe the array of rights enjoyed by a modern individual in relation to himself and to others. (O'Donovan, 1997). The story of the emergence of modern law and its reliance on relations based on contract is the story of the man who quite naturally has property in his person, who has self-ownership. Thus he has the right to his capacities and to the products of his labours.

Hegel and Locke philosophies have been studied and argued in modern legal literature to also demonstrate that property and personhood could be connected in at least two ways. Property in things other than oneself has been said to enhance personhood, because it establishes an extended sphere of non-interference with one's person. Margaret Jane Radin (1982), in a modern rendition of Hegel's thought, has called this 'property for personhood'. Property and personhood have also been linked in a more intimate manner by the assertion that persons may also be said to have property in themselves. Common to both approaches has been a desire to show how property interests express and secure the autonomy of the individual and hence their very personhood.

B. PROPERTY AS PERSONHOOD

1. Personhood and the Lockean Justification for Property

John Locke grounded his argument for property in labour. The U.S. Constitution's framers were familiar with Locke's writings, and gave expression to some of his ideas in the Declaration of Independence and the Constitution. (Locke, 1690, repub. 1967). The US courts continue to cite Locke, both explicitly and implicitly, in cases of intangible property rights. For example, in the case, *Ruckelshaus v Monsanto Co.*, 467 U.S. 986 (1984), the court held that trade secret rights are 'property' protected under the Takings Clause and

quoted Locke to support this proposition. Locke's argument that property rights should be tied to labour is a precursor of the common law doctrine of unjust enrichment. "Unjust enrichment involves the general principle that one person should not be allowed to unjustly enrich himself at the expense of another, but should be required to make restitution for property or benefits received." (Scott, 2003). Considering Locke's theory of property, its application to virtual worlds may be appropriate because his conception of property stemmed in part from his belief in an America of boundless, endless land. (Locke, 1689 repub. 2003). It is hardly surprising that his view of property can be pressed into service in this new, seemingly boundless environment called cyberspace, as it has been applied in similar arenas such as domain names. (*Kremen v Cohen*, No. 01-15899 (9th Cir. July 25, 2003)). Goldstein (1994) suggests that it has more generally been applied in the limitless, largely non-rival, arena of intellectual property. "Bubbling beneath all [intellectual property] ... is the intuition that people should be able to hold on to the value of what they create, to reap where they have sown." (Id.)

Locke thought a man could be a proprietor of himself. For, although he rejected the idea that persons could be the property of others, he explicitly endorsed the idea that we own ourselves - our persons and our labours. "Though the Earth, and all inferior Creatures be common to all Men, yet every Man has a Property in his own Person. This no Body has Right to but himself. The Labour of his Body, and the Work of his Hands, we may say, are properly his." (Locke, 1689 repub. 2003). Locke's central property thesis is that "whatsoever [man] removes out of the state that nature hath provided and left it in, he hath mixed his labour with, and joined to it something that is his own, and thereby makes it his property." (Id.)

Locke's property theory is a theory of dessert from labour; that is, the person who expended labour to render the "thing in nature" into valuable form deserves to reap its value. (Munzer, 1990;

Radin, 1982). The application of work and the expenditure of effort, at least in the protean world that was Locke's 'America,' justify the allocation of property interests. Players and avatars might assert they have a property claim in their virtual-world assets based on the Lockean labour-dessert theory. The assets in question emerge from the time and effort of the players. One might claim that playing a game is not labour. This is hardly strong argument in a world where professional athletes are paid fortunes to play games. As anyone who has slaved over a virtual forge will tell you, creating virtual-world property can involve at least as much tedium as any real-world work. In fact, the virtual work performed by users may closely mirror their real-world occupations. (Dibbell, 1998)

Locke notably employed the argument that we all naturally own ourselves as a justification for private appropriation of the commons. His view was that once we mix our labour (which we own naturally) with an object in the commons, we gain property in it. Self-ownership therefore provides a foundation for ownership of the external world. If someone else later takes this new product, this person harms the individual and thereby violates the first tenet. Therefore, the individual deserves a legally enforceable property right to protect the fruits of her labour. (Gordon, 1993)

Locke was unclear as to when someone has signalled her appropriation of property through her labour, i.e., when she has mixed her labour with material from the public domain and thereby created an enforceable right. (Olivercrona, 1974) Some argue that appropriative labour requires altering materials in the public domain in a way "that makes [them] usable and thus more valuable to humanity." (Id.) Locke did indicate that property ownership should only attach when it benefited, or at least did nothing to harm, the common good: "Labour being the unquestionable Property of the Labourer, no Man but he can have a right to what that is once joyned to, at least where there is enough and as good left in common for others."

(Locke, 1689 repub. 2003)

But a 'common good' requirement for property ownership still leaves a lot of room for interpretation. Locke argues that one person's joining of her labour with resources that God gave mankind ('appropriation') should not give that individual a right to exclude others from the resulting product, unless the exclusion would leave these other people with as much opportunity to use the common as they otherwise would have had. (Gordon, 1993) The problem with the above interpretation is that it strays from the personhood justification for property rights.

Locke's writings on the subject are sparse. As a result, Locke's common good requirement can easily be interpreted as a concern with public welfare in the aggregate. The requirement is satisfied if a system of property rights for labourers leaves the population better off as a whole than if there were no property rights. (Bartholomew, 2001) The labour justification for property rights does not have to clash with the personhood justification. A better way to interpret Locke's reasoning is to look at what the labourer (player) is hoping to achieve through her work. Appropriative labour is that which causes the labourer (player) to psychologically identify with her work. (Gordon, 1993)

Karl Olivecrona (1974) argues that Locke perceived the fruits of labour to be an extension of the labourer's (player's) personality. "By Property I must be understood here, as in other places, to mean that Property which Men have in their Persons as well as Goods," Locke explained. (Locke, 1689 repub. 2003) Locke defined appropriation as using labour to make an object a part of one's self. (Id.) Olivecrona (1974) writes that Locke unequivocally "expressed the idea that the personality is extended to encompass physical objects." Moreover, appropriative labour could encompass intangibles as well. Locke's seventeenth-century contemporaries understood property to include abstract things like an individual's religious faith. Why should property then not include such an abstract thing as virtual property?

In spite of this, all is not settled for a Locke-invoking avatar. Robert Nozick best summarized the standard objection made to Locke's vision: "If I own a can of tomato juice and spill it into the sea so that its molecules mingle ... do I thereby come to own the sea?" (Nozick, 1974; Zemer, 2006) The corporate owners of the virtual world might similarly argue that a player in their world could not claim property in any aspect of the virtual world, since his or her playing actions are little more than releasing tomato juice.

Two standard defences to this objection apply here. The first defence notes that Locke's theory only grants property where the "labour makes the far greatest part of the value of [the asset]." (Locke, 1689 repub. 2003) If the tomato juice made up the greatest part of the value of the sea, then we might think differently about granting maritime property rights to the tomato juice polluter. Within the virtual world framework, one could conclude that the player cannot claim property interests in the entire virtual world but might legitimately and reasonably claim them in some smaller part - the virtual castle, sword, or breastplate - in which his labour makes up the greatest part of the value. (Lastowka & Hunter, 2004; Raysman & Brown, 2005) This is the tack that Linden Lab's *Second Life* has chosen to take.

The second defence to the Nozickian objection is that any property claim in the sea (or any other common resource) applies only to the extent of the so-called Lockean Proviso. That is, the property claim can only occur to the point at which the property interest leaves "enough and as good" in common for others. (Id. citing Gordon, 1993) In contrast to physical resources such as the sea, the provision of property interests in virtual worlds does not reduce other property interests, since the world is essentially limitless. (Id.) I am not suggesting that any particular party should be granted ownership of virtual property, but simply noting that, in itself, the creation of a property right in virtual objects does not infringe on the ability of others to possess virtual objects. As a result, the Nozickian objection fails.

Locke's philosophy is consistent with protecting player's avatars and virtual property because it is harmful to take away a part of someone's personality. When an object has been appropriated and becomes part of the possessor's 'sphere of personality,' writes Olivecrona (1974), "it will be an injury to the possessor to deprive him of it.... For his own person (avatar) is exclusively his own."

2. Personhood and the Hegelian Justification for Property

Then there is Hegel's theory of property linked to self-ownership. (Hegel, 1952, trans. by Knox) He argued that in becoming a person one must put oneself into the external world and then re-appropriate the self through the appropriation of objects in the world. Taking the world unto ourselves is our method of completing our subjectivity and individuality, because it involves the purely subjective person externalising their personality and re-grasping it in the form of an external object. (Id.) In other words, a person does not have a concrete existence until she forms a relationship with something external. Self-actualization occurs by acting on an object. (Bartholomew, 2001) Property is 'embodied personality'. Property is only property insofar as it is occupied by a person's will. (Hegel, 1952, trans. by Knox) Property gives us the means of forming contractual relations with others. Through ownership we are able to recognise others as owners, and exchange our property. Property is therefore essential to the formation of social relationships.

Hegel's account of the sovereign individual is therefore quite different from Locke's. For Locke, the free and complete self-owning individual labours and, through labour, becomes an owner. For Hegel, it is only through the act of appropriation that a person realises their subjectivity, and becomes free: "Personality is that which struggles ... to claim the external world as its own." (Id.) The person therefore does not start as a self-owning entity. (Drahos, 1996)

Hegel did not believe that a person should gain an ownership right in property because of a wish or desire. There has to be some external manifestation of the will in the property; otherwise the property is not really reflective of the owner. (Bartholomew, 2001) One way to manifest one's will in property is to impose a form on the property: "When I impose a form on something, the thing's determinant character as mine acquires an independent externality and ceases to be restricted to my presence here and now and to the direct presence of my awareness and will." (Hegel, 1952, trans. by Knox)

Both personality and property in Hegel's account are complex entities, formed dialectically. One begins with pure subjectivity and pure objectivity, which may appear to be a relatively simple distinction between persons and the external world of objects. However, persons become self-owning by externalising themselves through the appropriation of objects. The person therefore becomes both pure subject, and object. (Id.) Similarly, the object, which starts as a mere thing, having no end-in-itself, becomes invested with the will and spirit of the appropriator. As long as the person's will remains in the object, it is property. (Id.) When abandoned, it returns to its former state of meaninglessness, rather like avatars and property in virtual worlds.

Hence, this theory plays out in the virtual world in an interesting way because it draws no distinction between the accumulation of real-world chattels or land and its virtual analogues. To the extent that Hegel's personality theory justifies private property in land or goods, it justifies property in virtual land or goods. The theory is predicated on the effect of the property interest on human needs like liberty and identity. These are not different just because the property at issue is virtual. (Lastowka & Hunter, 2004)

Margaret Radin (1982) built on Hegel's property theory to make moral distinctions in property disputes. She explains that 'personal property' is bound up with a person. Its loss causes pain that cannot be relieved by replacement. 'Fungible property,' on the other hand, is perfectly replaceable with other goods of equal market value. (Id.) She argues that the law should not recognize strong rights over fungible property because it is only held for instrumental reasons; it has no bearing on the possessor's personhood. Zealous enforcement of property claims should be reserved for personal property. (Id.) Social consensus already deems some property worthier of protection than other property. This distinction between personal and fungible property that explains why we enforce some property claims more strongly than others.

The personhood justification and Radin's moral scale for property rights may be applied to virtual worlds, and in particular to avatars. Although to some people owning a castle in Britannia or an X-Wing fighter on Tattooine is not a readily apparent form of ownership in the real world, the player who spent a tremendous amount of time and effort designing and building these things would feel that they are an expression of herself (or her avatar-self). When a player expresses ideas, her personality is externalized to the outside world, albeit a virtual world. I contend that the way in which a player lives out her adventures in a virtual world is similar to the way in which an artist/author creates a work of art, as opposed to merely performing with someone else's monkey. Ownership, even when the owner is no longer acting on the property she created, still fulfils an expressive component. When someone owns something she created - a sword, a song, or an avatar - the public recognizes that person as the inventor of a particular thing. (Bartholomew, 2001; Radin, 1982)

By continuing to hold onto a bundle of rights in her expression, the creator continues to make an affirmative act of personhood. (Hughes, 1998) The most valuable property a person can hold is her own personality. (Hegel, 1952, trans. by Knox)

One's personality is synonymous with the person in one sense, but in another sense it is defined only in its relation to society. "[A] person has a natural existence within himself and partly of such a kind that he is related to it as an external world," Hegel explained. (Id.) An individual's persona - the individual's public image - is a receptacle for her personality. (Hughes, 1998) Some people work on creating a public persona more than others. By endowing the individual with property rights in her persona, the law gives the individual economic protection for the most obvious external expression of her personality. The right of publicity protects celebrities from attempts by others to appropriate their personas. (Beverley-Smith, 2002)

Characters can be as personal to their creators as a public image might be to a celebrity. In this context, I refer to the adjectival form of the word character as defined by Oxford Dictionary (1975) as: "1. Of or relating to one's character. 2. (a) Specializing in the interpretation of often minor roles that emphasize fixed personality traits or specific physical characteristics: *a character actor.* (b) Of or relating to the interpretation of such roles by an actor: *the character part of the hero's devoted mother.* 3. Dedicated to the portrayal of a person with regard to distinguishing psychological or physical features: *a character sketch.*" Creators often feel a special relationship with their characters and infuse them with their personality in a way they cannot with other more tangible forms of property. As one author argues: "Creators and owners often identify so closely with their characters, intermingling their own personalities with those of their creations, that they become quasi-parents." (Helfand, 1992) In this was particularly so for the former stars of *Cheers*. Host, a bona fide licensee, had placed robots resembling the former stars from the television sitcom *Cheers* in airport bars modeled from the set. The stars sued for infringement and won. (*Wendt v Host International Inc.*, 125 F. 3d 806 (9ᵗʰ Cir. 1997)) Characters are particularly strong candidates for

Radin's category of 'personal property' that should be protected as more of the person is bound up in a character creation than in other 'fungible' objects.

Thus when it comes to avatars, personality theory would also seem to be strongly in favour of granting property rights. It is well documented that people feel connected to their avatar, not as a thing but as a projection of their self. As seen earlier, the concept of the cyborg - the mechanical extension of one's persona - is widely accepted. (Bukatman, 1993) One need only be attacked once in any first-person shooter game to realize how one projects a sense of self onto an avatar. Indeed, some users identify more with their online personas than their real ones. If, as personality theory would have it, property might be justified by reference to the effect on the self, it would seem that there is a normative basis for claiming property in virtual realty, virtual chattels, and, a fortiori, avatars. (Lastowka & Hunter, 2004)

Some have argued that a theory granting property rights in avatars based on the degree to which their creators identify with them does not justify broad alienability. (Lastowka & Hunter, 2004, citing, Reynolds, 2003) Nevertheless, we assume alienability for wedding rings or even nonessential body parts; but there are exceptions to the rule, even in tangible objects. Some are reluctant to consider human life the subject of property law. (Davies & Naffine, 2001) However, that should not apply to computer representations of people, no matter how lifelike the avatars might be. The property interest in avatars would be the property interest in the information which makes up the avatar, the hyper-real human.

Increasingly, individuals are moving online into mediated spaces; just as increasingly more of the physical world is becoming computer-mediated. Virtual worlds are the ultimate embodiment of a computer-mediated world existing entirely within a system of computers. Ubiquitous computing is the future of the physical world being entirely computer-mediated. By examining individuals as avatars in these virtual worlds, they may provide insight into how a future of increasing computer mediation will impact individuals in the real world. Escalating computer mediation of human activity provides mounting possibilities of interference with an individual's ability to act and be self-constituted. The capability of remotely monitoring and controlling physical objects provided by ubiquitous computing may make it possible to interfere with, and redistribute, personal property rights.

C. THEORIES OF PERSONAL PROPERTY

"There is nothing which so generally strikes the imagination, and engages the affections of mankind, as the right of property; or that sole and despotic dominion which one man claims and exercises over the external things of the world, in total exclusion of the right of any other individual in the universe." (William Blackstone)

Early legal theories described the term 'property' as the relationship of a person to a thing. Justin Graham (2002) describes "[t]echnological change [as] ha[ving] transformed nineteenth century conceptions of property as absolute dominion over a physical thing into property conceived as a limited bundle of rights in both material and non-material things." Later theorists attempted to describe 'property' as a complex collective of separate rights that have been 'bundled' together for ease of reference. (Id.) Hohfeld (1917) re-conceptualized 'rights' as claims and duties that between individuals in society, and argued that property is properly conceived as a bundle of these rights. Thus, property is the relationship of people to each other with respect to a thing. No particular 'stick' in this bundle is necessarily essential to make a thing the property of a certain person. The concept is merely a framework for analysing possible rights and obligations. (Mossoff, 2003) These rights and obligations include an integrated unity of the exclusive right to acquire, use, (Barr, 2005) exclude (*Loretto v Teleprompter Manhattan CATV Corp.*, 458 U.S. 419, 433 (1982) (describing the right to exclude as "one of the most essential sticks in the bundle of rights that are commonly characterized as property." Quoting *Kaiser Aetna v United States*, 44 U.S. 164, 176 (1979)) and dispose (Grant, 1995) of one's things? The complex institutions that have been created around the concept of property are omnipresent in our society today, but the pressing question remains whether there is a theoretical account of property that can sufficiently describe and guide these institutions, especially virtual institutions. (Mossoff, 2003)

Central to the operation of virtual worlds is a property system, with all of the familiar real world features of exclusive ownership, persistence of rights, transfer under conditions of agreement and duress, and a currency system to support trade in these property-based assets. (Lastowka and Hunter, 2004; Fairfield, 2005; Castronova, 2002) In the mid-eighteenth century, Blackstone envisaged property as an *in rem* right, but attributed to it an absolute status. (Blackstone) Since that time, scholars have disagreed in their interpretation of Blackstone's conception of the 'absolute,' with some regarding it as an anomaly (since Blackstone himself permitted the law to impose limitations on the right) and yet others as purposive hyperbole. (Burns, 1985; Rose, 1998; Kennedy, 1979) The noteworthy aspect of Blackstone's definition is its identification and use of the element of exclusivity. To Blackstone it was not enough that the individual claimed a power over the resource, it was vital that property also involved the exclusion of other individuals' rights over the same resource. (Id.) This strikes a major chord with those who live in virtual worlds.

Blackstone's understanding of property came to form the focus of analysis for generations of positivist scholars including John Austin, Jeremy Bentham and others. The main point lies in Blackstone's conception of 'dominion.' Superficially, there appeared to be a contradiction, given that the concept of dominium in Roman law derived from Roman law's absolutist (absolute, understood here in contrast to relative rights to possession) conception of ownership, which the common law had consciously rejected. (Birks, 1986) Subsequently, though, the process of identifying *in rem* rights together constituted this dominion.

At the turn of the 20th century, Wesley Hohfeld (1917) analyzed the concept of a 'right' into its respective components of correlative claims and duties between individuals in society. He developed a novel methodology of understanding legal relations, using what he called 'jural opposites' and 'jural correlatives.' Using a matrix consisting of rights, duties, privileges and a fourth variable (i.e., the no-right), Hohfeld set out to make the case for a consistent model of judicial analysis. He then applied this methodology to the analysis of *in rem* and *in personam* legal relations--which he termed, 'multital' and 'paucital' respectively. The crux of Hohfled's thesis in relation to property was that property consisted of a large mix of multital jural relations (i.e., rights, duties, privileges, etc.), not all of which could be mapped at any given point of time. (Id.) His analysis of property states that "what the owner of property has is a very complex aggregate of rights, privileges, powers and immunities," not in a thing (in rem) but rather against other people (in personam). (Id.)

Hohfeld's model eventually gave rise to what is today known as the 'bundle of rights' understanding of property, which grew to be immensely popular among the legal realists of the 1920s and 30s. Max Radin (1938) attempted to understand Hohfeld's analysis from a realist paradigm. While Hohfeld did not use the phrase 'bundle of rights', these later theorists have invariably tended to associate his views on property with the bundle conception. (Id.) The bundle conception basically consisted of the idea that property was a bundle of complex jural relations *in rem*. To an extent, this bundle conception diluted property of any substantive meaning it may have acquired in

legal discourses. Whereas even Blackstone had emphasized the element of excludability, the bundle metaphor merely recognized the 'right to exclude' as one among several rights and privileges accorded by the legal system to an owner.

The bundle metaphor, however, has demonstrably been of importance in functional terms, primarily in determining whether something had been removed from the bundle and was therefore short of full-property. It has found extensive use by American courts in eminent domain or 'takings' cases: see *Kaiser Aetna v United States*, 444 U.S. 164, 176 (1979); *Dolan v City of Tigard*, 512 U.S. 374, 384 (1994). However, it could never answer what full property was, at any given point of time. (Penner, 1996; cf. Merrill & Smith, 2001) As it was, this concept of property emphasized its function and its social relations. In doing so, the doctrine called attention to the more contingent nature of property which, in turn, had been the basis for the contention that property rights should be extended. (Harris, 1993) Today, theories of property reject the assumption that property is "objectively definable or identifiable, apart from social context." (Underkuffler, 1990) The focus has shifted to the function of property and the changing social relations reflected and constructed by new forms of property derived from the government. (Reich, 1964) Property in this wider sense included a whole range of intangibles, jobs, entitlements, occupational licenses, contracts, subsidies, and so on, that are the product of labour, time, and creativity such as intellectual property, business goodwill, and enhanced earning potential from graduate degrees. This idea was so prevalent that the analysis derived from Reich's conception of "New Property" formed the basis of the majority opinion in *Goldberg v Kelly*, 397 U.S. 254 (1970). In spite of the dilution of these new forms of property since *Goldberg v Kelly* and its progeny (*Bell v Burson*, 402 U.S. 535 (1971); *Perry v Sindermann*, 408 U.S. 593 (1972); *Morrissey v Brewer*, 408 U.S. 471 (1972)) as well as continued attacks on the concept, the legacy of 'new property' informs the concept of property with questions of power, selection, and allocation. (cf. *Bishop v Wood*, 426 U.S. 341, 347 (1976) (holding that the plaintiff's discharge from employment with the police department did not constitute a deprivation of a property interest); *Board of Regents v Roth*, 408 U.S. 564, 578 (1972) (holding that a non-tenured, one-year university teaching position was not a property right); Van Alstyne, 1977).

Reich (1964) argued "property is not a natural right but a construction by society" which echoes in current theories of property that portray the provision of property rights as a range of choices. The rejection of 'new property' on the ground that it is derived from the government rather than private sources is ultimately not persuasive, because as Reich (1964) further states, all property is a creation of law. A utilitarian framework of property analysis, which focused on analyzing property in terms of transaction costs and the allocative gains derived from the deployment of the institution itself, has been developed. Much of the scholarship in this area as also the entire law and economics movement can be traced back to the seminal work of Ronald Coase (1960) on transaction costs. This interpretation focuses on issues of relative power and social relations inherent in any definition of property. Hence, property is viewed as little more than a collection of use rights with respect to a resource and one that is capable of achieving allocative efficiency by ensuring the transfer of resources to higher valued uses. (Merrill & Smith, 2001b) While the bundle metaphor represented a form of 'conceptual realism', the utilitarian model posits itself as a form of 'economic realism'--making little effort to understand the institution of property in the form of an *in rem* right. (Id.)

Virtual economies have created real-world opportunities to get rich. Some denizens of virtual worlds buy virtual property at low rates from those who have no idea what the item is worth, then resell it on eBay for real-world profit. Some make a six-figure U.S. dollar income this way, and one or two individuals may make even more. For example, Julian Dibbell, in Play *Money: Diary of a Dubious Proposition,* (http://www.juliandibbell. com/playmoney/) wrote: "THE PROPOSITION: On April 15, 2004, I [Julian Dibbell] will truthfully report to the IRS that my primary source of income is the sale of imaginary goods -- and that I earn more from it, on a monthly basis, than I have ever earned as a professional writer."

As seen, the development of virtual worlds allows an opportunity for experimentation with legal relationships, transactions, and obligations that, in the real world, fall within the category of property. The existence of property within these worlds speaks to our inability to imagine any other way of structuring relationships between individuals under conditions of resource scarcity. (Lastowka & Hunter, 2004; Lehdonvirta, 2008) As technology changes, new uses of resources emerge. Property law protects emerging interests in property so that the emergent property interest may be productively used. (Demsetz, 1967; Hardin, 1975) One function of property is the guiding incentive to use resources productively as technology changes those incentives. "If the main allocative function of property rights is the internalization of beneficial and harmful effects, then the emergence of property rights can be understood best by their association with the emergence of new or different beneficial or harmful effects." (Demsetz, 1967)

Traditionally, the use of a physical object has been viewed as an exercise of the personal property right to use and to the quiet enjoyment of property. (Cunningham, Stoebuck, & Whitman, 1993) One purchases the object and uses it when one wants. The producer of the object does not maintain an interest in it, does not monitor its use, nor exercises any control over it. Most objects of personal property are treated this way. However, with advancing technology, such as virtual worlds and ubiquitous computing, this may change.

The remote monitoring and control of objects is becoming both possible and practical. Technology is developing the capacity to interfere with actions that have traditionally been viewed as exercises of personal property rights. This capacity to interfere with the exercise of traditional personal property rights will enable the displacement of property rights by creating a system in which rights in a physical object can be determined and enforced through technology and contract. For example, the greedy door of Philip Dick's story. This type of ubiquitous computing may promote a privately ordered system of rights to displace the publicly ordered system of property rights. A similar conflict has arisen in the ubiquitous computing counterpart, virtual worlds, in the context of objects that are not physical at all, but rather in objects that are entirely virtual.

"The information technology of virtual world systems allows for personal property rights in virtual world objects to be both easily reallocated by contract and controlled by a rights management system. Information technology makes the reallocation and control possible on a massive scale through automated means. The application of information technology, of computing ability, to virtual world objects occurs as a matter of course because virtual world objects are creatures of computers; they exist only through and within computers. The characteristics that flow from this relationship between virtual world objects and computing ability mimic the characteristics of physical objects in ubiquitous computing environments. It seems that the same interference, reallocation, and displacement of property rights currently possible with virtual world objects may apply to real world objects with the adoption of ubiquitous computing technologies." (Boone, 2008)

Between the rise of virtual worlds and the advances in ubiquitous computing technology a deeper examination of personal property rights is required. Are personal property rights traditionally enjoyed by the owner of an object are simply accidents stemming from the physical characteristics of that object? Have these physical characteristics made it impossible or impractical for the producer to monitor the object and control its use after ownership and possession have passed from the producer to the user? Locke's theory of property ownership is consistent with the views of Hegel and Radin. The products of labour are an extension of the labourer's personality. Appropriation, the point at which an individual's property right should be recognized, requires the infusion of the possessor's personality into an object by expending some labour on it. (Olivecrona, 1974)

Or, on the other hand, are the traditional personal property rights enjoyed by the owner of an object rather than being accidents, instead provide some benefit to society such that has decided to override technology-enabled private ordering in favour of property-based public ordering. Hegel and Radin also argue that property ownership should be linked to personal expressions in objects. Because characters are especially rich in personal expression, their creators deserve protection so they will continue to act on the outside world and not suffer harm from another party's misappropriation of their personal expression. This is important in a society that is progressively more mediated by technology. Ubiquitous computing may create the ability to interfere with the exercise of personal property rights and, thereby, create the ability to displace property as a rights ordering system.

D. PERSONHOOD INTERESTS & INTELLECTUAL PROPERTY

"Each person identifies with those capacities, physical and mental, to which he had direct access, and we see that this identification affords each person a normative sense of self." David Gauthier (1986)

Compelling as the arguments of Locke and Hegel are that people have a property interest in themselves, a deeper problem has been obscured. What constitutes 'personality' or a 'personhood' interest in a particular piece of property, especially when, as with intellectual property rights, you are dealing with creations of the human mind? The real world appears to be moving towards an economy primarily based on goods which take no material form. Virtual worlds have arrived at this point. As noted earlier, embodied virtuality is also on the rise. Computers are becoming embedded throughout the physical world simultaneously receding into the background and becoming universal in their connectivity. (Weiser & Brown, 1996) Ubiquitous computing has been described as the "colonization of everyday life" by computers and information technology. (Id.) Ideas and information once freed from constraints becomes something which happens in the field of interaction between minds or objects or other bits information or other ideas. They become an action which occupies time rather than a state of being which occupies physical space. As such, there has been an elimination of any predictable connection between creators and a fair reward the utility or pleasure others may find in their work. (Barlow, 2004)

An individual's personal identification with all of her physical and mental capacities could give rise to personal identification with the intellectual products of those capacities – without any reference to 'creativity'. For instance, if a person identifies with her own mental capacities, this may cause her to identify first, with the process of using those capacities, and then with the products of those processes. It is possible that someone would identify more with the processes, and less with the product. Both virtual worlds and ubiquitous computing environments are mediated by computing ability which forms the physical link.

Assume that the individual identifies with (1) their capacities; and thereby (2) the processes of using those capacities; and thereby (3) the intellectual products of these processes. One might conclude that step (1) is wrong, that the individual does not have any particular entitlement to identify with the talents with which she is endowed. One might further consider that even the ability to

expend effort to be determined by factors outside a person's control and hence a morally impermissible criteria for distribution. (Rawls, 1971) "The assertion that a man deserves the superior character that enables him to make the effort to cultivate his abilities is equally problematic; for his character depends in large part upon fortunate family and social circumstances for which he can claim no credit." (Id.)

This counter-argument fails in virtual worlds. Each person has chosen who and what they want to be. They have chosen, albeit from a pre-selected set of criterion, their capacities and the process of using those capacities. The pre-selected criterion is deemed to be an underlying intellectual product if the world creator and protected by copyright. By demanding payment for and creating code-based permissions, the world creator may be seen as granting a license to copy, transform or create joint or derivative works. Thus, the players may have acquired a particular entitlement to identify with these talents.

Justin Hughes (1998) in his article, *The Personality Interest of Artists and Inventors in Intellectual Property*, identified three separate personhood interests in intellectual property res: (1) creativity; (2) intentionality; and (3) identification as the source of the res. "Res is everything that may form an object of rights and includes an object, subject-matter, or status." (Black's Law Dictionary, 1990 citing *In re Riggles Will*, 205 N.Y.S.2d 19 (N.Y. App. Div. 1960)) They are as intrinsic to the virtual world as they are to the real world. He begins with creativity – a fundamental notion of copyright law – as a core personhood interest that blurs the notions of originality and personal expression. (Hughes, 1998) He refines this by following with intentionality. Black's Law Dictionary (1990) defines intent as "design, resolve, or determination with which a person acts" (*Witters v United States*, 70 U.S. App. D.C. 316, 106 F.2d 837 (D.C. Cir. 1939); "a state of mind in which a person seeks to accomplish a given result through a course of action" (*Wager v Pro, C.A.*,

195 U.S. App. D.C. 423, 603 F.2d 1005 (D.C. Cir. 1979)) and "a mental attitude which can seldom be proved by circumstances from which it may be inferred." (*State v Gantt*, 26 N.C. App. 554, 217 S.E. 2d 3 (N.C. App. Div. 1975)) Hughes (1998) ends with questioning whether merely being the source of res creates legitimate personhood interests that justify some sort of protection. These principles can be applied to both the players and corporate governors of virtual worlds in attempt to determine who has the stronger property rights in these creations.

1. Creativity

How fundamentally connected is creativity to individuality? Creativity as a characteristic is something we nurture in our children for their development as independent individuals. While looking at nearly interchangeable finger paintings, we praise them as original and unique. We envision that one of these children could be a new Jackson Pollock. All through our culture, our concepts of creativity, originality, and personal expression blur into one concept. This blurring occurs whether we are viewing kindergarten finger-paintings or Royal Albert Hall performances. In some cases, a work's origin may be very obvious and it may be obviously a powerfully original work - like Picasso's Les Desmoiselles d'Avignon when it was first viewed. Discussing this painting one commentator said, "the consequences of one individual act of perception were and remain incalculable ... This individual act of perception is recorded in a painting by Picasso, now called Les Demoiselles d'Avignon." (Read, 1974). The painting was 'recognized instantly' as a 'summit of achievement.' (Daix, 1993). One does not need much awareness of modern painting to recognize most of Picasso's work as Picasso or most of Pollock's work as Pollock.

Nevertheless, the identification of a certain work with a certain individual transpires with subtler expression, in a manner similar to a par-

ticular defensive play in a chess tournament, the arrangement of certain paintings at a retrospective, a particular style of lighting scenes in a film or a solution to a computer programming problem. In discussing the development of a few leading cinematographers from the Hollywood studio system of the 1930s, John Bailey said: "Coming out of that [studio system was] some really stellar people ... who had such strength and such individual voice that they kind of transcended whatever studio they happened to be working for. Today you can look back and very easily recognize their films from the look irrespective of the director." (Glassman, 1994).

In these understated cases, there is a groping for some new terminology like 'critical judgment' or 'intellectual insight.' All the same, it is difficult to ignore that a certain impression of personal style is what skulks behind the terminology. This view of 'style' is some aspect of creativity and personal expression. This remains true whether one adopts a 'modern' or 'post-modern' view of personality. Jeffrey Malkan (1997) discussed this problem with photographic images in his article *Stolen Photographs: Personality, Publicity, and Privacy*. Malkan observed that 'style' is a matter of what is 'on the inside' and quotes Cocteau's observation that "decorative style has never existed. ... Style is the soul. ..." (Id. at 833) If this is the case, then there is no wonder that the three ideas - creativity, originality, and personal expression – have become so completely entwined in law that there may be no simple or clear way to disentangle them, despite some courts' and commentators' attempts to keep originality and creativity conceptually separate and distinct.

In the beginning, the traditional Common Law approach towards the requirement of originality was developed in England and is still enforceable there. This approach has served as a baseline for all other Common Law-based systems, including the early days of copyright law in the United States. The British approach could be described both as pragmatic and practical. 'Originality' is equated with a minimum standard of labour, skill or judgment in the production of a work which must not be a copy of another work. There is no requirement of novelty or creativity in the protected work, but only a requirement for some basic degree of skill and labour in the production of a work that is not a mere slavish copy of another work.

Simon S. Stokes (2001) describes the standard required for a work to qualify as original as 'very low' and with no more than "trivial effort and skill ... required." The often cited case in this context is: *University of London Press Ltd. v University Tutorial Ltd.* [1916] 2 Ch. 601, 608-609, in which it has been declared that: "The word 'original' does not in this context mean that the work must be the expression of original inventive thought. Copyright acts are not concerned with the originality of ideas but with the expression of thought, and in the case of a 'literal work', with the expression of thought in print or writing. The originality which is required relates to the expression of the thought. But the Act does not require that the expression must be in an original or novel form, but that the work must not be copied from another work -- that it should originate from the author." Consequently, British courts have tended to acknowledge copyright in almost any work which has even a slight element of labour and skill invested in its production, and is not a simple copy of another work. Thus, the requirement of originality was acknowledged with regards to mundane factual compilations, (See *Ladbroke (Football) Ltd v William Hill (Football) Ltd* (H.L.(E.)) [1964] 1 W.L.R 273, 287, 289, 292, 1 All ER 465) such as a chronological list of sports' matches (See *Football League v Littlewoods* [1959] Ch. 637, 2 All E.R. 546, 3 W.L.R. 42); a transcript of a public speech as it was documented by a skilful journalist (See *Walter v Lane* [1900] A.C., 539); listings of programs to be broadcast (See *Independent Television Publications v Time Out* [1984] F.S.R. 64); and 'unoriginal works' which concentrate solely on the documentation of another work such as photographs of paintings or objects in a collection.

(See *Antiquesportfolio.com plc. Rodney Fitch & Co. Ltd.* [2001] FSR 345, at 352-354) The cases which did not meet this basic requirement were cases such as a slightly enlarged image produced by using a simple photocopier (See *The Reject Shop plc v Manners* [1995] FSR 870, at 876); or short slogans or titles. (See *Rose v Information Services Ltd.* [1981] FSR 254)

The notion of skill, however, could also be interpreted as referring to creative skill, as suggested by Prof. Sterling (1998): "The word 'skill' has an extensive import, and covers creative endeavour. So a United Kingdom judgement should have no difficulty applying the test of skill as requiring intellectual creation." If the choice and arrangement of source material demands more than a minimal standard of skill and labour, the final form of expression of the work will be entitled to a copyright which is independent and additional to the one which may exist in the source materials. (Cornish, 1999; Stokes, 2001)

This approach must be read alongside another basic principle of copyright law well established in the British system: the *idea-expression dichotomy* rule which excludes mere facts from the protection of copyright. Hence, copyright subsists only in a particular form of expression, in which ideas and facts are conveyed, and not in the abstracted form of the facts and ideas which are embodied within an expression. This basic rule is stated in many cases. For a recent House of Lords decision referring and applying the Idea-Expression Dichotomy, see *Designers Guild Ltd. v Russell Williams (Textiles) Ltd.* (H.L.(E.)) [2000] 1 W.L.R. 2416, at 2422-2423, [1 All E.R. 700]. For examples of factual information in context see *Walter v Steinkopff* [1892] 3 Ch. 489; *Express Newspapers v News (UK)* [1991] F.S.R. 36, at 41. The true nature of the protection granted to factual compilations was summarized clearly by the authors of *Copinger and Skone James -- On Copyright* (1999), who state that the merit of such works lies in the time and money spent in collecting and choosing the raw materials and it is this skill and effort that the law really intends to protect in this context: "The skill and effort is not literary in any conventional sense but as a matter of convenience it is protected as a literary work." Thus, intellectual creation or personal expression must be applied to the abstracted form of the facts in order for a copyright to subsist. This would then answer to the Oxford Pocket Dictionary's (1975) definition of original, ". . . not imitative, novel in character or style, inventive, creative, thinking or acting for oneself . . ."

The Privy Council case of *Interlego AG v Tyco Industries Inc.* [1988] 3 All E.R. 949 at 970 per Lord Oliver (appeal taken from Hong Kong) which held that "[s]kill, labour, or judgement merely in the process of copying cannot confer originality. . . [t]here must . . . be some element of material alteration or embellishment which suffices to make the totality of the work an original work."

In the 1991 *Feist* decision (499 U.S. 340), the U.S. Supreme Court unequivocally declared that 'originality' as employed in copyright law should be defined at least partially by means of creativity: "Original, as the term is used in copyright, means only that the work was independently created by the author (as opposed to copied from other works) and that it possesses at least some minimal degree of creativity. To be sure, the requisite level of creativity is extremely low, even a slight amount will suffice." In the statutory grant that "copyright protection subsists ... in original works of authorship," 17 U.S.C. §102(a)(1988 & Supp. IV 1992), 'original' is interpreted as having 'originality' or meeting the 'requirement of originality ....' (*Key Publications v Chinatown Today Publications*, 945 F.2d 509, 512 (1991))

The *Feist* decision has had influence beyond the borders of the United States and has reached other common law-based countries that have adopted the ruling of the United States Supreme Court, while abandoning their traditional leaning towards the British approach. In Israel, the Supreme Court in the *Interlego A/S v Exin-Lines Bros. SA* (C.A. 513/89, 48(4) *P.D.* 133) decision

adopted the *Feist* ruling with regards to both the interpretation of the originality requirement and the general rejection of the 'sweat of the brow' doctrine and the labour theory as a legitimate interest for establishing a copyright claim. In Canada, a Canadian Federal Court of Appeal withheld protection from a telephone directory arrangement (*Tele-Direct (Publications) Inc. v American Business Information, Inc.* (1997) 76 C.P.R. (3d) 296 (Fed. C.A.), rev denied, 1998). In *CCH Canadian Ltd. v Law Society of Upper Canada* (1999) 2 C.P.R. (4th) 129 (Fed. Ct.) a compiling of reported judicial decisions, including added headnotes and other matters, was found to be lacking the 'creative spark' essential to a finding of originality. By contrast, in another case, different facts, such as the selection of information useful for the community, the court allowed that it could be distinguishable from another telephone directory and as such original (*Ital-Press Ltd. v Sicoli* (1999) 86 C.P.R. (3d) 129 (Fed. Ct.) (telephone directory of Italian-Canadians in the Edmonton area)). Although other cases have restricted the *Tele-Direct* precedent to compilations and generally defined originality in more traditional common law terms. For example in *Hager v ECW Press Ltd.* [1998] 2 F.C. 287, 85 C.P.R. (3d) 289 (Fed. Ct.), the court recognized copyright protection in an interviewer's transcription of an interviewee's words.

This 'blurring' or 'linking' of creative-original-personal expression creates a multifaceted concept of creativity. The question becomes whether this blurring is the result of historical accident or to be expected. Did the law develop at a time when these ideas were culturally linked? If so, then even if the cultural links might have broken down over time, the conceptual links in jurisprudence might remain. (Hughes, 1988) This is the gist of the deconstructionist's interpretations about the single 'author' and the immutable 'text.' The deconstructionists rationalize that the 'solitary author-genius' is an invention of Romanticism that became entrenched in American jurisprudence in the nineteenth century. (Jaszi, 1992) In the new age of high technology and collaborative creative work, this theory needs to be displaced. Presupposing the 'solitary author-genius' echoes the creative process of past times, the deconstructionists give little evidence of how the current creative process is distinctive. The evidence the deconstructionists do assemble is of a complex conception of creativity in which the 'author-genius' skulks beneath intellectual property decisions. (Id.) Instead of being a historical accident, there is good reason to suppose that the links between creativity, originality, and personal expression is both inevitable and historically rooted. (Hughes, 1998) Many have explored how copyright law developed with, and came to rely on the Romantic notion of creative authorship, "an extreme assertion of the self and the value of the individual experience ... together with the infinite and the transcendental." (Jaszi, 1991 quoting *The Oxford Companion to English Literature,* M. Drabble ed., 5th ed. (Oxford: Oxford University Press, 1985) 842) The 'author' is seen as a historically contingent social construct that arose to capture the creative process in the nineteenth century and did not exist before that time. (Boyle, 1988) "The idea of [the] authorship is socially constructed and historically contingent." (Id.) This is an overstatement which may perhaps devalue copyright and its history. The preamble of the Statute of Anne, c. 19, clearly shows that the intent in 1710 was not solely utilitarian, but solidly anchored in the author's creativity: "encouragement of learned men to compose and write useful books . . . ." In general, the deconstructionists view "the persistent judicial reliance on author-reasoning as a method of resolving ambiguity and suppressing the complexity of the world." (Aoki, 1993)

Professor James Boyle (1988) has even argued that the author construct gets used in economic analyses of legal controls on information. "The values of romantic authorship seem to seep - consciously or unconsciously - into economic analysis. And because in most conflicts the paradigm of

authorship tends to fit one side better than the other, this romantic grounding provides economic analysis with at least the illusion of certainty. Authors tend to win." Thus, from the deconstructionist perspective, copyright law "is grounded on an uncritical belief in the existence of a distinct and privileged category of activity" (Jaszi, 1991) called authorship. However fascinating the historical account of romantic author-genius' arrival into Anglo American law may be, the courts, like art professors and theatre critics, are more concerned with creativity than authorship. Will this be the case for virtual worlds?

The U.S. Supreme Court has held that the Constitution established originality as a requirement for copyrightability. The Court asserted: "Originality is a constitutional requirement. The source of Congress' power to enact copyright law is Article I, 8, cl.8 of the Constitution, which authorizes Congress to 'secure for limited times to authors . . . the exclusive right to their respective writings.' In two decisions from the late 19th century - *The Trade-Mark Cases*, 100 U.S. 82 (1879); and *Burrow-Giles Lithographic Co. v Sarony*, 111 U.S. 53 (1884) - this Court defined the crucial terms 'authors' and 'writings'. In so doing, the Court made it unmistakeably clear that these terms presuppose a degree of originality." (*Feist*, 499 U.S. at 346) In *Feist* at 345, a unanimous Supreme Court defined originality by reference to creativity and stated that originality is the sine qua non of copyrightability. But it is important to remember the path to this conclusion. The U.S. Copyright Act, 17 U.S.C. §102(a) (1996), limits property rights to "original works of authorship." The U.S. Supreme Court explained that "original, as the term is used in copyright, means only that the work was independently created by the author (as opposed to copied from other works), and that it possesses at least some minimal degree of creativity." (*Feist* at 345) Some evidence suggests that the phrase 'minimal degree of creativity' should be interpreted to mean that the work is something more than a trivial variation of its precursors.

(*Alfred Bell & Co. v Catalda Fine Arts, Inc.*, 191 F.2d 99, 102 (2nd Cir. 1951))

The U.S. Supreme Court crammed the notion of creativity into the notion of originality in the context of using 'originality' as a requirement for copyright protection. Social scientists would argue that creativity is separate from originality; however, the Court was considering a judicial construct versus a social scientist exploring a social convention. Still, *Feist* is a starting point because the Court concludes that everything juridically original is also juridically creative. That logically entails the proposition that decided *Feist*: if something is not juridically creative, it cannot be juridically original. ("If j-original, then j-creative") "Juridically original" (j-original) and "juridically creative" (j-creative) should be distinguished as legal concepts from general social conventions. According to symbolic logic, the *Feist* decision is saying: if j-original, then j-creative, which is logically equivalent to if not j-creative, then not j-original." (Hughes, 1998) This equation (if j-original, then j-creative) was in reaction to a long line of case law that had supported the view that the requirement of originality was "little more than a prohibition of actual copying." (*Bell* at 103) This is a view unquestioned by scholars writing prior to *Feist*. "Copyright's threshold requirement of originality ... requires neither newness nor creativity, but merely creation without copying." (Litman, 1990; see also, Denicola, 1981) This juridical notion of originality, like the popular notion of originality, owes its currency to the idea of something's 'origin': if a song owes its origin to John, it must be original to John.

This measure of 'originality' dates back to Justice Story's early nineteenth century opinions (*Gray v Russell*, 10 F.Cas. 1035 (D. Mass. 1839) (Story, J); *Emerson v Davies*, 8 F.Cas. (D. Mass. 1845)) and gave us a fairly bright line test: if the work was the independent creation of someone, it was 'original' to that person. (VerSteeg, 1993; Olson, 1983) In the United Kingdom, Justice Petersen came to a similar conclusion in the

University of London Press case ([1916] 2 Ch. 601). This minimalist sense of 'original' - owing its origin to someone – will be explored later as the notion of 'sourcehood.' If the story owes its origin to Jedi Joe, Jedi Joe is the source of the story. If Jedi Joe owes his origin to LucasArts *Galaxies*, then LucasArts is the source of Jedi Joe. If, however, Jedi Joe owes his origin to Joe Dugger, then Joe Dugger is the source of Jedi Joe.

This derivation of 'originality' leads to a problem. Originality means that something could be juridically 'original' in the sense that it was not copied, but the thing might not be considered creative in the popular sense. Because American law makes originality the gate keeper of copyright protection, the *Feist* Court backed away from this narrow sense of 'original.' Instead, the Court embraced a formula tying originality with creativity.

The Second Circuit, in *L. Batlin & Son, Inc. v Snyder*, 536 F.2d 486, 490 (2d Cir. 1976) (en banc), was among those who had already explicitly linked originality to creativity while many copyright decisions had already required 'creativity' for copyright protection - meaning that it was either embedded in the notion of 'originality' or it stood as a separate requirement. The ambiguous place of the creativity requirement goes back at least to Justice Miller's formulation in *Trade-Mark Cases* that copyright protection applies to works "only such as are original, and are founded in the creative powers of the mind." *In re Trade-Mark Cases*, 100 U.S. 82, 94 (1879). This is contrary to the British theory found in *University of London Press Ltd.*, ([1916] 2 Ch. 601).

The Court in *Feist* adopts the formula 'if j-original, then j-creative' because this provides the more important rule, 'if not j-creative, then not j-original.' Embedding creativity in originality certainly makes the originality test more complicated than it would be as a mere test of sourcehood. (VerSteeg, 1993) In *Feist* at 347, the Court tells us only that creativity is not variations that are 'mechanical,' 'entirely typical' or 'garden variety.' Intellectual products that result from choices about composition that are obvious, inevitable, or 'age old practice(s)' do not count as minimally creative.

'Creativity' traces its etymological roots to the Latin verb *creo*, meaning 'to beget' or 'to give birth to.' The Latin root also means 'to make' or 'to produce' and is related to the verb *cresco* meaning 'to grow up' or 'to spring forth.' (Oxford Latin Dictionary, 1982) In a nutshell, the words' roots do nothing to help distinguish 'creating' from 'originating' or 'crafting' or being the source of something. A better starting point is that the idea of being the source of something, of originating something, and of creating something all relies on the idea of transforming existing materials into something that is identifiably different. This causes problems for Cory Ondrejka's (2005) theory that crafting is not creating.

Imagine that Bill Blacksmith purchases one hundred pounds of pig iron from Davey Dwarf, who dug the iron from a hillside on his farm. Bill uses fifteen pounds of the iron to make a sword; he sells this sword to Krull the Warrior. He also creates and donates five more swords to Krull (perhaps in exchange for protection). It is non-controversial that if someone asked you, knowing all this, 'what is the origin of the sword?' you would probably say 'Bill, the Blacksmith' and that the same reply would hold true if you substituted 'source,' i.e. 'what is the source of the sword?' If you rephrased the question into 'who created the sword?' you would again get 'Bill' as the answer.

Now consider if someone asked about the pig iron, i.e., 'what is the origin of the pig iron?' or 'what is the source of the pig iron?' This is more difficult. If you understood this question to be 'how did the pig iron get here?' you might answer 'Bill,' but it seems more likely that you would treat this as a question about the pig iron's provenance, i.e. 'where did it come from?' In that case, if someone asked you 'what is the origin of the pig iron?' you would probably say 'Davey' or 'Davey's farm.' Again, the same answer would come if 'source'

was substituted for 'origin.' The probable answer would be 'Davey' or 'Davey's farm.'

But what if someone asked who created the pig iron? The question might evoke 'God,' 'Nature,' or some explanation that Davey dug it up, but didn't 'create' it. This question gets a different answer because Davey does not seem to have transformed the materials available to him when he dug them up. But this still does not evince a great difference between the popular ideas of 'creating' and 'originating.' In fact, we could arrange a hierarchy of questions which, to increasing degrees, evoke the question of when an object first appears in the world (or first appears in the world in the form it now has): "What is the provenance of X?" "Where/who did X come from?" "What is the source of X?" "What is the origin of X?" "Who/what created X?"

Substitute Bill's sword or Davey's pig iron for X in this series of questions - the questions initially can be met with an intermediary answer ('the market,' 'the back of Bill's cart,' etc.). However, as you go down the list, what is increasingly demanded is an answer about when X first appears in the world identifiable as X. This would hold true if you ran through this list replacing X with a commercial star ship, an antique chest, or a manuscript, anonymous because the title page has been torn off. Point to a commercial star ship at a space station and ask where did it come from; its last stop - Tatoonine, Endor, Bespin - will be a fine answer. But point to the same star ship and ask who created it; nothing but " ? " will do as an answer. The moment when something first appeared in the world in its present form is synonymous with the moment when other things were transformed to the new thing.

The question becomes even more convoluted when set in virtual worlds. The above questions were answered within the boundaries of the virtual world. They can be answered by yet another manner when set in the 'real' world. Let X be a light sabre. "What is the provenance of X?" The maker of the light sabre or LucasArts? "Where/ who did X come from?" LucasArts or a galaxy far, far away? "What is the source of X?" George Lucas' fertile imagination or the Jedi Knight council? "What is the origin of X?" Again George Lucas' imagination or the Jedi Knight Master in the game? "Who/what created X?" I'm sure the Jedi Knight Master feels he has as much a right to claim creating the light sabre as did the computer programmer who created the software code.

The point of the hierarchy of questions is that it shows that both creativity and originality are rooted in the transformative process. The view that transformation or novelty is fundamental to creativity is also put forward in Robert Weisberg (1993). Weisberg provides a thoughtful survey of psychological efforts to explore creativity, particularly how it differs from regular thinking. But there are many details that need attention. First, there is the issue of whether the transformative process of 'creating' or 'originating' focuses on the materials actually at the disposal of the person or the total world of materials or elements possibly available. Notions of both creativity and originality are context-specific; they measure transformation by what the person actually had available.

"Whether or not there really is anything new under the sun, a creative act produces something new or novel in comparison to what the creator had encountered and known previously. If unbeknownst to the creator someone else had produced something similar or identical ... still the creator's act would have been an act of creation. All that matters is that the effects of this earlier discovery have not seeped through and become known to the new discoverer in a way that makes his act less novel. Calling an act 'creative' characterizes it only in relation to the materials it actually arose from, the earlier experiences and knowledge of the creator, not in relation to everything that has preceded it in the history of the universe." (Nozick, 1989) Taking Nozick's definition above, if Ted, the chess novice, hits upon the Evans gambit in a chess game today, as his opponent, I may call

his moves 'creative' or 'original' even though his moves are exactly how Captain W. D. Evans executed the game in the 1820s. (Id.)

George Lucas (2004) admits that his characters are traditional archetypes derived from mythology. He has a hero, Luke Skywalker, who follows the customary path of the mythological adventure. This path is a magnification of the formula represented in the rites of passage: separation – initiation – return. This is called the nuclear unit of the monomyth, a term taken from James Joyce's *Finnegans Wake* (1939). (Morong, 1994) "A hero ventures forth from the world of common day into a region of supernatural wonder: fabulous forces are there encountered and a decisive victory is won: the hero comes back from this mysterious adventure with the power to bestow boons on his fellow man." (Campbell, 1972) Lucas merely placed his character in a galaxy far, far away to pursue his monomyth. The first character that he meets on his journey is a wise man, Obi Wan Kenobi. He too is a traditional figure of mythology. His job is to provide the hero with amulets, in this case a light sabre, to help him overcome his future trials and obstacles.

These are just two examples from the *Star Wars* pantheon. Was George Lucas 'creative' or 'original'? I would argue that clearly he was. He has developed something new and novel compared to what came before. However, would the next player to join Lucas' virtual world be able to become a hero like Luke Skywalker? He would be a different person/character. He would pursue his own unique monomyth within the virtual world. He would be an avatar which reflected another source of inspiration rather than solely George Lucas.

On the other hand, Mihaly Csikszentmihaly (1994) explains with regard to Rembrandt and a master forger that only "Rembrandt's work is creative because he introduced some variations in the domain of painting at a certain point in history, when those variations were novel (original) . . . The very same variations a few years later were no longer creative, because then they simply reproduced existing forms." (Hughes, 1998) Returning to our player and his personal and unique avatar and using Csikszentmihaly's definition, has he developed something novel (original) or is he simply reproducing an existing form created by LucasArts? Csikszentmihaly's definition of creative differs from Nozick's not in the test - which remains a test of identifiable difference - but in the reference set used for the test. Whereas Nozick refers to what the creator had encountered and known previously, Csikszentmihaly compares to all that has come before.

Whether the standard is an identifiable difference from what the creator had encountered or from all of what was known previously, the popular measure for the 'original' or the 'creative' still seems to be whether the thing seems identifiably different to us, not the creator. This is a problem for game players who feel they 'make' (create or craft?) their characters unique and identifiable. LucasArts, on the other hand, merely sees that their prototype characters are dressed differently. No transformation is apparent to LucasArts; nothing in the virtual world looks much different than the pre-existing conditions.

Complex characters require hundreds of hours to create, and although the game developers have created the potential for these characters to exist by programming them into the software code, they do not actually appear in the game until a player has invested a considerable amount of time in overcoming game obstacles to build the character. (Stephens, 2002) In addition, the game developers have only created a skeleton of this complex character. They have not developed a player's specific character because the player exclusively controls some features of the character. (Fitch, 2004) For example, when a character forges relationships and alliances with other characters in the game, the game developer has no control over these aspects of the character.

The development of in-game objects, such as houses, also requires a significant time investment by players. (Id.) Again, the game developers have created the potential for the existence of these in-game objects in the software code, but these objects do not actually exist in the game until a player pursues them. With houses, the player also uses individual creativity in developing the in-game object by designing the layout and appearance of the house. Players provide more than trivial variations on the *Star Wars* story. They are creating a new story. This is no longer a game. Reality is being socially established. Events are observed and have consequences. Events 'really happen' in a space that has been meticulously authenticated. For players, what happens in *Galaxies* is authentic, as much as what happens in the movies is authentic - even more so, because it happens to them.

Can it be said then that creativity/originality requires a transformation not arising from the background order, but from the person who causes the transformation? Thus, there is a connection between creativity/originality and the personal - personal expression, personal intention, and personal reflections. LucasArts created the background order by opening up the *Star Wars* universe to others with *Galaxies*, but it is the players who transform this world by their personal expressions, personal intentions, and personal relations.

Many artists base their art on their own personal experiences. Justin Hughes (1998) cites the following examples. Diego Rivera's affair with his wife's sister, Christina, was discovered because of the way he painted Christina's image into a mural at the Mexican National Palace - in an 'ecstasy pose,' while the extraordinary paintings of his wife, Frida Kahlo, reflected her own experiences - spinal injuries from a car accident, a miscarriage, and struggles with Catholicism. Edward Munch's first major work, *The Sick Child*, recalls the death of his sister Sophie from tuberculosis. It was a scene he would repaint six times in his life. Ibsen was even more direct in transforming personal experiences into literature. He was known to abruptly start inviting individuals to dinner parties, and then just as unceremoniously drop them from his social list, once he had enough of their manners, speech, and attitudes to create a character.

As Bono, lead singer of U2 remarked, "musicians, painters, whatever, they have no choice but to describe where they live." (Pareles, 1997) This is what the players in the virtual worlds are doing. Although what can you do about tribute bands in real life or virtual worlds? Currently, *Second Life* has *U2 in SL* in which all four of the band members' avatars carry the names of their real life counterparts. The tribute band is a commercial violation that Linden Labs ought to be cracking down on contends Csven Concord, a resident of *Second Life*. Csven argues that, "Not only are *U2 in SL* guilty of trademark or other IP rights violation (both the band name and Bono's name are trademarked), but they are also crossing LL's Terms of Service, which specifically forbids giving your avatar the name of another person or a trademarked entity."

They are artists of their own characters and stories. Thus, a connection between creativity and personal experience may be inferred. This connection could be one of practicality and prudence; the most successful creators staying close to what they know. Kahlo herself explained that many of her paintings were self-portraits "because I am the subject I know best." However, originality is something more than creativity conveniently spliced to personal memories. Most people move uncritically from a belief that intellectual works reflect personal experiences to a belief that intellectual works are personal expressions. (Hughes, 1998)

When a player is creating his own character within a virtual world, he is likely to stay close to what he already knows. Nevertheless, many players create avatars which not only reflect but improve on their own characteristics. It follows then that the presentation of one's own persona in the virtual world resembles to some extent the player's real-life identity. This mechanism is referred to as transference. (Suler, 2002) It con-

sists in transferring concealed emotions – often unconsciously – to the fictitious character. In addition, it is important to consider how personal expression may be something different from repeating or reproducing personal experiences. The possibility of modelling the characters played in the virtual world is not only a mechanism supporting identification, the player also has an active role in modulating the transmissions that reach him, and has control over them.

A player does not merely faithfully reconstruct a situation from his personal past - memory regurgitation – which would be an act of personal reflection. Instead he presently watches the screen to determine what actions he should take or what decisions to make. Obviously, it is easier to identify ourselves with something we have partly created rather than by pictures imposed on us by someone else. This transmission modulation enhances the gaming experience. Otherwise, it would reflect personal experiences as though the person was a passive, if imperfect, mirror of extra-person reality; a sort of secondary identification similar to a cinematic experience. Paradoxically, this sort of identification relies on distance while in the case of games, there is something more than just intimacy. (Filiack, 2003)

It is certainly easy to believe that an intellectual work is a personal reflection of the individual especially in games where identification is replaced by *introjection* – the subject is projected inward into an 'other'. We do not need a complete imitation to confuse the 'other' with the 'self'. (Morse, 1994) The subject (player) and the 'other' (avatar) do not stand at the opposite sides of the mirror anymore – they become one. While using an electronic medium in which subject and object, and what is real and imagined, are not clearly separated, the player loses his identity, projecting himself inward, becoming the 'other', and identifies with the character in the game. (Filiack, 2003)

Personal experiences reflect in this intellectual work because they are deep causes in the course of events that produce the work. During the game, the player's identity ends in disintegration, and the merger of user's and character's consciousness ensues. There is the possibility that personal reflection, personal expression, and creativity should all collapse on one another, i.e., that 'creativity' is only a fancy covering for observation - the direct reproduction of things we have experienced. (Hughes, 1998) Whatever creativity is, it relies on - uses as fuel - the personal experiences of the creator. Something more than those experiences must be produced; otherwise, it cannot be said that the individual has been creative. Hence, creativity and originality are so intertwined. What is this 'more'? How and in what sense is it expression of the individual? (Id.)

Robert Nozick (1989) suggested that "for a product to be creative it must not only differ from what came before but also stand in no specific obvious relationship to its predecessors." He proposes that when a new object is derivable from predecessors by "mechanical application of a clear rule" it stands in a kind of "specific obvious relationship" to that predecessor and it is not creative. (Id.) I have previously described how an avatar is created. One begins with the software code of the skeleton or shell of a character. This would be copyright protected by the company. One transforms this character by experiencing the virtual world in which it exists. This could be considered a derivative work.

According to Nozick, individual avatars and their stories, no matter how unique and new to the galaxy, would not be considered creative as they are only the mechanical application of the rules of engagement in the MMORPG. Thus, regardless of how transformative the process, which has, in fact, produced an identifiably new character, it will not be considered creative because of the mechanical rules which govern the software of these virtual worlds and avatars. I disagree. The recombining of infinite (or seemingly infinite) attributes and relationships which an avatar may acquire will produce a story/character unique and

original to that player; albeit, this formulation could be considered mechanical in nature. Many psychological descriptive accounts of creativity could still reduce creativity to a 'mechanical' activity - at least for a sufficiently large mind. For example, if creativity is the combination of 'remotely associated' ideas - a view put forward by Keith Simonton - then one only needs to mechanically combine more and more remote ideas to get something creative; if it involves 'lateral thinking' - the view of Edward deBono - then one needs only keep recombining patterns laterally to get something creative. (Weisberg, 1993)

Creativity has also been described as 'a form of therapy' by authors such as Graham Greene. "Art is a form of therapy. Sometimes I wonder how all those who do not write, compose, or paint can escape the madness, the melancholia, the panic-fear inherent in the human situation." (Berman, 1995) This could explain why so many artists describe their work as critical to their psychological well-being – "a physical and spiritual necessity." (Hughes, 1998 citing, Sam Francis Exhibition, Jeu de Paume Museum, Paris (Jan.1996)) This is very true in virtual worlds as players choose to spend a tremendous amount of time building and refining their avatars. "The creative work and product come to stand, sometimes unconsciously, for herself or for a missing piece or part, or for a defective one, or for part of a better self. The work is a surrogate for the creator, analogue of her, a little voodoo doll to tinker with and transform and remake in something analogous to the way she herself, or a part, needs to be transformed, remade, or healed... Important and needed work on the self is modelled in the process of artistic creation and symbolized there." (Nozick, 1989)

This returns us to Locke's theory above in which the fruits of one's labour are perceived to be an extension of the labourer's (player's) personality. (Olivecrona, 1974) As avatars require much time and effort, they are shaped as much by player psychological needs as by advances in computer hardware and software. (Rehak, 2004) The gaming experience could be said to reflect an on-going work of art. This view corresponds with John Dewey's (1980) work in *Art as Experience*. Although he was dealing mainly with artistic production, he believed that much about artistic and inventive production was the same. His work explores the various ways in which creativity is the interaction of old personal experiences and the new environment. (Id.)

Each creative agenda bears, through the individual's interests, the imprint of her respective personal experiences. Each adventure the player has allows her to acquire new skills and attributes. Each adventure adds to her cumulative experience and thus to her creative agenda of becoming a more powerful wizard or a stronger warrior. Dewey (1980) has a stronger view of creativity as synthesis in which both perception and imagination are the synthesis of old experiences stored in memory and new circumstances being experienced by the individual: "[an] experience becomes conscious, a matter of perception, only when meanings enter it that are derived from prior experiences. Imagination is the only gateway through which these meanings can find their way into a present interaction; or rather ... the conscious adjustment of the new and the old is imagination." Further, "experience is rendered conscious by means of that fusion of old meanings and new situations that transfigures both (a transformation that defines imagination)" (Id.)

"The junction of the new and the old is not a mere composition of forces, but is a recreation in which the present impulse gets form and solidity while the old, the 'stored,' material is literally revived, given new life and soul through having to meet the new situation. It is this double change that converts an activity into an act of expression. Things in the environment that would otherwise be mere smooth channels or else blind obstructions become means, media. At the same time, things retained from the past experience that would grow stale from routine or inert from lack of use, become coefficients in new adventures and put on raiment of fresh meaning. Here are all the elements needed to define expression." (Id.) This sums up the virtual world experience very neatly.

Dewey's view is that both the subjects our minds engage and what we do with those subjects are the results of personal experience being reworked in the present tense. Because each of us is a unique experiential time line, whatever we produce constitutes personal expression. Each of us is a unique order of experiences and each new creation might somehow be predictable and mechanical while staying beautiful and unique. (Noziak, 1989)

Does copyright protection subsist in massively consensual hallucinations? Can individuals create something copyrightable in these alternative galaxies known as virtual worlds? An author must contribute expression that is 'original'; or an author must contribute distinguishable variations - variations that are greater than merely trivial - to a pre-existing work. (VerSteeg, 1996) So for example, LucasArts creates the galaxy's structure and the various races of characters possible; however, the players craft "original" characters and experiences. This will be explored in more detail in Chapter 6.

2. Intentionality

Intentionality is used here as a counterpart to 'creativity' and as a constituent part of 'personality'. (Hughes, 1998) Philosophers and jurists have struggled with the idea of 'intention' and the ways to characterize the process of forming and having intentions. Return to Black's Law Dictionary (1990) definition of intent as "design, resolve, or determination with which a person acts." (*Witters v United States*, 70 U.S.App.D.C. 316, 106 F.2d 837 (D.C. Cir. 1939)) This definition is similar to the Oxford Pocket Dictionary's (1975) definition of intent as well. Intent and motive should not be confused. Motive is what prompts a person to act, or fail to act. Intent refers only to the state of mind with which the act is done or omitted. (Black's, 1990)

A common theme in philosophical discussions of intentions is a sense of their 'nowness' - that an intention is a desire or decision being put into action. "Intending to do something is to be already in the process of doing it, even if merely by having undergone a re-arrangement of the causal powers within oneself in the direction of the action one intends to do." (Castaneda, 1975) Charles Taylor (1989) further states that "awareness of [an] intention incorporates, and may be nothing more than, our awareness of what we are doing intentionally." To the degree that an intention is separate from the 'spirit' of an action, this might help us distinguish intention from the creative impetus behind a project. While desire can be described as an intentional state, the important difference between a 'desire' and an 'intention' is that the latter is operational. One can 'desire' some end without doing anything to achieve that end, but 'intending' something connotes making a plan and putting it into action. An intention includes an awareness of a personal goal, awareness of a means to achieve that goal, and a commitment to pursue that means with personal actions. (Hughes, 1998)

There is no question that artistic works that seem imbued with creativity also seem imbued with the artist's intention or purpose. As such, "[w]here the work constitutes a work that has both artistic intent and aspects of craftsmanship; it will attract copyright protection as a work of artistic craftsmanship." (*Lambretta Clothing Co Ltd v Teddy Smith (UK) Ltd* [2003] RPC 41, 2003 WL 21353286 (Ch D), [2003] EWHC 1204, [2004] EWCA Civ 886) Dewey remarked that: "no matter how imaginative the material for a work of art, it issues from the state of reverie to become the matter of a work of art only when it is ordered and organized, and this effect is produced only when purpose controls selection and development of material." This returns us to the concept of authorship in British copyright law. The author

of a work is the person who creates it. (CPDA 1988 s 9(1)) In most work, this is self-evident. Author has also been defined at the person who gathers or organizes the material contained within a work and who selects, orders, and arranges that material. This was in reference to compilations in the case of *Waterlow Publishers Ltd v Rose* [1995] FSR 207.

The United States Supreme Court has defined the word 'author' twice; but only in dicta. First in *Community for Creative Non-Violence v Reid*, 490 U.S. 730, 737 (1989), "As a general rule, the author is the party who actually creates the work, that is, the person who translates an idea into a fixed, tangible expression entitled to copyright protection." (citing 17 U.S.C. §102) Next in, *Burrow-Giles Lithographic Co. v Sarony*, 111 U.S. 53, 58 (1884): "An author. . . is to whom anything owes its origin; originator; maker. . ." Generally speaking, cases that have defined 'author' for purposes of copyright have focussed their inquiry on one basic question: Has the putative author produced something that is copyrightable? There are two versions of what is really the same 'rule' of copyright law that have led courts to ask this question.

One version of the 'rule' comes from Justice Thurgood Marshall's statement in *Community for Creative Non-Violence v Reid:* "As a general rule, the author is the party who actually creates the work, that is, the person who translates an idea into a fixed, tangible expression entitled to copyright protection." (citing 17 U.S.C.A. §102) The other version of the 'rule' comes from the discussion of joint authorship in Professor Goldstein's treatise (1994) on copyright law: "A collaborative contribution will not produce a joint work, and a contributor will not obtain a co-ownership interest, unless the contribution represents original expression that could stand on its own as the subject matter of copyright." According to Professor Goldstein, in order to be an 'author,' one must contribute something that is independently copyrightable. Taken together, courts have used these two versions to forge the rule that a person must fix his idea in a tangible medium of expression in order to be considered an 'author'. Prof. Versteeg (1996) called this hybrid rule the Marshall-Goldstein approach.

The Marshall-Goldstein approach has a certain logical appeal. The U.S. Copyright Act could not be clearer: "Copyright protection subsists ... in original works of authorship fixed in any tangible medium of expression, now known or later developed, from which they can be perceived, reproduced, or otherwise communicated, either directly or with the aid of a machine or device." (17 U.S.C.A. §102(a) (1996)) In order to be subject to copyright protection, a work must be fixed in a tangible medium. Because a work cannot be copyrightable unless it is fixed, it stands to reason that a person cannot be considered an author for purposes of copyright unless he has fixed his work in a tangible medium. *Childress v Taylor*, 945 F.2d 500 (2nd Cir. 1991), serves as an illustration of this definition of 'author.'

In *Childress*, Clarice Taylor, an actress who had built a reputation by impersonating the black entertainer 'Moms' Mabley, approached the plaintiff, Alice Childress, a playwright, and convinced Childress to write a play about the life of 'Moms' Mabley. (Id. at 502) Taylor researched Mabley and provided her research to Childress. Subsequently, Childress asked Taylor for additional biographical information and then routinely consulted with Taylor as the writing of the play evolved. During this process, Taylor recommended detailed scenes, jokes, and characters for the play. According to the Second Circuit, "Taylor contributed facts and details about Moms Mabley's life and discussed some of them with Childress. However, Childress was responsible for the actual structure of the play and the dialogue." (Id.) The Second Circuit affirmed summary judgment for Childress on the basis that the intent necessary for joint authorship was lacking. (Id. at 507-8) The U.S. Copyright Act, 17 U.S.C.A. §101 (1996), defines a 'joint work' as "a work prepared by two or more authors with the

intention that their contributions be merged into inseparable or interdependent parts of a unitary whole." Thus, in order to be considered 'joint authors,' the putative joint authors must manifest this intention. (Id. at 507)

Nevertheless, the Court also addressed the definition of 'author' in dicta. (Id. at 506) After all, "by definition the party raising the joint authorship claim (or defence) must be an 'author' of the copyrightable work." (*Respect Inc. v Committee on the Status of Women*, 815 F. Supp. 1112, 1120 (N.D. Ill. 1993)) The *Childress* decision at 504 recognized that the authorship question in the context of joint authorship is particularly sensitive and difficult: "Care must be taken to ensure that true collaborators in the creative process are accorded the perquisites of co-authorship and to guard against the risk that a sole author is denied exclusive authorship status simply because another person rendered some form of assistance. Copyright law best serves the interests of creativity when it carefully draws the bounds of 'joint authorship' so as to protect the legitimate claims of both sole authors and co-authors."

Judge Newman noted that "[a] more substantial issue arising under the statutory definition of 'joint work' is whether the contribution of each joint author must be copyrightable or only the combined result of their joint efforts must be copyrightable." (*Childress* at 506) Judge Newman concluded, "The case law supports a requirement of copyrightability of each contribution." (Id.) *Childress* established that in order to be considered an 'author,' one must contribute something that is copyrightable. (VerSteeg, 1996; Lape, 1997)

The Seventh Circuit adopted this position in a case which provides another example of this approach to defining 'author,' *Erickson v Trinity Theatre, Inc.*, 13 F.3d 1061 (7th Cir. 1994), Erickson involved a claim of joint authorship by a theatre performing the plays of a playwright. Although playwright Karen Erickson was the sole writer of the plays in question, the Trinity Theatre argued that its actors had contributed a great deal to the finished products and, therefore, it should be deemed a joint author. The conditions in *Childress* and the conditions surrounding the development of Erickson's plays are analogous. Here, the actors contributed ideas and provided suggestions. Their contributions simply developed in a different manner than in *Childress*. Taylor presented a rather stronger case. She could identify specific material contributed by her. The Trinity actors, with one exception, were could not identify any specific contributions they had made.

The Court suggested that "even if two or more persons collaborate with the intent to create a unitary work, the product will be considered a 'joint work' only if the collaborators can be considered 'authors'." (Id. at 1068) The Court emphasized that the U.S. Copyright Act dictates that a 'joint work' be 'prepared by two or more authors' by citing 17 U.S.C. §101 (1994). The Court then quoted Justice Marshall's dictum in *Reid* at 737 stating, "An author is 'the party who actually creates the work, that is, the person who translates an idea into a fixed, tangible expression entitled to copyright protection'." The Court then latched onto the phrase "fixed, tangible expression" and quoted the U.S. Copyright Act's definition of 'fixed.'

As to the requirement of fixation, §101 states that "[a] work is 'fixed' in a tangible medium of expression when its embodiment in a copy or phonorecord, by or under the authority of the author, is sufficiently permanent or stable to permit it to be perceived, reproduced, or otherwise communicated for a period of more than transitory duration." The *Erickson* Court concluded at 1072 that "to qualify as an author, one must supply more than mere direction or ideas." Applying these rules of law, the Court determined that the Trinity Theatre could not be a joint author: "In order for the plays to be joint works under the Act, Trinity also must show that actors' contributions to Ms. Erickson's work could have been independently copyrighted." (Id.) The Court punctuated its decision with an almost irrefutable maxim of copyright law: "Ideas, refinements, and suggestions, standing alone, are not the subjects of copyrights." (Id.)

A similar case in the United Kingdom, *Brighton and another v Jones* [2004] EWHC 1157, concerning the play *Stones in His Pockets* involved similar issues. Miss Jones had been commissioned by Dubbeljoint Theatre Company to write a play called *Stones in His Pocket*. Miss Brighton was the director of the play which was originally produced in 1996. Miss Jones was credited as the author of the play in the publicity materials. Miss Jones wrote the original script in 1996 and in 1999 rewrote the original play. Two separate copyrights subsisted for these two 'dramatic works'. The 1999 version was a commercial and critical success. Miss Brighton claimed joint authorship of the 1996 script on the basis of contributions she had made in rehearsals. Consequently, she alleged that Miss Jones had breached that right when she created the 1999 script. Miss Brighton claimed that she had sent a draft opening script to Miss Jones before she had started work on the 1996 script. Miss Jones closely followed the storyline (but not the precise words) to the end of the opening draft. Miss Brighton claimed that the draft was a dramatic work in its own right and that she was the owner.

The court held that the basic provisions of the CDPA ss 9 and 10 as to ownership were qualified to the extent that under s 104(2), there was a presumption that the author named on the work was the actual author. Miss Jones had been; however, Miss Brighton failed to prove that she also was named. (*Brighton* at 1158) It was further established that copyright infringement ('altered copying') existed if B took A's story and wrote a play based on it but did not have a licence from A to do so. (*Designers Guild Ltd v Russell Williams (Textiles) Ltd* [2000] 1 WLR 2416 at 2422H and 2431D; *Ravenscroft v Herbert* [1980] RPC 193; and *Harman Pictures NV v Osborne* [1967] 1 WLR 723) The court held that Miss Jones had indeed used a significant part of the draft in the 'altered copying' sense, but not in the 'language copying' sense. She accepted that this was true and actually quite extensive. The court, however, reject Miss Brighton's claim stating that she had given Miss Jones an implied open-ended licence to use the work. (*Brighton and another v Jones* [2004] EWHC 1157)

The court then explored the claim of joint authorship. Joint authorship under CDPA s 10(1) requires 'collaboration … in which the contribution of each author is not distinct from that of the other author or authors.' Miss Brighton's case was that this provision applied to the manner in which rehearsals had proceeded. The court went on to review the case law required: (i) a person claiming joint authorship needed to have made a significant contribution to the creation of the work; (*Robin Ray v Classic FM plc* [1998] FSR 622) (ii) the contribution had to be a contribution towards the creation of the work; (*Fylde Microsystems Ltd v Key Radio Systems Ltd* [1998] FSR 449) and (iii) a person can become a joint author without putting pen to paper, so long as someone else has effectively written what that person has created. (*Cala Homes (South) Ltd v Alfred McAlpine Homes East Ltd* [1995] FSR 818) During rehearsals, the actors might improvise or Miss Brighton might suggest dialogue, but Miss Jones would put it down in her own words. The court determined that Miss Brighton's claims failed despite her contributions during rehearsals because the words were composed by Miss Jones. Any changes made on the basis of Miss Brighton's input were not considered significant enough. Also, she did not establish that her contribution was in the work rather than in its interpretation and theatrical presentation. (*Brighton and another v Jones* [2004] EWHC 1157)

Thus, one might say that the person's intentionality is intention in the process which led to creation of the res, not intention in the res itself. This, in turn, leads us from an exploration of the artist's expression into exploration of her intentions, i.e., "what was she trying to express?" easily becomes "what was her intention?" To John Dewey (1980), purpose was as keenly connected to one's personality as creativity: "Purpose implicates in the most organic way an individual self. It is the purpose he entertains and acts upon that an individual most completely exhibits and realizes his most intimate selfhood. Control of material by a 'self' is control by more than just 'mind': it is control by the personality that has mind incorporated within it." However, not just any intent is enough for a personhood interest in intellectual products; the individual must intend to produce some form or shape that does not yet exist.

Once again Lockean philosophy may be invoked. The artist/author must have the intention of being identified with her original work which has been set down in a fixed manner. This appropriative labour has caused her to psychologically identify with her work. (Gordon, 1990) Her personality interest might arise from being the source of the directed labour. The scientists who made an important discovery from the hypothalamus gland characterized their work in much the same terms of highly directed labour: "nobody before had to process millions of hypothalami . . . . The key factor is not the money; it's the will . . . the brutal force of putting in 60 hours a week for a year." They likened the experience to "fighting Hitler . . . you have to cut him down." (Latour & Woolgar, 1986) Or it can be applied to players in a virtual world. Take this account of one user's virtual toils:

John Stolle had to procure the money for the deed to his new castle. To acquire the money, he sold his old house. To buy that first house, he spent hours manufacturing virtual swords and armour to sell to a steady customer base of about three dozen fellow players. To find and then maintain these customers, he was obliged to bring [his avatar's] blacksmithing skills up to Grandmaster level. To reach that rank, Stolle spent six months blacksmithing to the exclusion of all else. He clicked on hillsides to mine ore, returned to his forge to click the ore into ingots, clicked again to transform the ingots into swords and armour. Then he returned to the hills to start the process all over again. Each time he improved [his avatar's] skill level a small fraction of a percentage point.

Pause for a moment and reflect on this story. Consider what was going on here. Every day, month after month, a man came home from a full day of bone-jarringly repetitive work with a jack hammer and then sat up all night doing finger-numbingly repetitive work with 'hammer' and 'anvil'. He paid $ 9.95 per month for this privilege. If one were to ask Stolle why. He would reply: "Well, it's not work if you enjoy it." (Dibbell, 2003) He clearly identifies with his creations. Would he not be surprised to learn that he may not actually own the fruits of his labour? He might even be shocked to learn that he is merely a joint author of a vast consensual hallucination. The idea of a vast consensual hallucination comes from Rushkoff's *Cyberia*. (1994)

So how should one determine the ownership of the virtual assets created in these spaces? Currently, the two most prevalent ways in which to deal with the issue lay in intellectual property law and contract law. Both these approaches carry with them a set of presuppositions about whose intentions should be protected. This set of presuppositions then defines how the rights of players/crafters should be balanced against the rights of designers/creators. The European Commission's Green Paper on Copyright in the Knowledge Economy (COM (2008) 466/3) is considering an exception for user-generated content on the basis that it is "transformative" and would follow the trend which the United States is following. One must note, however, that transformative use alone is not a defence to copyright infringement but a factor when determining a fair use defence under §107 of the U.S. Copyright Act. This will be discussed further in Chapter 6.

3. Sourcehood

Besides creativity and intentionality, there may be another personality interest: identification as the source of the res. (Hughes, 1998) I suggest that

this is a more basic aspect, but one which may resonate closely with players in a virtual world. The idea of 'sourcehood' takes two forms. The first is the purely private self-identification with the res. This is a private belief that one is the source of the res. (Id.) An example would be a player creating a distinctly unique avatar as opposed to accepting a generic avatar. On the other hand, it could be the computer programmer who created the code to allow avatars to acquire blue dye which, in turn, would allow them to have blue hair. Contrast this with the desire for the attention of others, recognition, or social place; a person who wants others to identify her and might try to achieve this recognition by 'marking' things as her own. (Hegel, 1952; Gordon, 1993) These markings could be the symbols a craftsman uses to identify his goods or it could be the marks that a guild might use to identify its members. This 'sourcehood' interest, being identified as the source of some intellectual work, may be a personality justification.

One of the main justifications for intellectual property rights, especially copyright, is the belief that "an author's or inventor's sense of worth and dignity require public acknowledgment by those who use the writing or discovery. . . ." (Hettinger, 1989) Certainly, the personhood interest in intellectual property is most often protected with a guarantee of social recognition: the right of attribution. (Berne Convention, article 6bis) Attribution rights protect sourcehood interests; however, in America these rights are not as developed as in Europe. In the United States, the default position is that a source of intellectual property res does not have a right of attribution as noted in *Cleary v News Corp.*, 30 F.3d 1255 (9th Cir. 1994). In *Vargas v Esquire, Inc.*, 164 F.2d 522 (7th Cir. 1947), the court held that an artist could not claim a right of attribution against a magazine where the artist granted the magazine all rights to his drawings in exchange for monthly compensation). In a further example, *Nelson v Radio Corp. of Am.*, 148 F. Supp. 1 (S.D. Fla. 1957), the court denied a singer a right of attribution in the context of a master/servant relationship between recording company and singer and absent agreement to provide label credit.

Although, self-identification and the desire for recognition from others are conceptually distinct, one can imagine creative people who identify with their work and do not want social recognition. Perhaps, an artist wants to avoid social recognition in order to maintain greater creative freedom. Or perhaps, an individual wants to relate to others via a different identity provided by their avatar. In MMORPGs, this is where the aspect of role-playing is at its height. Virtual worlds are the domain of liquid identities. Even so, these two notions - self-identification as the source of a res and desire for social recognition through the res - are rarely disentangled. They are combined on the assumption that the person seeks social identification for those things with which she already self-identifies. The notion of identity is compelling when studying culture; "self" is the measure of reality. (Filiack, 2003) Protecting this "self" takes the form of social mores as much as laws.

If the right of attribution is limited in our mores and laws, then so is the extension of any other rights (i.e. to control the intellectual property res) relating to one who self-identifies with that res. This section explores some of the situations in which self-identification might arise from 'sourcehood' and how that can be extrapolated into virtual worlds. Further there are situations where a person is the source of some valuable intellectual property but something about the situation disallows a justification based upon creativity or intentionality. (Hughes, 1998)

A sourcehood interest could also arise through labour or effort, even though that effort has not led to anything apparently creative. This is likely to be an argument in videogames. Intentionality, though, may still provide an adequate justification for a personality interest. A sourcehood interest could also come from being the passive source of

valuable genetic information; this is the *Moore v University of California*, 793 P.2d 479 (Cal.1990), problem. Virtual worlds are analogous to this problem. LucasArts' computer programming code can be seen as being the equivalent to the genetic code in Moore's spleen. The game players would then be analogous to the doctors at UCLA. In both situations, the legal system does not grant protection - and therefore does not seem to recognize a personhood interest - unless other elements are present. The juxtaposition does not have to be unprotected 'sources' from protected 'geniuses'; the undervaluing of 'sources' may be rooted in the idea of human agency as the ingredient that removes something from the Lockean commons. (*Holmes v Hurst*, 174 U.S. 82 (1899); *Jeffreys v Boosey*, 10 Eng. Rep. 681 (H.L. 1854))

Moore v Regents of University of California is an interesting case. Doctors at UCLA Medical Centre had removed Moore's spleen in the course of cancer treatment, and then used Moore's cells to create a patented cell-line. The California Supreme Court held that the doctors may have breached their fiduciary duty to Moore, but that Moore had no property interest in his own body's cells. The *Moore* majority was not concerned with the moral dimension of extending property rights over living tissue; nor did the court question the propriety of the patents issued to the physicians who had cultured Moore's spleen cells. Instead, the majority opinion called Moore's own claim to have a property interest in the biological materials derived from his own body 'novel' and 'problematical at best.' (793 P.2d 479 (Cal.1990)) The majority opinion completely skips over the Lockean theory regarding a person owning his own body which provides the first step in a labour theory of property which has influenced American law since the Founding Fathers.

This issue is still hotly debated in Europe. Even though most industrialized countries agree that non-naturally occurring micro-organisms are patentable, only a few allow patents for larger, non-natural organisms. In the early 1980s, the U.S.

Supreme Court held in *Diamond v Chakrabarty*, 447 U.S. 303 (1980) that genetically engineered, single-cell organisms not found in nature were patentable. This decision did not expressly address the patentability of multi-cellular or naturally occurring animals. Nonetheless, under the authority of the Court's decision in *Chakrabarty*, the U.S. Patent and Trademark Office announced it would accept applications for and grant patents on such animals. The U.S. Patent and Trademark Office, in fact, issued a patent on the 'Harvard Oncomouse,' a mouse genetically engineered to be highly susceptible to human cancer.

The European Patent Office determined that the Harvard Oncomouse was not an unpatentable 'animal variety.' The EPO stated that each patent application for higher life forms will be examined individually, and the grant of the Harvard Oncomouse patent does not open European protection for all higher life forms. Dissemination of unwanted genes, cruelty to animals, environmental risks, and benefits of the invention will be considered in granting such an application. (See 11 Biotech. L. Rep. 150-53 (1992) for a reprint of the European Patent Office's statement.) (Kimbrell, 1995; Helfgott, 1992)

James Boyle (1996) criticized the *Moore* opinion for its inexplicable discussion of uniqueness as a requisite for a property right in human cells. The *Moore* court (at 490) focused on the genetic code for production of lymphokines, finding that this tiny part of Moore's gene code could not be different from anyone else's. The proper focus of analysis, however, was not the gene code, but the cells (or whatever aspect of the cells - possibly including code) that were responsible for Moore's higher than normal level of lymphokines production. Even if the court had done a tighter factual analysis, there would be no justification for the court's uniqueness requirement on Moore's property claim. Uniqueness is a requirement only of patent law; it is not required for most other property regimes and certainly not for rights to one's own labour – one's own bodily toil. One

irony of the *Moore* case is that the conventions of the scientific community did a better job of recognizing Moore's contribution than the legal system did: as issued, the patent covers the 'Mo cell line.'

To Boyle, *Moore* is a case in which 'sources' of new intellectual property are undervalued while the manipulators who use source material are aggrandized by the 'author' construct. (Boyle, 1996; *cf.,* Fairfield, 2005) This point is reinforced by the dissent's comment that "no one can question Moore's crucial contribution to the invention." (*Moore* at 511) The *Moore* court emphasized the patented work of the UCLA researchers in producing a cell line from Moore's cells, opining that "adaptation and growth of human tissues and cells in culture is difficult - often considered an art" and that the patent granted to the cell line applied to the results of this "inventive effort ... not the discovery of naturally occurring raw materials." (Id. at 492)

The patent rights of the UCLA researchers do not bear directly on property rights to the source material. The amount of art a sculptor puts into a work would not alter property rights to the original bronze or marble. The sculptor might own the copyrightable image of the work yet still be liable for stealing the marble. LucasArts would make this argument against the rights of players in their characters and the objects associated with those characters. No matter the amount of time and energy a player expends on creating their avatar, goods, homes, and adventures, nothing would alter the property rights to the underlying computer code that LucasArts supplied in the first place. However, by analogy, just as the UCLA researchers acquired rights in their manipulation of Moore's genetic code, so should players receive rights in their manipulation of LucasArts' computer code. The great difference, however, is that people have no conscious personal experience, creativity, or intentionality embedded in their genetic codes. Does a personhood interest in this information arise nonetheless because you are the source of the information? Should the personhood interest arise because there is a conscious personal experience, creativity and intentionality in the actions of the players?

The issue that could have been confronted is whether Moore had a property right to his cells - does Locke's theory of self-ownership extend to the cellular level or does 'ownership' simply make no sense when applied to body parts? The majority opinion fails to get to the root questions of cell ownership; and thus, to when and where ownership begins.

The connection between genetic information and persona has not gone unnoticed. Stephen Mortinger, (1990) pointed out that "a cause of action for appropriation of the commercial value of a person's genetic structure [is not] far removed from the Court's current recognition of the right of a person to claim appropriation of his unique likeness or persona. Moore's experience has been analogised to that of Bela Lugosi's heirs and Mr. Lugosi's portrayal of Dracula. In *Lugosi v Universal Pictures*, 603 P.2d 425 (Cal. 1979), a majority of the California Supreme Court held that Lugosi's heirs could not prevent Universal Studios from licensing an image of 'Dracula' that clearly included Lugosi's likeness. Lugosi had granted Universal a right to use his likeness in promoting specific Dracula films. Universal had discovered, as Disney had with Mickey Mouse, that the 'Dracula' character - particularly Lugosi's rendition of it - was a valuable property separate from any films in which it appeared. Universal widely licensed the Lugosi-Dracula character for merchandise unconnected to any re-release or promotion of the films. Lugosi's heirs argued that Lugosi's grant to Universal did not extend to such uses. (Id.)

The majority found that Lugosi's right to control his name and likeness was personal, and, therefore, nondescendible. This left Universal free to exploit the Lugosi-Dracula image after Lugosi's death. The majority concluded that "neither society's interests in the free dissemination of ideas nor the artist's rights to the fruits of his own labour would be served" by recognizing the right to descend to Lugosi's heirs. (Id.) The court also justified their non-descendibility ruling by "the difficulty in judicially selecting an appropriate durational limitation" if heirs were allowed to inherit a property right in a likeness. (Id.)

The *Lugosi* case is not easily analyzed as a 'source' versus 'author' battle. In *Lugosi,* the original author plays no part because the character created by the author, Bram Stoker, had already entered the public domain. On one hand, the case centred on a popular artiste's battle against an anonymous collaborative institution. On the other hand, that artist, Lugosi, was clearly using someone else's material. The only hint of Mr. Lugosi being an underappreciated 'source' may have been Justice Mosk remarking that Lugosi "was a talented actor but ... he was not a playwright, an innovator, a creator or an entrepreneur." (Id. at 432) He further went on to note that 'merely playing a role' creates no property interest in that dramatic role. (Id.)

This would be a very strong argument for LucasArts. Although Bram Stoker did not have a role in the litigation, George Lucas certainly would have. He is the playwright, the innovator, the creator, and entrepreneur of the original *Star Wars* oeuvre. There is no doubt of his property rights in that. However, there is an equally strong argument in favour of the players. The players write the persistent and interactive adventures they portray. They are the on-going innovators of *Galaxies*. They create stories and goods daily. Entrepreneurialism is an intrinsic aspect of virtual worlds.

As Justice Bird pointed out in her dissent, when Universal granted licenses, it "specifically authorized the use of Lugosi's likeness from his portrayal of Count Dracula." (Id. at 435, Bird, J. dissenting) Universal did this even though other actors had played the Dracula role in other Universal films. She recognized that the right of publicity could have justifications separate from privacy and similar to that of other intellectual property. She was correct that this was a case about an image. (Id.) Justice Mosk took a misstep when he reasoned that Lugosi's "performance gave him no more claim on Dracula than that of countless actors of Hamlet who have portrayed the Dane in a unique manner." (Id. at 432) He missed the point. The issue was not whether Lugosi's heirs had rights over the Dracula role, but whether Lugosi's heirs had rights over the Lugosi-Dracula image.

The present level of technology, we can understand that image as a compendium of information. It could be digital information used to create the image on a computer; it could also be genetic information which largely (although not completely) constituted Lugosi's physiognomy coupled with some information on make-up. This may seem to oversimplify the case because the Lugosi-Dracula image was rooted in an intentional, dramatic performance. But the simplification is justified by the widespread use of the image separate from the films and the fact that many consumers of the image - particularly young people - have no experience with Lugosi's dramatic performance as Dracula. This is what arguably makes any personhood justification for protecting the Lugosi-Dracula image so different from protection for the images of Madonna, Prince, Julia Roberts or Princess Leia. In those cases the individual's image and overall persona is a product imbued with intention and purpose. (Fisher, 2004)

But the rise of the image of Lugosi-Dracula, an image sold to teenagers who do not know who Bela Lugosi was, seems comparatively accidental. Separated from Lugosi's dramatic performances, Lugosi's vampirical likeness becomes a possible sourcehood example, one in which we might want to recognize a personhood interest even where no creativity or intentionality is at play. George Lucas recognized this when he first started putting together *Star Wars*. He wanted complete and utter control of the licensing rights to all the characters, creatures, and stories. (Lucas, 2004)

E. THE PROBLEM OF LABOUR

Beyond examples like the *Moore* case, a final area of case law may offer some insights into the sourcehood justification of personality interests. Intellectual property law is rich in cases holding that mere labour or effort does not lead to intellectual property protection. Justice Brennan cautioned against seeing protectable interests arising from labour in the 1985 case brought against the *Nation* for printing excerpts of former President Ford's memoirs:

Limiting the inquiry to the propriety of a subsequent author's use of the copyright owner's literary form is not easy in the case of a work of history. Protection against only substantial appropriation of literary form does not ensure historians a return commensurate with the full value of their labours. The literary form contained in works like "A Time to Heal" reflects only a part of the labour that goes into the book. It is the labour of collecting, sifting, organizing, and reflecting that predominates in the creation of works of history such as this one. The value this labour produces lies primarily in the information and ideas revealed, and not in the particular collection of words through which the information and ideas are expressed. Copyright thus does not protect that which is often of most value in a work of history, and courts must resist the tendency to reject the fair use defence on the basis of their feeling that an author of history has been deprived of the full value of his or her labour. A subsequent author's taking of information and ideas are in no sense pirating because copyright law simply does not create any property interest in information and ideas. (Harper & Row Publishers Inc v Nation Enters., 471 U.S. 539, 589 (1985))

The 'tendency' against which Brennan warns might be couched as the 'labour' problem - whether protectable (personality) interests can arise from seemingly non-creative labour that produces valuable works. (Hughes, 1998) The "collecting, sifting, and organizing" that constitutes such a large part of some works is a kind of activity which does not seem to be creative. Yet researchers feel justified in having a deep personality interests in their own work.

One could say that learning to play the MMOR-PGs is akin to "collecting, sifting and organizing" information about the new virtual world. The player is gathering skills, strength, and powers. As suggested earlier, this type of labour involves a certain amount of intentionality. It is clearly a goal-directed, conscious activity. In research based cases though, the intentionality - the will behind the research - may belong to someone else. If the purpose, approach, and design of the research is completely determined by an employer and the research activity is not judged creative, does the researcher have any personhood interest in the results just from being the source of the labour? In virtual worlds, the will behind the research is that of the player not the game company. Although it can be argued that the purpose, approach and design of their research is determined by the game company. The question remains whether or not the results of that research activity can be judged as creative. In both scenarios, perhaps the researcher/player can only achieve a right of attribution.

This leads to another area of arguably non-creative, non-intentional labour, painstaking reproduction. (Id.) Hughes emphasizes that the reproduction must be painstaking. For purposes of my argument this may not be necessary as the underlying computer code make any creation synchronized with the entire virtual world. When painstaking reproduction takes nature as its subject, there was no problem distinguishing the res from its underlying inspiration. No matter how realistic, a painting is distinguishable from the meadow or fruit bowl it portrays. What happens when painstaking reproduction takes virtual nature as its subject? Now these skills of painstaking reproduction are focused on an object which is already the subject of intellectual property rights. How can we grant property rights to character X,

a painstaking reproduction of character Y, without compromising the intellectual property rights to Y? The games themselves have a built-in remedy for this problem. For example, no one can be the character of Darth Vader. However, someone can attempt to become a Dark Lord in his own right.

Gracen v Bradford Exchange, 698 F.2d 300 (7th. Cir. 1983), is an interesting case in this regard. An artist who had realistically recreated Dorothy from The Wizard of Oz on collector's plates was unable to stop her image from being reproduced without her permission. Bradford had sponsored a contest to create a collector's plate image of Dorothy; the arguably contradictory contest instructions stated that Bradford sought the artist's 'interpretation' of Dorothy but that this interpretation of "Judy/Dorothy must be very recognizable as everybody's Judy/Dorothy." (Id. at 301) Gracen had won the contest originally. However, when Gracen and Bradford failed to agree on the price for Gracen's work, Bradford hired another artist to copy Gracen's work. Gracen sued, claiming that the second artist had, at Bradford's direction, pirated her copyrighted image of Dorothy. Gracen lost on summary judgment - later affirmed on appeal - on the basis that Gracen's image had insufficient variation from the Dorothy images in the film. "The prize for faithful accuracy doomed Gracen's copyright suit ... The court condemned Gracen for achieving precisely her creative goal." (Wiley, 1991) Gracen should have had some copyright recognized and that, in general, copyright should be rewarded where the artist has painstakingly reproduced something. (Id.)

It is enlightening to note that faithful reproductions like Gracen's work are often shoehorned into the 'creativity' model. Bradford had originally praised Gracen's painting of the Wizard of Oz, saying that it "was the one painting that conveyed the essence of Judy's character in the film ...." (*Gracen* at 301) The idea of 'conveying' or 'capturing' the 'essence' of something is very much in the romantic spirit of defining an author. The difference between a northern European Renaissance painter and Gracen is that the romantic painter was usually capturing the 'essence' of some aspect of nature or human activity, whereas Gracen was capturing the essence of prior, protected art. (Wiley, citing E.H. Gombrich, 1984)

Let us consider this scenario in a slightly different light. The call has gone forth for artists/players to create or capture the essence of *Star Wars* characters. They are given generic characters with which to begin, a wookie or a female human. The player has been told that they cannot become or re-create the characters Chewbacca or Princess Leia. However, Chewbacca has pretty standard looking fur and blue eyes. Only the adventures he has be on with Han Solo mark him out as a unique wookie. Princess Leia is also a pretty standard looking female with brown hair and eyes in a hooded white dress. Does her hairstyle or clothing mark her out as unique or again is it her adventures that make her unique?

Not all games have cared about this. See, *Marvel Enterprises Inc and Marvel Characters Inc. v NCSoft Corp, NC Interactive, Inc. and Cryptic Studios, Inc.*, No. CV 04-9253-RGK (unreported, Central Dist. Calif.) In the defendants' game, players design and create superheroes, which they can then use to interact with other players within the virtual city 'Paragon City'. The game contains a character creation system which guides players through the superhero design process. Marvel claims that this character creation system allows and encourages players to create heroes that are similar to, or identical in appearance to, Marvel's well-known comic book characters.

What can a player do to make their character unique or derivative of the original characters? It is possible that the practical problem of sorting out rights between the original and derivative work compels the *Gracen* conclusion. Perhaps, the *Gracen* case was not persuasive because we feel there was little or no personality interest in her work. The term 'creative' was just misplaced. No one would ask Gracen what her Dorothy 'meant' because it was an image so undistinguishable

from the Dorothy of the movies that no one would have thought it to be a different creation. It will be interesting to see if anyone creates an image or character that is indistinguishable from the *Star Wars* movies. It will also be interesting to see what the court determines in the *Marvel* case.

The next point is really the problem. As long as high fidelity copying could only be done by humans - and a very few, dedicated humans - it was easy to believe that some very subtle but nonetheless unique work went into 'capturing' the 'essence' of the image. While contemplating the modern advent of the 'author' construct, Boyle (1988) thought that "the most cursory historical study reveals that 'medieval church writers actively disapproved of the elements of originality and creativity.'" He then quoted Ernst Goldschmidt's (1969) conclusions that medieval theologians "valued extant old books more highly than any current writings or books and they put the work of the scribe and the copyist above that of the author. The real task of the scholars [was] ... a discovery of great old books, their multiplication and the placing of copies where they would be accessible to future generations of readers."

Goldschmidt's (1969) conclusion about the relative position of scribes and authors describes something more than the lower station occupied by authors in pre-modern times; his comment must be read against the technological level of medieval times. Prior to the printing press, the accurate scribe or copying provided a very valuable, uniquely human skill. In the technological situation our players find themselves, they have been given a template upon which they must create a unique variation. Does this make them a scribe in George Lucas' universe or authors of their own destinies?

To a medieval pair of eyes, the scribe's work seemed far less 'mechanical' than it does to us. To return to one of Nozick's (1974) ideas - the juxtaposition of the creative and the mechanical - if scribe copying seemed less mechanical back then, it probably seemed more 'creative' back then.

What is the proper analogy? Perhaps in medieval times, the scribe's skills appeared like the airline pilot's skills appear to us: we know what the pilot does, we know that pilots do the same thing again and again, but we also think that each time they land a plane they employ skill, finesse, and intuitive judgments unavailable to most of us and not yet reduced to mechanical algorithms. This is analogous to what goes on is virtual worlds. We know Jedi knights go on adventures and maintain the peace in the universe. But each adventure they have requires that they employ skill, finesse, and intuitive judgement. Scribes were, in the medieval context, understandably special, as are Jedi knight in the virtual context.

Has technology foiled this equation? It is no accident that realism in painting waned as photography waxed. It has become harder to see 'personality' in painstaking reproductions of images or sounds. What personal meaning can be conveyed in doing what a machine can do? And as our machines have become more clever and adept, the problem has become more severe. Reproduction remains, however, a means by which we can see the sourcehood interest in very non-creative labour and where the legal system does not permit rights to flow from that interest. Gracen had an understandable attachment to her work - something Judge Posner may have implicitly recognized in permitting her to continue to use her Dorothy image in her own portfolio. At the margins, we might find that the fair use doctrine, for example, gives some breathing space to sourcehood interests in reproductions - but not much. (Hughes, 1998)

F. CONCLUSION

Property rights are conventionally justified in terms of economic efficiency, but in the sphere of intellectual property such justifications, however convincing, do not have a strong empirical basis. (Greene, 2004) 'Personhood' interests can also be used to justify property rights or, in some cases,

rules bending or mitigating the effect of property rights. Behind the shield of property rights, personhood flourishes in our homes, automobiles, clothes, computers, and the things we collect - be it art, baseball cards, music, pottery, virtual swords, light sabres, or trophies. In the world of artistic and scientific creations, personhood interests take a different turn. It often seems that an individual's personality is already 'expressed' in an intellectual property res. Courts have recognized the 'personal expression,' 'creativity,' 'genius,' and 'intellectual labour' of intellectual property - all intimating that protection of the creator's personhood interests is at issue.

But beyond saying that someone's personality is expressed in an intellectual work, is there anything more we can say about the personhood interests? This chapter has argued that creativity or personal 'expression,' personal 'intention,' and 'sourcehood' are three candidate conditions for personhood interests, with varying degrees of protection possible for each. Along the way, creativity has been presented as a complex notion that serves as an equally good explanatory device for recent copyright cases which deconstructionist scholars have criticized as relying unduly on the 'romantic author' construct. I have proposed that the concept of intentionality may explain personality interests in research programs and photojournalism. This sort of personality interest may help explain occasions when we grant property protection as well as occasions when courts deny rights, but we feel a tug of regret that we cannot grant those rights.

In the end, the process of intellectual exploration - whether it is modern painting, Darwin's voyages, or gaming in virtual worlds - may be much the same. Whether we call it a profession or a preoccupation, when we return to the same activity again and again, what we learn in the exploratory process transforms us. In this spiral of activity we explore, digest, create, transform ourselves, and explore again.

REFERENCES

Aoki, K. (1993). Adrift in the Intertext: Authorship and Audience Recording Rights. *Chi.-Kent L. Rev., 68*(805).

Baker, J. H. (1990). *An Introduction to English Legal History* (3rd ed.). London: Butterworths.

Barlow, J. P. (2004). *Selling Wine Without Bottles: The Economy of Mind on the Global Net.* Retrieved from http://www.eff.org/Misc/Publications/John_Perry_Barlow/Html

Barr, W.P. (2005). The Gild That is Killing the Lily: How Confusion Over Regulatory Takings Doctrine is Undermining the Core Protections of the Takings Clause. *Geo. Wash. L. Rev., 73*(429).

Bartholomew, M. (2001). Protecting the Performers: Setting a New Standard for Character Copyrightability. *Santa Clara L. Rev., 41*(341).

Bentham, J. (1931). *The Theory of Legislation.* Amsterdam: Thoemmes Cortinuum.

Berman, L. (1995). An Artist Destroys His Work: Comments on Creativity and Destructiveness . In Panter, (Eds.), *Creativity and Madness: Psychological Studies in Art and Artists.* New York: AIMED.

Beverley-Smith, H. (2002). *The Commercial Appropriation of Personality.* Cambridge, UK: Cambridge University Press. doi:10.1017/CBO9780511495229

Birks, P. (1986). *The Roman Law Concept of Dominium and the Idea of Absolute Ownership. Acta Juridica 1. Black's Law Dictionary. (1990).* St. Paul, MN: West Publishing.

Blackstone, W. (n.d.). *Commentaries on the Laws of England* (Vol. 2).

Boone, M.S. (2008). Ubiquitous Computing, Virtual Worlds, and the Displacement of Property Rights. *I/S: J. L., & Pol'y for Info. Soc'y, 4*(91).

Boyle, J. (1988). The Search for an Author: Shakespeare and the Framers. *Am. U. L. Rev., 37*(625).

Boyle, J. (1996). *Shamans, Software, and Spleens: Law and the Construction of the Information Society.* Boston, MA: Harvard University Press.

Bukatman, S. (1993). *Terminal Identity: The Virtual Subject in Post-Modern Science Fiction.* Durham, NC: Duke University Press.

Burns, R.P. (1985). Blackstone's Theory of the Absolute Rights of Property. *Cin. L. Rev., 54*(67).

Campbell, J. (1972). *The Hero with a Thousand Faces.* Princeton, NJ: Princeton University Press.

Castaneda, H. (1975). *Thinking and Doing.* New York: Springer Publishing.

Castronova, E. (2002). *On Virtual Economies.* The Gruter Institute of Working Papers on Law, CESifo Working Paper No. 752.

Coase, R. H. (1960). The Problem of Social Cost. *The Journal of Law & Economics, 3*(1). doi:10.1086/466560

Cornish, W. (1999). *Intellectual Property -- Patents, Copyright, Trade Marks and Allied Rights* (4th ed.). London: Sweet & Maxwell.

Csikszentmihaly, M. (1994). *The Evolving Self.* New York: Perennial.

Cunningham, R., Stoebuck, W., & Whitman, D. (1993). *The Law of Property* (2nd ed.). New York: LexisNexis Publishing.

Daix, P. (1993). *Picasso Life and Art* (Emmett, O., Trans.). New York: Harper Collins.

Davies, M., & Naffine, N. (2001). *Are Persons Property? Legal Debates about Property and Personality.* Dartmouth, MA: Ashgate.

Demsetz, H. (1967). Toward a Theory of Property Rights. *The American Economic Review, 57*(347).

Denicola, R.C. (1981). Copyright in Collections of Facts: A Theory for the Protection of Nonfiction Literary Works. *Colum. L. Rev., 81*(516).

Dewey, J. (1980). *Art as Experience*. New York: Perigee Books.

Dibbell, J. (1998). *My Tiny Life*. New York: Henry Holt & Co.

Drabble, M. (Ed.). (1985). *The Oxford Companion to English Literature* (5th ed.). Oxford: Oxford University Press.

Drahos, P. (1996). A Philosophy of Intellectual Property. Ch 4 'Hegel: The Spirit of Intellectual Property' citing Hegel, Philosophy of Right s. 39, Dartmouth, MA: Aldershot.

Fairfield, J. (2005). *Virtual Property*, Indiana University School of Law – Bloomington, Legal Studies Research Paper Series, Research Paper Number 35.

Filiciak, M. (2003). *Hyperidentities – Post-modern Identity Patterns in Massively Multiplayer Online Role-Playing Games in Mark J.P. Wolf & Bernard Perron edited 'The Video Game Theory Reader*. London: Routledge.

Fisher, C. (2004). Interview. *Star Wars Trilogy* [Motion Picture]. Bonus Materials. United States: LucasFilm.

Fitch, C. (2004). *Cyberspace in the 21ˢᵗ Century: Mapping the Future of Massive Multiplayer Games*. Retrieved from http://www.gamasutra.com/features/20000120/fitch_04.htm

Garnett, K., James, J. R., & Davies, G. (1999). *Copinger and Skone James -- On Copyright* (14th ed.). London: Sweet & Maxwell.

Gauthier, D. (1986). *Morals by Agreement*. Oxford: Oxford University Press.

Glare, P. G. W. (Ed.). (1982). *Oxford Latin Dictionary*. Oxford: Oxford University Press.

Glassman, A. (1994). *Visions of Light*. Retrieved from http://www.imdb.com

Goldschmidt, E. P. (1969). *Medieval Texts and their First Appearance in Print*. Cheshire, CT: Biblo-Moser.

Goldstein, P. (1994). *Copyright's Highway: Gutenberg to the Celestial Jukebox*. New York: Hill and Wang.

Gombrich, E. H. (1984). *The Story of Art* (14th ed.). Boston, MA: Phaidon Press.

Gordon, W. (1990). Toward a Jurisprudence of Benefits: The Norms of Copyright and the Problem of Private Censorship. *U. Chi. L. Rev., 57*(1009).

Gordon, W. (1993). A Property Right in Self-expression: Equality and Individualism in the Natural Law of Intellectual Property. *Yale L.J., 102*(1533).

Graham, J. (2002). Preserving the Aftermarket in Copyrighted Works: Adapting the First Sale Doctrine to the Emerging Technological Landscape. *Stan. Tech. L. Rev.* (1).

Grant, D.L. (1995). Western Water Rights and the Public Trust Doctrine: Some Realism About the Takings Issue. *Ariz. St. L. J., 27*(423).

Greene, K. J. (2004). Abusive Trademark Litigation and The Incredible Shrinking Confusion Doctrine – Trademark Abuse in The Context of Entertainment Media and Cyberspace. *Harv. J. L. & Pub. Pol'y, 27*(609).

Halewood, P. (2008). On Commodification and Self-Ownership. *Yale J.L. & Human., 20*(131).

Hardin, G. (1968). The Tragedy of the Commons . In Ackerman, B. (Ed.), *Economic Foundations of Property Law*. New York: Aspen Publishing.

Harris, C.I. (1993). Whiteness as Property. *Harv. L. Rev., 106*(1709).

Hegel, G. W. F. (1952). *Philosophy of Right* (Knox, T. M., Trans.). Oxford: Oxford University Press.

Helfand, M. (1992). Note, When Mickey Mouse is as Strong as Superman: The Convergence of Intellectual Property Law to Protect Fictional Literary and Pictorial Characters. *Stan. L. Rev., 44*(623).

Helfgott, S. (1992). Claim Practice Around the World: A Comparison of How Inventions Are Claimed. *J. Proprietary Rts, 4*(9).

Hettinger, E.C. (1989). Justifying Intellectual Property. *Phil., & Pub. Aff., 18*(31).

Hohfeld, W. (1917). Fundamental Legal Conceptions as Applied in Judicial Reasoning. *Yale L.J., 26*(710).

Hughes, J. (1998). The Personality Interest of Artists and Inventors in Intellectual Property. *Cardozo Arts & Ent L. J., 16*(81).

Jaszi, P. (1991). Toward a Theory of Copyright: The Metamorphoses of Authorship. *Duke L.J., 41*(455).

Jaszi, P. (1992). On the Author Effect: Contemporary Copyright and Collective Creativity. *Cardozo Arts & Ent. L. J., 10*(293).

Joyce, J. (1939). *Finnegan's Wake*. New York: Viking Press, Inc.

Kant, I. (1930). *Lectures on Ethics* (Infield, L., Trans.). London: Methuen and Co.

Kennedy, D. (1979). The Structure of Blackstone's Commentaries. *Buff. L. Rev., 28*(205).

Kimbrell, A. (1995). *Life for Sale*. Utne Reader.

Lape, L. (1997, Fall). A Narrow View of Creative Cooperation: The Current State of Joint Work Doctrine. *Albany Law Review*.

Lastowka, G., & Hunter, D. (2004). The Laws of the Virtual World. *Calif. L. Rev., 92*(1).

Latour, B., & Woolgar, S. (1986). *Laboratory Life: The Construction of Scientific Facts*. Princeton, NJ: Princeton University Press.

Lehdonvirta, V. (2008). *Real Money Trade of Virtual Assets: New Strategies for Virtual World Operators,* Helsinki Institute for Information Technology (HIIT). Retrieved from http://www.hiit.fi/u/vlehdonvirta

Litman, J. (1990). The Public Domain. *Emory L.J., 39*(965).

Locke, J. (1689). *Two Treatise of Civil Government and A Letter Concerning Toleration* (Shapiro, I., Ed.). New Haven, CT: Yale University Press.

Locke, J. (1690). *Two Treatises of Government, Second Treatise* (Laslett, P., Ed.). 2nd ed.). Cambridge, UK: Cambridge University Press.

Lucas, G. (2004). Interview. *Star Wars Trilogy* [Motion Picture]. Bonus Materials. United States: LucasFilm.

Malkan, J. (1997). Stolen Photographs: Personality, Publicity, and Privacy. *Tex. L. Rev., 75*(779).

Merrill, T.W., & Smith, H.E. (2001). The Property/Contract Interface. *Colum. L. Rev., 101*(773).

Merrill, T.W., & Smith, H.E. (2001b). What Happened to Property in Law and Economics? *Yale L.J., 111*(357).

Morong, C. (1994 Winter). Mythology, Joseph Campbell, and the Socio-Economic Conflict. *The Journal of Socio-Economics.*

Morse, M. (1994). What do cyborgs eat? Oral Logic in an Information Society . In Bender, G., & Duckrey, T. (Eds.), *Culture on the Brink: Ideologies of Technology*. Seattle, WA: Bay Press.

Mortinger, S. A. (1990). Comment: Spleen for Sale, Moore v Regents of the University of California and the Right to Sell Parts of Your Body. *Ohio St. L. J., 51*(499).

Mossoff, A. (2003). What Is Property? Putting The Pieces Back Together. *Ariz. L. Rev., 45*(371).

Munzer, S. (1990). *A Theory of Property*. Cambridge, UK: Cambridge University Press.

Nozick, R. (1974). *Anarchy, State, and Utopia*. Chicago, IL: Basic Books.

Nozick, R. (1989). *The Examined Life*. New York: Simon & Schuster.

O'Donovan, K. (1997). With Sense, Consent, or Just a Con? Legal Subjects in the Discourses of Autonomy . In Naffine, N., & Owens, R. (Eds.), *Sexing the Subject of Law*. Sydney, Australia: Law Book Company.

Olivecrona, K. (1974). Appropriation in the State of Nature: Locke on the Origin of Property. *Journal of the History of Ideas, 35*(211).

Olson, D.P. (1983). Copyright Originality. *Mo. L. Rev., 48*(29).

Ondrejka, C. (2005). Escaping the Gilded Cage: User Created Content and Building the Metaverse. *N.Y.L. Sch. L. Rev., 49*(81).

Pareles, J. (1997, February 9). Searching for a Sound to Bridge the Decades. *N.Y. Times*, B34.

Penner, J.E. (1996). The Bundle of Rights Picture of Property. *UCLA L. Rev., 43*(711).

Poster, M. (1999). Theorizing Virtual Reality . In Ryan, M.-L. (Ed.), *Cyberspace Textuality: Computer Technology and Literary Theory*. Southbend, IN: Indiana University Press.

Radin, M. (1938). A Restatement of Hohfeld. *Harv. L. Rev., 51*(1141).

Radin, M.J. (1982). Property and Personhood. *Stan. L. Rev., 34*(957).

Radin, M. J. (1996). *Contested Commodities*. Chicago, IL: University of Chicago Press.

Rao, R. (2007). Genes and Spleens: Property, Contract or Privacy Rights in the Human Body? *The Journal of Law, Medicine & Ethics, 35*(371).

Rawls, J. (1971). *A Theory of Justice*. Boston, MA: Bellnap Press.

Raysman, R., & Brown, P. (2005, August). Computer Law (virtual property law). *New York Law Journal*.

Read, H. (1974). *A Concise History of Modern Painting*. London: Thames and Hudson.

Rehak, B. (2003). Playing at Being: Psychoanalysis and the Avatar . In Wolf, M. J. P., & Perron, B. (Eds.), *The Video Game Theory Reader*. London: Routledge.

Reich, C. (1964). The New Property. *Yale L.J., 73*(733).

Reynolds, R. (2003). *IPR, Ownership and Freedom in Virtual Worlds*. Retrieved from http://www.ren-reynolds.com/downloads/RReynolds-IPR-CRIC-2003.doc

Rose, C.M. (1998). Canon's of Property Talk, or Blackstone's Anxiety. *Yale L.J., 108*(601).

Rushkoff, D. (1994). *Cyberia: Life in the Trenches of Hyperspace*. New York hypertext Ed. Retrieved from http://www.rushkoff.com/cyberia/

Sam Francis Exhibition. (1996 January) Jeu de Paume Museum, Paris.

Scott, R. (1981). *The Body as Property*. London: A. Lane.

Scott, R. (2003). *Contract Law and Theory* (3rd ed.). New York: LexisNexis Publishing.

Stephens, M. (2002). Sales of In-Game Assets: An Illustration of the Continuing Failure of Intellectual Property Law to Protect Digital Content Creators. *Tex. L. Rev., 80*(1513).

Sterling, J. A. L. (1998). Creators' Rights and the Bridge Between Authors' Rights and Copyright. In INTERGU (Ed.), Shutz von Kulture und geistigen Eigentum in der Informationsgesellschaft. Amsterdam: Nomos Verlag.

Stokes, S. (2001). *Art and Copyright*. Oxford: Hart Publishing.

Suler, J. (2002). Identity Management in Cyberspace. *Journal of Applied Psychoanalytic Studies, 4*(455).

Taylor, C. (1989). *Sources of the Self: The Making of Modern Identity*. Cambridge, UK: Cambridge University Press.

The Pocket Oxford Dictionary. (1975). Oxford: Clarendon Press.

Underkuffler, L.S. (1990). On Property: An Essay. *Yale L.J., 100*(127).

Van Alstyne, W. (1977). Cracks in The New Property: Adjudicative Due Process and the Administrative State. *Cornell L. Rev., 62*(445).

VerSteeg, R. (1993). Rethinking Originality. *Wm., & Mary L. Rev., 34*(801).

VerSteeg, R. (1996). Defining 'Author' for Purposes of Copyright. *Am. U.L. Rev., 45*(1323).

Weisberg, R. (1993). *Creativity: Beyond the Myth of Genius*. New York: W.H. Freeman & Company.

Weiser, M., & Brown, J. S. (1996). *The Coming Age of Calm Technology*. XeroxPARC. Retrieved from http://www.ubiq.com/hypertext/weiser/acmfuture2endnote.htm

Wiley, Jr., J.S. (1991). Copyright at the School of Patent. *U. Chi. L. Rev., 58*(119).

Zemer, L. (2006). The Making of a New Copyright Lockean. *Harvard Journal of Law & Public Policy, 29*(3), 891.

Chapter 5
Virtual Property in Virtual Worlds

"If nature has made any one thing less susceptible than all others of exclusive property, it is the action of the thing power called an idea, which an individual may exclusively possess as long as he keeps it to himself; but the moment it is divulge, it forces itself into the possession of everyone, and the receiver cannot dispossess himself of it. Its peculiar character, too, is that no one possesses the less, because every other possesses the whole of it. He, who receives an idea from me, receives instruction himself without lessening mine; as he who lights his tape at mine, receives light without darkening me. That ideas should freely spread from one to another over the globe, for the moral and mutual instruction of man, and improvement of his condition, seems to have been peculiarly and benevolently designed by nature, when she made them, like fire, expansible over all space, without lessening their density at any point, and like the air in which we breathe, move and have our physical being, incapable of confinement or exclusive appropriation. Inventions then cannot, in nature, be a subject of property." — Thomas Jefferson, 1813

DOI: 10.4018/978-1-61520-795-4.ch005

INTRODUCTION

Digital technology is detaching information from the physical plane, where property law of all sorts has always found definition. Throughout the history of intellectual property law, the proprietary assertions of thinkers and inventors have been focused not on their ideas, but on the expression of those ideas. The ideas themselves, as well as facts about the phenomena of the world, were considered to be the collective property of humanity. One could claim franchise, in the case of copyright, on the precise turn of phrase used to convey a particular idea or the order in which facts were presented. Law protected expression. To express was to make physical. One did not get paid for the idea but for the ability to deliver it into reality. The value was in the conveyance and not the thought conveyed. In other words, the bottle was protected, not the wine. (Barlow, 2004)

In the realm of virtual reality, a similar situation is occurring. Many "objects" are being created in worlds that are owned and operated by large corporations who own the underlying code which enables "objects" to be created. In other words, the code is the bottle and the "objects" are the wine. A virtual object is given its meaning at the level of code, even if that meaning is only fully realized in the context of the environment. Divorcing anything from its necessary context (i.e., music without anything to play it) creates an illusion of non-existence. It is the context of virtual worlds that give virtual property its existence, and successful legal protection of virtual property depends on careful consideration of this context. The virtual world interface and the virtual property rely on each other, but their co-dependence does not make them less "real" unless one or the other ceases to exist at the code level. So long as there is careful delineation as to how far virtual property rights extend, many of the problems raised by virtual property's uniquely digital nature may be avoided. Hence, both the bottle and the wine may be protected.

A. THE ACQUISITION OF VIRTUAL PROPERTY

A quick review of how one acquires virtual property might be useful, because everything your avatar will need costs money. (Salem & Zimmerman, 2004; Bartle, 2004) Not only will you have to furnish your avatar's tables, chairs, grape arbour and a toilet, but all of the objects and chattels in your place are subject to wear and tear. If you want to keep attracting guests, you will have to refresh the buffet, unblock the toilet, and fix the broken pool table. All of these services have a price. Property in today's virtual worlds is not confined to virtual realty. Houses are merely one aspect along with weapons, suits of armour, pig iron, lumber, tables, chairs, plants, magic scrolls; or any other virtual item a virtual character of Britannia might want or need which can be bought at auction. A pair of sandals starts at $5; an exceptionally badass battle-axe goes for $150; and a well-located fortress would be priced at about $1,200. (Dibbell, 2003) A simple

calculation puts the total of these transactions at approximately $3 million per year. (Castronova, 2002)

Still you want to acquire a home to your avatar. There are a few ways to go about this. The first way involves spending about 40,000 gold coins and receiving a small house property deed, which is essentially a building permit. (Dibbell, 2003) Building a truly appealing home or tavern requires one to purchase walls, windows, and perhaps a pool table, all of which cost quite a lot of simoleons. One must spend time and effort to build up enough online wealth to afford the materials. To do this, one could try killing monsters with your weapons, a risky and uncertain prospect. Or one could become a skilled labourer, like a blacksmith. This means sitting in front of the computer clicking on iron ore deposits, carting them back to a forge, and knocking out breastplate after breastplate. If you do this for days on end, you will eventually accumulate enough of the local currency to afford to build your first hut. In addition to this 'click-slavery' of toiling over a virtual red-hot forge, you will need to pay real money - between ten and thirteen U.S. dollars - month after month for a subscription charge to the virtual world of your choice. (Dibbell, 2003) This is known as 'click slavery' because you are slaving over your mouse for hours and hours in a mind numbing fashion.

This method assumes that the best way of obtaining something is going to the place where it is made and then building it yourself. By analogy, consider the choice faced by a Briton in search of a Javanese totem or Incan blanket. She could travel to those places, study the art of making totems and blankets, and after years of toil produce her heart's desire with her own hands. Most people would regard this as insanity. (Lastowka & Hunter, 2004) Alternatively, one can buy a completed tavern, built by property speculators who, like their real-world counterparts who buy prime land early, throw up an anodyne house that appeal to a broad range of would-be owners, and sell it off. (Planet Modz Gaming Network)

Another way to acquire these assets is to log on to eBay and buy your self a rather nice house in Britannia, just like Joe Dugger, mentioned earlier. There is nothing unusual about his transaction. At any given time, many Britannian houses are listed for sale online for various prices. To make this trade requires that both players be able to connect both in the virtual world and in the real world. Within the virtual world, the seller's avatar hands over the item being traded to the buyer's avatar. Back in the real world, the buyer/player transfers real money to the seller/player. They may use cash, if they actually meet in real life. However, more often they will use one of the usual forms of payment systems the modern financial world has devised: a credit card, a money order, a check, or credits with a respected third party. (Stephens, 2002) James Grimmelmann (2005) also posed the question, "What distinguishes the world of exchanged promises to pay and complex intermediated financial instruments from a virtual world?"

As mentioned above, this is only a small percentage of the total wealth created annually by the residents of Britannia. For each item or character sold on eBay and other web sites, numerous other items and characters are traded within the game itself. Some bartered, but most bought with Britannian gold pieces, a currency that in 2002 was readily convertible into US legal tender at about 40,000 to the dollar, a rate that puts it on par with the Romanian lei. (Castronova, 2002) The goods exchanged number in the millions, nearly every one of them brought into existence by the sweat of some player's virtual brow. Magic weapons won in gruelling quests, custom-crafted furniture built with tediously acquired carpentry skills, characters made powerful through years of obsessive play - taken as a whole, they are the gross national product (GNP) of Britannia. (Id.)

Foreign exchanges in currency and direct investment operate constantly between the virtual worlds of Britannia, Rubi-Ka, Blazing Falls, and Norrath, on the one hand, and real-world bank accounts in the United States, Canada, Australia, and Korea, on the other. (Terdiman, 2004) The mechanics of it are simple. Possessing some valuable asset in the virtual world (say, a million simoleons or a level fifty avatar), I list it for sale in the section of eBay devoted to such auctions. The auction winner uses eBay payment mechanisms (Visa, Mastercard, PayPal) to transfer the agreed price in the real world. I then agree with the auction winner on a meeting place in the virtual world, and when we meet there I hand over the in-world property. (Stephens, 2002) This practice is so common that one can now establish reliable U.S. dollar prices for various virtual-world properties. The amount of trade is so vast that it is possible to analyze the economies of virtual worlds in the same way that real-world national economies are analyzed. (Castronova, 2002; Simpson, 1999; Barzel, 1997; Lehdonvirta, 2008)

Others look at the business potential of avatar shopping from another angle. Mindark, a private Swedish company, aspires one day to use avatar-based shopping to build a global network monopoly in internet interface. *Project Entropia* is a virtual world in which every object that an avatar may own will be available for sale direct from the company for the player to own also. (Damgaard, 2002) This move envisions making corporate peace with the auction markets by making them completely unnecessary. Their scheme is to create a virtual world of colossal scale, so that millions can use it at any time. The virtual world would be without charge, but people would be allowed to use their credit cards to make transactions within the virtual world. The world designers would then wait for the society and markets to develop, and invite Earth retailers to open three dimensional stores in the virtual space. This is still being developed. It took a leap forward with the sale of a space resort. At that point, your Lara Croft doppelganger avatar will be able to follow up her tough day of adventuring with a run into the nearby virtual Land's End -- to buy Lara's owner a new dress, for real money. Land's End offers customer's the ability to create a virtual model of themselves which can try on virtual clothes which can, in turn, be purchased in reality. (see, My Virtual Model at www.landsend.com and follow the links.)

The commercial potential of virtual worlds is striking, and well worth noting. The exchange rate between Norrath's currency and the United States dollar is determined in a highly liquid currency market, and its value in 2002 exceeded that of the Japanese Yen and the Italian Lira. The creation of dollar-valued items in Norrath occurs at a rate such that Norrath's GNP per capita in 2002 easily exceeded that of dozens of countries, including India and China. (Castronova, 2002) Mindark wants to tap into that kind of market. In the past, the discovery of new worlds has often been the event of the century for both the new world and the old. The new world typically has a precursor, an unlucky explorer who has become lost and has wandered aimlessly about in strange territory, but who has had the wit and good fortune to document what he has seen, his impressions of the people, and the exciting dangers he has faced, for an audience far away. (Id.)

As such, the industries that produce these shared virtual reality environments have continuously and rapidly evolved. Advances in connectivity (bandwidth) and interfaces (haptic devices, heads-up displays) have been driven by technology. The amount of available content (narratives, folklores, back stories) has unfolded as huge corporations have begun to transform deeply enmeshed cultural icons into virtual reality spaces. The video game industry has begun to surpass the motion picture industry in gross revenues. According to the Los Angeles Times, game industry revenues were $9.35 billion in 2001, of which $3 billion was for hardware. Total Hollywood box office revenues in 2001 were $8.4 billion. The video game industry had $8 billion dollars in sales in 2004 which translates into an $18 billion impact on the U.S. economy. Estimates call for video game sales to grow to $15 billion

by 2010. (Reuters May 10, 2006: *Study: Video Games Worth $18 Billion to U.S.*)

Sony preserves the world of *Star Wars* Jedi Knights. Sony, Microsoft, Electronic Arts, and others compete in the realm of Tolkienesque worlds of elves and hobbits. Electronic Arts maintains a vastly popular virtual world of *Sims* whose beings/characters would be unremarkable and frankly dull except for the fact that they exist only in a cyberspace reality. As the phenomenon continues to develop, the cumulative amount of time devoted to shared virtual reality spaces is likely to rise from today's tens of thousands of person-years into the hundreds of thousands or perhaps millions. (Sellers, 2006; Terdiman, 2006)

B. CRAFTING VS. CREATING

The craving to create and customize is a significant force. In Britannia, the popular fantasy world operated by *Ultima Online*, players who would like to embellish their homes must come up with convoluted yet sophisticated strategies for amalgamating in-world objects in order to produce images that look like real world items. For example, there are several different techniques for assembling pianos that involve dozens of different objects, ranging from wooden crates and chessboards to fish steaks and fancy shirts. (*Ultima Online* Renaissance Playguide, 2000) Other forms of user created content are Mods. Mods are a user modification of the source art, 3D characters, environments, or game engine of a commercially produced video game. David Kushner (2003) describes the process of game "modding", or directly modifying the fame's code to allow new forms of gameplay or other significant changes. For a general background on Modding, see Wikipedia, Mod (Computer Gaming), http://en.wikipedia.org/wiki/Mod_(computer_gaming). Note that wikipedia. org is a collaborative information website which can be edited by its visitors, and so its content may be updated frequently. In practice, much

Mod-related information is exclusively available on such websites and electronic forums. Modding is generally a decentralized endeavour that relies heavily on collaboration via the internet. Those working on the same project may often never meet in person, or even reside in the same country. The digital dissemination of Mod-related information and discussion reflects this trend.

Mods fall back on the fact that many first person shooter games, and some other adventure games, allow players to modify the content via some combination of artwork and game play. The more adaptable the engine or platform is, the more variety in the mods. So an original first person shooter game can be morphed into anything from a driving game to architectural walkthroughs. There are websites that provide an audience and reviews for these mods. This web-community operates as a training ground or boot camp for artists and developers who want to work on games. An example of this would be PlanetQuake Featured Mods at http://www.planetquake.com/features/motw.

John Diamond is a professional game designer who went by the call sign "Irritant". A common ritual in the gaming culture is to use a professional nickname reminiscent of fighter pilot's call-signs. Ten years ago, this moniker turned out to be prophetic. In 1997, Irritant and other programmers were working on an amateur project involving Mods called "Alien Quake". It was a planned Mod of the Id Software game "Quake" where the original game's environments and the monsters that had populated them would be entirely replaced by the characters, environments and sounds depicted in the Alien movie franchise. (Mogul Interview, 2004) In the vernacular of modders, this extensive level of alteration was referred to as a "Total Conversion". However, Twentieth Century Fox, owner of the rights to the Alien films, was not happy. It demanded complete destruction of all the work of Irritant and his team. The previous homepage of the "Alien Quake" project now displays (and has done so for nearly ten years) simply the following message:

"The Alien Quake project has been discontinued by 20ᵗʰ Century Fox. I received an email on April 11ᵗʰ, 1997, form a 20ᵗʰ Century Fox representative that ordered us to cease all activity. The Alien Quake project was using copyrighted material without permission and this make Alien Quake an unauthorized and illegal production. Therefore, you are herby ordered to remove all you Alien Quake files from your computer storage. You must also remove all references to Alien Quake from any www pages or internet sites you keep or maintain. All distribution of Alien Quake is illegal and you should know that the Alien Quake team is under an obligation to report the name and URL of any distributor to 20ᵗʰ Century Fox. Please let us know if you know the URL of a distributor or potential distributor. Thank you for your cooperation." (Former Alien Quake Homepage, http://student. nada.kth.se/~nv91-gta/quake/.)

The reaction spawned a term among later Modders for such heavy-handed legal tactics: Irritant was the first person to get "Foxed". (Smith, 2001; Binary Bonsai, 2004)

The distinction between the Quake mods and the Britannia piano is a particularly significant point. The Quake mods allowed the players to change the behaviour of the game; whereas, the Britannian piano cannot be played. It looks like a piano, but it is only a stack of crates, a chessboard, and fish sticks. This is an obvious yet very useful example of the difference between craft and creation. Ironically, in a medium where these user content contributions are more significant than in other previous mediums, the law has generally been reluctant to grant formal protection (such as ownership) to these contributions. This reluctance is in part due to the legal analysis that has focused principally on the computer code underlying the game, rather than on the player's experience of the game. This distinction is particularly interesting when compared to the existence of doctrines (involving artistic appropriation and fair use) that have developed in other media to balance the rights of the original creators of intellectual property with subsequent creators' rights to expressive re-imaginings of that original material. A comparable case can be found in *Mattel v MCA Records*, 296 F.3d 894 (9th Cir. 2002). The Danish band, Aqua, released a song entitled "Barbie Girl" with lyrics that included "I'm a blonde bimbo girl/dress me up/make it tight/I'm your dolly." Mattel sued MCA records for trademark infringement. The United States Court of Appeals for the Ninth Circuit held that "Barbie Girl" was not purely commercial speech and therefore fully protected under the First Amendment. (Meikle, 2002) It demonstrates what would need to change as to which bits would need protection is which context.

The malleable nature of these games and the connectivity of the internet have encouraged a phenomenon no other medium of mass entertainment has embraced so completely: a symbiosis of content creation. There are fan-created stories involving popular fictional characters, such as those archived at FanFiction.Net, http://www.fanfiction.net which has an extensive history as well. However, evidence of any re-incorporation of such fiction into new content produced by the character's original creators is extremely rare, in comparison to the commonplace incorporation of Modded content (or hiring of Mod programmers) by a game's original developers. (Kushner, 2003) While commercial entertainment software companies design and publishers release the initial game product, the players of the games are themselves responsible for creation of additional content, which then contributes to, expands, and sometimes eclipses the original game and its player experience. (Hyman) Many players were purchasing the game "Half-Life" simply to be able to play the user-created Mod "Counter Strike". Because technology requirements, Mods are generally only created for games played on PCs. Microsoft has recently announced the "XNA Creators Club", which allows individuals to create and release games for use on its Xbox 360 game console for others to download and play – but only by other

subscribers to the Club (at $100 per year). (Duffy & Carless, 2007) Some hold that crafting is not creating in the realm of MMORPGs. Crafting is merely the process of 'levelling' or advancing your character or avatar through repetitive generation of game objects. Levelling relies on a complicated system of skills and progressions that permits the player to acquire new abilities, travel to new portions of the world, and generally become more powerful. (Crafting Level 1 at http://starwarsgalaxies.station.sony.com/content) The objects generated through crafting are selected from the repository provided by the game developers. These object may be used by the crafting player, sold to other human players within the game or sold to non-player characters ('NPCs') added to the game by world developers solely to act as buyers. These automated buyers are essential because player levelling causes large quantities of items that are not useful or desired to be generated, so the NPCs are needed to drain the unwanted items from the system. (Ondrejka, 2005; Castronova, 2006)

In the real world, objects or goods are created out of component parts of lesser value. A piano, for example, may be built from timber, wire, and ivory (or plastic nowadays). Even though raw materials may have negligible value, the end product piano may be exceedingly valuable due to time and effort added in order to create not only a functional piano, but a beautiful and perfectly pitched piano. This vital type of added value is intrinsic in the real world but is conspicuously absent from virtual worlds. Again, the Britannia piano cannot be played.

For the reason that most crafting systems involve the gathering of 'raw materials,' and newer MMORPGs are adding more complicated schemes, the crafting being accomplished gives the appearance that value is being added in the same way as real-world creation. This may not be accurate. Game developers use crafting based on 'raw materials' to slow the rate of production, to limit the crafting of the best items, and to extend the life of content by obscuring which items are the best. (Id.) Production is slowed because players must take the time to acquire the correct combination of raw materials. Crafting of the best items is limited through artificial scarcity of raw materials. (Id.) The players must search through a larger design space which, in turn, takes more time to discover the items. This adds to the slower spread of items through the community.

Nevertheless, the players are still merely picking from the set of objects that the world developers constructed for the game. Competitive pressures merged with communication between players will force rapid convergence onto the best items. The value of some of these items will be increased due to scarcity, but this is fundamentally different from the value added in real world creation. Players cannot truly innovate because they are still just choosing from the items supplied by the developers. (Ondrejka, 2005)

Developers believe that they are creating new worlds in which communities can be formed and stories can be told. Players see this in a slightly different light. They use the game platform to create identities, have adventures, and tell their own stories. This altering process could be compared to starting with the pieces of a chessboard, incorporating a pair of dice, and creating a game like "Risk". (Baldrica, 2007) The technologies for producing animated motion pictures and building virtual worlds have been converging. The design of movies and virtual worlds are similar; however, virtual worlds require interactivity. Interactivity makes virtual worlds a better medium for the communication and exchange of ideas than motion pictures. Not only can the game designer exercise his imagination in the creation of new worlds, but so do the players. Motion pictures allow images to be viewed by a mass audience; but multiplayer online games convert that mass audience into active participants and storytellers. (Metz, 1982)

Virtual worlds permit contingent events, path dependencies, and cumulative effects. In short, they permit the development of histories. They allow the players to formulate new meanings, to engage in new adventures, to take on new personas, to form new communities, and to express themselves and interact with and communicate with others in ever new ways. (Balkin, 2004) "A virtual world is a computer-simulated environment intended for its users to inhabit and interact via avatars. This habitation usually is represented in the form of two or three-dimensional graphical representations of humanoids (or other graphical or text-based avatars). Some, but not all, virtual worlds allow for multiple users. The world being simulated typically appears similar to the real world, with real world rules such as gravity, topography, locomotion, real-time actions, and communication. Communication has been in the form of text in current examples of an online world. One perception of virtual worlds requires an online persistent world, active and available 24 hours a day and seven days a week, to qualify as a true virtual world. Although this is possible with smaller virtual worlds, especially those that are not actually online, no massively multiplayer game runs all day, every day. All online games include downtime for maintenance that is not included as time passing in the virtual world. While the interaction with other participants is done in real-time, time consistency is not always maintained in online virtual worlds. For example, *EverQuest* time passes faster than real-time despite using the same calendar and time units to present game time." (http://en.wikipedia.org/wiki/Virtual_world)

Many (not all) virtual worlds allow avatars to be modified over time. Many (not all) of those modification allow the avatar to achieve more, or to achieve it more easily, to wield greater power within the virtual world, or just to see cool things in the game. (Salem & Zimmerman, 2004; Bartle, 2004; Grimmelman, 2004) Sometimes, it is the virtual objects that come into the avatar's possession that provide the benefit. These objects could be virtual currency, virtual weapons, virtual gadgets, and so on. It matters not whether these increased possibilities are treated as attributes of the avatar or as a distinct virtual item. They are always desirable. They could be confirmation of success, the keys to unlocking Jedi mastery, or markers of social status. As such, for most all the reasons that people lust after possessions in the real world, they lust after possessions in virtual worlds. (Id.; Bartle, 1996; Yee, 1999-2004) A thriving trade follows. (Dibbell, 1995; Simpson, 1999) As history has demonstrated, where there is capital, there is law to protect it. In the case of *Morissette v United States*, 342 U.S. 246 (1952), the Supreme Court remarked that, "Stealing, larceny, and its variants and equivalents, were among the earliest offences known to the law that existed before legislation."

Thus players accumulate not just experiences but property. "Property [being] nothing but the basis of expectation," according to Bentham, "consist[ing] in an established expectation, in the persuasion of being able to draw such and such advantage from the thing possessed." (Munzer, 1990, citing Bentham) Curiously, although Bentham argued strongly for the constructed nature of property, he considered the absence of property -- poverty -- to be natural: "Poverty is not the work of the laws; it is the primitive condition of the human race. . . ." Munzer (1990) characterizes the idea of property-as-'thing' as the popular conception and property-as-relations as "the sophisticated version of property." He also notes that "property, conceived as a legal structure of Hohfeldian normative modalities, makes possible legal expectations with respect to things." (Id.) The relationship between expectations and property remains highly significant, as the law "has recognized and protected even the expectation of rights as actual legal property." (Powell, 1990) Munzer (1990) argues that property cannot be equated with expectations, but that expectations are part of the psychological dimension of property. This theory does not suggest that all expectations give rise to property, but those expectations in tangible or intangible things that

are valued and protected by the law are property. The bits of code which players collect in the perceived shape of goods are expectations that those goods are really owned by them. "A commodity is a commodity. If it is worth something, people are going to work hard to make the money. In China, there is a matter of fact attitude about it." (Robbie Cooper quoted by Twist, 2005) In fact, the difficulty lies not in identifying expectations as a part of property, but in distinguishing which expectations are reasonable and therefore merit the protection of the law as property. (Harris, 1993) Joseph Sax asserts: "The essence of property law is respect for reasonable expectations. The idea of justice at the root of private property protection calls for identification of those expectations which the legal system ought to recognize." (Sax, 1980) Virtual property may not be protectable from a loss of context. For example, would it be reasonable to enjoin a game company from terminating games simply because there are participants that own virtual property in them. This could be seen as being unconscionable for the courts to force game companies to continue operating a game so that participants could keep using their virtual property. It is conceivable that a game's virtual property will someday be of greater value than the ownership of the game itself.

For example, in *Project Entropia* there have been sales of $26,000 and $100,000 for virtual property. Consider a case where a game company is losing $1 million per year running a game, the game itself is worth $2 million, and the virtual property in the game is worth $100 million. Such a case provides a quandary insomuch as there is more value in continuing the game than in allowing it to cease operations. However, it would be unconscionable to force the game company, for whom the game is losing money, to continue funding its operation. Would it be better to allow the game company to tax the virtual property, thereby making up the yearly loss? How much tax would be justifiable or quantifiable? Should the courts force an auction of the game, thereby providing a market mechanism for game continuation to the virtual property owners? Should the government take over operation of the game? A scenario like this is unlikely to happen in the commercial game development context, where the game provider has the opportunity to increase subscription fees (similar to a tax) and sell virtual property itself to create additional revenue streams. There is, perhaps, no good solution in the context of freely available games. MindArk uses this approach with *Project Entropia*, which gives free accounts to anyone and charges in-game currency for items. In some other game companies, the game provider itself sells in-game currency and virtual property for real money. (*Entropia Universe*, http://www. entropiauniverse.com)

There is another difficulty when determining the line between change of context and loss of bits. If a game provider replaces one virtual sword with another, is it a prohibited deletion? If a game provider replaces a virtual sword with a virtual gun, is it a deletion? If a game provider replaces a virtual sword with virtual armour, is it a deletion? If a game provider replaces a virtual sword with gold, is it a deletion? Deleting an item completely from a character account should be prohibited. However, what about deleting one characteristic of a virtual sword, such as the ability to automatically slay a certain type of monster? Is that a deletion of virtual property or just changing context?

Bits should be protected from effectively complete devaluation. Game companies should not be allowed to continue to provide a game (continuation of the context) but prohibit the use of, or completely devalue, the existing virtual property. This will be an area of great debate. Suppose that a game company introduces a type of virtual armour in a game. Users determine a way to use the armour to make their in-game characters effectively invincible, thereby making the armour very valuable. This is a problem for the game company, which strives to keep a game 'balanced.' "Balancing" a game refers to ensuring that no particular type of virtual property is sig-

nificantly more powerful than other alternatives. However, there is value to the virtual property, and if the game company deletes the armour, then the users will lose this value, which would be similar to the situation in which the virtual property is lost or stolen. The game company should, however, be allowed to modify the context of the bits by changing the unbalanced aspects of the armour. However, this raises the question: what is the line between total devaluation and partial devaluation? Is it the case that when the context of the invincible armour is changed, so that it is only as good as other armour, its value is so much lower that it is effectively valueless? Perhaps. These are the borderline questions that should go to fact finders to make the decision.

Recently the *World of Warcraft* was hit by a mysterious rampant plague. It began as a new especially challenging dungeon was opened which featured a dungeon boss, called Hakkar the Soulflayer, who cast a spell called Corrupted Blood (a reference to *King Lear*). Such powerful spell attacks are not unusual in this game world. But what happened next was just plain weird. When infected adventurers returned to town at the end of their quest, they inadvertently passed along the Corrupted Blood infection to those nearby. "The most interesting thing about this 'outbreak' is perhaps the reaction of the *World of Warcraft* players. Instead of being angry about the deleterious effects of a bug, many are treating this as an exciting and unprecedented event in the *World of Warcraft* universe. It would be even more interesting if epidemiologists in the real world found that this event was worthy of studying as a kind of controlled experiment in disease propagation." Jeremy Reimer on Ars Technica (2005) was quoted as saying.

Although the existence of certain property rights may seem self-evident and the protection of certain expectations may seem essential for social stability, property is a legal construct by which selected private interests are protected and upheld. In creating property 'rights,' the law draws boundaries and enforces or reorders existing regimes of power. Singer (1992) argues that, in deciding what contract and what property rights to enforce, the state endorses the power of one party over the other or prevents one party from exercising power to the detriment of the other. Thus, the state makes allocative decisions in all transactions, public or private. The inequalities that are produced and reproduced are not givens or inevitabilities, but rather are conscious selections regarding the structuring of social relations. In this sense, it is contended that property rights and interests are not 'natural,' but are 'creation[s] of law.' Justice Holmes's dissent in *International News Service v Associated Press* stated that "[p]roperty, a creation of law, does not arise from value. . . ." 248 U.S. 215, 246 (1918).

C. THE ALLOCATION OF RIGHTS

Professor Joshua Fairfield (2005) in an article entitled *Virtual Property* has taken up the utilitarian justification of property rights in virtual world objects and expanded upon it with a law and economics justification. First, he posits that property rights are generally granted in newly emerging resources in order to provide incentive for their proper development and use. (Id. at 1065) Next, he reasons that due to the interdependent nature of virtual environments, improper allocation of property rights in virtual environments can lead to an undesirable anti-commons. (Id. at 1076) The overlapping property rights in an anti-commons prevents anyone from making beneficial use of the property thus reducing overall value. Therefore, property rights ought to be allocated in a manner that cuts across potential conflicts and allows the use of the object to which the property rights attach. Because virtual world objects define such a useable object, they are the proper unit in virtual environments to which property rights should be attached. (Id. at 1077)

From the virtual world creators' point of view, the company produces the game and provides ac-

cess to the servers on which it operates, "runs" the world and therefore owns everything. For example, in the Everquest User Agreement and Software License, Sony claims to own the entirety of a player's character: "We and our suppliers shall retain all rights, title and interest, including, without limitation, ownership of all intellectual property rights relating to or residing in the CD-ROM, the Software and the Game, all copies thereof, and all game character data in connection therewith. You acknowledge and agree that you have not and will not acquire or obtain any intellectual property or other rights, including any right of exploitation, of any kind in or to the CD-ROM, the Software or the Game, including, without limitation, in any character(s), item(s), coin(s) or other material or property, and that all such property, material and items are exclusively owned by us."

When a player makes a character in EverQuest or some other MMORPG and grows it into a powerful entity, the company typically claims to own the character and its possessions as its intellectual property to the same degree it claims to own the copyrighted computer code used to generate the image of the character on the player's screen. So, one of the conditions of use for the game is that Sony requires all players to agree that they do not own the character via a lengthy End-User License Agreement ("EULA") that pops up every time they start the game which a player must click through in order to enter Norrath. The Everquest license reads, in part: "You acknowledge and agree that you have not and will not acquire or obtain any intellectual property or other rights, including any right of exploitation, of any kind ... in any character(s), item(s), coin(s) or other material or property, and that all such property, material and items are exclusively owned by us." (Id.)

Although Sony encourages most economic activity when goods and services are exchanged for plat (in game currency), the EULA forbids the same sales for U.S. dollars. "You may not buy, sell or auction (or host or facilitate the ability to allow others to buy, sell or auction) any Game characters, items, coin or copyrighted material." (Id.) In fact, Sony asserts that efforts to sell the character, the character's equipment, the character's plat, or even to offer to power-level (or accept an offer to be power-levelled) for real-world profit gives it the right to terminate a player's access by giving the character itself the (in-game) death penalty for the commercial activities of the player in the real world. The EverQuest EULA states:

"We may terminate this Agreement (including your Software license and your Account) and/or suspend your Account immediately and without notice if you breach this Agreement or repeatedly infringe any third party intellectual property rights, or if we are unable to verify or authenticate any information you provide to us, or upon gameplay, chat or any player activity whatsoever which we, in our sole discretion, determine is inappropriate and/or in violation of the spirit of the Game as set forth in the Game player rules of conduct, which are posted at a hotlink at www.everquestlive.com. If we terminate this Agreement or suspend your Account under these circumstances, you will lose access to your Account for the duration of the suspension and/or the balance of any prepaid period without any refund." (Id.)

Furthermore, Sony claims that it has actively sought out and banned players who farm plat for the purpose of selling it for U.S. dollars. (Posting of Smed (John Smedley President, Sony Online Entertainment) to Everquest II Official Forums) From Sony's perspective, such a ban is likely deemed necessary to prevent a breakdown of the virtual world itself. This is not entirely accurate. The use of U.S. dollars to purchase virtual-world goods does not cause the virtual world economy to break down. It merely changes the game's atmosphere. Real-world wealth can replace in-game effort. This can taint the successes of those who "work" for their items within the game's environment. Thus, according to Sony, such a ban on a secondary market is necessary because it preserves

the quality of the primary market. Under the rule of reason, an otherwise anticompetitive restraint may be deemed pro-competitive if the product would cease to exist without such a ban. The U.S. Supreme Court held in *Nat'l Collegiate Athletic Ass'n v. Board of Regents*, 468 U.S. 85 (1984) that such a claim is a fairly standard defence in many antitrust cases, such as in a horizontal joint venture.

Virtual property rights in all of the virtual worlds are demarcated by EULAs. An in depth look at these contracts will be provided in Chapter 7. However, a brief look at the divergent types of virtual worlds is needed here. They can be labelled as property-opposed worlds, the virtual world creators who openly reject virtual property rights, in contrast to property-endorsing worlds, whose creators have granted property rights. Since virtual worlds first began, a huge market for virtual products has emerged. However, most virtual world EULAs prohibit the trade of virtual products outside the virtual environment. They further deny any property claims players may assert against them, even within the virtual environment. Unfortunately, any legal dispute between users and operators over virtual property in such worlds would likely be decided by these agreements.

1. Property-Opposed Worlds

The EULAs of property-opposed worlds deny all virtual property rights which may allow for a claim against a virtual world creator. World of Warcraft (WoW), the most popular virtual world in the United States, is a good example. Blizzard Entertainment, which owns and operates World of Warcraft, includes the following in its EULA §8:

"You may not purchase, sell, gift or trade any Account, or offer to purchase, sell, gift or trade any Account, and any such attempt shall be null and void. Blizzard owns, has licensed, or otherwise has rights to all of the content that appears in the Program. You agree that you have no right or title

in or to any such content, including the virtual goods or currency appearing or originating in the Game, or any other attributes associated with the Account or stored on the Service. Blizzard does not recognize any virtual property transfers executed outside of the Game or the purported sale, gift or trade in the "real world" of anything related to the Game. Accordingly, you may not sell items for "real" money or otherwise exchange items for value outside of the Game."

The contract is clearly adamant that the players do not have any right to the accounts for which they pay, let alone to any virtual property within those accounts. As such, players have no right to buy, sell, gift, or trade any such goods. This provision is regularly breached. Elsewhere in the EULA, Blizzard asserts that it owns all objects in the game, and that it may terminate user accounts at any time, for any reason. (§7 WoW EULA)

Another highly popular world is owned by NCsoft, the operator of Lineage. The Lineage User Agreement § 4(d) also strictly limits user rights which includes the following: "[Y]ou agree that you do not own the account you use to access the service, the characters NC Interactive stores on NC Interactive servers, [or] the items stored on these servers ...." Lineage, in contrast to WoW, allows players to upload their own content into the virtual world. Nonetheless, the EULA limits a player's rights even as to her own content. She must agree to grant the operator a perpetual right to do essentially anything the operator wants with the player-created content. (Id. § 6(c))

These EULAs are representative of property-opposed virtual worlds. Their terms deny users any claims to virtual property. A pragmatic argument in favour of virtual property rights would be to point out that players are trading over $200 million in virtual property, they must be relying on property rights. A related policy argument would be that courts should protect virtual property rights because failing to do so would destroy an otherwise viable market. (Westbrook, 2006)

From an outside point of view, players seem to have exclusive possession of their virtual products along with an ability to transfer those products to others. According to this argument then, to deny the existence of property rights under such circumstances would be ignorant or naïve.

The virtual world operates disagree. First, trade among players may suggest the existence of rights; but there is no clear underpinning structure to these rights between players and operators. Second, the very conditions that give rise to putative property rights are controlled by the virtual world operators, themselves. Despite appearances, the virtual world operators know that they possess the virtual products insofar as they possess the entire world. They can prohibit transfer by changing the code. They can destroy any value virtual products might have by providing identical goods to every player. They can even destroy all products by shutting off the world completely. On the other hand, doing any of these things may destroy their business.

2. Property-Endorsing Worlds

As stated earlier in this work, Linden Lab's Second Life purports to be different. Second Life announced that it would protect the virtual and intellectual property rights of its residents. Linden Lab's CEO, Philip Rosedale, has said, "We like to think of Second Life as ostensibly as real as a developing nation .... If people cannot own property, the wheels of western capitalism can't turn from the bottom." (Baage, 2006) To the users of his world, Rosedale says, "You create it, you own it--and it's yours to do with as you please." (Id.) Linden Lab even sells virtual land directly to users, who can have their own island for $1,675 plus $295 per month. (Second Life--Land: Islands) Linden Lab appears strongly committed to protecting the virtual property rights of Second Life residents.

The simplest way for residents to create objects is by clicking an option that opens a small winder where the resident can find a set of building tools. The resident then selects from primary building blocks choices called graphic primitives, or "prims". The resident controls and manipulates the dimensions of the prims, attaches other prims to it, then colours the result object. A separate function allows the application of a variety of textures to various parts of the object as desired. Each object that is created can then be fashioned together similar to Legos in order to create more complex objects. A function also allows the user to create an exact replica of this object. This replicating facility allows for easier building of complex objects. For example, it allows the residents to create lots of bricks in order to build a structure. There a basic templates for the less experienced residents as well. The physics of these prims are also geared to the physics of the virtual world, so that residents can have a reliance on ordinary physical characteristics. For example, permeability and density are embedded into objects so that a wall to a building cannot ordinarily be penetrated.

There is also a simple script that allows users to write code which allows their objects to move. So, once a resident has created a car, she can then use this script to allow for motion and steering commands. The resident can also create a balloon to follow them or candles that will burn down and out. There is an area called Svarga where whole ecologies grow up seedlings, to tree, flower, and then die along with the bees that then re-pollinate and start the process of rebirth. When a resident wants to create or continue working on a creation, they can access the platform provided tools through an edit option which re-opens the building tools window. If the resident does not want to leave their creation unattended (and many areas of Second Life do not allow unattended objects to be left), then the resident stores her creation in an inventory folder. If she would like others to be able to interact with her creation, then she must rent or purchase land. On this land, the resident may create her own landscapes and set rules, permitting or banning activities such as building or commerce by non-authorized residents. (Marcus, 2008)

A careful reading of the Terms of Service suggests, however, that Linden Lab's protection of residents' property is not as vigorous as it first seems. The Terms of Service state: "[Linden Lab retains] the perpetual and irrevocable right to delete any or all of your Content from Linden Lab's servers and from the Service, whether intentionally or unintentionally, and for any reason or no reason, without any liability of any kind to you or any other party ...." Linden Lab retains the right to destroy content in a virtual world where everything is content. To the extent that this license term is valid, residents have no claim against Linden Lab even for the loss of all of their property. While Linden Lab is happy to sell you an island for almost $2,000, the Terms of Service emphasize: "Linden Lab does not provide or guarantee, and expressly disclaims ... any value, cash or otherwise, attributed to any data residing on Linden Lab's servers." In other words, the virtual world operator has no obligation to protect the value of players' property, and it reserves the right to do anything it wants with that property. This includes the right to copy, use, reproduce, or analyze user content for almost any reason. (Terms of Service)

The seeming disparity between Rosedale's statement and the Terms of Service may be reconcilable. Rosedale and Linden Lab are committed to virtual property rights insofar as they are committed to protecting and fostering a resident's stock of in-world goods, and to protecting a resident's in-world property rights against the infringement of other users. In short, Linden Lab is committed to protecting property in resident-resident conflicts but not in operator-resident conflicts. Linden Lab may be expressing, in part, a commitment to respect residents' intellectual property rights as well as resident-resident virtual property rights. This commitment would not preclude them from deleting resident-copyrighted designs, for example, and would be consistent with its EULA. The case of *Bragg* discussed below demonstrates Linden Lab's commitment to protecting residents' rights.

The case shields residents from those who wish to obtain property through questionable or fraudulent means. Moreover, Linden Lab's failure to protect all possible residents' property claims may just be a necessary precaution. They may not be able to remain in business if faced with the risk of a server failure deleting vast amounts of resident property, and opening them up to millions of dollars in liability.

D. WHICH RIGHTS WITHIN THE 'BUNDLE' SHOULD BE ALLOCATED TO VIRTUAL PROPERTY?

Returning to Wesley Hohfeld's (1917) bundle of rights theory, his analysis of property states that "what the owner of property has is a very complex aggregate of rights, privileges, powers and immunities," not in a thing (in rem) but rather against other people (in personam). Accepting that what one creates in the virtual world is owned by that creator, what would that actually entail? The Terms of Service serves as the framework for the virtual world. It will set out the rights of the player and create the tools to protect them.

1. The Right to Exclude

The right to exclude protects property owners from various kinds of trespass, and has been held by the U.S. Supreme Court in *Kaiser Aetna v. United States,* 444 U.S. 164 (1979) to be "one of the most essential sticks in the bundle of rights that are commonly characterized as property." This right becomes interesting in a virtual environment due to the availability of code-based exclusionary measures. With regard to personal property creations in Second Life, once a resident has created her object, she controls the permissions that allow or not other residents from certain types of activities including subsequent transfers, modifications, and identical copying. The permissions are enabled by clicking boxes on the editing menu. If a resident allows others to modify her object, the any resident has access to the object and can edit and modify it using the same tools in the same manner as the original creator. Upon transfer of an object, the new resident-owner may set any of the enabled permissions for subsequent transfers.

With regard to virtual real property, another way to express the right to exclude is the right to visit. The most basic rule for virtual real estate is to allow all residents access to all areas. However, this would render ownership meaningless. So, the virtual world operators must allow owners the ability to choose who is allowed to enter their property. Unfortunately, trespass remains a problem. In Second Life, a French political party's virtual headquarters was the target of a protest that developed into a riot and minor war. The disruption was so severe that portions of the party's virtual headquarters were destroyed, and it had to relocate its in-game headquarters. (New World Notes, 2006) Despite the damage to the building and the forced relocation, the party had no recourse for the trespass or the destruction of its virtual property. This sort of situation will become more commonplace in virtual worlds as more real world entities establish a virtual presence. Resolving this problem in a virtual environment requires very little legal intervention with a right to visit permission.

The right to visit is usually perpetual, non-transferable, and subject to revocation by the owner. An example of the types of permissions would be the distinctions between the following: Visitor, Guest, Resident, Tenant, Acquaintance, Associate, Friend, Ally, Partner, and, of course, Owner. Each of these can be further customized with respect to the number of permissions, and to special object with their own special rules. This would include being able to automatically exclude specific avatars. This takes the form of an eject button (the equivalent of throwing a specific person out of a club), or a ban function (the equivalent of an unbreakable "No Trespassing" sign that would apply only to select avatars or to everyone but select avatars).

2. The Right to Possess

Possession is a more complicated right to resolve in the context of virtual environments. Due to the unique digital nature of virtual property, it is capable of being possessed in two distinct ways: (1) in the real world, and (2) within the virtual environment. More importantly, it is capable of being possessed in both ways simultaneously, since even as users possess the virtual property within the environment, the developer's possession of the actual data remains uninterrupted. Keith Hunt (2007) proposed a "co-possession" approach that would allow both the developer and the player to simultaneously possess the virtual property depending on whether the player was actively logged in. Co-possession can be thought of as a type of joint tenancy, except that parties would be granted asymmetric interests based on a bailment standard. Bailment is "the rightful possession of goods by one who is not the owner." (Black's Law Dictionary, 1990) As a result of this possession, the bailee (possessor) owes the bailor (owner) a duty of care. Applied to virtual worlds, the developer would be considered a bailee that possesses the virtual property for the entirety of its existence. Players, in contrast, should only be considered to possess virtual property whenever logged in, since that is the only time they are able to transfer, delete or otherwise modify the virtual property. (Balkin, 2004)

Co-possession becomes most important while the player is logged into the virtual world. During this time, both parties can manipulate the virtual property (i.e., delete it, alter it or transfer it). Thus, both should be considered to possess it. During co-possession, the player would be solely liable for anything that happened to the data within the virtual world (i.e., for "handing" it to another character). Developers would be liable for anything

that happened to the data outside the context of the virtual world (i.e., a hacker moving virtual property from one player's data file to another's). This would, in turn, limit the developers' liability to risks it can be expected to control. (Hunt, 2007)

3. The Right to Transfer

The free alienation of virtual objects occurs even in property-opposed virtual worlds so long as the transfers are based on the local currency, and within the context of the game. Some companies have attempted to ban out-world transfers with limited success. So although the world is Tolkienesque, the Middle Earth trappings are mostly superficial from a cultural perspective. The transfer of virtual chattels remains as familiar as the transfer of real chattels. If your avatar wants to sell her invulnerable chain mail armour, she is free to do so. If she wants to seek multiple in-game buyers, there are well-known markets within each world where she might peddle her goods. These change regularly. Finally, if your avatar dies, others can strip the armour from her lifeless body and make it their own. However, rules vary from world to world.

In Second Life the right to transfer virtual goods is highly encouraged. Adding to the total collaborative experience is the point of Second Life. Residents post and provide scripts which are either given away or sold within and outside the platform through a library-themed forum, in-world instructions that residents post at various locations, and simple in-world inter-avatar interaction. In practice, any and all property from Second Life can and is transferred (sold) on sites such as eBay. In direct contrast to property-opposed worlds, Second Life believes that this is good for their business, and they have developed a friendly relationship with eBay. This is of comfort to the businesses who wish to conduct their business within Second Life.

E. CURRENT LEGAL DEVELOPMENTS IN VIRTUAL PROPERTY RIGHTS

It is one thing for property to be recognized within a virtual world; quite another for this fact to have any significance in the real world. Yet, property interests in the virtual worlds bleed over into the real world, and assets accumulated in a virtual world sometimes have value in the real world. (Lastowka & Hunter, 2004; Castronova, 2001) A gamer, David Storey of Australia, spent £13,700 on an island in *Project Entropia* and has recouped his investment according to the game developers. The character, Deathifier, made his money back in under a year by selling land to build virtual homes as well as taxing other gamers to hunt or mine on his island. (BBC News, 2005/11/09; Market Wire, Nov. 8, 2005) Already, cases have been filed over the ownership of various virtual assets. For example, a California company called BlackSnow Interactive set up a "point-and-click sweatshop" in Tijuana, Mexico. (The Unknown Player, 2003) Their business plan was based upon the disparity between the value of labour in first and developing worlds as well as between real world and virtual world. The possibility of arbitrage existed and created an incentive for this type of indirect employment. If the effective hourly wage is greater in Norrath than in the real world, then it is possible to extract this differential. (Press Release, 2002) So, they hired locals to sit and play *Dark Age of Camelot*. The 'employees' would generate a lot of in-game wealth and assets. This is called "gold farming." (Barboza, 2005) BlackSnow would in turn sell these items at on-line auctions.

They were caught by the webmasters and their accounts terminated. Mythic Entertainment, the owner of *Dark Age of Camelot*, attempted to prevent the commoditization of their world by forcing eBay to remove all in-world virtual items from their auction listings based upon a theory of intellectual property infringement. (The Unknown Player, 2003) BlackSnow brought suit against FunCom.

(*Blacksnow Interactive v Mythic Entertainment, Inc.* (U.S. Dist. C.D. Cal.)) Blacksnow's lawyer threw down the gauntlet: "What it comes down to is, does a ... player have rights to his time, or does Mythic own that player's time? It is unfair of Mythic to stop those who wish to sell their items, currency or even their own accounts, which were created with their own time." (Dibbell, 2003) Though the plaintiff dropped the case when its other legal problems forced a hasty retreat, the issues it raised remain. Virtual 'property' has real-world value.

However, the threat to the dealers from the games companies remains. For example, Sony declared a ban on the *EverQuest* auction market and got eBay to enforce it. (Smith, 2001) They then created StationExchange, a site which allows players to auction in-game items to each other for real-life money. Sony takes a service charge of $1 per item listed for auction. (see Sony's description of the process at http://www.stationexchange.station.sony.com) The resulting uproar and push for a class action lawsuit centred on the claim that, although Sony owns the virtual item, the players own their time and labour that procured the items. As such, the virtual items should be freely alienable by the players. Apparently, the class action suit never developed and an opportunity to litigate this issue was lost. (Smith, 2001) But even apparently market-friendly efforts can play havoc with the traders' livelihoods. Recently Electronic Arts announced that *Ultima* players could now, for a mere $29.95, order their own custom-built, high-level characters straight from the company. This is frowned on by some such as James Hebert (2005) who reported GuS Tovar, 14. a San Diegan who plays the online game Guild Wars saying "I frown upon it due to the fact that the game should be just as difficult for everyone. People who can afford to buy (millions in) gold can just dominate."

Bragg v. Linden Research, Inc., Pa. Magis. Dist. Ct., Chester Cty., No. CV-7606, complaint filed 5/2/06, highlights some of these issues, and was thought that it could become the first case in a United States court to test virtual property rights. Marc Bragg, the plaintiff, accumulated Second Life property worth thousands of dollars, some of which he purchased through a loophole in an auction system, and some of which he accumulated through legitimate means. However, when Linden Lab learned of Bragg's questionable dealings, it seized all of Bragg's in-game assets, including land, items, and roughly $2,000 in real-world money on account. Because of his exploitation of the auction system, Bragg is not a particularly sympathetic plaintiff, and the case was likely to turn on whether Bragg violated the Terms of Service rather than on the general question of whether users can assert virtual property claims against operators. Still, Linden Lab's willingness and potential ability to seize and sell off a user's assets cast doubt on whether it supports strong user rights.

Bragg and the Second Life Terms of Service demonstrate that Linden Lab's commitment to virtual property rights is not absolute. Linden Lab's CEO tells users that their virtual goods are theirs to do with as they please. At the same time, Linden Lab reserves the right to delete any content at any time, for any reason, or take and sell the virtual property of those users Linden Lab believes to be in violation of the Terms of Service. If users want to retain robust virtual property rights, Second Life is not a perfect world.

In Asia, the first litigation involving virtual property was successfully completed. (Xinhua Online, Dec. 19, 2003) In 2003, a young man who played in the virtual world of *Hongyue* (*Red Moon*) became basically invincible via hard work stockpiling a vast collection of biological weapons and purchasing thousands of hours of game play. One day, while he was not logged in, a hacker broke into his account and stole everything. He went to the game designers and requested the identity of the hacker, but they refused to give it to him. He then went to the police to no avail. So, he filed suit in a Chinese court where he won. The court ruled

that he was to have his virtual object returned to him. (China Daily, Nov. 20, 2003)

Implicit in this last case is that the player has a property right in virtual objects that could be recognized in a real-world court. This is one of the most interesting features of the property systems of the virtual worlds. They closely mirror the real world, or at least the subset known as the Western capitalist economy. Private property is the default. Entrepreneurs and tycoons feel right at home. The timeworn metaphor of property as a bundle of rights, chiefly the rights to use, exclude, and transfer, applies to virtual chattels as well. (Lasktowka & Hunter, 2004 citing Honore, 1961)

REFERENCES

Baage, J. (2006, December 21). Five Questions with Philip Rosedale, Founder and CEO of Linden Lab, Creator of Second Life. *DIGITAL MEDIA WIRE*. Retrieved from http://www.dmwmedia.com/news/2006/12/21/five-questions-with-philip-rosedale-founder-and-ceo-of-linden-lab-creator-of-second-life

Baldrica, J. (2007). Mod as Heck: Frameworks for Examining Ownership Rights in User Contributed Content to Videogames, and a More Principled Evaluation of Expressive Appropriation in User Modified Videogame Projects. *Minn. J. L. Sci. & Tech., 8*(681).

Balkin, J. (2004). Virtual Liberty: Freedom to Design and Freedom to Play in Virtual Worlds. *Va. L. Rev. 90*(2043).

Barboza, D. (2005, December 9). Ogre to Slay? Outsource It To The Chinese. *N.Y. Times*, A1. Retrieved from http://www.iht.com/articles/2005/12/08/business/gaming.php

Barlow, J. P. (2004). *Selling Wine without Bottles: the Economy of Mind on the Global Net*. Retrieved from http://www.eff.org/Misc/Publications/John_Perry_Barlow/HTML/idea_economy

Bartle, R. (1996). Hearts, Clubs, Diamonds, Spade: Players who suit MUDs. *Journal of MUD Research, 1*(1). Retrieved from http://www.mud.co.uk/richard/hcds.htm.

Bartle, R. (2004). *Designing Virtual Worlds*. Berkeley, CA: New Riders Publishing.

Barzel, Y. (1997). *Economic Analysis of Property Rights* (2nd ed.). Cambridge, UK: Cambridge University Press. doi:10.1017/CBO9780511609398

BinaryBonsai.com. (2004). *Being Foxed*. Retrieved from http://binarybonsai.com/archives/2004/07/20/cease-and-desist/

(1990). *Black's Law Dictionary* (6th ed.). St. Paul, MN: West Publishing.

Castronova, E. (2001 December). *Virtual Worlds: A First-Hand Account of Market and Society on the Cyberian Frontier*. CESifo Working Paper Series No. 618.

Castronova, E. (2002). *On Virtual Economies*. The Gruter Institute of Working Papers on Law, CESifo Working Paper No. 752.

Castronova, E. (2006 April). Geekonomics. *Wired Magazine*.

Daily, C. (2003, November 20). *Lawsuit Fires Up in Cases of Vanishing Virtual Weapons*. Retrieved from http://www.chinadaily.com.cn/en/doc/2003-11/20/content_283094.htm

Damgaard, I. (2002). *Legal Implications of the Project Entropia: Conducting Business in Virtual Worlds*. Juridiska Institutionen Handelshögskolan vid Göteborgs Universtiet. Retrieved from http://www.handels.gu.se/epc/archive/00003250/

Dibbell, J. (2003 January). The Unreal Estate Boom: 79th Richest Nation on Earth Doesn't Exist. *Wired Magazine*.

Dibbell, J. (2003) Serfing the Web: Blacksnow Interactive and the World's First Virtual Sweat Shop. *Wired Magazine*. Retrieved from http://www.juliandibbell.com/texts/blacksnow.html

Duffy, J., & Carless, S. (March 2007). For the People, By the People, Game Developer. *Entropia Universe*. Retrieved from http://www.entropiauniverse.com

Everquest User Agreement and Software License. (n.d.). Retrieved from http://eqlive.station.sony.com/support/customer_service/cs_EULA.jsp

Fairfield, J. (2005). *Virtual Property*. Indiana University School of Law – Bloomington, Legal Studies Research Paper Series, Research Paper Number 35.

Grimmelmann, J. (2004). Virtual Worlds As Comparative Law. *N.Y. L. Sch. L. Rev. 49*(147).

Grimmelmann, J. (2005). *Virtual Borders: The Interdependence of Real and Virtual Worlds*. Yale Law School Information Society Project.

Harris, C.I. (1993). Whiteness as Property. *Harv. L. Rev. 106*(1709).

Hebert, J. (Oct. 9, 2005). Online Gamer? Buy Your Way to the Top. *San Diego Union-Tribune*, F-3.

Hohfeld, W.N. (1917). Fundamental Legal Conceptions as Applied in Judicial Reasoning. *Yale L.J. 26*(710).

Honore, A. M. (1961). Ownership . In Guest, A. G. (Ed.), *Oxford Essays in Jurisprudence* (1st ed.). Oxford: Oxford University Press.

Hunt, K. (2007). This Land is not Your Land: Second Life, Copybot, and the Looming Question of Virtual Property Rights. *Tex. Rev. Ent. & Sports L. 9*(141).

Jefferson, T. (1813). A Letter to Isaac McPherson. *The Founders' Constitution, 3*(1), Section 8, Clause 8, Document 12. Retrieved from http://press-pubs.uchicago.edu/founders/documents/a1_8_8s12.html

Kushner, D. (2003). It's a Mod, Mod World: For Computer Game Developers, Encouraging Users to Modify Copyrighted Material is Good for Business. *Spectrum Online*. Retrieved from http://www.spectrum.ieee.org/careers/careerstemplate.jsp?_ArticleId=i020203

Lastowka, F.G. & Hunter, D. (2004). The Laws of the Virtual World. *Calif. L. Rev., 92*(1).

Lehdonvirta, V. (2008) *Real Money Trade of Virtual Assets: New Strategies for Virtual World Operators*. Helsinki Institute for Information Technology (HIIT). Retrieved from http://www.hiit.fi/u/vlehdonvirta

Lineage User Agreement. (n.d.). Retrieved from http://www.lineage.com/support/terms.html

Marcus, T. D. (2008). Fostering Creativity in Virtual Worlds: Easing the Restrictiveness of Copyright for User-Created Content. *J. Copyright Soc'y U.S.A, 55*(469).

Market Wire. (2005, November 8). *Press Release, Virtual Island Purchase of $26,500 Recoups Investment in First Year With Room for Ongoing Profit*. Retrieved from http://www.marketwire.com/mw/release_html_bl?release_id=100596

Meikle, E. (2002, October 21). Barbie Goes to Court. *Brand Channel.com*. Retrieved from http://www.brandchannel.com/features_effects.asp?pf_id=127

Metz, C. (1982). *The Imaginary Signifier: Psychoanalysis and the Cinema. (Celia Britton trans.)*. Bloomington, IN: Indiana University Press.

Mogul. (2004). Interview with John Diamond, Founder of COR Entertainment. *Planetquake.gamespy.com*. Retrieved from http://planetquake.gamespy.com/View.php?view=Articles.Detail&id=346

Munzer, S. (1990). *A Theory of Property*. Cambridge, UK: Cambridge University Press.

New World Notes. (2006, November 15). Retrieved from http://nwn.blogs.com/nwn/2006/11/second_life_clo.html

News, B. B. C. (2005, November 9). *Virtual Property Market Booming*. Retrieved from http://news.bbc.co.uk/go/pr/fr/-/1/hi/technology/4421496.stm

Ondrejka, C. (2005). *Changing Realities: User Creation, Communication, and Innovation in Digital Worlds*. Retrieved from http://www.themisgroup.com/uploads/Changing% 20Realities.pdf

Online, X. (2003, December 19). *Online Game Player Wins 1st Virtual Properties Dispute*. Retrieved from http://news.xinhuanet.com/english/2003-12/19/content_1240226.htm

Planet Modz Gaming Network. (n.d.). Retrieved from http://www.planetmodz.com/index.php

Powell, J.A. (1990). New Property Disaggregated: A Model to Address Employment Discrimination. *U. S.F. L. Rev. 24*(363).

Press Release: Blacksnow Interactive Sues Mythic in Federal Court for MMORG Player's Rights. (n.d.). Retrieved from http://www.kanga.nu/archives/MUD-Dev-L/2002Q1/msg00363.php

Salem, K., & Zimmerman, E. (2004). *Rules of Play: Game Design Fundamentals*. Cambridge, MA: MIT Press.

Sax, J. L. (1980). Liberating the Public Trust Doctrine from Its Historical Shackles. *U.C. Davis L. Rev., 14*(185).

Second Life--Land. *Islands*. (n.d.). Retrieved from http://secondlife.com/community/land-islands.php

Second Life--Terms of Service. (n.d.). Retrieved from http://secondlife.com/corporate/tos.php

Sellers, M. (2006, January 9). *The Numbers Game*. Retrieved from http://terranova.blogs.com/terra_nova/2006/01/index.html

Simpson, Z. B. (1999). *The In-game Economics of Ultima Online*. Retrieved from http://www.mine-control.com/zack/uoecon/uoecon.html

Singer, J.W. (1992). Re-reading Property. *New Eng. L. Rev. 27*(711).

Smed (John Smedley President, Sony Online Entertainment). (n.d.). Message posted to Everquest II Official Forums. Retrieved from http://eqiiforums.station.sony.com/eq2/board/message?board.id=stex&message

Smith, A. (2001, February 12). 3D Realms Fences in Foxing Fans. *The Register*. Retrieved from http://www.theregister.co.uk/2001/02/12/3d_realms_fencing_in_foxing/

Smith, A. (2001, January 25). Everquest Class Action Threat Over Auction Spat. *The Register*. Retrieved from http://www.theregister.co.uk/2001/01/25/everquest_class_action_threat_over/

Stephens, M. (2002). Sales of In-Game Assets: An Illustration of the Continuing Failure of Intellectual Property Law to Protect Digital Content Creators. *Tex. L. Rev., 80*(1513).

Terdiman, D. (2004, January 23). Virtual Cash turns into Real Greed. *Wired Magazine*.

Terdiman, D. (2006, December 14). 'Second Life' hits second million in eight weeks. *Cnet News*. Retrieved from http://news.com.com/2061-10797_3-6143909.html?part=rss&tag=2547-1_3-0-5&subj=news

The Unknown Player. (2003, June 5). *Have you Guys missed Me? Blacksnow sure has*. Retrieved from http://www.unknownplayer.com/modules.php?op=modload&name=News&file=article&sid=1517

Twist, J. (2005, October 27). Picturing Online Gaming's Value. *BBC News*. Retrieved from http://news.bbc.co.uk/go/pr/fr/-/l/hi/technology/4360654.stm

Ultima, O. R. P. (2000). Retrieved from http://www.uo.com/guide/renaissance.pdf

Westbrook, T. J. (2006). Comment, Owned: Finding a Place for Virtual World Property Rights. *Mich. St. L. Rev., 2006*(779). Wikipedia, Mod (Computer Gaming), http://en.wikipedia.org/wiki/Mod_(computer_gaming).

Wikipedia, Virtual World, http://en.wikipedia.org/wiki/Virtual_world

World of Warcraft: Terms of Use Agreement. (2009). Retrieved from http://www.worldofwarcraft.com/legal/termsofuse.html

Yee, N. (2004). The Daedalus Project. Retrieved from http://www.nickyee.com/daedalus

Chapter 6
Intellectual Property and Virtual Worlds

"There can be no doubt that communications pervade contemporary social life. The audio-visual media, print and other communications technologies play major parts in modern human existence, mediating diverse interactions between people. Moreover, they are numerous, heterogeneous and multi-faceted. Equally, there can be no doubt that communications are dynamic and ever-changing, constantly reacting to economic and popular forces." (Cobley, 2004)

INTRODUCTION

As stated previously, virtual worlds are created by computer code which is designed to act like real world property. (Fairfield, 2005) Also noted earlier was the emergent certainty that digital technology is detaching information from the physical plane, which, in turn, disrupts the foundations of property law. The next question posed was, should this virtual property be protected and regulated in the same manner as real world property? The answer was perhaps. However, first, another aspect of property law should be considered, intellectual property.

A good deal of computer code is just one step away from pure idea. Like ideas, it is non-rivalrous; that is, one person's use of the code does not stop another person from using it. (Fairfield, 2005) This kind of code is deemed to be protected by intellectual property law. (Lessig, 1999; Geist, 2003; O'Rourke, 1997) Intellectual property protects the creative interest in non-rivalrous resources. Richard Posner (2000) noted: "Intellectual property is characterized by heavy fixed costs relative to marginal costs. It is often very expensive to create, but once it is created the cost of making additional copies is low, dramatically so, in the case of software, where it is only a slight overstatement to speak of marginal cost as zero. Without legal protection, the creator of intellectual property may be unable to recoup his investment, because competitors can free-ride on it; and so legal protection can expand output rather than, as in the usual case of monopoly reduce it."

DOI: 10.4018/978-1-61520-795-4.ch006

Multimedia creators rely heavily on this theory. (See e.g., *Davidson & Associates, Inc., et al v. Internet Gateway, et al.*, No. 4:02-CV-498 CAS (U.S. Dist. Ct., E. Dist. Missouri, 2004)). There is a different kind of multimedia which is upsetting this theory, multi-author interactive online role-playing games. MMORPGs bring another type of code into existence; one which is designed to act more like land or chattel than like ideas. A type of code more prevalent on the internet than the first type of code and which uses most of the internet's resources. This type of code is rivalrous, if one person owns and controls it, others do not. (Fairfield, 2005) In fact, it makes up the structural components of the internet itself. For example, domain names, URLs, websites, email accounts, and virtual worlds. The chattel-like code creates virtual property akin to real life property. It demands protection too. (Bradley and Froomkin, 2005)

At the moment virtual property is governed under a system where initial rights are allocated to traditional intellectual property rights holders, and subsequent rights are governed by license agreements called End User License Agreements (EULAs). The traditional intellectual property rights holders have been systematically eliminating any emerging or potential virtual property rights which game players may be entitled to by the use of EULAs. This is causing an imbalance in resources and rights. The common law is a complex system which has evolved over time to encode many different factors into its rules. In particular, the law of contract and the law of property have traditionally balanced each other. The law of contract permits parties to realize the value of idiosyncratic preferences through trades. The law of property traditionally limits the burdens that parties may place on the productive use or marketability of high-value resources by means of contract. (Merrill and Smith 2001) At the moment, emergent useful property forms in cyberspace are being eliminated by contract.

Copyright law has been the first line of defense for the games companies, but the protection afforded to the games companies can be equally applied to the games users. The Federal Court of Australia, *Galaxy Electronic Pty Ltd v Sega Enterprises Ltd* (1997) 145 ALR 21, held that visual images created by playing a video game fell within the Australian statutory definition of 'cinematographic film'. The question is, nevertheless, who is creating the film: the games company who provide the backdrop and venue or the players who provide the dialogue, action, and plot. The structure and building-blocks are the legal property of the creator-company; however, each character is the embodiment of a player's story.

A. VIRTUAL WORLD ARCHITECTURE

An understanding of the technology is important to determine where and when the real world law would interface with the virtual world. Online role-playing games use a type of client/server architecture. This means that two physically separate computer programs control the game. (Salem & Zimmerman, 2004) One computer program operates on the player's personal computer, and another computer program operates on a centralized server that multiple players may access simultaneously using the Internet. (Id.)

The computer program on the server controls the logic of the game and maintains the state of the game. Software logic generally is defined as 'the sequence of instructions in a program.' (TechEncyclopedia at http://www.techweb.com/encyclopedia) The game logic is the set of instructions that defines the types of objects that appear in the virtual world and the events that can occur in the game. For example, the game logic defines the appearance and power of a particular weapon and determines what a character must do before advancing to a new skill level. Copyright would likely vest with the game company. The state of the game is the state of the virtual world at any time and includes the number of players in the world, the identity and assets of those players, and the time of day effective in the virtual world. (Id.)

The player controls a character from his personal computer; the server program must accept messages from the player's personal computer to determine the current state of the player's character. (Salem & Zimmerman, 2004; Bartle, 2004) As such, copyright would likely vest with the game player. Only the server knows the activities of all characters in the game, the server program must send messages to each player's personal computer to update the state of the game for that player. (Id.) As such, copyright would likely vest with the game company. To maintain the state of a player's character, the server program must operate a character database. (Ragaini, 2002) The character database contains the name, profession, and skills of the character associated with each player and a list of the assets possessed by that character. (Id.) As such, copyright would likely vest with the game player. Although the character database identifies the assets the player possesses, the database does not store the appearance or functionality of those assets. The database stores only the location of the code defining the appearance or functionality of the asset. Copyright would likely vest with the game company as would also perhaps a *sui generis* database right.

Items of value to players, such as virtual armour, swords, currency, etc., are represented in a database as integers. Game companies maintain that the game player should be afforded no protection for the integer as a numeric concept. Further, they believe that the game player should be afforded no protection for the database containing either the integer or the physical server on which the integer resides. The game company believes that it should receive protection for these assets. The CDPA, s 3A (as amended by the Regulations), defines a database for copyright protection as: A collection of independent works, data or other materials which – (a) are arranged in a systematic or methodical way, and (b) are individually accessible by electronic or other means.

Moreover, there is also the possibility of gaining a sui generis database right protection which would come into existence automatically upon creating the database. To benefit from the database right protection, there must have been a substantial investment in obtaining, verifying, or presenting the contents of the database. (Regulation 13(1)). This is an equally strong argument for the game companies as well as the game players. Each player is creating their own personal database which has required a substantial investment in time, money and energy.

The protection afforded to the game player should be for the particular integer (bits) as used in the game (context). (Meehan, 2005) If the game maker changed or upgraded the game and altered the underlying representation, then an equivalent representation would be made (e.g., a different integer stored in a different database), and it would be the new representation that would be protected. Additionally, the game player does not have a right to that integer outside of the context of the game, and in particular outside of the context of the player's account for that game. (This makes for interesting arguments regarding e-Bay and other outside sales.) Another player may, for example, have the same virtual light sabre and therefore have protection over an equal integer stored elsewhere (in the context of the other player's account). Likewise, if the game is migrated (moved) to a different physical server, the player has a right to the migrated bits, the new bits representing her account, and not to the bits on the old server. (Id.)

To put this into context, multiple players may possess a light sabre. Only one copy of the software code that defines the appearance of a light sabre exists in the server memory, and the location of that code in the memory has an address. The character database only stores this address to represent the asset. When a player loses the light sabre, the server program simply deletes its address from the list of assets associated with that player's character; when a player gains a light sabre, the server program adds its address to the list.

So when should 'bits in context' be protected? Game players feel that bits in context should be protected from theft or loss. A case has already presented itself in China where a user's virtual property (the bits) in an online game (the context) was lost. This was allegedly due to a hacker. The Chinese court ordered the game company to restore the bits. (*Li Hongchen v Beijing Arctic Ice Technology Development Co.*; Knight, 2003) In addition to any related civil or criminal charges based on the fraud or theft, the remedy for loss of virtual property would be replacement. This would be where possible, replacement of the virtual property, as opposed to providing a monetary equivalent. This relieves the court of trying to determine the real-world value of virtual property and will preclude placing a potentially extreme monetary burden on the responsible party.

Although the game logic pre-defines many assets such as swords and potions, more complex assets such as houses are not pre-defined because the player has the freedom to design and build the asset. (*Ultima Online* Renaissance Playguide, 2000) Copyright would likely vest with the game player or in the alternative, a design right or possible trademark. The more complex assets are composed of simpler, pre-defined assets. (Id.) For example, a house is composed of walls, floors, and furniture. The game logic pre-defines a variety of walls, floors, and furniture, and the player selects the types and configuration of these simpler assets when building a house. If the player owns a house, the character database represents the house as a list of the addresses that identify the location of code defining the simple assets composing the house. Copyright would likely vest with the game company. As seen earlier, Second Life adopted a novel approach to this issue. They stated that they would retain the rights in the back office source code, but the front end code and user generated designs, materials, and content would go to their respective owners/creators.

The computer program on the player's personal computer controls the messaging that occurs between the player's computer and the server program. (Salem & Zimmerman, 2004; Bartle, 2004) The computer program also presents the player's view of the game world, which includes displaying the game graphics and playing sound. (Kines, 2001; King, 2001) Technology has evolved to a point where plausible interactive characters are now the norm. Game characters have individual recognizable faces, are equipped with cool-looking weapons, and roam visually impressive environments. (Ragaini, 2002)

B. HOW WOULD COPYRIGHT BE APPLIED?

Although all aspects of intellectual property law could be used in determining ownership in a virtual world, copyright is the current focus. In the United States, "Copyright subsists, . . ., in original works of authorship fixed in any tangible medium of expression, now known or later developed, from which they can be perceived, reproduced, or otherwise communicated, either directly or with the aid of a machine or device. Works of authorship include the following categories: (1) literary works; (2) musical works, including any accompanying words, (3) dramatic works, including any accompanying music; (4) pantomimes and choreographic works; (5) pictorial, graphic, and sculptural works; (6) motion pictures and other audiovisual works; (7) sound recordings; and (8) architectural works. (17 U.S.C. §102)

In the United Kingdom, the following are protected subject matter for copyright purposes: original literary works are defined as any work, other than a dramatic or musical work, which is written, spoken or sung – these include databases and computer programs, including preparatory design material for computer programs; films;

databases; the typographical arrangement of published editions of literary, dramatic or musical works; sound recordings; broadcasts; and cable programmes. (Copyright, Design, and Patents Act 1988, ss 1-8) Literary, dramatic, musical and artistic works and films are sometimes be collectively referred to as 'author works', and the other categories (apart from databases) are grouped as 'media works'. The distinction rests on a number of points, of which the most important conceptually is the idea that the second group relies essentially on the operation of machinery and technology where the first depends upon an individual as creator.

Recently, European Commission has been debating "Copyright in the Knowledge Economy. (Green Paper on Copyright in the Knowledge Economy COM (2008) 466/3) The Commission wishes to "foster a debate on how knowledge for research, science and education can best be disseminated in the online environment." (Id.) The debate is actually far wider than indicated. In fact, it goes to the very heart of copyright in the European Union by tackling the nature and extent of the exhaustive list of non-mandatory exceptions to the copyright protection set out in Directive 2001/29 OJ LI67 (InfoSoc Directive). A relevant and key question here is whether a copyright exception should be created for user-generated content on the basis that it is "transformative". The principle is important in light of the Gower's Review which recommended exceptions for creative, transformative, or derivative works and caricature, parody or pastiche. (Gower's Review of Intellectual Property, 2006)

First, virtual worlds consist of mainly images and text; and thus, the most obvious choice is copyright. There is no requirement of formality necessary for copyright to vest in each creation. The categories of elements that may receive copyright protection under a current understanding of copyright law are as follows: text (fiction and code), digital images, building designs, music, computer generated works, and multimedia/data-

base. Secondly, as players craft visual and textual avatars and objects in virtual worlds, copyright is directly implicated. There is the possibility of derivative works. There is also the argument to be made that a transformative work has been created.

1. Text: Fiction

Within most virtual spaces, players interact textually with each other and with their world. He may have discussions with other players, examine items more fully, or do battle - and this entire experience is textual. Because virtual worlds attempt to create three-dimensional worlds, text is most commonly incorporated in player interactions, although it remains integral in many other ways.

Fictional texts are at the very core of copyright law, extending protection to original literary "works of authorship fixed in any tangible medium of expression." (CDPA 1988, ss 1-8; 17 U.S.C.A. s.102(a) (1996)) The two issues that must be addressed in determining whether these virtual fictions are copyrightable are whether they are original and whether they are fixed in a tangible medium.

The originality requirement remains a low hurdle. The United States' Supreme Court in *Feist Publications, Inc. v Rural Telephone Service Co.*, 499 U.S. 340 (1991), held that "the requisite level of creativity is extremely low; even a slight amount will suffice." Likewise, the United Kingdom's court in *Ladbroke (Football) Ltd v William Hill (Football) Ltd.*, [1964] 1 WLR 273, maintained a similarly low hurdle that "only that the work should not be copied but should originate from the author." As long as the fictional texts are even remotely creative, they pass this requirement for originality. While the bar is indeed set low, short phrases (*Magic Mktg, Inc. v Mailing Services of Pittsburgh, Inc.*, 634 F. Supp. 769, 772 (W.D. Pas. 1986) holding that short words and phrases on envelopes 'do not exhibit a sufficient degree of creativity to be copyrightable.') and simple shapes (*John Muller & Co. v N.Y. Arrows Soccer*

Team, Inc. 802 F.2d 989, 990 (8th Cir. 1986) holding that a simple logo for a soccer team did not demonstrate 'certain minimal levels of creativity and originality.') remain unprotected by copyright. Much of the textual dialogue is indeed quite short and may fail to pass this low hurdle. While each individual phrase may not itself merit copyright protection, the dialogue in its totality would most likely be sufficiently original to garner copyright protection.

Providing a greater quandary is the requirement that the work of authorship be fixed in a tangible medium. (CDPA, s.3(2) and s. 178; 17 U.S.C. §102) Much of the textual interplay is quite transitory; unless a character records conversations or events, the text will be lost. It may not be necessary that a work be recorded to be considered fixed. In the United States, the Ninth Circuit held in *MAI Systems Corp. v Peak Computer, Inc.*, 991 F. 2d 511 (1993), that a computer program is copied when the software is temporarily stored in RAM. If a RAM copy suffices as fixation for purposes of infringement, it could be argued that it should suffice for purposes of granting copyright. Another important aspect of MMORPGs is that every time a player creates a new character, that character is put into a database. That character is forever maintained in the continuity that is the game fiction. Every character must be fixed for this alternate reality to maintain continuity and game play.

There is no doubt that the fiction, if it clears the hurdles of originality and fixation, should receive copyright protection. But there is yet another hurdle which was discussed earlier: determining authorship. Players become members of collective dramas. One way to solve the problem is to consider the entire collective fiction as a compilation. Authorship of the whole could be granted to all participants, while each player would retain authorship of his personal contribution to the fiction, as long as it met the requirements for originality and fixation. (*Macmillan & Co. Ltd. v K & J Cooper* (1923) 40 TLR 186) Another solution would be to consider the collective drama as a joint work of authorship, thereby granting ownership of the whole to all participants, as long as each participant made copyrightable contributions and intended to be a co-author. (CDPA ss 10 and 88(5); 17 U.S.C.A. §101 (1996))

2. Text: Code

Virtual worlds are created by code. The creators of these worlds write software code that, when run, creates a shared virtual space. As discussed earlier, players may write code. In virtual worlds, players create mods that represent their characters and environments. While the interface provides a useful environment for creation, it also serves to insulate players from code; each act of creation using the interface creates underlying code, invisible but essential. This code, although invisible to its creator, may be protected by copyright. On the whole, copyright law treats software as a type of literary work and grants copyright in the code that makes up a piece of software. This principle was established under international law by article 10 of the TRIPS Agreement (Trade Related Aspects Of Intellectual Property Rights), which reads (art. 10(1) TRIPS): "Computer programs, whether in source or object code, shall be protected as literary works under the Berne Convention (1971)." The TRIPS Agreement is Annex 1C of the Marrakesh Agreement Establishing the World Trade Organization, signed in Marrakesh, Morocco on 15 April 1994. Though by tradition, WTO member states have interpreted international treaties in subtly different way when enacting or revising national laws.

The United States follows the general thrust of international and most national laws stating: "A 'computer program' is a set of statements or instructions to be used directly or indirectly in a computer in order to bring about a certain result." (17 USC §101B) The Third District U.S. Court in *Apple Computer, Inc. v Franklin Computer Corp.*, 714 F.2d 1240 (3rd Cir. 1983), held that "a computer program, whether in object code or source code, is a 'literary work' and is protected from unauthorized copying, whether from its object or source code version." The written code is therefore protected as a 'literary work' as long as it meets the other requirements of originality and fixation. The judgement also re-enforced that "it is only the instructions themselves" that are covered. This scope excludes two areas: the idea for a program as opposed to an individual express expression as recorded in code; and data upon which instructions operate. This follows the House Report accompanying 17 U.S.C. §102(b) which states: "Section 102(b) is intended, among other things, to make clear that the expression adopted by the programmer is the copyrightable element in a computer program, and that the actual processes or methods embodied in the program are not within the scope of the copyright law." (H.R. Rep. No. 1476, 94th Cong., 2d Sess. 57 (1976), reprinted in 1976 U.S.C.C.A.N. 5659, 5670.)

The European position is slightly more ambiguous. The European 'Software Directive' (Council Directive 91/250/EEC of 14 May 1991 *on the legal protection of computer programs* Official Journal L 122, 17/05/1991 P. 0042 – 0046) states "the term 'computer program' shall include programs in any form." The United Kingdom's implementation of this directive into law provides no explicit definition of software whatsoever. Instead the Copyright, Designs and Patents Act, s 3(1), as amended by the Copyright (Computer Programs) regulations 1992, defines a 'literary work' variously as: "A table or compilation other than a database, a computer program, preparatory design material for a compute program, a database." British law thus relies heavily on case law rather than legislation to define the scope of software, and case law (at least in respect of software) rests heavily on the interpretive procedures and definitions created in American courts. (Lemley, 1995)

The defining case in the United Kingdom is *Richardson v Flanders*, [1993] FSR 497, High Court . In this case the judge, Ferris J, establishes

a scope parallel between 'the detail of certain routines' and 'the plot of a book or other literary work' which mirrors arguments in the Third Circuit case *Whelan v Jaslow*, 797 F.2d 1222, 230 USPQ 481 (3d Cir. 1986), cert. denied, 479 U.S. 1031 (1987), a case that set out certain idea\expression tests which set limits on the scope of the application of copyright to code in the form of source or object code. Ferris J also applies tests established in the case of *Computer Associates v Altai*, 775 F. Supp. 544, 20 USPQ 2d 1641 (E.D.N.Y. 1991) which, amongst other things, deals with the nature of non-literal copying of a computer program.

First, the originality requirement would be satisfied as long as the code demonstrated 'some creative spark' or reflected the author's personality. (*Apple Computer, Inc. v Franklin Computer Corp.,* 714 F.2d 1240 (3rd Cir. 1983)) However, if development tools are used, the generic code generated may not demonstrate any creative spark or the author's personality. However, this creativity could be evidenced by unique, player-defined attributes and descriptions embodied in the code and reflected in the virtual creation. Hence, any creativity embodied in the code would depend on the degree of creativity that the player used during the process of creation. Creativity would lie in the type of object created, the attributes assigned to that object, and the descriptions accompanying that object. Therefore, the code that renders a rock, designed by the player with the assistance of a design environment, would probably not be sufficiently creative, assuming the rock is just an ordinary rock; however, the code underlying a well-defined character, similarly designed by the player with the aid of a development environment, would probably evidence sufficient creativity. Second, the fixation requirement would offer no hurdles here, because the code would be maintained in internal storage on the server.

3. Building Designs

One of the advantages of virtual space is the ability to construct your world as you imagine it, independently of economic considerations. Many players build houses or even cities. (Damer, 1998) These buildings are often elaborately designed and constructed. For example, a resident of Britannia created a three storied home with nine rooms, a rooftop patio, and walls of solid stonework. Works of architecture are an subcategory of artistic works under the CDPA s 4(1)(b). They are defined as a building or model for a building. In turn, a building is defined as including 'any fixed structure and a part of a building or fixed structure'. The copyright also exists in the architect's plans and drawings. The 1990 Architectural Works Copyright Protection Act P.L. 101–650, 104 Stat. 5089, 5133 and 17 U.S.C. §101 (2000) states that "An 'architectural work' is the design of a building, architectural plans, or drawings. The work includes the overall form as well as the arrangement and composition of spaces and elements in the design, but does not include individual standard features."

There is a possibility that a two-dimensional representation of a building could be the design of a building embodied in a tangible medium of expression. To the extent that the building design demonstrates the author's personality, there is a good argument that such building designs are protected by copyright. Granting a copyright in the building design would offer broader protection than that offered by pictorial and graphic representations; it goes beyond the mere visual representation to the arrangement and composition.

4. Digital Images

Virtual environments are abounding with images. These digital images may take many forms, ranging from photos to creative art, and may be used to illustrate places or represent characters. Artistic works are at the heart of copyright protection. Copyright law includes 'pictorial, graphic, and sculptural works' among the defined categories of 'works of authorship.' (CDPA ss 1-8; 17 U.S.C. §102(a)(1996)) Digital images qualify as pictorial or graphic works. Again, the only remaining issues are originality and fixation. According the Jacob LJ in *Nova Games Ltd. v Mazooma Productions Ltd.*, [2007] RPC 589 para 16, "all the things falling within the artistic work category have one thing in common in that they are all static, non-moving. Although a screen display shown during the playing of a computer game is undoubtedly a graphic work, there is no separate copyright in a series of such images." This view is supported by the existence of films as a separate category of copyright work which is seen to protect computer games. (Id.)

Under the U.S. Copyright Act, a work is 'fixed' when "its embodiment in a copy . . . is sufficiently permanent and stable to permit it to be perceived, reproduced, or otherwise communicated for a period of more than transitory duration." (17 U.S.C. §101) As further explained in the legislative history, "the definition of 'fixation' would exclude from the concept purely evanescent or transient reproductions such as those projected briefly on a screen, shown electronically on a television or other cathode ray tube, or captured momentarily in the 'memory' of a computer." (H.R. Rep. 94–1476 52-53 (1976))

This was put to the test in *Stern Electronic v Kaufman*, 669 F.2d 852 (2nd Cir. 1982). The owner of rights in an arcade video game sued a competitor for infringing the copyright in the audiovisual work comprising the game. The competitor defended on the ground that it had not copied the underlying computer code, merely the screen display images. These images failed to meet the fixation and originality requirements. Judge Newman acknowledged this but noted that:

"many aspects of the sights and the sequence of their appearance remain constant during each play of the game. These include the appearance (shape, colour, and size) of the player's space-

ship, the enemy craft, the ground missile bases and fuel depots, and the terrain over which (and beneath which) the payer's ship flies, as well as the sequence in which the missile bases, fuel deports, and terrain appears. Also constant are the sounds heard whenever the player successfully destroys an enemy craft or installation or fails to avoid an enemy missile or laser. It is true, appellants contend, that some of these sights and sound will not be seen and heard during each play of the game in the event that the player's spaceship is destroyed before the entire course is traversed. But the images remain fixed, capable of being seen and heard each time a player succeeds in keeping his spaceship aloft long enough to permit the appearances of all the images and sounds of a complete play of the game. The repetitive sequence of a substantial portion of the sights and sounds of the game qualifies for copyright protection as an audiovisual work." (Id. at 855)

As long as the work demonstrates the author's personality and is fixed, then copyright law will protect the image. What does this mean for a video game designer? The U.S. Copyright Office has ruled that "all copyrightable expression owned by the same claimant and embodied in a computer program, or first published as a unit with a computer program, including computer screen displays, is considered a single work and should be registered on a single application form. . . . Ordinarily, where computer program authorship is part of the work, literary authorship will predominate, and one registration should be made on application Form TX. Where, however, audiovisual authorship predominates, the registration should be made on Form PA." (Registration and Deposit of Computer Screen Displays, 53 Fed. Reg. 21, 817-18 (1988))

5. Music

Many virtual worlds use music in various ways as part of the experience. It may be included to provide ambiance to particular locales or may serve as a soundtrack to a particular quest or adventure. Both players and designers may use music to enhance the virtual world. The musical sequences, which are generally played in continuous loops, come in one of two forms: borrowed and original. The player or designer may incorporate borrowed music into his space for which another may already retain a copyright. But to the extent the music is original to the virtual space, it may warrant copyright protection for the author.

Musical works and sound recordings in the United Kingdom are protected works of authorship under CDPA 1998 ss 1 and 5A(1). The CDPA gives no guidance as to what a musical work is, but this has yet to cause a problem in practice. A sound recording is defined as "(a) a recording of sounds, from which the sounds may be reproduced, or (b) a recording of the whole or part of a literary, dramatic or musical work, from which sounds reproducing the work or part may be produced, regardless or the medium on which the recording is made or the method by which the sounds are reproduced or produced."

Musical works and sound recordings in the United States are protected works of authorship under 17 USC 102(a)(2), (a)(7). A copyright of musical works protects the underlying musical score – 'the sequence of notes, and often words, that a songwriter or composer creates.' (Reese, 2001) Copyright in a sound recording protects the 'fixation of a performance of someone playing and singing a musical work.' (Id.) To the extent the musical composition passes the tests for originality and fixation, it will be protected by copyright as a musical work and possibly as a sound recording. The registration of sound recordings does not extend to the art contained on the album cover either. (*Jefferson Airplane v Berkeley Systems*, 32 U.S.P.Q.2d 1632 (N.D. Cal. 1994))

In so far as a musical work is incorporated into an audiovisual work, it is not covered by the protection offered to sound recordings. 17 U.S.C. 101, defines 'sound recording' as excluding the sounds accompanying a motion picture or other audiovisual work. Audiovisual works receive their own protection. 17 U.S.C. 101, 102 (a)(6), defining 'audiovisual work' and listing it as a defined work of authorship.

6. Multimedia/Audiovisual

Virtual environments display an audiovisual feast. Virtual worlds are rich with images and sound played in combination to create a unified cyber experience. The player, through his participation, creates part of the audiovisual exhibition, while other aspects are inherent in the world itself, ingrained in the design of the creator. The player may manoeuvre his character, in combination with other characters, through an established quest or adventure to create a multimedia experience, which if recorded may be watched as a movie.

In the United Kingdom, multimedia experiences are possibly protected by copyright law. They will be protected by copyright in so far as their parts are protected by copyright; the work as a whole might fall within the UK's generous definition of a film; or the compilation may attract a type of database protection. 'Film' is defined as 'a recording on any medium from which a moving image may by any means be reproduced' and they include the film soundtrack. (CDPA, s 5B) In system terms an avatar or piece of virtual chattel is individuated by an entry in a data set - generally held in a database. This raises the question of whether an avatar or virtual chattel is a database in legal terms and thus what rights would be afforded to whom. The law of copyright in the United Kingdom, pre-1988, provides for copyright in a 'compilation' as distinct from the rights the may be held in any individual part of that collection. The test for where copyright subsists in a collection is that there has been sufficient 'skill, industry or experience applied in the production of the collection' (*Ladbroke (Football) Ltd v William Hill (Football) Ltd* [1964] 1 WLR 273)

Post-1988, the law incorporated the European Union Database Directive which defines a database as a legal object for the first time and created a *sui generis* database right. Council Directive No. 96/9/EC of 11 March 1996 (O.J. No. L77, 27.3.96, page 20) *on the legal protection of databases* enacted into UK law under The Copyright and Rights in Databases Regulations 1997 which amended The Copyright, Designs and Patents Act 1988. Under the directive a database is defined as "a collection of independent works, data or other materials arranged in a systematic or methodical way and individually accessible by electronic or other means." (s 1(d)) The directive defines that copyright subsists if and only if "[the databases] which, by reason of the selection or arrangement of their contents, constitute the author's own intellectual creation." (s 3(1)) Similarly the Directive grants a *sui generis* database right, this time to a 'maker' (not author) such that "qualitatively and/or quantitatively a substantial investment in either the obtaining, verification or presentation of the contents to prevent extraction and/or re-utilization of the whole or of a substantial part evaluated qualitatively and/or quantitatively, of the contents of that database." (s 7(1)) The directive goes on to provide rights in respect of extraction and re-utilization.

Databases do not exist in the legal ontology of American copyright. There is no *sui generis* right in databases either. Hence the situation is akin to the pre-1988 situation in the United Kingdom with a databases being seen as a collection, falling under the general provisions for literary work as interpreted in case law. As mentioned earlier, the foundation case in the interpretation of copyright in collections is *Feist v Rural Telephone Service*, 499 US 340 (1991) *Feist* established that just as copyright does not subsist in facts alone - it does not subsist in collections of facts simply in virtue of the effort taken to compile them. That is, *Feist* rejected the 'sweat of the brow' test as basis for copyright. Now, while *Whelan v Jaslow*, 797 F.2d

1222 (1986), overturned an argument from *Baker v Seldon*, 101 U.S. 99 (1879), the idea\expression dichotomy ruled out copyright in a form, holding that "blank forms may be copyrighted if they are sufficiently innovative that their arrangement of information is itself informative." *CCC Information Services v Maclean Hunter Market Reports*, 44 F.3d 61 (2d Cir. 1994) later ruled that copyright could subsist in both items within the collection and the collection as a whole stating 'listings also embody sufficient originality to pass Feist's low threshold. These include: (1) the selection and manner of presentation of optional features for inclusion'

On the other hand, multimedia is explicitly protect by copyright law as an audiovisual work (17 U.S.C. 102), which is defined as "works that consist of a series of related images which are intrinsically intended to be shown by the use of machines or devices ... together with accompanying sounds, if any, regardless of the nature of the material objects ... in which the works are embodied." (17 U.S.C. 101) This provision has been used to protect the audiovisual experience of video games, which seems an apt analogy for virtual space.

Thus, electronic games are protected under copyright law as audiovisual works, as per *Lewis Galoob Toys, Inc. v Nintendo of America, Inc.* 964 F.2d 965, 967 (9th Cir. 1992). The Court in *Micro Star v FormGen Inc.*, 154 F.3d 1107 (9th Cir. 1998), held that copyright protection encompasses the game art and the game story. Copyright also protects the object and source code as literary works as determined in *Apple Computer, Inc. v Franklin Computer Corp.* 714 F.2d 1240, 1249 (3rd Cir. 1983). As with the protection of all literary works, however, copyright protects only the literal aspects of the code - the actual language used and the organization of that language - not the functional aspects of the code. (*Whelan v Jaslow Dental Lab*, 797 F.2d 1222, 1225 (3rd Cir. 1986)) So does it matter whether a computer game is treated as literary work or an audiovisual work?

Manufacturer's Technologies, Inc. v CAMS Inc., 706 F. Supp. 984 (D. Conn. 1989) approached the protectability of screen displays by treating "the single registration of a computer program as accomplishing two interrelated yet distinct registrations; one of the program itself and one of the screen displays or user interface of that program, to the extent that each contains copyrightable subject matter."

From its beginning, *Galaxies* has been shaped by continuous communication between prospective players and the design team on the game's community Web site. In contrast to the official movie site, where trailers, announcements and images pour out from the studio to a keen audience, the official game site is used for collecting player feedback more than for dropping hints and tidbits. It has the atmosphere of a town hall meeting, with producers acting like city council members and placing tricky issues up for public debate. Creative input has been actively sought by LucasArts. Players are as much a constituency as an audience. They are the creators of this experience, even more so than the original artists and programmers. (Turner, 1995)

Does this make *Galaxies* a 'joint work'? According to the *Childress* Court, it would.

The Copyright Act, 17 U.S.C.A. §101 (1996), defines a 'joint work' as "a work prepared by two or more authors with the intention that their contributions be merged into inseparable or interdependent parts of a unitary whole." According to the *Brighton* court, it probably would be too as collaboration amongst the players would not be distinct. Players dedicate the majority of their leisure time to this game, this place, this story. It is their story. Players can point at what they have created and accomplished with the building blocks provided by LucasArts. LucasArts, on the other hand, has taken some of these aspects of the games and grafted them back into the films. This is the ultimate *Star Wars* wish fulfilment. The player does not just to watch and imagine this universe, but actually is a living, breathing part of it. That means that thousands of people recognize that you are part of it. George Lucas acknowledges that you are a Corellian smuggler/bounty hunter en route to Yavin 4, with a cargo of contraband and a grudge.

7. Computer Generated Works

The concept of a computer-generated work is specifically referenced in British law. "In the case of a literary, dramatic, musical or artistic work which is computer-generated, the author shall be taken to be the person by whom the arrangements necessary for the creation of the work are undertaken." (CPDA s 9(3)) "Computer-generated," in relation to a work, means that "the work is generated by computer in circumstances such that there is no human author of the work." (CPDA s178) This provision in the Act was created to reflect that fact that in an increasingly computerised society a growing number of works my fall outside copyright as no human author is directly responsible for the creation of the work. (Millard, 2002) As with 'computer program' the term 'computer-generated' is not defined further.

However in the case of *Express Newspapers v Liverpool Daily Post & Echo*, [1985] 1 WLR 1089, the work under consideration was seen to fall within the scope of computer-generated. In this case, a computer program was used to generate unique five letter sequences which were printed on 22 million cards as part of a competition called Millionaire of the Month. Council for the defence argued that as there was no human author, copyright did not subsist – hence the defendant was free to publish the winning sequence is their newspaper. Justice Whitford defined the role of the computer as instrumental, saying "The computer was no more than a tool" and rejected the defence argument stating "it would be to suggest that, if you write your work with a pen, it is the pen which is the author of the work rather than the person who drives the pen." In the ruling the author of the work was adjudged to be the programmer. (Id.)

Express v Liverpool Daily Post establishes that in practice copyright can subsist in computer-generated works under British law. Moreover the case seems to suggest that a work is computer-generated when the computer is in sense acting on its own to produce the actual works. In this case, an algorithm was used to select each of the five letter sequences rather than a human making any decision or creative act in each case. Most relevant to the matter at hand, the ruling seems to interpret "arrangements necessary for the creation of the work" as the use of a computer program, as opposed to the creation of that program. While Justice Whitford's pen analogy supports this reading of the Act (i.e. it is the user of the pen not the designer or maker of the pen that is the author), the ruling is slightly ambiguous as the person adjudged to be the author was both the user of the program and the programmer.

In contrast, American laws lack the categories provided under British law. Hence each option for authorship (user, developer-publisher, user and developer-publisher, computer or no one) has to be examined individually on the basis of case law. Currently, there are arguments to support each interpretation of authorship. The arguments for user and developer-publisher are as follows:

Users: could argue that a computer program is effectively an instrument of user in a relationship that is akin to a 'work for hire' agreement. This interpretation of computer as tool is supported by the final report of The National Commission on New Technological Uses (CONTU) of Copyrighted Works commissioned by the US Congress in 1974. However, the final report of the National Commission on New Technological Uses of Copyrighted Works (1978) did not take this view, suggesting instead that copyright might rest with the computer. (Glasser, 2001)

Developer-Publishers: could argue that a computer-generated work is a derivative work of the program in which they hold copyright. The force of this argument depends very much on the nature of the final work and its relationship to the original program. In *MicroStar v FormGen,* 154 F.3d 1107 (9ᵗʰ Cir. 1988), the Court considered the nature of addition levels created for the game Duke Nukem 3D and whether they constituted an enhanced game. The Court ruled that they did as they incorporated pre-existing protected works. Stephens (2002) further argued that if we try to apply this to virtual items we will find that they are not derivative as they 'simply expedite the realization of a more advanced form of the pre-existing work.'

Returning to *Stern Electronics*, Judge Newman comments that the player's participation does not nullify copyright protection for a video game. But in the court acknowledged that the exact video output being protected varied with each game, depending on the particular person playing the game and what actions she took. So who is the author of a video game? CONTU took a traditional copyright approach to the question. "If a work created through application of computer technology meets the minimal test of originality, it is copyrightable." (CONTU Report at 45) With regard to authorship, CONTU explained as follows:

Computers are enormously complex and powerful instruments which vastly extend human powers to calculate, select, arrange, display, design, and do other things involved in the creation of works. However it is a human power they extend. The computer may be analogized or equated with, for example, a camera, and the computer affects the copyright status of a resultant work no more than the employment of a still or motion –picture camera, a tape recorder, or a typewriter. Hence, it seems clear that the copyright problems with respect to the authorship of new works produced with the assistance of a computer are not unlike those posed by the creation of more traditional works. . . .

Finally, we confront the question of who is the author of a work produced through the use of a
computer. The obvious answer is that the author is one who employs the computer. The simplicity of this response may obscure some problems, though essentially they are the same sort of problems encountered in connection with works produced other ways.

One such problem is that often a number of persons have a hand in the use of a computer to prepare, for example, a complex statistical table. They may have varying degrees and kinds of responsibility for the creation of the work. However, they are typically employees of a common employer, engaged in creating a work-for-hire, and the employer is the author. When the authors work together as a voluntary team and not as employees of a common employer, the copyright law with respect to works of joint authorship is as applicable here to works created in more conventional ways, and the team itself may define by agreement the relative rights of the individuals involved.

To be used in the creation of a work, a computer must be controlled by a program and must ordinarily utilize data input from other sources. Both the program and the data may be copyrighted or parts of copyrighted works. The question has been raised whether authorship or proprietorship of the program or data establishes or may establish a claim of authorship of the final work. It appears to the Commission that authorship of the program or of the input data is entirely separate from authorship of the final work, just as authorship of a translation of a book is distinct from authorship of the original work. It is, of course, incumbent on the creator of the final work to obtain appropriate permission form any other person who is the proprietor of a program or data base used in the creation of the ultimate work. The ultimate use of a program or data base might limit or negate the author's claim of copyright in the ultimate work, just as a failure of a translator to obtain a license from the proprietor of the translated work might prevent securing copyright in and making use of the translation. But this is not a question of authorship itself, and the author of the original work does not become the author of the translation merely because it is made from the original work without permission. Here, too, the situation with respect to works produced by the use of a computer does not appear to differ from that with respect to works otherwise created. . . .

However, the Commission recognizes that the dynamics of computer science promise changes in the creation and use of author's writings that cannot be predicted with certainty. The effects of these changes should have the attention of Congress and its appropriate agencies to ensure that those who are the responsible policy makers maintain an awareness of the changing impact of computer technology on both the needs of authors and the role of authors in the information age. . . .

CONTU Report at 45 – 46

This reasoning provides an interesting segue into derivative works and transformative works. Residents of virtual worlds may soon be able to argue more convincingly that their goods and characters are not solely derivative, but, in fact, transformative works which will attract independent rights in themselves.

8. Derivative Works

The game industry is not keen to concede that players are joint authors. Instead, they prefer to classify videogame play as a potentially-infringing derivative work. To constitute a derivative work, "the infringing work must incorporate in some form a portion of the copyrighted work." *Litchfield v Spielberg*, 736 F.2d 1352, 1357 (9th Cir. 1984), *cert. denied*, 470 U.S. 1052 (1985) In addition, the infringing work must be substantially similar to the copyrighted work. (Id.) "Even if a player did not use items already created by the game company but modified them in a wholly new way,

the resulting works would at best be unauthorized derivative works and hence unprotectable by copyright. . . ." (Gourvitz, 2006).

In many instances, computer game software manufacturers encourage the development of 'add-on' software so as to make their products more attractive to users and to build larger networks of users. The case that supports this position is not directly on point. In *Micro Star v Formgen, Inc.*, 154 F.3d 1107 (1998), the Ninth Circuit classified user-created levels for *Duke Nukem 3D*, a pioneering first-person game released in 1996, when sold in bulk by Micro Star to be infringing derivative works. Judge Kozinski held that the user-created levels were derivative works of the original story. "A copyright holder holds the rights to create sequels . . . and the stories in the [files containing the user-level information] are surely sequels, telling new (though somewhat competitive) tales of Duke's fabulous adventures."(Id. citing *Trust Co. Bank v MGM/UA Entm't Co.*, 772 F.2d 740 (11th Cir. 1985)) The Court further held that because Micro Star's distribution of the derivative works failed to qualify as fair use, then the implied license of Formgen which was given to individual players did not apply to Micro Star. Formgen specifically limited any license by including a written licence that states, "Any new levels the players create 'must be offered [to others] solely for free.'" (Id.) Micro Star went too far when it collected and commercially distributed these levels.

It is unfortunate that Judge Kozinski did not consider that the user-created levels as joint works but relied upon the case regarding sequels. However, the cases are distinguishable in that the *Trust Company* case is missing an important element which was clearly present in the *Micro Star* case. "The distinction [between a derivative work and a joint work] lies in the intent of each contributing author at the time his contribution is written." (Chisum & Jacobs, 1999); *Weissmann v Freeman*, 868 F. 2d 1313, 10 U.S. P.Q. 2 1014 (2nd Cir. 1989)) In *Trust Company*, the original author conveyed her intent that no sequels were to be written. Margaret Mitchell, author of *Gone with the Wind*, was adamant that her story was complete as written. "Ms. Mitchell was opposed to any effort to carry on the story of Rhett and Scarlett beyond the end of the novel, primarily because she believed that any resolution of what happened to Scarlett and Rhett would undermine the integrity of the original story." (*Trust Bank* at 742) MGM tried to argue that Ms. Mitchell and her heirs contractually conveyed sequel rights to the movie studio. (Id.) Ms. Mitchell's intent was among other things, a critical element in the Court's affirmation of the ruling against MGM. The author's intent in *Trust Company* is in sharp contrast to the *Duke Nukem* scenario where Formgen, by providing the means and encouragement, intended that players would build new levels that would act as 'sequels' to the game.

On the other hand, it was held in *Lewis Galoob Toys, Inc. v Nintendo of American, Inc.*, 964 F.2d 965 (9th Cir. 1992) that the Game Genie device and program manufactured by Galoob which allows the player to alter up to three features of a Nintendo game is not an infringing derivative work. The Game Genie is inserted between the game cartridge and the Nintendo Entertainment System which then block the value for single data bytes sent by the cartridge to the system. It does not alter the data stored in the game cartridge. Its effects are temporary. (Id.) The court concluded that "even if the audiovisual displays created by the Game Genie are derivative works, Galoob is not liable because the displays are a fair use of Nintendo's copyrighted displays." (Id.) "The doctrine of fair use allows a holder of the privilege to use copyrighted material in a reasonable manner without the consent of the copyright owner." (*Narell v Freeman*, 872 F.2d 907 (9th Cir. 1989)) Further, "an attempt to monopolize the market by making it impossible for others to compete runs counter to the statutory purpose of promoting creative expression and cannot constitute a strong equitable basis for invocation of the fair use doctrine." (*Sega Enterprises Ltd. v Accolade, Inc.*, 977 F.2d 1510 (9th Cir. 1992)

As seen in the United Kingdom, a computer program is protected as a literary work with all the provisions attached to it. Here, the concern is with the making of an adaptation. An adaptation is defined by s21(3)(ab) of the 1988 Copyright, Design, & Act Patents as an arrangement or altered version of the program or a translation of it. For computer programs, a translation includes: ". . . a version of the program in which it is converted into or out of a computer language or code or into a different computer language or code." (CDPA s21(4)) There is also the fair dealing defence of decompilation. (CDPA s50B) A lawful user of a computer programme may copy it or adapt it if that is necessary for his lawful use. This would be a difficult defence for a virtual world resident to use in the United Kingdom. The interfaces of the computer programme for the world is already known and available. It would be a matter of contract as to what use of it could be made. In the United States, the fair use defence would have more scope.

Today's virtual worlds are different from the game at issue in *Micro Star* in one very important way. A user playing an unmodified version of Duke Nukem 3D always stepped into the shoes of Duke himself, and no matter how well or poorly he played, his experience was the (admittedly repetitive) story of Duke's "fabulous" adventures. (154 F.3d 1112) Most virtual worlds, on the other hand as has been described in earlier chapters, require the player himself to create a protagonist for his game experience, an avatar. The game's creator provides a world with a back story and setting, but such details are not generally the focus of the gameplay. Thus, while it is possible for a resident of the world to create his own story which allegedly infringes not only the audiovisual aspect of the game, but the protectable story elements of the virtual world as well, it is equally possible for him to simply use the world in the same way a shoestring budget filmmaker might use an empty lot or city street. In the latter case, the fair use analysis would focus exclusively on the allegedly infringed audiovisual work, while in the former the story, and possibly copyrighted characters, are also allegedly infringed, complicating the analysis of the "purpose" of the secondary work under fair use. (Reid, 2009)

The heart of virtual worlds' appeal lies in their interactive nature. The fact that the player gets to play within the events of the game and control those events rather than just sit passively and watch is the difference between traditional audiovisual works and these new derivative works. The interactive nature of the audiovisual work comprising the game's copyright is relevant because they are a medium which presupposes and encourages some amount of creative, transformative input from the player. A fair use analysis will be made later in this chapter to further justify players' rights in their creations.

9. Transformative Works

A final major way in which a copyright could possibly subsist is by the player using the game technology in an unanticipated expressive way in a 'meta' creative process. For example, the player uses the game engine, graphics, or other elements to create a new expression which is no longer a game. An example of this is Red v Blue (Rooster Teeth, 2007). These are a series of short films entirely created within the videogame *Halo* by recording in-game actions and their actions. These videos have been release for sale as DVD compilations, and full clips are available at http:// rvb.roosterteeth.com/home.php. Think of it as using modified or even original chess pieces to stage a play by Shakespeare then filming it and releasing it on DVD. Other creative endeavours include using the game environments as virtual art projects or even interactive training tools. For example, Velvet Strike, a violence-awareness project where artists log into game servers and, rather

than engaging in virtual battle, instead decorate the virtual environment with logos promoting peace. Another is example is the United States Marines' use of a Modded version of the game *Doom* as a way to train their soldiers. (Riddell, 1997) This last type of appropriated use seems to fall most closely in line with the rationale of protected artistic expression embodied in the case of *Mattel v MCA*, 296 F.3d 894 (9th Cir. 2002) in which the protections of a copyrighted work are balanced against the social value of transformative fair use of that copyrighted work.

The difficulty lies in drawing a line within the twilight overlap of the derivative market entitlements secured to copyright holders under 17 U.S.C. §106(2) (2006) and the transformative fair uses protected and fostered in the "breathing space" created by §107. (*Campbell v Acuff-Rose Music, Inc.*, 510 U.S. 569 (1994) To a certain extent, this may simply reduce to a policy judgment about how far the penumbra of exploitative entitlement of a given work need extend in order "[t]o promote the Progress of Science and useful Arts," while not "stifling the very creativity which that law is designed to foster." (Id.) The open-ended formulation of the fair use doctrine concedes that this line will never be bright, but can still be drawn with consistency in similar factual scenarios.

What is 'authentic' and what is 'official' are no longer precisely one and the same. Not only will the players compose hundreds of thousands of new characters free from licensing review, but those characters' actions will become to all intents and purposes part of the *Star Wars* myth, regardless of whether they are officially absorbed into the canon. Because *Galaxies,* unlike a child's room strewn with action figures, is, in fact, that massively consensual hallucination discussed earlier.

10. Characters

While copyright in the audiovisual works embodied by the output of video games is a source of potential infringement claims, courts have also found copyright in characters. (Nimmer, 2008) As noted earlier, video games have placed players in the position of a main character almost since their inception. The increasing sophistication of the stories told and the characters that inhabit them has risen along with the audiovisual capabilities of the systems running game software. (Bartle, 2004) As such game makers can present players with an array of very visually and aurally distinct characters, which in turn increased the likelihood that the characters themselves may be subject to copyright protection.

Judge Learned Hand remarked in *Nichols v. Universal Pictures Corp.*, 45 F.2d 119 (2nd Cir. 1930), "that the less developed the characters, the less they can be copyrighted." In *Walt Disney Productions v. Air Pirates*, 581 F.2d 751 (9th Cir. 1978), the court found cartoon characters such as Mickey Mouse and Donald Duck copyrightable, noting that while "it is difficult to delineate distinctively a literary character . . . [w]hen the author can add a visual image . . . the difficulty is reduced." (Id.) Further, "a comic book character, which has physical as well as conceptual qualities, is more likely to contain some unique elements of expression." (Id.) This idea was reinforced by Judge Posner in *Gaiman v. McFarlane*, 360 F.3d 644 (7th Cir. 2004). A writer of an issue of the comic "Spawn" sued the artist of the same issue, alleging joint authorship in several characters. (Id.) Discussing "Count Cogliostro," one of the characters at issue, the court noted first that the script and dialogue written by plaintiff would not alone have made the Count distinct enough to grant him copyright protection, but that the writing combined with the artist's visual rendering of the character was enough to create a character sufficiently delineated to be protectable. (Id.) The court also distinguished "stock" characters (not protectable) with a distinct character like the Count (protectable). (Id.)

Some virtual worlds have a selection of distinctly named (and often times voiced) charac-

ters. However, the players themselves are often required to create their own characters. They are offered "stock" visual models which have been designed by the games' creators, but the name, actions, and many other subtleties of the character's story are the product of the player's interaction with the game. As have been seen, copyright in characters raises many interesting issues both in terms of infringement, and in terms of potential joint authorship with players.

C. RIVALROUSNESS AND THE FIRST SALE DOCTRINE

The extent of a copyright holder's rights has been a question in the law since at least 1908 when *Bobbs-Merrill*, 210 U.S. 339 (1908), established the principle of the first sale doctrine. The United States Supreme Court held that a copyright holder who sells to a wholesaler could not bind a downstream retailer to selling at a given price, even if the book itself explicitly included such a price-maintenance claim. (Id. at 351-52) The case involved the sale by R.H. Macy of a book entitled *The Castaway*. R.H. Macy priced the book at 89¢ despite the fact that the publisher, Bobbs-Merrill, had explicitly printed in the book itself that it should be sold for no less than 99¢. However, this proto-EULA was rejected by the U.S. Supreme Court who argued: "[T]he copyright statutes, while protecting the owner of the copyright in his right to multiply and sell his production, do not create the right to impose, by notice . . . a limitation at which the book shall be sold at retail by future purchasers, with whom there is no privity of contract." (Id. at 350)

The U.S. Supreme Court further stated that the purpose of the copyright laws was to prevent unauthorized copying of the work in question and to grant the sole right to sell the copies into the market, but "[t]o add to the right of exclusive sale the authority to control all future retail sales, by a notice that such sales must be made at a fixed sum, would give a right not included" in the copyright statute. (Id. at 352)

Since then, new technologies, such as file-sharing networks like Napster, have emerged which challenged the fundamental concept of the first sale doctrine. These networks provide the means by which purchasers of recorded music can provide their friends with free copies of the same music. The recording industry sued Napster, arguing that Napster's network infringed the music publishers' right to control the reproduction and distribution of their copyrighted materials. (*A&M Records, Inc. v Napster, Inc.*, 239 F.3d 1004, 1014 (9th Cir. 2001)) The U.S. federal court agreed, finding Napster had violated the rights of the copyright holders and that Napster did not possess any legitimate defence. (Id. at 1024-28)

Even before Napster arrived on the scene, software manufacturers had developed a tool for circumventing the first sale doctrine. Software is not sold, but rather is licensed. What you buy is not the software on the CD, but the right to install and use it. Furthermore, just as in *Bobbs-Merrill*, the consumer does not sign any contract, but is deemed to be bound by a EULA that he 'agrees to' by tearing open the shrink wrap or clicking 'Agree' when starting up a game on his computer. The U.S. Supreme Court rejected Bobbs-Merrill's claim that a printed notice in the book sufficed to bind a downstream purchaser. (Loren, 2004)

Whereas the need for protection against Napster-style file-sharing of copyrighted material without consent of the copyright holder is understandable, the parallel need in other forms of digital intellectual property is not as transparent. Napster created copyright issues because it facilitated users' ability to violate the copyright holder's right to prevent duplication while providing virtually costless duplication with widespread distribution. (*A&M Records*, 239 F.3d at 1014) Economists would describe the consumption of shared files as perfectly non-rivalrous. (Demsetz, 1988) Sharing a copy of the latest Scissor Sister

single does not impede the sharing party from using it, nor does it prevent him from providing it to an infinite number of other parties. The U.S. federal court in *Napster* sought to prevent the sale of copyrighted materials where the seller could have his cake and eat it too. For example, the seller can keep a song to listen to and still sell the song over and over again.

Rivalrousousness is what distinguishes *Napster* from *Bobbs-Merrill*. When R.H. Macy sought to sell *The Castaway* for 89¢ rather than 99¢, it transferred the copy of the book to the purchaser and could not resell that same copy to another customer. To sell a second copy, it needed to purchase a second copy. And to sell a third copy, it needed to purchase a third copy. (Schwartz & Bullis, 2005) As the U.S. Supreme Court in *Bobbs-Merrill* at 350 concluded, by selling the book at less than the copyright holder wished, it had not infringed upon the copyright holder's right to prevent duplication. In contrast, Napster did infringe on this right, not because it gave the music file away for free, but because after giving the music away for free, it could give it away for free again and again. As the appellate court in *Napster* said, the record companies "seek to control the reproduction and distribution of their copyrighted works, exclusive rights of copyright holders," which is fundamentally compatible with *Bobbs-Merrill*'s hundred-year-old logic. (*A&M Records*, 239 F.3d at 1027 (emphasis added))

The rise of the MMORPGs takes this question to the next level. (Schwartz & Bullis, 2005; Fairfield, 2005) How far does Sony's software copyright extend into the economic activity within both its virtual world and in real world dealing of virtual objects? The question as to how much control Sony ought to have over a player's use, rental, or even sale of in-game items or the character itself is the concern. It may seem like the issues surrounding an have much in common with the logic of the *Napster* decision, both being products of the internet. However, the *EverQuest* sword is really much closer to *Bobbs-Merrill* than it is to *Napster*, because of the fundamental issue of rivalrousness. In this important dimension, the goods and services for sale in Norrath are no different from the books for sale in 1908.

Just because something is digital should not necessarily qualify it for DMCA or other special protection. (Reese, 2003) The Copyright Office itself has adopted a wait-and-see approach to the impact of the DMCA on the first sale doctrine. Any electronic copy of the Scissor Sisters' song, 'Comfortably Numb' in a raw MP3 format is infinitely duplicable and nearly costless while any particular instance of a special magical *EverQuest* sword as it exists in Norrath is not. MP3 is standardized format for compressing digital music. The term 'raw' here is used to distinguish a file on which no coding restrictions have been placed, in contrast with, say, a 'tethered' download that cannot be removed from the first computer that receives it. If an *EverQuest* sword is sold for 40,000 gold pieces or for $31.50, the seller no longer has the sword. The player can get another but must engage in the same time-consuming hunting that netted the first one and in competition with other players seeking to acquire this fairly rare item. This is no different than the bookstore acquiring a new copy of the book it just sold, but it is very different from a file-sharer, who continues to have her downloadable copy available for copying.

Under mandate from Congress, the Register of Copyrights (2001) has taken on the question of whether there is a digital first sale doctrine and how changes in technology may change the historical line where copyright holders' rights terminate. They concluded that "the tangible nature of a copy is a defining element of the first sale doctrine and critical to its rationale." (Id. at § B.1.a.) Thus, whether an item is digital or not is immaterial. What matters is whether it exists in a physical embodiment. By this rule, a legally purchased, raw MP3 of 'Comfortably Numb' is not re-sellable, but a legally purchased CD of the same digital music is.

Usually, tangibility and non-rivalry are highly concurrent. Most things with a physical embodiment can be consumed non-rivalrously. The opposite does not hold true. Mere intangibility does not need to imply non-rivalry. As a matter of economics, what matters is not whether the item can be touched, but whether it can be shared. (Imparato, 1999) An infinitely reproducible MP3 of 'Comfortably Numb' cannot fit into a *Bobbs-Merrill* world, but an MP3 of 'Comfortably Numb' with digital rights management that makes its consumption rivalrous, does fit the framework and should be treated no differently. Thus, according to economists, the special *EverQuest* sword in Norrath is intangible but rivalrous, and consequently fits more closely with its tangible property cousins than other, non-rival digital media. (Schwartz & Bullis, 2005; Fairfield, 2005)

Focusing on tangibility obscures the real issue that the first sale doctrine is a crude attempt to delineate the boundary between intellectual and physical property. Historically, the line was articulated as first versus second sale. This boundary corresponded conveniently with the point at which the content was put into physical form. So intellectual property rights such as the content of a book or the music of song is both an intangible good and intellectual property while the physical embodiment, namely a printed book or a compact disc, is physical property that the purchaser can resell just like any other property. However, it is not the tangibility of the good that matters; it is merely the rivalrous nature. In a pre-digital world, the distinction was unnecessary, simply because the concepts of tangibility and rivalry concurred. (Id.)

An infinite number of people can have a book's content in mind. Only one person can have a given copy of that book in hand at once. Changing the boundary to the point at which the product moves from non-rivalrous to rivalrous gives identical answers for non-digital questions, but when the framework is turned to digital products, rivalry, rather than tangibility, gives a more coherent framework. (Id.)

This is more than just the point at which the first sale doctrine can apply; this is the point at which physical property law can apply. The first sale doctrine is the line after which intellectual property rights no longer apply. Since the *EverQuest* sword exhibits all of the important characteristics of a physical book, the legal framework that best fits is to treat it like a book, not like the content of the book. Although it lacks tangibility, it has rivalrousness, and thus economically, it is physical property and not intellectual property. Such digital products share every relevant attribute of physical property except they are not really physical. Nevertheless, the economics of rivalrous consumption make it clear that mere intangibility is not enough to make a rivalrous product into intellectual property. (Imparato, 1999)

Thus, the same framework that adjudicates the rights of those who want to sell used books, used cars, and used compact discs, fits used digital swords. Special treatment for new digital technologies can be reserved for the relatively new phenomenon of non-rivalry, where intellectual property law should be applied. The most appropriate legal paradigm for the rest, whether virtual or truly physical property, are the laws of physical property, such as the first sale doctrine's recognition that embodiment creates rivalry and thus ends certain intellectual property rights. (Schwartz & Bullis, 2005; Fairfield, 2005)

The significant distinction of rivalry is sometimes missed in discussions of the merits of the sale of goods. Opponents of these sales question how they could be justified if simply giving away free stuff, a sort of light sabre-for-each-player program, would be seen as ruining the games. The question seems a legitimate one because if every gamer had instant access to a light sabre and anything else they wanted, one very important quality of MMORPGs--advancement through the acquisition of higher skills and better weapons--would be lost. However, this is a false analogy because the replacement of gold coins with U.S. dollars does not suddenly make the light sabre

non-rivalrous. "One large thing we've been doing is developing the technology behind catching farmers. We recently banned a bunch of people for breaking the EULA.... This is something we are vigilant about ... in fact, I think it's fair to say brutally vigilant." (Smed posting, 2005)

Even the argument that real-money transfers spoil the gaming experience for others makes more sense from the physical property framework that rivalrous consumption suggests. Although network effects, where the utility one user gets depends on the number of other users of a given network, are fairly well studied in economic literature, it is uncommon to consider situations in which a given intellectual property consumer's utility is affected by the nature of others' use. However, in physical property the phenomenon is common. One tenant's quiet enjoyment of an apartment is highly dependent on her upstairs neighbours' respect for that quiet. One farmer's soil erosion efforts are highly dependent on his upstream neighbours' activities. And many gamers claim their enjoyment of their accomplishments is highly dependent on their neighbours' respecting the dividing line that keeps the virtual world separate from the real. Professor Richard Bartle (2005) has said: "Most of the players hate this kind of activity, really, really hate it. As far as they're concerned, they're playing a game.... [a]nd if someone comes along and turns it from a game into work, they think: 'I work all day, and now my fun is being spoilt by these people buying success.'" This is an argument of physical property, more akin to pollution than piracy.

No matter how modern the virtual world, if its game structure preserves rivalrous consumption, the old world legal framework works perfectly well. What is new about the digital era is not that it is computerized, but that it is often non-rivalrous. Where goods are non-rivalrous, new laws and new protections may be needed and the first sale doctrine may be extremely detrimental to the copyright holder's ability to control duplication. (Liu, 2001) But just putting a sale into a virtual world like Norrath does not make it non-rivalrous, as long as you cannot swing your sword and sell it too. (Id.; Schwartz & Bullis, 2005; Fairfield, 2005)

D. INFRINGEMENT OR FAIR USE

"Freedom is participation. Freedom is distribution. Freedom is interaction. Freedom is the ability to influence and be influenced in turn. Freedom is the ability to change others and to be changed as well." (Balkin, 2008) The tension between copyright protection which provides a copyright owner with exclusive rights and the public's need for the free and "fair use" of such work for certain purposes has long been the subject of disputes. Fundamentally, copyright protects a copyrighted work from commercial exploitation by others without the permission of the copyright owner. Yet, the protection is not, and cannot, be absolute in order to achieve the goals of a free and productive society. (Sanders, 2009)

The doctrine of fair use was codified in the United States Copyright Act of 1976. Congress restated the common law traditions by crafting the provision for certain limitations on the exclusive rights granted to copyright owners. Under §106, the owner of an original work is granted the exclusive right to reproduce the copyrighted work in copies and prepare derivative works based upon the copyrighted work. Notwithstanding such exclusive rights, §107 provides for certain limitations where particular kinds of uses of a copyrighted work do not constitute infringement. This includes, for example, for purposes of criticism, comment, scholarship or research. The fair use criteria set forth in this provision is considered illustrative rather than exhaustive. To assist in understanding the fair use provision in its entirety, Congress identifies the following four factors as necessary considerations in determining whether fair use is applicable:

- The purpose and character of the use, including whether such use is of a commercial nature or is for non-profit educational purposes.
- The nature of the copyrighted work.
- The amount and substantiality of the portion used in relation to the copyrighted work as a whole.
- The effect of the use upon the potential market for or value of the copyrighted work.

In *Campbell v. Acuff-Rose Music, Inc.*, the U.S. Supreme Court's most recent case to discuss the fair use analysis in depth, the Court cautioned that "[t]he task is not to be simplified with bright-line rules, for the statute, like the doctrine it recognizes, calls for case-by-case analysis." (Id. at 577) The Court went on to state that in drafting the statute, Congress declined to create presumptive categories of fair use, even for the examples listed in the text, "intend[ing] that courts continue the common-law tradition of fair use adjudication." (Id.) Consequently, taken individually, none of the four factors is dispositive to the fair use analysis. "All are to be explored and the results weighed together, in light of the purposes of copyright." (Id. at 578) Judge Pierre Leval's (1990) article *Toward a Fair Use Standard* was cited extensively by the Court. He proposed that the four factors simply supply a framework for answering the overriding question of whether a given use would serve the "objectives of the copyright." (Id.) Hence, fair use doctrine requires courts to view a given use though the lens of these purposes and "to avoid rigid application of the copyright statute, when, on occasion, it would stifle the very creativity which that law is designed to foster." (*Campbell* quoting *Stewart v Abend*, 495 U.S. 207 (1990))

In keeping with this prohibition on reducing fair use to a bright-line test, §107 provides no guidance on how much weight each factor should receive. Indeed, the case-by-case approach called for has led courts to adjust the relative weight accorded to each factor based on the specifics of the case before them. (See for example, *Castle Rock Entertainment, Inc. v Carol Publishing Group, Inc.*, 150 F.3d 132 (2nd Cir. 1998); *Sony Corp. of Am. v Universal City Studios, Inc.*, 464 U.S. 417 (9184)) While the weight accorded each factor is impossible to determine outside a specific factual context, the case law postdating the enactment of the 1976 Act helps to define the rough contours of each factor.

1. The First Factor: The Purpose and Character of the Use

The first factor of §107 requires the court to look at "the purpose and character of the use, including whether such use is of a commercial nature or is for nonprofit educational purposes." Judge Leval (1990) called this factor "the soul of fair use." He argued, "the strength of the [would-be fair user's] justification must be weighed against the remaining factors, which would focus on the incentives and entitlements of the copyright owner." (Id.) The statutory language also asks courts to consider the commercial or non-profit nature of the use. (§107(1)) The commerciality of the use weighs against fair use in some contexts. (*Sony Computer Entertainment of America, Inc. v Bleem*, 214 F.3d 1022 (9th Cir. 2000)) However, the U.S. Supreme Court has retreated from imbuing such commercial nature with a presumption of unfairness. (*Campbell* at 584) Moreover, the significance of the first factor wanes when the use is highly transformative. (Id.) Leval (1990) argued that the key inquiry of the first factor is the extent to which the secondary use is "transformative." The question turns on "whether the new work merely supersedes the objects of the original creation, or instead adds something new, with a further purpose or different character, altering the first with new expression, meaning, or message." (*Campbell* at 579) This formulation acknowledges that all creative activity builds, to some extent, on prior

work. At the same time it draws a line (though not a bright one) at the point where the original work is no longer being used as "raw material, transformed in the creation of new information, new aesthetics, new insights and understandings," (Leval, 1990) but rather is simply being copied and repackaged in an attempt "to get attention or to avoid the drudgery in working up something fresh . . . ." (*Campbell* at 580)

As stated earlier, the concept of "transformative" use is imprecise because of the fact-intensive nature of the fair use analysis. As such, there is a likelihood of the term being applied in a legally conclusory manner because this first factor often provides the main measure of the nature and magnitude of the secondary user's justification for copying. In turn, there may be a finding of transformative character whenever they are already inclined to a finding of fair use. When considered along with the fourth factor of the fair use test, however, the idea of transformative purpose gains workable criteria. (Reid, 2009)

2. The Second Factor: The Nature of the Copyrighted Work

The second factor (§107(2)) deals with the extent to which the original work is of the sort that copyright was designed to encourage and protect. The analysis comprises two dichotomies: that between published and unpublished works and that between factual and creative works. (Reese, 2008) The general rule has been that the scope of fair use is narrower for unpublished than for published works, and narrower for creative works than for factual works. (*Blanch v Koons*, 467 F.3d 244 (2nd Cir. 2006) A line of cases, beginning with *Harper & Row, Publishers, Inc. v. Nation Enterprises*, 471 U.S. 539 (1985) interpreted the published/unpublished dichotomy uncompromisingly against the copying of unpublished works. This caused Congress to add to § 107 the following clarifying language: "The fact that a work is unpublished shall not itself bar a finding of fair use if such finding is made upon consideration of all the above factors." The first factor usually overrides the creative/factual aspect of the second factor, however, such that a transformative use of a creative work will usually be found to be a fair use. (*Koons* at 257 quoting *Bill Graham Archives v Dorling Kindersley Ltd.*, 448 F.3d 605 (2nd Cir. 2006))

3. The Third Factor: The Amount and Substantiality of the Portion Used

The third factor is "the amount and substantiality of the portion used in relation to the copyrighted work as a whole." (*Campbell* at 586) This is related to the purpose of the copying, as addressed under the first factor. (Id.) The court examines the amount taken and determines whether it is excessive in light of the purpose of the use. Consequently, the acceptable amount varies greatly with the facts of a given case. Furthermore, both the quantitative and qualitative amount of the copying is relevant. (Id.) This factor is also sometimes linked to the fourth factor, as a larger or more qualitatively significant taking often (but not always) signals that the use is substituting for, rather than transforming, the original. (Id.)

4. The Fourth Factor: The Effect of the Use upon the Potential Market for or Value of the Copyrighted Work

This factor tends to be considered the most important factor by various courts and commentators even though the U.S. Supreme Court clearly stated in *Campbell* (at 578) that no single factor is dispositive and that "[a]ll [factors] are to be explored . . . ." This factor requires courts to examine "not only the extent of market harm caused by the particular actions of the alleged infringer, but also 'whether unrestricted and widespread conduct of the sort engaged in by the defendant . . . would result in a substantially adverse impact on the potential market' for the original." (Id.)

Additionally, the fourth factor "take[s] account . . . of harm to the market for derivative works, defined as those markets that creators of original works would in general develop or license others to develop." (*Castle Rock* at 145 citing *Campbell*)

In other words, subsidiary markets which originate from the licensing of authorized derivative works, based on the original work, may be harmed if the use at issue simply creates an unauthorized derivative work. Nevertheless, the first factor is incorporated into this analysis because subsidiary markets for transformative uses do not fall under the protection of the fourth factor. Basically, the court must decide if the copyright holder is entitled to control the type of use at issue. If she is, then the alleged infringer has injured this right by taking for free something for which she should have paid. Economic harm is found under this factor only when "the secondary use usurps or substitutes for the market of the original work [or its derivatives]" and not simply when "the secondary use suppresses or even destroys the market for the original work or its potential derivatives" (*Castle Rock* at 145) (as with negative criticism or review which quotes the work). (*Campbell* at 591)

Overall, the fair use doctrine creates a "breathing space" for certain subsidiary or derivative uses of a work by declining to recognize the copyright holder's entitlement to control (or exploit) the markets for these uses. In determining which of these uses fall into this breathing space, the first and the fourth factors merge to create a sliding scale. The use slides out of the market for derivatives (where the fourth factor recognizes harm) and into the breathing space (where the fourth factor does not recognize market harm) as the degree of its transformative purpose under the first factor increases. (*Castle Rock* at 145) "The more transformative the secondary use, the less likelihood that the secondary use substitutes for the original." (Id. citing *Campbell*) However, the relationship between these two factors is in danger of being circular. That is, transformative works are less likely to be market substitutes for the original or its derivatives because the law does not recognize (for fair use purposes) the existence of markets for works deemed transformative. Hence, the *Campbell* Court's limitations as to which markets were to be recognized under the fourth factor. This represented a first step in attempting to avoid it by providing meaningful criteria for discriminating between transformative and non-transformative uses. (Reid, 2009)

E. REGISTERING INTELLECTUAL PROPERTY IN SECOND LIFE

Because this area of law is not entirely settled, residents of Second Life have taken matters into their own hands. The Second Life Patent & Trademark Office (SLPTO) was founded by two Second Life Residents in 2008. FlipperPA Peregrine (Tim Allen in the real world) and Michael Eckstein set up the SLPTO to help residents protect their intellectual property online without the need for a lawyer. Second Life residents may register their creations with images, a description, a time stamp, and other identifying information. If a dispute arises, the SLPTO will provide the relevant facts from its database as a neutral third party; not, it must be noted, as a legal authority. Registration is free. All the resident must do is make a list of the patents and trade marks they wish to register. The resident is then offered the SLPTO Vault programme in which the resident may store their creations as well as access and communicate with the Vault. Once registered, the next step is to set a price for them so that fellow residents may buy licences. This is known as selling a limited edition. To sell a 'limited edition' (similar to a compulsory license), the resident must grant permissions and download the script from the SLPTO website. As items sell, the Vault is automatically updated with transaction and financial details. (Gupte, 2008)

REFERENCES

Balkin, J. (2008). Digital Speech and Democratic Culture: Theory of Freedom of Expression for the Information Society.

Bartle, R. (2004). *Designing Virtual Worlds*. Berkeley, CA: New Riders Publishing.

Bartle, R. (2005) Virtual Worldliness: What The Imaginary Asks of The Real. *N.Y.L. Sch. R. 19*(1).

Bradley, C., & Froomkin, M. (2005). Virtual Worlds, Real Rules. *N.Y. L. Sch. L. Rev. 49*(103).

Cobley, P. (Ed.). (2004). *Routledge Introductions to Media and Communications*. Abingdon, UK: Routledge.

Damer, B. (1998). *Avatars!* Berkeley, CA: Peachpit Press.

Demsetz, H. (1988). *Ownership, Control, and the Firm: The Organization of Economic Activity*. London: Blackwell.

Fairfield, J. (2005). *Virtual Property*. Indiana University School of Law – Bloomington, Legal Studies Research Paper Series, Research Paper Number 35

Geist, M. (2003). Cyberlaw 2.0. *B.C. L. Rev. 44*(323).

Glasser, D. (2001). Copyrights in computer-generated works: Whom, if anyone do, we reward? *Duke Law & Technology Review, 24*.

Gourvitz, E. (2006). Virtual Gaming Worlds Test Boundaries of Intellectual Property Law, Panellists Say. *Electronic Comm. & L. Rep. (BNA), 11*(143)

Gupte, E. (2008). Register your IP rights at the SLPTO. *Managing IP.* January

Imparato, N. (Ed.). (1999). *Capital for Our Time: The Economic, Legal, and Management Challenges of Intellectual Capital*. Stanford, CA: Hoover Institution Press.

Kines, M. (2001). *Planning and Directing Motion Capture for Games*. Retrieved from http://www.gamasutra.com/features/20000119/kines_01.htm

King, B. (2001) *Making Those Games Sound Right*. Retrieved from http://www.wired.com/news/games/0,2101,53156,00.html

Lemley, M. (1995). Convergence in the Law of Software Copyright? *High Technology Law Journal, 10*(1).

Lessig, L. (1999). The Law of the Horse: What Cyberlaw Might Teach. *Harv. L. Rev., 113*(501).

Leval, P. (1990) Toward a Fair Use Standard. *Harv, L. Rev., 103*(1105).

Liu, J. (2001). Owning Digital Copies: Copyright Law and The Incidents of Copy Ownership. W&M L. Rev., 4.

Loren, L.P. (2004). Slaying the Leather-Winged Demons in the Night: Reforming Copyright Owner Contracting with Click Wrap Misuse. *Ohio N. U. L. Rev., 30*(495).

Meehan, M. (2005). *Virtual Property: Protecting Bits in Context*. Stanford Law School's Legal Studies Workshop. Retrieved from http://lasso.textdriven.com/blog/lsw/2005/12/06/bits-in-context

Merrill, T.W. & Smith, H.E. (2001). The Property/Contract Interface. *Colum. L. Rev., 101*(773).

Millard, C. (2002). Copyright . In Reed, C., & Angel, J. (Eds.), *Computer Law*. Oxford: Oxford University Press.

Nimmer, M., & Nimmer, D. (2008). *Nimmer on Copyright*. New York: Westlaw.

O'Rourke, M.A. (1997). Legislative Inaction of the Information Superhighway: Bargaining in the Shadow of Copyright Law. *B.U. J. Sci. & Tech. L. 3*(193).

Posner, R. (2000) *Antitrust in the New Economy*. U. Chicago, John M. Olin Law and Economics Working Paper No. 106.

Ragaini, T. (2002). *Post Mortem: Turbine Entertainment's Asheron's Call*. Retrieved from http://www.gamasutra.com/features/2 0000525/ragaini_02.htm

Reese, R.A. (2001). Copyright and Internet Music Transmissions: Existing Law, Major Controversies, Possible Solutions. *U. Miami L. Rev. 55*(237).

Reese, R.A. (2003). The First Sale Doctrine in the Era of Digital Networks. *B.C. L. Rev. 44*(577).

Reese, R.A. (2008). Transformativeness and the Derivative Work Right, *Colum. J.L. & Arts, 31*(467).

Reid, C. (2009). Fair Game: The Application of Fair Use Doctrine to Machinima, *Fordham Intell. Prop. Media & Ent. L.J., 19*(831).

Riddell, R. (1997). Doom Goes to War: The Marines are Looking for a Few Good Games. *Wired*. Retrieved from http://www.wired.com/wired/archive/5.04/ff_doom_pr.html

Rooster Teeth. (2007) *Red v Blue*. Retrieved from http://rvb.roosterteeth.com/home.php

Salem, K., & Zimmerman, E. (2004). *Rules of Play: Game Design Fundamentals*. Cambridge, MA: MIT Press.

Sanders, A.J. (2009). Case Comment: J.K. Rowling and the Lexicon. *E.I.P.R., 45*.

Schwartz, A.D. & Bullis, R. (2005). Rivalrous Consumption and the Boundaries of Copyright Law: Property Lessons from Online Games. *Intell. Prop. L. Bull., 10*(13).

Smed (John Smedley President, Sony Online Entertainment). (2005). Message posted to EverQuest II Official Forums. Retrieved from http://eqiiforums.station.sony.com/eq2/board/message?board.id=stex&message.id=76&view=by_date_ascending&page=1

Stephens, M. (2002). Sales of In-Game Assets: An Illustration of the Continuing Failure of Intellectual Property Law to Protect Digital Content Creators. *Tex. L. Rev., 80*(1513).

Ultima Online Renaissance Playguide. (2000). Retrieved from http://www.uo.com/guide/renaissance.pdf

United States Copyright Office. (2001). *DMCA Section 104 Report*. Retrieved from http://www.copyright.gov/reports/studies/dmca/sec-104-report-vol-1.pdf

United States Copyright Office. (2001). *Executive Summary Digital Millennium Copyright Act, Section 104 Report*. Retrieved from http://www.copyright.gov/reports/studies/dmca/dmca_executive.html

Chapter 7
Contract Law and Virtual Worlds

"Apart from the educational aspects and training of programmers there are commercial benefits. Manufacturers have realized that they are more likely to improve their sales if their new machines can win at chess than if they can invert nonsensical matrices. The lay purchaser is more likely to prefer a chess program (which he believes he understands) as a measure of the power and speed of a machine. Indeed, as consoles become more and more common, then eventually computers will become as available as the television set. If so, it is very likely that future generations will use them in their leisure time to interact with game playing programs. The commercial profits of such entertainment could well exceed that of any "useful" activity.

Unfortunately, at the moment, most people who wish to play games with computers do not have the eminence of a Turing, et al. Rather than convince the 'reader', they have to convince the firm that such work is useful. A word of advice: do not say you wish to 'play games'. Much better is a wish to study 'dynamic technique of search and evaluation

in a multi-dimensional problem space incorporating information retrieval and realized in a Chomsky Type 2 language." (Bell, 1972)

INTRODUCTION

Software companies offering subscriptions to virtual worlds want protection for their intellectual and economic investment. As such, companies condition entry to their worlds upon acceptance of a EULA which will generally impose strict restrictions on rights of participants. Professor Julie Cohen's (1998) explanation in 'Lochner in Cyberspace' illustrates how private contracts routinely extend beyond real world law. 'Lochnerism' describes judicial activism in the sphere of economic legislation. It comes from the case, *Lochner v New York*, 198 U.S. 45 (1905). "For an example of the use of the term in the present context, consider the following: Many commentators have recognized the similarities between the Court's current approach to structural media regulation and its approach to economic and social legislation during the *Lochner* era. Importing content neutrality and tiered scrutiny into the

DOI: 10.4018/978-1-61520-795-4.ch007

constitutional analysis of structural regulation has opened the door to deep economic review." (Burnstein, 2004 pp 1057-1058; Benkler, 2003 pp 201-205) Compare the assertion that First Amendment defences of the right of databases to control access to their contents have "some fairly strong parallels" with "the traditional conception of Lochner." (Richards, 2005 pp 1212-13) This can be seen to extending to virtual worlds via these complex agreements with their 'click-wrap format' which discourage a complete review of their terms. Click-wrap agreements are online interactive contracts similar to shrink-wrap licenses. Shrink-wrap licenses are often used for software, where a consumer is deemed to agree to the license when he removes the plastic shrink-wrap packaging from the product box. Click-wraps appear on-screen and the participant must either agree or disagree to the terms before advancing to the next screen. Click-wrap agreements are of the shrink-wrap license. (Casamiquela, 2002, pp 477-80; Lemley, 1995) The motivation for the explosion of software licensing agreements remains in dispute. There are those who believe EULAs benefit corporations and consumers alike, while critics bemoan its influence on the application of intellectual property law.

EULAs attempt to regulate a number of different aspects of both law and gaming environments, including: gamer etiquette, game rules, privacy policies, business policies, and real world law of contracts and intellectual property. The extent of these restrictions suggests that any efforts to limit the impact of real world law must first recognize the way in which the EULA's use of contract law unavoidably shapes all aspects of virtual worlds.

Dr. Richard Bartle (2004) is a strong advocate of maintaining game space via EULAs. He believes that the potential real world problems can be avoided by following three design principles: (1) the notion that virtual worlds are game-like spaces; (2) the necessity of the virtual world's evolution; and (3) the exploration of identity. He believes virtual worlds should be a place. A place

that allows players to do whatever they want to do (within the context of its physics) and be whatever they want to be (within the context of their own personality). (Id.) These three design principles dovetail neatly with the virtual freedoms described by Professor Jack Balkin (2004) as constituting virtual liberty.

Return to the key question regarding the interface between virtual world laws and real world laws. How should the law safeguard and shield the independence of virtual worlds and those who play within them, including the ability of players in those virtual spaces to cultivate and impose their own norms?

A. FREEDOM TO PLAY AND DESIGN

Legal regulation of virtual worlds is gaining more interest as more and more people flock to virtual worlds and invest their time and resources there. The next section reviews the idea of regulation and freedom in virtual space. (Balkin, 2004) There are three. First is the freedom of players to take part in virtual worlds and to network with one another through their avatars. The second freedom is for game designers to design, build, and maintain a virtual world; this freedom would be called the freedom to design. Finally, there would be a shared right between the designers and players to construct and enhance the game space together; and hence, deemed the freedom to design together.

1. Freedom to Play

Games are difficult to define. Game scholar, Johan Huizinga (1971), identifies them using the idea of irrelevance. If it involves a moral consequence, it cannot be a game. "Whatever is transpiring, if it genuinely matters in an ethical or moral sense, cannot be called a game." (Id.) Rather, he believes that games are places where we only **act** as if something matters. Without a doubt, play-acting seriousness can be one of the most central purposes in a given game. According to Huizinga, if some consequence really does matter in the end, the game is over. In effect, the sole act of moral consequence that can occur within a game is the act of ending the game. (Id.) By rejecting its 'as-if' character, destroying the fantasy, and thereby breaking the magic circle of shared illusion, the game ends. It is no longer of consequence. The magic circle of shared illusion transpires in a specific place, specifically intended for the game. "Games", he says, "happen in designated spaces." (Id.)

Online games allow a gamer to choose variables – 'the possibility space' – within a range of pre-determined constraints – 'the topography of that space.' (Pearce, 2002) With virtual worlds, society seems to have begun an exploration of the dimension of significance that may be attributed to a game. Gamers are interacting with other gamers in such a way as to determine their own game and that of each other, within the series of parameters set by the game provider. As a result of the increased randomness of game play, gamers spend a greater period of time playing online games, giving rise to a feeling that they have 'invested' in the game. Consequently, this contributes to the gamers' sense of entitlement in and to aspect of the game. (Carter, 2002)

Virtual worlds also offer a type of freedom: freedom to do, to be, to realize. "Strictly speaking, this should be 'virtualized,' in the sense of making the imagination non-imaginary (i.e. 'real' under normal circumstances, but 'virtual' here). Designers want freedom in the designing of virtual worlds every bit as much as players want freedom in the playing." (Bartle, 2004) For each player who is satisfied to regard the virtual world as a game, there is another who cheerfully buys and sells the game's swords, armour, and gold pieces for U.S. currency on eBay. For each player who is not concerned if the virtual world is hacked and accounts are fleeced, there is another who believes the breach is a computer crime of the worst kind. For each player who sleeps like a log after being

expelled from a guild, there is another who thinks about suicide. (Castronova, 2004/05)

This broad spectrum of significance and the ensuing emotional reaction that people manifest in virtual worlds provide an incentive for the state to regulate and prosecute virtual crimes. But has something got lost in translation? Perhaps, the standing of these places as stadiums and the activity taking place within them is a game. Just ask Andres Escobar, the Columbian soccer star, who kicked the ball into his own net and thereby knocked his country out of the 1994 World Cup, if a game is really just a game. He was killed a week later by an enraged fan on the street outside a Columbian bar. (Berkowitz, 1994) When sport includes and unites a society, society endorses the seriousness of the consequence of the sport. It becomes meaningful only because society thinks it is meaningful.

A similar scenario occurred in June of 2005 in Shanghai, China. Qui Chengwei was a player in a game called Legend of Mir II. (Krotoski, 2005) In the course of his game playing, Qui and a friend succeeded in a difficult quest, which rewarded them with a sword – the Dragon Sabre – a virtual weapon. They subsequently lent the weapon to Zhu Caoyuan, who, without permission, sold the Dragon Sabre in an online auction for the equivalent of $870 U.S. dollars. (Id.) Qui, needless to say, was very upset at the loss of his 'property' and so approached the authorities to file a theft report. He was given no remedy since Chinese laws did not recognize his virtual goods as a type of property. Seeing as there was no recourse, Qui hunted down Zhu; and during their confrontation, he stabbed Zhu to death. A 'real world' murder occurred. Qui was prosecuted and received a death sentence which was suspended due to his voluntary surrender to police shortly after committing the murder. (Id.)

Millions are playing in virtual worlds. Their activities in these virtual worlds look very much like activities that take place in the real world, sometimes tragically so. And as such, the players believe their actions have consequences in the virtual world, which can then bleed over into the real world. However, at present, these new virtual worlds are considered distinct play-spaces, where the customary rules of government, law, and economics do not apply. This distinctiveness is a large part of the appeal.

Dr. Richard Bartle's (2004) first design principle can be applied here: (1) the notion that virtual worlds are game-like spaces. This is otherwise known as the game conceit. When games are played, the participants agree to submit for the short term to a set of rules which restricts their behaviour (i.e., limits their freedom). In return, they obtain whatever benefits the game offers. The boundary separating the game world from the non-game world is known as the magic circle. (Huizinga, 1975) Virtual worlds are not necessarily games; nevertheless they use the game conceit. Some freedoms must be relinquished for a time in order that new freedoms can be experienced during that time. The subject of giving up selected freedoms to gain greater freedoms has a long history in Philosophy, stemming in the main from Thomas Hobbes', *Leviathan* ch. 14. This shall not, however, be discussed here except to note that the debate exists. For example, in the real world, a girl may find it difficult to participate in group conversations because she is very self-conscious and fears rejection. She is willing to accept the rules of a virtual world in order to interact with other people in a situation where rejection does not matter so much. She, thus, gains a freedom that she does not have in the real world. She can use this experience to gain confidence and harness it back in the real world.

But what happens when someone does not play by the rules? Dr. Bartle (2005) uses the example of three people playing the game Cluedo. You are close to winning when the person playing Ms. Scarlet abruptly turns to the person playing Rev. Green and says, "I'll give you £20 if you show me your cards." Rev. Green accommodates, Ms. Scar-

let forks out the money, and promptly proclaims that Colonel Mustard did it in the conservatory with the rope. Few players would be happy if this happened to them. There are no written rules in Cluedo about bribery; however, there are unwritten rules against this type of behaviour because it stops the game from being a game. (Salem & Zimmerman, 2004) You would probably choose not to play with Rev. Green again, and you would probably tell all your friends not to play with Ms. Scarlet.

In a virtual world, what can one player do if another player is suspected of bribing a third player or otherwise going beyond the confines of 'play'? One could simply stop playing with those they regard as cheats. This would have the disagreeable consequence of needing to stop playing with perhaps all the other people, some of whom may have become very good friends. Perhaps one's friends would also stop playing, and then everyone could relocate to another virtual world where the game conceit has not been violated. Regrettably, there is no guarantee that the cheats would not follow them to this new world (anonymously or otherwise). So the players can either: grin and bear the situation; try to prevent the troublemakers from playing (or at least repeating their scam); or quit completely in disgust. (Bartle, 2005)

In the beginning, virtual world designers in their small virtual worlds could deal with these characters on an individual basis by speaking to them and clearing up the problem. The designer would inform the player that it was unfair to the other players if they continued to conduct themselves in the manner they were. After which they would be politely requested to stop. Most would understand and oblige. Those that did not were reminded that the 'wizard' had his finger on the obliterate button for their avatar and could erase them utterly if he so desired. The proprietors of these worlds have extraordinary power over participants such that their 'magical' level power has led them to be described as wizards or gods. The justification for doing this was quite simple and reflects the rationalization used by people who break the unwritten rules.

Virtual worlds are unlike board games in that their written rules are coded into them. Board games have certain unwritten rules coded into them, too, by their mere physical existence. In Cluedo, for example, you cannot make your character occupy two rooms simultaneously because the universe does not permit it. Such rules are unwritten because they do not need to be written--they cannot be broken anyway. In these games, all that restrains a player from moving their token more than the dice roll indicates, is the attention and awareness of the other players. In a virtual world, you do not get to fly unless the code says you do.

The subversive player claims that the code alone defines the virtual world. There is no recognition of the reality of unwritten rules (i.e., the game conceit). Their opinion is that if the code allows them do it, they may, justifiably, do it. They argue that this was how standard computer games operated, and thus this was how virtual worlds should operate. If an activity is not permitted, why did the software not prevent them from doing it in the first place? This idea explored further under the Freedom to Design.

Further, they argue that in ordinary computer games it was the program, not the players, which defined the rules. Only the code could determine what they did. These mechanisms for rule enactment are complemented by mechanisms of rule enforcement. Participants who violate the rules can be expelled from the virtual world--harkening back to the practice of ostracism from ancient and medieval cities. (Johnson & Post, 1996; Milgrom, North & Weingast, 1990) Such forced exit works through a combination of legal and technical means. Because breaking a rule is a violation of a participant's contract, it permits the virtual world provider to punish participants that break the rules, even by cancelling the contract with them if necessary. For example, the *Second Life*

Terms of Service state, "Any violation by you of the terms of the foregoing sentence may result in immediate and permanent suspension or cancellation of your Account. You agree that Linden may take whatever steps it deems necessary to abridge, or prevent behaviour of any sort on the Service in its sole discretion, without notice to you." *Second Life* Terms of Service § 5.1.

Sony Online Entertainment's Terms of Service are similar: "Without limiting the foregoing, SOE shall have the right to terminate this Agreement with you, effective immediately, and/or terminate or temporarily suspend your access to all or any part of The Station, without notice, in the event of any conduct by you which SOE, in its sole discretion, considers to be unacceptable, or for conduct that SOE believes is a violation of the terms and conditions contained herein or any policies or guidelines posted by SOE on The Station, or for other conduct which SOE believes, in its sole discretion, is harmful to SOE, other Station Members or other users of The Station. SOE reserves the right to deny registration of any individual as a Station Member and to deny access to The Station to any individual." Sony Online Entertainment Terms of Service § 10. Because access to virtual worlds is restricted by means of username and password, providers can use a technical measure-- software code--to invalidate that participant's access privileges and thereby enforce the legal consequences stemming from the breach of contract.

Another example of a technical fix is offered in the following scenario. Using foul language would be no problem because it was sanctioned by the rules as determined by the code. If it was not sanctioned, then the communication commands could be removed. Removing the communication commands, however, would have spoiled the virtual world. Instead, one wizard came up with the idea of a command called the FOD ('Finger of Death'). If people used foul language, they were FODed. Their characters crumbled into dust and blew away. Using the subversive player's logic, the program allowed the designer to do it, so it must be allowable. It did not permit anyone else to do it unless a flag was set on their avatar. (Bartle, 2005)

However, expulsion as an enforcement mechanism is a more effective because participants in virtual worlds incur significant social and financial costs when they are forced to leave. They not only have to leave behind a network of friends and their accumulation of social and other capital, but also are forced to abandon the persistent narrative that they have constructed around their avatar. For example, in *A Tale in the Desert*, Rules of Conduct, it states: "We do not have a policy against offensive behaviour, but be aware--if you offend the other players; they have the power to punish you. They can even exile you permanently from the land of Egypt--game over, don't come back. If you choose to behave in a way that is annoying to other players, we will not protect you from the wrath of the other players."

There are additional financial costs: the required use of credit cards for payment of the virtual world's monthly fees ensures that individual participants are linked to specific credit cards (and thus, by approximation, people), making it difficult for individuals to re-register for a virtual world from which they have been banished. While it is not impossible to sign up again with a different credit card, it would still be a costly choice, as one would still have lost everything connected with the previous avatar. For example, Mr. Bungle, the evil protagonist of Julian Dibbell's (1998) famous account, "A Rape in Cyberspace," rejoined the community as Dr. Jest after being 'toaded' -- that is, officially deleted from the servers. This practice could become difficult over time if virtual world providers work together with credit card companies. Moreover, forced exit is an efficient mechanism of enforcement, because it is cheaper for providers to banish a user than for participants to lose access to their virtual world. (Mayer-Schönberger, 2003)

The mechanisms for rule enactment (either through software or through an extension of the contract with the users) and rule enforcement (either directly through behaviour restricting code or indirectly through provider action facilitated by technical means to restrict access) provide the necessary foundation for governance in virtual worlds to function. These means, however, do not necessarily incorporate the procedural and other qualities that we are accustomed to seeing in the real-world rulemaking and enforcement space. (Mayer-Schönberger & Crowley, 2006)

In sum, virtual world proprietors want to have complete control over their virtual world vested in the mechanics of that world. As long as this design principle is respected, administrators feel they can protect the game conceit. If the game designers are denied unconditional control, then the game conceit must be protected another way. If not, the virtual world would be just another extension of the real world.

Let us return to the analogies to professional sports. As in a MMORPG, professional athletes are acting within the context of what is popularly considered a game, or at least not 'real life'. In *Hackbart v Cincinnati Bengals, Inc.,* 601 F.2d 516 (10th Cir. 1961), the Tenth Circuit considered whether an intentional blow struck in the context of a football game gave rise to tort liability. (Id. at 518) Hackbart was a professional football player for the Denver Broncos. (Id. at 519) During an in-game play against the Cincinnati Bengals, Hackbart blocked Charles Clark, a Bengals player, by throwing his body in front of him. Hackbart remained kneeling on the ground. (Id.) Clark, infuriated by the block as well as an interception during the preceding play, struck Hackbart with his right forearm with enough force to cause a severe neck fracture. (Id.) In deciding Hackbart's tort claim, the district court found in favour of the defendant, reasoning that football is not so much a game as a "species of warfare[,] and that so much physical force is tolerated and the magnitude of the force exerted is so great that it renders injuries not actionable." (Id.) The United States Court of Appeals reversed and remanded the case, finding that "there are no principles of law which allow a court to rule out certain tortuous conduct by reason of general roughness of the game or difficulty of administering it." (Id. at 520) In fact, the rules of the game specifically prohibited the type of misconduct in which Clark engaged. (Id. at 521)

Another case in which game play was in opposition to the rule of law was *PGA Tour, Inc. v Martin,* 532 U.S. 661 (2001). The United States Supreme Court resolved a conflict between the Americans with Disability Act and the rules of professional golf. Casey Martin was a talented golfer who had been afflicted with Klippel-Trenaunay-Weber Syndrome, a degenerative circulatory disorder, since birth. (Id. at 664-65) The disease atrophied his right leg and resulted in his inability to walk an eighteen-hole golf course. 'Conditions of Competition and Local Rules' are a set of bylaws applicable to the PGA professional tours. They require all players to walk the course. (Id. at 666) Martin's request to use a golf cart during a tournament was denied, and he filed suit under the Americans with Disabilities Act. (Id. at 644-69) The Court performed a thorough analysis of the rules of golf in order to resolve whether a departure as requested by Martin "might alter such an essential aspect of the game of golf [so] that it would be unacceptable even if it affected all competitors equally." (Id. at 682) Eventually, the Court affirmed a decision in favour of Martin, stating, "we have no doubt that allowing Martin to use a golf cart would not fundamentally alter the nature of petitioner's tournaments." (Id. at 690)

One can surmise from the above cases that game-related transgressions of law will not be analyzed in a vacuum. The rules of the game were deemed valid considerations by the courts in both cases. Like other games, MMORPGs are governed by rules. "The rules are written (embodied in the code) and unwritten (embodied in the expectations of players). People can deny the existence of unwritten rules, but they cannot deny the existence of coded rules." (Bartle, 2004) In the interest of role playing, players are given considerable scope in crafting their character within the virtual world. One can be a thief, and one will not have to go to jail. (*Ultima Online* Support, Harassment Policy and Reporting, http://support.uo.com.harass.html) "[A]nthing considered a valid play style in *Ultima Online* is not considered harassment. An avatar who steals from other players, however, will be marked as a 'criminal'. (*Ultima Online*, Britannian Etiquette, http://www.uo.com/newplayer/newplay_2.html) A player can escape from his boxes, those on the company's organization sheet as well as the cubicles that chillingly evoke them in real-space. In these worlds, a player can be whoever he wants to be. Jennifer Mnookin (2001) identified this facet of cyberspace at an early point: "Labeling LambdaMOO a 'mere' game is the easiest way to free what happens in LambdaMOO from external legal oversight." Unfortunately, these new virtual worlds have begun to suffer bit by bit an intrusion of meaning that wears away their claim to special legal treatment, and may possibly diminish their ability enrich their participants.

In some games, nefarious exploits making unorthodox use of in-game mechanics have been the object of grudging praise. In the MMORPG EVE Online, a science fiction oriented game focusing on space combat, players role-playing as pirates stole an entire dreadnought warship. The scale of this operation has been compared to purloining the 'Death Star' of *Star Wars* fame, or in real world terms, pilfering an entire aircraft carrier. All virtual warships in EVE Online feature an automatic anti-collision system to prevent them from inflicting damage on each other in congested environments. With the help of a spy, the pirates waited until the target battleship was unoccupied by any enemy personnel. Then pirate ships manoeuvred close enough to the target to bump it out of its dock with their anti-collision shields. Pirates landed their own pilot aboard the ship and proceeded to fly it away. All the while, the pirates had another group staging a diversion to draw attention away from the heist. The dreadnought was worth about two to five million units on in-game currency. The administrators of EVE Online have given their tacit approval by allowing the feat to stand un-punished. The true brilliance of the operation was the bandits' employment of an emergent property of EVE Online, using the anti-collision system in a new and interesting way not contemplated by the designers. An even more celebrated heist in EVE Online netter $16,500 worth of virtual goods, when the assets of an entire virtual corporation were looted in conjunction with the assassination of its CEO in an in-game contract killing of the CEO's player's avatar. (Wallace, 2005)

Ironically, the players do this to themselves by not keeping the distinction between game and life clear, as did Mr. Qui. They tend to wreck the illusion that is the game. As meaning leaches into these play spaces, their significance as play spaces will decay. Though the professional sports precedents could possibly be useful to a court in adjudicating certain game-related disputes, both *Hackbert* and *Martin* are distinguishable from *Qui*. In those two cases, the issues were confined to events within the field of play. In *Qui*, the facts imply that Zhu did not simply use a 'steal' capability provided by the game's designers. Thus, Zhu's motivation was not to role play a thief in the context of the game. His acts broke the boundary between the virtual and real worlds, and Qui justifiably de-serves consideration for a real world legal remedy.

Thus, the first freedom is the freedom of the players to interact with each other in the virtual world, both as a game and as life. The right to participate in the virtual world through one's avatar is the 'freedom to play.' (Castronova, 2004)

2. Freedom to Design

One way to protect this freedom has been for game companies to demarcate specifically the worlds they create. Game designers control these worlds through two basic devices – code and con-tract. They can write or rewrite the software that shapes the physics and metaphysics of the game world and set parameters about what players can do there. (Balkin, 2004) Through code they can transform aspects of the virtual landscape, confer or deny powers to players, and remove players from the world. Unfortunately, the agreements that govern the virtual worlds have lengthened to reflect the complexity of the interaction between participants and proprietors. (*Star Wars Galaxies*, Policies Index) Tension pervades the governing agreements. Virtual worlds tend to be controlled by authoritarian proprietors and populated by crowds of participants searching for unscripted interaction. Whilst the anonymity of online communities has been known to encourage mischievous participant behaviour, the nearly absolute proprietary power encourages a tendency toward arbitrary rulemak-ing and exclusion. (*BBSBBS: The Documentary* (2005))

The business success of virtual worlds stems from their capacity to draw customers who are keen to pay an ongoing fee to hang out in their virtual world. That forces virtual world builders to offer a form of entertainment that is unceas-ingly more attractive than the competition. The primary business challenge game designers face is the escalating cost of creating virtual worlds. The cost of excellent art continues to increase faster than the market is expanding, especially as the MMORPGs require vastly more art assets than the majority of stand alone video games. (2008) MMORPGs are huge. They must be endowed with hundreds of hours of game play to hundreds of thousands of players. This translates into large teams and lengthy development cycles, often involving thirty or more developers working for at least two years. (Ondrejka, 2004)

Virtual world designer Raph Koster (2009) has observed that as a game designer, "[y]ou have to give players a sense of ownership in the game. This is what will make them stay--it is a 'barrier to departure.' . . . If they can build their own buildings, build a character, own possessions, hold down a job, feel a sense of responsibility to something that cannot be removed from the game--then you have ownership." This concept is known as 'stickiness' to game designers. Raph Koster (2009) further noted that "[a] role play-mandated world is essentially going to have to be a fascist state." Other virtual world designers have expressed similar concerns. (Rickey, 2003)

This leads us to the second design principle of Dr. Bartle (2004): (2) the necessity of the virtual world's evolution. New content is inserted, old content is renovated, exploits are shortened, bugs are eliminated, and game play is rebalanced. If virtual world designers were unable to be fascist dictators and to adjust to their virtual world, that world would become tired, boring, subjected to unfair exploits and its game play would become completely disjointed. World designers would also not be able to deal with crises as they occurred, such as when a user breaks the rules or creates an unplanned innovation or behaviour that threatens to erode confidence in the virtual world.

For example, Sony Online Entertainment had to perform such an intervention when an *EverQuest* user devised an ingenious scheme that threatened to introduce the online equivalent of the Industrial Revolution to the economy and thereby devalue the in-world currency. (Sandoval, 2000; Terdi-man, 2004) When *EverQuest* users gain sufficient experience, they can produce virtual goods, like virtual swords. These virtual goods can then be sold in a virtual store in *EverQuest* for a fixed price. Through a shortcut, one user was able to produce and sell many virtual goods in a short period of time, simultaneously amassing huge wealth for himself and devaluing both manual labour and the in-world currency. In essence, the user had caused an industrial revolution, threatening the savings of hundreds of thousands of users. Sony intervened and modified the software to stop the shortcut from working. This type of intervention is possible because of the complete control pro-

viders retain over their worlds. Such stabilization is valued by users who have a substantial investment in the virtual world. While it is possible for this comparatively settled state to be achieved, one with few bugs and exploits remaining and an adequate amount of player-generated content for it to maintain its novelty; it would take a long time to get a virtual world into this arrangement. Still intermittent changes would still be required.

Modifications to a virtual world affect different avatars (and hence different players) in different manners. Consider a virtual world that has two types of warriors, the Rebel Alliance soldiers and the Jedi Knights. The Jedi Knights have similar powers as the Rebel Alliance soldiers except for being more powerful against evil foes. After awhile, the world designer observes that there are numerous Jedi Knights and few Rebel Alliance soldiers. Because there are so many Jedi Knights, there are fewer evil creatures available to kill because they are all dead. The Jedi Knights could kill non-evil creatures, but this would be more difficult and somewhat pointless for them so they do not want to do it. Instead, they complain about how boring the virtual world has become, and that there should be more evil creatures. (Bartle, 2005)

The world designer can tackle this problem in many ways. Adding more evil creatures is just one way. At the end of the day, the core problem is that there is an incentive for players to be Jedi Knights rather than Rebel Alliance soldiers, but no disincentive. If more players were Rebel Alliance soldiers (or fewer were Jedi Knights), the problem would disappear. Thus, the world designer determines to make a modification such that Jedi Knights are weaker against non-evil foes. Jedi Knights are not attacking these anyway, so should not care. Players now have a choice to play as Rebel Alliance soldiers (and be equally effective against all kinds of foes), or as Jedi Knights (and be more effective against evil foes but less effective against non-evil foes). The virtual world should be better as a result. (Id.)

On the whole, even the smallest modifications to game play can have implications throughout the entire virtual world, affecting things not immediately connected to them. In-context economies are particularly affected in this regard. An "in-context economy" is one designed into the virtual world; whereas an "out-of-context economy" contains elements the virtual world knows nothing about (e.g., US dollars). Any slight correction in the way that a non-player character calculates the value of a light sabre would affect the price that it paid for light sabres, which in turn has an impact on the amount a light sabre craftsman could afford for raw materials, and so on. A non-player character ('NPC') is a character in a virtual world that is controlled by the virtual world itself (using artificial intelligence techniques). This contrasts with a player character ('PC'), which has a human being controlling it. The ramifications gradually disseminate throughout the virtual world as supply and demand. As a result of the new light sabre-valuation policy, there is a 0.01% fall in the price of platinum in a distant galaxy. This adjustment would not be noticed by most players, but it could genuinely aggravate the merchant who has 100,000 units of platinum in a warehouse there. If this could be predicted (which is possible, if perhaps unlikely), would it be a motive not to make the initial modification to the way the non-player character values a light sabre? (Bartle, 2004; Salem & Zimmerman, 2004)

Virtual world designers must account for all of these things when deciding whether or not to modify their virtual world. Any adjustment that bestows something to one group of players will by definition withdraw something from another group. A shrewd designer will justify what is happening and why. He will prepare the players for the amendments while giving them the opportunity to voice objections. In the end though, the designer must determine what is best for the virtual world as a whole. Nonetheless, no matter how fair virtual world overseers try to be; they cannot please all their players all the time. Intermit-

tently, they must modify the virtual world which some, if not all, players will find distasteful. If this design principle is followed, and virtual world designers are able to discount players' opinions, they can continue to develop and improve their virtual worlds. Anything that served to limit this process would limit the virtual world's evolution.

On the other hand, Linden Lab chose to go against this design principle and granted intellectual property rights to their participants who created content. In a Press Release, *Second Life Residents to Own Digital Creations*, at http://lindenlab.com/press_story_12.php; Terms of Service and End User License Agreement for *Second Life* § 5.3, at http://secondlife.com/tos.php stated that "[p]articipants can create Content on Linden's servers in various forms. Linden acknowledges and agrees that, subject to the terms and conditions of this Agreement, including without limitation the limited licenses granted by you to Linden herein, you will retain any and all applicable copyright and/or other intellectual property rights with respect to any Content you create using the Service". This has forced its competitors into a difficult position. They can either continue to invest heavily in content development and accept the economic disadvantages of competing directly against the content that *Second Life*'s players are creating, or follow Linden Lab's lead and grant intellectual property ownership to their own participants. Participants too, now face a choice. They can either choose virtual worlds that permit them to retain their intellectual property rights (like *Second Life*), or cede ownership to the virtual world provider in exchange for rich content that a central team of professionals creates for them. (Mayer-Schönberger & Crowley, 2006)

Paradoxically, the very innovation that energizes *Second Life*'s strategy influences the choices participants will make, thereby creating a mechanism that prevents the company from becoming too dominant in the marketplace. Whenever virtual world participants retain their intellectual property rights, they experience lower switching costs. If they ever choose to exit one virtual world, they can simply port their information goods to a competitor. They would use the export function of one virtual world to extract the digital representation of their intellectual property from the virtual world they want to exit. This would create files containing the intellectual property, which then could be imported through a technical feature of the virtual world to which they want to migrate. (Ondrejka, 2005) Exiting participants, nonetheless, lose their social network, and thus incur some transactional cost. However, they can at least take the fruits of their creative labour with them.

An analogy for this situation would be that traditional virtual worlds do not permit their emigrants to take any property with them, while *Second Life*-like providers let emigrants leave with their belongings. Conceivably, one could envision what could happen if a group of *Second Life* participants ever becomes disaffected with Linden Lab's management of the virtual world. They would take their content en masse and move to a different virtual world, leaving behind a barren virtual space. In this case, the loss of every player who switches away from *Second Life* is felt more directly and immediately than in worlds where all intellectual property is owned by the provider.

Hence, a universe of virtual world providers following the *Second Life* model will approximate a situation in which the public votes with their feet more so than jurisdictions in the real world. Participants who are willing to pay more--either in terms of capital (monthly fees) or time investment--will expect more from the virtual world that they choose. Others may prefer a less sophisticated world at a cheaper price. In abstract terms, Charles Tiebout (1956) famously described such a universe of people who use perfect residential mobility to choose the jurisdiction in which they wish to settle, based solely on their preferences. "If consumer-voters are fully mobile, the appropriate local governments, whose revenue-expenditure patterns are set, are adopted by the consumer-voters." (Id.)

If the practice of granting intellectual property rights spreads among virtual world providers, the question will then arise as to how will these providers compete with each other? It will not be on content, because they will not control content anymore. Possibly, they will be able to compete on size; thus, by extension, on the availability of user-supplied content. In addition, network externalities make some virtual worlds more attractive for people to join: joining a larger community provides more possibilities for interaction and expansion of one's social network than joining a smaller virtual world. Predictably, this network effect leads (at least initially) to strong first-mover advantages: whoever attracts the most users first is likely to attract more in the future. New competitors must offer a significantly better deal than the first mover in order to either attract users to switch to their virtual world, or to attract new people to join. However, virtual worlds will have lost 'stickiness' due to lowered switching costs, leaving virtual world providers with less control over size. Price will still be an option. Participating in a virtual world takes time and effort. Such investment is difficult to make for multiple virtual worlds in parallel. Users may, however, sometimes tire of a virtual world and thus migrate to another one after a period of time. This tendency has even created new markets for 'migration services' like Playvault, which offers to transfer and convert game money from one virtual world to another. See Playvault.com, http://www.playvault.com On the other hand, with no content and no population to control, they will face the fate of commodity providers even more quickly.

Service has become the point of stickiness for virtual world providers. For example, providers could offer superior content creation tools and a more attractive user environment (with easy capabilities to search objects and places in the virtual world), and thereby--temporarily at least-- achieve competitive advantage. In the long term, however, such a strategy may be undermined by the development of cross-world, cross-platform tools providing services from content creation to search. Related to this and facilitated by the granting of intellectual property rights is that virtual worlds may also compete on the regulatory frameworks they provide.

Given the increasing costs of development, the high failure rates of new worlds, and the rising expectations of participants, developers incorporate significant risks into governing agreements. (Terdiman, 2005 & 2004) Some commentators have suggested that virtual worlds are free to evolve, unrestrained by real world laws. (Lastowka & Hunter, 2004) However, those same commentators acknowledge the degree to which virtual world lawmaking is determined by both the developers' control of code and governing agreements. (Lastowka & Hunter, 2004) The power to construct the law of a virtual world could be the privilege to determine every aspect of that space. (Reynolds, 2005)

Virtual worlds are governed by rules. The rules are written (embodied in the code) and unwritten (embodied in the expectations of the players). People can deny the existence of unwritten rules, but they cannot deny the existence of coded rules. (Bartle, 2004) If the code says that you cannot walk across water, you cannot walk across water. If the code says you can shoot arrows around corners, you can shoot arrows around corners. If the code says the wizard (world designer) can eradicate your avatar, he can eradicate your avatar.

Players may be able to single out which cultural norms to obey, but they do not get to single out which rules of the virtual world's physical universe to obey--and the world designer's authority in a virtual world is personified in those rules. One will not use foul language, because if you do you will be obliterated. A player will not do anything that the virtual world designer does not want them to do, because if they do the player will be obliterated. Some things that virtual world proprietors object to are understandable. For example, virtual world for counselling rape victims (and there are such places) might dismiss journalists who turn up

faking having been raped in order to get a story. Some are more ambiguous. For example, a virtual world created for worshipers of religion X (and there are such places, for different values of X) might dismiss members of religion Y who turn up hoping to participate in a ritual or service. Some are completely arbitrary. For example, I don't like the cut of your jib. Nonetheless, all are part of the laws of the virtual world. If you participate, they are enforced with the same authority as any other law. As such, it would follow that anything the virtual world permits its players do, they can in fact do. The decision of whether a player does something or not is entirely tempered by what the virtual world lets its more powerful players do should they dislike what that player has done. For most virtual worlds, the virtual world proprietors are fair and reliable. Those who are not have fewer players.

The other way world designers can regulate the space is by engaging in a centralized process of lawmaking through a form of non-negotiated, infinitely modifiable, proprietor-friendly regulation called EULAs or Terms of Service (ToS) which players must sign in order to participate in the virtual world. In most cases, the EULA covers rules about proper play, appropriate behaviour, and decorum in the virtual world. These are aspects of the game which are difficult to control via code. The game designer can discipline players who violate the EULA, take away their privileges and powers, or even kick them out of the game space and eliminate their avatars.

The inspiration and spirit of specific virtual worlds sometimes conflict incongruously with these governing agreements. For example, to enter the virtual world of *Anarchy Online*, a user must agree to abide by an extensive array of rules. This list includes is the anti-anarchistic admonition that "[y]ou will always follow the instructions of authorized personnel while in *Anarchy Online*." (Rules of Conduct Within *Anarchy Online*, http://anarchy-online.com/content/corporate/rulesofconduct.html) The only implication of a lawless, anarchistic society in *Anarchy Online* is the difficulty a potential user encounters in trying to find the EULA, which appears to be only available to purchasers. Likewise, the infernally named virtual world Helbreath the Heldenian prohibits participant actions, such as organizing into antireligious groups, among other behaviours. Helbreath USA, Conduct Rules, at (9), http://www.helbreathusa.com/rules.php: "You may not organize any guilds or groups that are based on, or espouse, any ... anti-religious ... or other hate-mongering philosophy." While technology may be seen as a significant constraint on behaviour in the digital world, given the truly digital environments of virtual worlds, private contract law is actually the most significant limitation. (Lessig, 1999) Professor Lawrence Lessig (2000) has argued that code is law in cyberspace.

Not all share this view. Judge Frank Easterbrook (1996) sees no urgency in harmonizing either the procedural or substantive Internet law. He argues that Internet law is nothing more than everyday cases whose only common element is the incidental use of a new technology. In Easterbrook's opinion, devoting time and effort to studying "the law of the Internet" makes as much (or as little) sense as studying "the law of the horse." He explains that: "Lots of cases deal with sales of horses; others deal with people kicked by horses; still more deal with the licensing and racing of horses, or with the care veterinarians give to horses, or with prizes at horse shows. Any effort to collect these strands into a course on 'The Law of the Horse' is doomed to be shallow and to miss unifying principles." Judge Easterbrook concludes that Internet law is not a proper subject for empirical study and that we should "let the world of cyberspace evolve as it will, and enjoy the benefits." (Id.) Similarly, Joseph Sommers (2000) contends that "[e]ven if the Internet or personal computer has the promised transformative social impact, they are unlikely to generate a characteristic body of law."

If 'code is law' were true, what need would EULAs serve? Proprietors could simply encode all restrictions. (Bartle, 2004) But contrary to some of the more enthusiastic proponents of the 'code is law' movement, software code is not able to regulate all online behaviour. First, software is not sufficiently advanced to grasp the semantic meaning of text. (Dreyfus, 1992) This problem is well known in the context of filtering illegal content on the Internet. For instance, the Censorware Project (1997) reports that the software filter Cyber Patrol also blocks access to sites like the MIT Project on Mathematics and Computation, the University of Arizona, the U.S. Army Corps of Engineers Construction Engineering Research Laboratories, and AAA Wholesale Nutrition, a provider of bodybuilding products. (Pelz, 2002) For example, veiled threats made by one participant of a virtual world to another may not be recognized by the virtual world's software and may not trigger the software code that filters the message. Second, not every human conflict can be avoided through regulation of behaviour. Conflicts are bound to arise even in the most restricted virtual worlds. Third, participants demand a certain degree of freedom to interact. (Koster, 1998) If behaviour is constrained too narrowly, it will act as a disincentive for people to join and stay in the virtual world.

Because software code can only limit and not eliminate conflict, virtual world providers must apply more old-fashioned governance mechanisms to deal with conflicts that cannot be constrained through modifications to the underlying code: codifying social norms into written rules and providing effective enforcement of these rules. Enactment of such a means of governance is relatively straightforward with the use of EULAs. Participants agree to be bound by the rules and regulations in that contract. Providers thus have a mechanism to set the rules they deem necessary.

Another explanation for the dominance of governing agreements is the relative ease and cost-effectiveness of writing a document of rules compared to the effort involved in creating a complex behaviour-controlling code. For example, James Grimmelmann (2005) points out that code cannot adequately address participant manipulation of coding errors that endow the user with unexpected powers. Additionally, experiments in technology, such as speech filters, have shown some of the difficulties in attempting to encode such restrictions.

EULAs represent an important interface between real world law and virtual world law. These agreements, governed by real world law, are the primary instrument of law employed by proprietors in the virtual world. The game designer's freedom to design and the players' freedom to play are often synergistic. The EULA and the code create the social contract and architecture of the virtual world. They allow people to play within it. Without EULAs, these 'games' are not games at all. They are mere suburbs of the metropolis Earth. Regions which must be guarded, regulated, policed and taxed just like the Earth. Thus, it can be said that the players' freedom to play is the freedom to play within the rules the game designers have created.

3. Freedom to Design and Play Together

Dr. Bartle's (2004) third design principle - the exploration of identity – is intrinsic to the concept of freedom to design and play. Many people interact in virtual worlds in order to explore their identity. Virtual worlds allow this by providing the players an experience equivalent to a hero's journey. Joseph Campbell (1949) wrote quite a bit about the hero's journey in *The Hero with a Thousand Faces*. Essentially there is a pattern followed by much of myth, ancient and modern, that takes an individual on a journey to a world of adventure (i.e., a virtual world in this case) where challenges are met, foes defeated, aspects of the self confronted, and identity asserted. As a

result, the individual is a more complete person than they were before they made the journey. In virtual worlds, the undertaking of a hero's journey is, for many players, the ultimate source of the fun they derive from playing.

Although not all virtual worlds provide this, for example *Second Life,* most do. Likewise, not every player has this apparent motivation or at least does not actually realize it. In particular, designers playing virtual worlds do not see them in the same way as do regular players. This is similar to the way that movie directors take different things from a movie than do regular movie-goers. In virtual worlds designed to steer players along their hero's journey, the notion of achievement is critical to success. Players must feel that that they are progressing, that this progress is worthwhile, and that there is some definite goal that indicates they have 'won.' Unfortunately, few modern commercial virtual worlds actually have this final step, mainly because developers are afraid that once players feel they have won they will stop playing (although, perversely, this is not really something that need concern them). However, the idea of 'winning' is still a pervasive expectation of most players. Most virtual worlds have a system of swift comparison between avatars--normally an organization of levels, with higher-level avatars being more advanced than lower-level ones. Even though, technically, MMORPGs do not have such a system or mechanism like this to expedite a hero's journey, it helps. If they do have such a system, then they are implicitly propounding a hero's journey whether they intended to or not. For the most part, this is the intention.

An essential item to observe at this point is that the avatar signals the progress of the player. Usually, a player who is nearing the end of their hero's journey will utilize a very high level avatar. Players use their relative standing to ascertain their ranking in the social hierarchy. A higher ranking avatar is 'better' than you, just as you are 'better' than a lower ranking avatar. Players embark on activities in the virtual world that improve their avatars and raise them up to higher levels, in so doing they demonstrate to other players (but mainly themselves) just how wonderful a player they are turning out to be. This benefits all players who are on a hero's journey. If this metric, that some players are better than others, is not accepted, then a player cannot hope to utilize that same metric to ascertain the progress in play of their future-selves over their current-self. (Bartle, 2004; Salem & Zimmerman, 2004)

This value system would collapse if there was not a compelling equivalence between an avatar's level and its player's experience. The issue is not so much that a low-level avatar must have a low-experience player operating it; the vital conclusion is that a high-level avatar must have a high-experience player operating it. If this reasoning were not true, then when a player became a high-experience player, how would others (but especially himself) recognize that achievement? This is what renders virtual worlds fun and exciting. This persistent competition and collaboration among the players, Professor Yochai Benkler (2003) has also characterized it as the freedom 'to play together.' James Grimmelmann (2003) offers the related concept of a 'free-as-in-speech-game,' which he distinguishes from a 'free-as-in-speech-game platform.' Virtual world designers also completely appreciate this. As such, they attempt, via design, to allow only those avatars belonging to players who genuinely are good at what they do to reach the higher levels. This preserves the integrity of the social order, which in turn, sustains the players' sense of development and reinforces their growing sense of self-actualization. A virtual world in which the lucky roll of a die could instantly turn a newcomer into a mighty warrior would remove all pretence that rank meant anything. Unless the players of this world could find some other way to measure their relative progress, it would become a very disappointing and dispiriting place for those on a hero's journey. The perception must be of fairness.

Virtual world proprietors endeavour to safeguard the integrity of the level chain of command. If they detect that a player is taking advantage of some unplanned or inadvertent design feature that leap-frogs them to higher levels, they not only must track down the bug and fix it, but also confiscate all benefits that the player has acquired from it. Generally speaking, if a player discovers an exploit and informs the administrators without having taken advantage of it, they will be rewarded for their honesty. Unfortunately, also generally speaking, players do not tend to do this and are thus subject to the full fury of the administrators when they are found out. This could possibly mean that the world designer's will reduce the avatar by several levels, but it can also include recalling in-world property or in-world currency wrongfully obtained. The interesting question is the definition of 'wrongfully acquired.' Who decides it is wrong? What makes some actions in the virtual world 'exploits' when other, similar actions, are not?

For this reason, platform owners seek out the opinions of the player community about how to improve the game and to make it more fun to play, how different features can be tweaked, and how loopholes can be eliminated. They also ask for suggestions as to how previously unanticipated forms of player behaviour, which are thought to be unfair or not in the spirit of the game, can be prevented through code or prohibited by the EULA. The game designers cannot make everyone happy because the suggestions are often contradictory. Some players may want to have a certain behaviour prohibited while others want it to become a legitimate part of the game. (Musgrove, 2006)

Virtual worlds are designed to be indefinite. Designers are delighted when they realize that their virtual world responds logically to a situation which they had not envisioned. For example, all virtual warships in *EVE Online* (2005) feature an automatic anti-collision system to prevent them from inflicting damage on each other in congested environments. Nefarious exploits making unorthodox use of this in-game mechanics have been the object of grudging praise. With the help of a spy, some pirates waited until the target battleship was unoccupied by any enemy personnel. Then pirate ships manoeuvred close enough to the target to bump it out of its dock with their anti-collision shields. They landed their own pilot aboard the ship and proceeded to fly it away. All the while, the pirates had another group staging a diversion to draw attention away from the heist. The dreadnought was worth about two to five billion units of in-game currency. The scale of this operation has been compared to purloining the 'Death Star' of *Star Wars* fame or, in real world terms, pilfering an entire aircraft carrier. The administrators of *EVE Online* have given their tacit approval by allowing the feat to stand unpunished. The true brilliance of the operation was the bandits' employment of an emergent property of *EVE Online*, using the anti-collision system in a new and interesting way not contemplated by the designers.

Needless to say, the effects were unintended. It gave players a quick and easy way to wealth. The question is: should this be considered as a feature or an exploit? The designers could have modified the virtual world's code so as not to allow this to happen again or make it possible yet more difficult to accomplish again. From an abstract point of view, there is little difference between a feature (easy logs) and an exploit (easy treasure). In some virtual worlds, this could be the reverse; easy treasure (a feature) and easy logs (an exploit). Either way, the virtual world's designers should be the ones making this judgement call. If they are not in a position to determine what is or is not an exploit, exploiters/pirates will triumph and the achievement mechanisms and hierarchy will collapse.

Not all exploits are in the code. Some exploits take place where the code cannot gain access -- in the real world. If a player acquires an advantage in the real world which the game designers deem to be dishonest or unfair, proprietors ought to be

allowed to take action in the virtual world to preserve the achievement system. For example, they hack into the client software to reveal information to which they should not be privy. This could ultimately mean annihilating avatars acquired through hacked clients.

Those virtual world systems and their administrators, who maintain unambiguous, precise, authorized procedures by which the comparative experience of players (via their avatars) may be judged or determined, have a responsibility to maintain the integrity of those procedures. So as to be able do this, the virtual world proprietors must have the freedom to eliminate what they perceive to be short-cuts and to nullify the effects of what they determine to be deviant behaviour whenever these situations surface -- even if they arise in the real world. (Bartle, 2004) As long as this design principle is appreciated, virtual world proprietors mat uphold the basic integrity of the achievement structure. If their capacity to intervene as they deem necessary were taken away, then either another means of upholding the hierarchy must be created or some other hierarchy must be employed. If not, the virtual world will cease to function as a valuable location for identity exploration.

4. Servitude

"There are gods, and they are capricious, and have way more than ten commandments. Nobody knows how many because everyone clicked past them." (Koster, 2006)

In some ways, virtual worlds represent some of the most sophisticated online communities because of the potential for interaction and creativity. (Kosak, 2002)

As modern-day governing agreements evolve from earlier virtual world models, EULAs will continue to influence future online communities. Evidence of this influence is demonstrated by the fact that aspects of virtual world EULAs resemble the governing agreements of earlier technologies, such as Internet service providers. (Braman & Lynch, 2003)

Present-day virtual worlds thereby provide a model for a possible future of 'walled' Internet communities governed by private law. Like a software company, a virtual world proprietor "consistently imposes restrictive mass-market click-wrap licenses on its customers, who never learned to expect anything more." (Gibson, 2004)

Julian Dibbell (2003) compares EULAs to constitutionalism, suggesting that the "relation between the game companies and their paying 'citizens'" comes "close enough to blur the line between designing a game and framing a constitution." Edward Castronova (2002) described "the political structure of every virtual world" as consisting of "a group of all-powerful executives surrounded by mobs of angry, harassing suppliants." It has been suggested, most EULAs are far closer to a satire of the U.S. Constitution as EULA than a constitution. (Eisenberg, 2005) U.S. constitutional rights would be different under a EULA-type agreement modification format. An update to the Fourth Amendment using this format would read, "This amendment affects the Unreasonable Search and Seizure section of the Agreement. Under the new terms of this section, the right to unreasonable search and seizure shall not be abridged." (Id.) After attending an *EverQuest* player convention, Dibbell (2003) suggested that EULAs are "effectively renegotiated on a daily basis," because he witnessed dedicated participants complaining to proprietary representatives who were carefully taking notes on the participant concerns. However, Dibbell ignores the absence of any possible negotiation for the average potential participant who is confronted with the choice of whether or not to accept governing agreement terms by clicking the 'I accept' button. There is a big difference between a proprietor being aware of participants' concerns and participants having

the ability to negotiate their rights prior to their taking effect.

Professor Jack Balkin (2004) has put forward the concept of the 'company town' to apply to virtual worlds. The concept is based on the United States Supreme Court's description in *Marsh v Alabama,* 326 U.S. 501 (1946). A company town is one in which a business privately owns all of the public spaces, such as pavements and streets. *Marsh* established that privates businesses are held to the same standards for the protection of constitutional rights in these once-public spaces on the grounds that the private actor had become the state actor by usurping the traditional role of the state. (Id. at 508) Hence, a business can only restrict speech on its privately-owned pavements to the same extent that the state can limit speech on its public pavements. (Id.) Although the argument is fairly abstract at the moment, it would change the way EULAs are interpreted.

For example, *The Sims* was the first mass-market game to exploit user-created content. The game allows the player to control the lives of a number of avatars who go about their day attempting to find happiness. Some believe that possessions bring happiness, and thus, fill their homes with better furniture like stereo equipment and pianos. This is the focal point of their existence. (Herold, 2003) The game designers at Electronic Arts (EA) grasped that the players would be able to provide more content to each other than the designers could generate. So, they released tools to create content before the game was distributed. EA now claims that over 80% of the content in use was created by players. (Twist, 2005) This desire to customize their world extends to other games which do not support this kind of interaction.

Some players customized it into a darker world. Several underage users of the virtual world allegedly began engaging in explicit online sex chats with adults in exchange for simoleons. (Goldman, 2005) Peter Ludlow, a University of Michigan philosophy professor who styled himself a virtual world reporter and published the Alphaville Herald which chronicled newsworthy events and stories in Alphaville, the Sims Online's largest city, reported on this situation and his stories began receiving attention in the real-world press. EA responded by terminating Ludlow's account and thereby preventing him from existing or even accessing the virtual world. It did this under the pretext that his avatar maintained a commercial website for the Alphaville Herald in violation of the *Sims'* EULA. This EULA was agreed upon by Ludlow and EA, and the EULA gave EA the right to terminate the user account at its discretion. (Id.) This is censorship plain and simple.

Second Life made a strategic adaptation which altered the landscape of virtual worlds. It was no longer another virtual Disneyland, in which consumers experience what the company has provided for them. Linden Lab created a marketplace instead. Everybody could build and own property which could be utilized for one's own gain. However, returning to the case of Mark Bragg who was stripped of all his property in Second Life for engaging in dodgy land speculation. A player could take advantage of the online auction interface by going to unlinked URLs and prematurely starting land auctions that would not be visible to players who did not know how to access them. This allowed the player who initiated the auction to purchase land without having to face competing bides, allowing him to pay a significantly lower price. (Craig, 2006) In spite of the likely finding of illegality, Bragg paid Linden Labs $300 for a parcel of land called 'Taessot' upon which Bragg built a nightclub. (*Bragg v Linden Lab,* Pa. Magis. Dist. Ct., Chester Cty., No. CV-7606, complaint filed 5/2/06) Linden Labs acted promptly upon becoming aware of this practice of its users. In doing so, they froze Bragg's account, deleted his avatar, and denied him access to all of his virtual property. Two months later, they removed his name from the title of 'Taesoot' without compensation him, and prepared it for future resale. (Id.) Bragg attempted to negotiate with Linden Lab to no

avail, and then brought an action which included violation of consumer protection statutes, fraud, and breach of contract. (Id.) Bragg alleged that he relied upon statements made by Linden Lab, which indicated that property rights in *Second Life* were inviolable. In particular, Bragg cited to their press release in which Linden Lab altered its Terms of Service to "allow[] subscribers to retain full intellectual property protection for the digital content they create." (Press Release, Linden Lab, *Second Life Residents to Own Digital Creations* (Nov. 14, 2003)) In the same release, Phillip Rosedale said: "We believe our new policy recognizes the fact that persistent world users are making significant contributions to building these worlds and should be able to both own the content they create, and share in the value that is created. The preservation of users' property rights is a necessary step toward the emergence of genuinely real online worlds." (Id.) According to Bragg's complaint this statement and other like it were made primarily to attract players to the game by promising them rights in their virtual property and that those statements induced Bragg to invest in *Second Life*. Bragg's dispute with Linden Labs illustrates another limitation of EULAs, one in which property disputes are not easily adjudicated.

With this shift in ownership of property, Linden Lab undermined the traditional concept of stickiness based on control. The maximum control that traditional virtual world providers enjoy implies ownership over everything about and within the game, including any virtual property created by the players. As a result, users who want to switch to a different virtual world face huge costs. Nothing they have built in one virtual world--friendships, reputation, and identity, not to mention any savings in virtual currency--can be transferred to another world. This combination of lock-in and control makes it relatively easy for virtual worlds to retain their users. (Johnson, 2006) Before *Second Life*, competition among virtual worlds was largely about first-time users, as most people tend to belong to only one virtual world at a time. (Id.)

Since the grant of property ownership in *Second Life*, competition among virtual worlds is also about retention. Thus, the interaction between the game designers and the player community assists both the freedom to design and the freedom to play. It is the obvious aspect of the freedom to design together. However, all of these freedoms seem to rely, and rely heavily, on the flexibility of their End User License Agreements.

C. END USER LICENSE AGREEMENTS

"They say possession is nine-tenths of the law . . . I do know this: the remaining one-tenth is storytelling. Some say that the law is overwhelmingly concerned with questions of property. . . Fascinated by the power and scope of the intellectual property question, I failed to notice the beauty, if it's not too ridiculous to call it that, of the EULA question, which is that it's not about possession at all. In some fundamental way, it's about the same thing virtual worlds are about: creation, invention, the conjuring of abstract universes, the telling of stories. It's about that other tenth." (Dibbell, 2003)

People joining virtual worlds have the power of choice based on a number of factors, including good governance and favourable contractual terms. They can choose the society in which they want to live by migrating their online activities from place to place with much greater ease than real-world immigrants can move their physical lives. Virtual world providers who operate within this market-dynamic measure their success in terms of the size of their user base, and they consequently pursue two goals: attracting people to join their virtual world, and retaining them over time. The EULA is an intrinsic aspect of this process. However, there are some who think this is the most vital aspect of the creation of virtual

worlds and others who feel that EULAs hinder the growth of virtual worlds.

1. Proponents

Proponents claim that license agreements afford real advantages to players because of their efficiency, information, and variety of rights. EULAs 'promote efficient software transactions' by incorporating standardization of contract on a 'mass market scale.' (Gomulkiewicz & Williamson, 1996) By encouraging more efficient transactions, the price is lowered for the players. While the ensuing agreements may be 'contracts of adhesion,' standardized contracts offered to consumers of goods and services on essentially 'take it or leave it' basis without affording the consumer a realistic opportunity to bargain and under such conditions that the consumer cannot obtain the desired product or services except by acquiescing to the form contract. (*Cubic Corp. v Marty*, 185 C.A.3d 438 (Cal. Ct. App. 1986); *Standard Oil of Calif. v Perkins*, 347 F.2d 379 (9th Cir. 1965)) Most players "rather than relying on their own negotiating skills or knowledge of the relevant law," would be "better served by relying" on these contracts to protect their interests. (Gomulkiewicz & Williamson, 1996) The courts generally recognize that these contracts are not the result of traditionally 'bargained' contracts, so the trend is to relieve parties from onerous conditions imposed by such contracts. However, not every such contract is unconscionable. (*Lechmere Tire and Sales Co. v Burwick*, 277 N.E.2d 503 (Mass. 1972)) Since the Seventh Circuit in *ProCD v Zeidenberg*, 86 F.3d 1447 (7th Cir. 1996), courts have been willing to uphold shrinkwrap licenses as satisfying the assent requirements of contract law.

EULAs also provide valuable information to end users. Consumers do not tend to be familiar with copyright law, neither rights they are granted, nor what rights are denied. The EULA puts into writing contract terms and conditions which notify the end user of the "relationship between the parties and the range of rights available to each party." (Miller, 2003) Even though the EULA can impart valuable information, the player remains in ignorance of his rights if he does not read it. (Id.; Dibbell, 2003) Generally, it remains unlikely that courts will avoid any clauses in a EULA for unconscionability as long as players do not care about intellectual property rights because they use the virtual world for entertainment not income. This is changing as business is booming in virtual worlds these days.

Licensing agreements present a guaranteed definite bundle of rights to consumers at the lowest price. Occasionally, EULAs grant players more rights than they would have had under traditional intellectual property law. For example, many licensing agreements permit the user to make and use a second copy of a licensed program, which would be an infringing activity under copyright law. (Gomulkiewicz & Williamson, 1996) Furthermore, software licensing agreements clarify the collection of rights regarding products that are frequently protected by numerous and various intellectual property laws by generating a single document itemising these rights.

Although companies may withhold rights that players would have been guaranteed under intellectual property law, this refusal generally is intended to protect corporate investment. The rights withheld tend to be ones that most players would never employ. "The law should not force mass market software publishers to burden the price of their software by requiring publishers to offer rights which most users are not interested in acquiring." (Gomulkiewicz & Williamson, 1996) At the State of Play Conference in November 2003, Linden Lab made what turned out to be an important strategic move. It granted its users the right to own the intellectual property to their creations, and thereby introduced the concept of transferable property into their virtual world. In the *Second Life* Terms of Service, Linden "acknowledges and agrees that ... you will retain any and

all applicable copyright and/or other intellectual property rights with respect to any Content you create using the Service." *Second Life* Terms of Service, *supra*, § 5.3. However, in the same section, Linden also reserves some rights, such as "a royalty-free, fully paid-up, perpetual, irrevocable, non-exclusive right and license to use and reproduce (and to authorize third parties to use and reproduce) any of your Content" for marketing or support purposes. Id. Further, Linden states generally that all data on its servers are subject to deletion, alteration or transfer. See id. § 4.3. (Ondrejka, 2005)

Because virtual worlds are nothing but information, if users can own their intellectual property in virtual worlds, they can own whatever they build and create. Hence, 'property' is information, and 'power' is the ability to control information. (Nimmer & Krauthaus, 1994; Barlow, 1994) The creation and protection of property is a central function of government. The virtual world has become a company town. "Economists describe [information as] 'public goods'. Once released, further disseminations of information cannot be prevented without the aid of law." (Nimmer & Krauthaus, 1994) As the for-profit corporations are now fulfilling all of the municipal functions that are normally provided by the state, these corporations are now subjected to the same legal requirements as a state actor. (Balkin, 2004)

The impact of *Second Life*'s decision to grant intellectual property rights extends to yet another level. When players leave, they experience lowered switching costs. This is not just true between virtual worlds, but also between a virtual world and the real world. For example, one software programmer took a game he created in *Second Life* to the real world and sold it in the real world to a start-up offering games for mobile phones. The programmer made both virtual and real money by commercializing his software in both realms. (Grimes, 2005) They are like merchants moving from one marketplace to the next, or holders of resources (such as capital) selecting a suitable jurisdiction in a time of globalization. If participants can join a virtual world and port their extant informational property to that environment, virtual world providers have less incentive to offer their own content. *Second Life* will soon offer its users a technical means to 'export' intellectual property created in *Second Life*. Users will then be able to take objects they have created in *Second Life* and export them into a file format that users can use in other software packages, and presumably other virtual worlds. Linden Lab feels this will stimulate users to create in *Second Life*-- they will not have to fear that their creations' fate is tied to Second Life. (Cory Ondrejka, CTO, Linden Lab, Remarks at the Berkman Center Luncheon Series (Nov. 27, 2005))

Virtual world providers may evolve from content providers to facility providers - that is, providers of virtual space or real estate, which will be filled by the informational property that its participants either bring along from other worlds or create while they are members. These conditions, in turn, weaken virtual world providers' ability to use content to retain customers. There are three primary strategies by which they can differentiate themselves and gain a competitive advantage:

1. **Content:** Virtual world providers may offer a more immersive experience and convincing simulacrum than their competition, with better graphics and richer content. Because creating new content takes time and effort and requires a significant, continuous investment in product development, differentiating on product are both the most obvious and the most costly strategy. It requires a continuous and expanding revenue stream, which can be generated either by attracting more users or raising the price for the existing user base. The revenue stream will have to increase over time, as established virtual world providers with their growing legacy software foundation face new competitors, which use the latest in software tools. Thus,

modifying and adapting existing virtual worlds to meet the demands of users who compare it to the latest new virtual realms becomes more expensive over time.

2. **Price:** Virtual world providers may lower their price, attracting users by offering a more affordable experience. Given relatively high fixed costs and relatively low recurring costs, virtual world providers may find this an attractive option. However, this strategy has a significant downside, as the market for virtual worlds has shown limited price elasticity. Joining a virtual world generally entails a significant time investment: users must not only acclimate to the software and the geography of the virtual space, but also build both relationships with new people and trustworthy reputations for their avatars. The differential between the relatively small monthly fee of $12 paid to a virtual world provider and the value associated with time invested in a virtual world translates into price inelasticity, and may explain why many virtual world providers offer their subscriptions at roughly the same price points. (Koster, 2005) He estimated the cost of building a top-flight game at $12 million in 2005.

3. **Regulatory Framework:** Finally, virtual world providers may compete by offering users a virtual environment more aligned to users' expectations and demands. For example, a company could provide its users with a more user-centric rule-making and enforcement framework; though, as the cases of LambdaMOO and MediaMOO exemplify, devising a suitable governance structure is difficult. For an analysis of the complex implications of such regulatory competition in the area of U.S. environmental regulation. For example, Richard L. Revesz (1992) stated: "[I]nterstate competition can be seen as competition among producers of a good--the right to locate within the jurisdiction.

These producers compete to attract potential consumers of that good--firms interested in locating in the jurisdiction." A real-world example of a jurisdiction courting investors is the Emirate of Dubai, where businesses domiciled in a government-sponsored business park called Dubai Internet City are promised to be issued a "Certificate of Incorporation ... within mere hours." (Dubai Internet City, Incorporation Services) Similarly situated Singapore is trying to attract businesses by entirely committing itself to excellence in serving its citizens. (Ma, 2000) Ma attributes Singapore's economic success at least partly to its modernized public service. At the same time, competition for existing users heats up due to a newfound ability for users to take their intellectual property with them when they migrate from one virtual world to another.

Providers can refuse to follow the *Second Life* model. They can continue to compete on the content they design and offer in their virtual worlds. Nevertheless, once tens of thousands of users start designing their own content, and possess all the incentives inherent in the ownership of the intellectual property rights to their creations, the comparatively limited amount of content that providers create in-house with dozens or at best hundreds of employees cannot sustain any provider's competitive edge. At the 2005 Austin Game Conference, *Second Life* engineer Jim Purbrick was quoted as saying that the 60,000 then members of the world were creating content equivalent to what 300 full-time designers could develop. (Terdiman, 2005) Network effects will only intensify this problem. Users will join the virtual worlds with the most content and activity. As the ability of providers to compete through content they control slowly erodes, they will eventually be forced to switch to an alternative differentiation strategy. Unfortunately for these world creators, lowering prices will not be a long-term solution for traditional virtual world

providers competing with virtual world providers that grant intellectual property rights. Because *Second Life*-type providers do not have to create their own content, these virtual world providers can use the resulting savings either to lower user fees or to create an even better environment. In September 2005, *Second Life* dropped its monthly subscription model entirely, substituting this model with fees associated with buying and maintaining land. CNET News.com estimates that these land-use charges are netting Linden Lab $400,000 per month. (Id.) Conversely, traditional providers will have to continue to invest in content creation. The resulting cost disadvantage will make it impractical in the long run for traditional providers to compete on price.

While new users may choose worlds like *Second Life*, the high switching costs for users of traditional virtual worlds is likely to dissuade them from moving to *Second Life*-type worlds, at least in the short run. In spite of that, due to network externalities, each user who does make the switch to a *Second Life*-type world lowers the benefits for all other users of their original virtual world by lowering the revenue stream available to the traditional providers for creating new content. Network externalities make some virtual worlds more attractive for people to join: joining a larger community provides more possibilities for interaction and expansion of one's social network than joining a smaller virtual world. It has become widely accepted that, according to the so-called Metcalfe's law (1996), the value of a network is proportional to the square of the number of users. Over time, the traditional virtual world providers may find themselves in a challenging double spiral of progressively lower revenue available for content creation and diminishing network value due to falling numbers of participants. (Gartner, 2000) It may not happen immediately, but, over time, economics may force traditional virtual worlds to follow *Second Life*'s lead.

For a short analysis of how this dynamic operates within a power law relationship, regulating the populations of virtual worlds, see a comment by Raph Koster on TerraNova (2005): "Back in 2003 I did a graph of available MMORPGs in the Western market (which meant it included a few Asian games). What I found was a power-law distribution typical of a network effect. One characteristic of these distributions over time in many domains is that the curve is essentially invariant. For example, the curve of "biggest cities in the US" has always been the same shape. The #1 city has always been x times larger than the #2 city, and so on, although which cities these were has changed over time. When a city rose in population or declined, it was as if the other cities 'knew' what new numbers to adjust themselves to in order to retain the proper shape of the curve. According to this theory, once you get bigger than the biggest game, you're on an inevitable path to the next 'station' on the graph. Once you fall in size, you're on a track to shrink until you fit the curve."

Another argument is that 'play' conditions are a commons area which affords a persuasive conceptual foundation for the game EULAs as they are currently written. EULAs imagined and described as contracts that inhibit individuals from whittling away the play-ness of the space, for the benefit of all users. (Catronova, 2004) In other words, the right kind of EULA can make everyone happy. The fact that virtual worlds are marketed as 'play' or 'games' should not change the fact that a contract has been made. In *SEC v SG, Ltd.*, 265 F.3d 42 (1st Cir., 2001), the court considered whether a 'virtual stock market' 'game' was essentially a real stock market for purposes of SEC fraud regulations. The district court characterized the purchases of virtual shares as a "clearly marked and defined game", that was not part of the commercial world, and thus beyond the ambit of federal securities law. (Id. at 47) However, the First Circuit reversed, finding the virtual stock market qualified as an investment contract within the SEC's jurisdiction. (Id. 48 -55) Of particular interest was the court's dismissal of the defendant's

claim that their virtual market was only a 'game' and not a real commercial instrument: "We do not gainsay the obvious correctness of the district court's observation that investment contracts lie within the commercial world. Contrary to the district court's view, however, this locution does not translate into a dichotomy between business dealing, on the one hand, and games, on the other hand, as a failsafe way for determining whether a particular financial arrangement should (or should not) be characterized as an investment contract. . . . As long as the [relevant legal test] is satisfied, the instrument must be classified as an investment contract. Once that has occurred, 'it is immaterial whether the enterprise is speculative or non-speculative or whether there is a sale of property with or without intrinsic value.' It is equally immaterial whether the promoter depicts the enterprise as a serious commercial venture or dubs it a game." (Id. 47 – 48, citations omitted)

Properly enforced EULAs make every virtual world its own parallel legal universe protected and insulated in so far as possible from the incapacity of current law to imagine its strangeness and possibilities. The missing link in the law is a broad policy position that play spaces are a unique collective good and part of the collective commons, whose value can only be maintained under specific restraints on individual behaviour. The EULA created the restrictive legal regime that is *Dark Age of Camelot*. *Dark Age of Camelot* is one of the world's fastest-growing online role-playing games based on the King Arthur legends, Viking mythology and Celtic lore. There are prohibitions against buying and selling goods and characters on eBay. It has a standard clause stipulating that copyright to everything the player says or does is within its purview. This perhaps ought to have a separate and distinct legal standing as a document that establishes a place of play. The issue is that *Dark Age of Camelot* has no unique value at all as a place of play unless the EULA is effective. (Miller, 2003) Without the EULA, *Dark Age of Camelot* is not a play space. It would be like a suburb of Bradford -- a place that used to be marshland, but now has houses, businesses, and athletic fields, all of which are entirely indistinguishable under law from the house, businesses and athletic fields of Bradford itself. Yet, there is nothing mentioned about such examples of play, in current law. No law pronounces how or when this can be done. Virtual worlds can be viewed as a specific case of David R. Johnson and David Post's (1996) general argument that cyberspace is unique and separate enough to warrant special legal treatment.

Meanwhile, the EULA may effortlessly provide the fundamentally open alternate reality of an online marketplace like *Second Life*. A place where the buying and selling of virtual items and virtual real estate is promoted; and the users retain all intellectual property rights. As for that rather interesting point, the EULA can generate interesting parallel realities outside the sphere of games. A prime example is the General Public License which is the legal keystone of Linux and other open-source software. For all intents and purposes, it is a EULA – as are the various licenses designed by Creative Commons to fashion out a place for other alternatives to copyright. However, community that lacks a "practical agreement on a conception of justice must also lack the necessary basis for political community." (MacIntyre, 1990) Virtual worlds are inhabited by representatives of all different nations and cultures. Each has its own definition of justice. EULAs permit each community to define its own concept of justice. Therefore the convergence between law, justice, and contract is also relevant in the context of private law-making or legislation between individuals. (Id.) In a society which promotes individual autonomy, justice may be defined as keeping one's agreements. In essence, this would be contract as justice. (Rosenfeld, 1985) This approach to defining social norms of behaviour is that justice is accomplished without any authority imposing its view of social good on unwilling individuals. (Id.) In a society which operationally defines justice

as a function of contract, no one may force his views on others. Nor can anyone be compelled to do anything that he has not previously agreed to do. Therefore, the only just institutions are those that are agreed upon by each member of society (or in this case the world designers.) (Id.)

2. Critics

Code and authoritarian EULAs can become the primary law that participants encounter, and they remain subject to arbitrary decision-making by proprietors. (Balkin, 2004) This power imbalance and lack of effective means of redress suggest significant governance problems. The absence of law also leads to disputes between participants, particularly as participants spend more and more amounts of time in virtual worlds. (Terdiman, 2005) Critics complain that software licensing intends to shield the companies to the disadvantage of both the consumer and the function of intellectual property law. Intellectual property law strikes a careful balance between the rights of intellectual property owners and the rights of users. (Lemley, 1995)

Legally binding license agreements, for example access to a database which the user would agree to, compel these users to conduct themselves in a manner which is far more restricted than copyright law would have required. McManis, (1999) contends that unless the proposed Article 2B is altered, it will result in securing 'all of the benefits of federal copyright law, with none of its limitation'. As such, vendors who draft EULA provisions often seek to expand their rights and limit the rights of participants. EULAs are drafted by corporate attorneys to safeguard corporate interests in corporate products. Any supposed benefit to players is merely a happy consequence which also happens to be for the security of corporate concerns – "to prevent people from hacking into or altering the program's source code." (Rolston, 2000)

Hence, the EULA is a powerful tool for controlling ownership in virtual space. Reading a software licensing agreement can be a disturbing experience. Not only is it disturbing, but it may strip you of ownership in your creative works in a virtual world. However, software publishers/ game designers who offer access to commercial virtual worlds use licensing agreements to protect their economic interests. Through the use of these agreements, most designers deny ownership to participants who exercise their creativity. (Miller, 2003)

The *Ultima Online* License Agreement, in outlining a subscriber's rights in paragraph 5(b), explains that the player relinquishes all rights to personally-created works of authorship: "You acknowledge and agree that all characters created, and items acquired and developed as a result of game play are part of the Software and Service and are the sole property of Origin Systems." The player not only loses any rights of copyright claims to the character or item that he creates, but he also transfers ownership of his creation to the software publisher. This remains true against the author, even if the character or item is uncopyrightable. The transfer meets the statutory requirements set out in section 204 of the Copyright Act: it is in writing and signed, at least digitally. (17 U.S.C. §204(a) (2000))

Ultima Online is not alone. *EverQuest*, in paragraph 8 of its EULA, claims all intellectual property relating to the game: "We and our suppliers shall retain ownership of all intellectual property rights relating to or residing in the CD-ROM, the Software, and the Game." While this language appears at first blush to be inclusive than that of the *Ultima Online* Agreement, Sony's enforcement of its EULA has demonstrated stronger application:

"Sections 7 and 8 of this Agreement provide that we own all property rights in the game, subject to your license to play the game. To further emphasize these points, effective immediately, the following language shall be added to the end of section 9 of the User Agreement and as a section in the EverQuest rules of conduct: "You may not

sell or auction any EverQuest characters, items, coin or copyrighted material.""

While this may not serve as a complete transfer of copyright in player creations, the player's rights have been limited, and the aggressive stance taken by Sony in protecting the rights embodied in their EULA suggests that they encompass a very broad reading of their claim to intellectual property in the game. (Sandoval, 2000) Although the EULA may function to effectively transfer ownership of the copyright from the player to the hosting company, the author does retain the right to cancel transfer – but only after 35 years. (17 U.S.C. §203(a)(3) (2000)) For a gamer's internet game creation, this is a life sentence. In 35 years, his creation will be worthless. The provisions for cancelling transfer do not provide the gamer with any practical tools for recapturing ownership of his creations.

Sony Online Entertainment has had to reverse its negative stance towards player-to-player auctions of virtual objects. After long and bitter opposition to the sale of *EverQuest* objects on eBay and IGE, Sony Online Entertainment saw that market demand and revenue opportunities of virtual object sales were too great to ignore. (Smedley, 2005) In July 2005, Sony launched Station Exchange, a site which the Senior Vice President and CFO, John Needham, characterized as 'SOE-bay.' (Zelfden, 2005) In its first three months of operation, Station Exchange had $540,000 in real money transfers of virtual objects, with Sony taking a ten percent commission on each transaction. (Parloff, 2005) Sony Online now plans to roll out the auction model to its other virtual worlds, and may even add a product that will have no monthly subscription fee, but will derive its revenues from selling virtual objects and services to its players. (Grimwell, 2005)

By acknowledging the existence of saleable virtual property and directly profiting from its existence, Sony has opened itself up to the arguments of equity. If Sony can profit, then player ought to be able to develop a stake in the fruits of their labour by creating virtual property. In an attempt to avoid liability for harm to players' property, Sony strictly disclaims any right of a player to establish a virtual property interest: "You promise, therefore, that you will never assert or bring any claim or suit against SOE, its licensor(s), any Sony Company, or any employees of any of the above, which is related to or based on (I) a claim that you 'own' any virtual goods in any game, (II) a claim for the 'value' of virtual goods if SOE deletes them (and/or terminates your account(s) . . . (III) a claim for the 'value' of virtual goods that you may lose if SOE does anything that it is entitled to do pursuant to any provision of the exchange agreement, this agreement, the game's rules of conduct, SOE's terms of service and/or (IV) a claim that the 'value' of any virtual goods has increased or decreased by virtue of any game modification that SOE has made or will make. All of the above applies whether on an exchange enabled server or on a non-exchangeable server."

Sony wants to have it both ways. They want to retain control of the game narrative by explicitly maintaining the ability to delete or modify virtual property at any time, while profiting from the exchange of virtual goods on its server. They rely purely on this EULA which feebly attempts to prevent players from forming any expectations of 'owning' virtual property by expressly denying a player's ability to do so. "You agree that SOE retains the unfettered right to modify its games and all aspect of characters, items, and coin (collectively 'virtual goods') therein. . . . You further acknowledge that SOE can and will, in its discretion, modify features, functions or abilities of any element of the game or any Virtual Goods substantially more effective or functional, or less effective or functional, more common or less common, or eliminated entirely."

Despite the uncertainty of fundamental questions about the nature of virtual property, the vast majority of virtual worlds exist in a property paradigm. As Professor Lastowka and Professor Hunter (2004) note, "[t]he real property systems within all of these worlds mostly conform to the norms of modern private property systems, with free alienation of property, transfers based on the local currency, and so forth," which is unsurprising given that virtual worlds are largely the productions of 'property-owning corporations.' Unfortunately, this endorsement by world designers of alienability of property within the world, while discouraging alienability outside, provides confusion within the world. Further confusion arises for participants who are not allowed to own property within their virtual worlds because there are virtual world proprietors who do allow customers to have property rights within and without their virtual worlds. In a Press Release, *Second Life Residents to Own Digital Creations*, Linden Labs stated that "[p]articipants can create Content on Linden's servers in various forms. Linden acknowledges and agrees that, subject to the terms and conditions of this Agreement, including without limitation the limited licenses granted by you to Linden herein, you will retain any and all applicable copyright and/or other intellectual property rights with respect to any Content you create using the Service."

Again, there is both confusion and hypocrisy in the way virtual world designers attempt to restrict out-of-world sales of virtual items. When Blizzard Entertainment, the proprietor/designer of *World of Warcraft*, (2004) stated that it did "not allow 'in game' items to be sold for real money" and that it would take any and all actions necessary to stop this behaviour," they justified the statement by arguing that such trading "is illegal, but it also has the potential to damage the game economy and overall experience for the many thousand of others who play *World of Warcraft* for fun." This pronouncement prompted one *World of Warcraft* participant to contrast personal experience of selling game items from other virtual worlds with the stern warning from Blizzard. The participant asked, "Is it illegal to sell your account when you're done playing the game? I know that in other games like D2 [Diablo II] and EQ [*Ever-Quest*] people sold their accounts with high level characters on E-Bay [sic] and other similar sites . . . was that illegal?" The apparent confusion of this participant's question reflects the fact that issues of property represent a serious dilemma within virtual worlds.

This dilemma is compounded by problems of unequal and incomplete enforcement. Strict proprietor/designer pronouncements regarding property rights, like Blizzard Entertainment's, suggest that proprietors are either concerned that they will have an enforcement problem if they do not attempt to use law-based intimidation, or that the situation appears in danger of slipping out of their control. (Terdiman, 2004) This is a reasonable fear considering the ease of transfer of virtual world items. (Castronova, 2003) The suggestion has been made that proprietors are hypocritical in their treatment of sellers of virtual property. Generally they enforce the trading prohibition, but allow the most dedicated participants, their best customers, to engage in transactions without legal consequences. Prof. Dan Hunter (2004) argues that virtual world companies "are often two-faced in their opposition to secondary market trading. Publicly, the Blizzards and Sony Onlines of the world say these virtual worlds are role-playing games and that the users want the games to be about play, said Hunter. 'If you talk to them in private,' he said, 'they will accept, or at least start to tell you, a significant number of the power players--the guys they count on to drive the world--if you didn't allow the transfer of these things, they would just head off into another (game)." To other participants, uneven enforcement of property transfer prohibitions by proprietors undermines participant motivation to obey the system. Uneven enforcement producing lack of faith in the governing system is one of the general consequences of an autocratic and arbitrary central rule. (Ostrovsky, 2005)

C. RAMIFICATIONS

Lastowka and Hunter (2004) argue that "We will likely see courts rejecting [End-User License Agreements (EULAs)] to the extent that they place excessive restrictions on the economic interests of users. And since there is already so much money and property at stake in these worlds - and there will be significantly more in the future - we can expect a large number of lawsuits rooted in these property-rights disputes."

Let us return to *Project Entropia*. Recently, *Project Entropia* sold a virtual space resort, located in the "treacherous but mineral rich Paradise V asteroid belt." MindArk has a unique business model in which they allow people to play their game for free and simply charge them real dollars for in-game currency. Once in the game, players can create wealth by killing monsters and retrieving treasure from the corpses worth pennies or tens of cents. Some of the treasures on the monsters' corpses, however, are worth the equivalent of over $1000. The wealth that a player has in the game can be transferred out of the game. MindArk will a player you in real-world currency when the player requests a withdrawal. (BBC News, 2006) The space resort will provide the purchaser with 1000 virtual apartment deeds; 100 virtual store deeds in a virtual shopping mall; taxation rights; land management, event management, and marketing management systems; and a landing point for new avatars. New arrivals, or "newbs," can choose to start their experience in the virtual world of *Project Entropia* at the space resort. The advantage for the space resort owner of hosting new arrivals is that the new arrivals will invariably spend in-game money, which the space station owner can withdraw from the game, essentially converting it to real-world money. The space resort was originally set for a $0.10 starting price with a pre-auction buyout price of $100,000. Within a few days of the announcement, the buyout price was met by Jon 'NeverDie' Jacobs, who is known as Skalman in-game. Construction on the space resort is scheduled to be complete by 21 December 2005.

So what did Mr. Jacobs purchase? According to the EULA, "MindArk retains all rights, title, and interest in all parts including, but not limited to Avatars and Virtual Items." (*Project Entropia* EULA, Section 6 "Ownership and Transactions.") The contract further reads: "As part of your interactions with [*Project Entropia*], you may acquire, create, design, or modify Virtual items, but you agree that you will not gain any ownership interest whatsoever in any Virtual item and you hereby assign to MindArk all of your rights, title and interest in any such Virtual item." (Id.) If MindArk retains all rights to all virtual items, including the space station, then what did the company sell to Mr. Jacobs for $100,000? One may argue that MindArk sold the right for Mr. Jacobs to "play space resort owner." However, his purchase has real world implications. He can sell the 1000 virtual apartment deeds and the 100 virtual store deeds for in-game currency and then withdraw the in-game currency from MindArk, thereby converting the currency into real-world money – all within the limits of the EULA. If this is possible, then he must own something. Of course, if Mr. Jacobs own only those rights to play space resort owner, then he may be selling the right to play apartment owner when he sells the apartment deed to another player in the game.

This has a number of implications. First, it appears that, notwithstanding the language of the EULA, MindArk is selling some right in the property to Mr. Jacobs. This is not the case of a player-to-player sale of goods on eBay which the game company has not sanctioned, though these too must be considered in a virtual property regime. Here, there is a case where the game company is presumably hoping to profit off of the creation and sale of a particular part of a virtual world. Mr. Jacobs has agreed to purchase that virtual property. One can argue that Mr. Jacobs has agreed to the EULA and therefore knows that he is purchasing nothing more than a right to play. He should un-

derstand that he does not *own* anything. He should have thought about the fact that the EULA clearly states that the game provider retains all rights to the space station.

However, one might also consider what the game company is really selling. The website on which the auction was hosted clearly states that 'ownership interest' in that virtual space station includes 1000 apartment deeds, 100 shop deeds, and other virtual items. (Space Resort for Sale by Public Auction) Is this in direct conflict with the End User License Agreement? If the assignment of all virtual property rights in the EULA controls the interpretation of any 'ownership interest' listed in the offer, or if the represented 'ownership interests' were merely rights to play certain aspects of the game in the first instance, then the question remains: Again, what did Mr. Jacobs buy?

Consider this hypothetical: The EULA suggests that MindArk can sell the virtual space station to Mr. Jacobs and terminate his account the next day for no reason. *Project Entropia* EULA, Section 5, "Termination" states that "MindArk may terminate [Mr. Jacobs' account] upon notice … [and] without reason . . ." According to the EULA, he owns merely a right to play 'space station owner' but little else. Can the rights transferred really be so ephemeral?

Perhaps, since the EULA had already been signed at the time the offer was made, it is possible that a court would interpret the offer, insomuch as its terms conflicted with the EULA, to supersede the terms of the EULA. If this is the case, then the ownership interest of Mr. Jacobs may be less ephemeral. The offer for sale, under the heading of 'ownership rights' offered, e.g., 1000 'Apartment Deeds' and a "[s]pawning point for newcomers to *Project Entropia*[, which] will enable the owner to market his Space station Resort outside *Project Entropia* so that the newcomers will arrive directly at the resort . . ." How do the terms of the offer interact with the terms of the EULA? The situation is not entirely clear. It is possible to read the

1000 apartment deeds as implying a right to sell the leases to other players. The sale of the deeds to Mr. Jacobs may indicate that he has the right to retain his account, or at least the ability to sell the deeds, thereby at least partially overriding the termination clause of the EULA.

The 'spawning point' term may provide more evidence of overriding the termination clause of the EULA. The term implies that the owner should be able to market his space station to new players, which implies that he will have a continuing ownership right of some sort. If he has a right to market the space station over time, then a court may find that Mr. Jacobs has a right to continue playing the game, or otherwise maintain pecuniary control over the space station, in opposition to the termination clause. (Meehan, 2005)

Additionally, the plain terms of the offer may also override the EULA's 'ownership interest' term. The EULA states that the players of the game cannot 'own' any virtual item. However, the offer clearly includes 'ownership interests.' The question remains, however, what, exactly, is 'owned?'

Notwithstanding the extent to which offer for the space station overrides some of the terms of the EULA, if MindArk acted on the termination clause of the EULA and Mr. Jacobs sued Mind-Ark, then the court may perceive the EULA or the effective contract governing the sale under the EULA as unconscionable. This is likely to be Mr. Bragg's course of action in *Bragg v Linden Lab,* Pa. Magis. Dist. Ct., Chester Cty., No. CV-7606, complaint filed 5/2/06.

Unconscionability requires both procedural and substantive unconscionability. The EULA, in light of such sales, may be seen as substantively unconscionable, since the terms are clearly favourable to MindArk. Procedural unconscionability would be harder to prove. Mr. Jacobs received information on the clause when he clicked-through the EULA. One may be able to argue that Mr. Jacobs would not have an ability to understand the terms of the contact. However, the contract

is not overly complex or obscure. The strongest case for procedural unconscionability may lie in the combination of unequal bargaining power, MindArk's likely take-it-or-leave it posture, and the lack of business necessity for the harsh terms. First, there is clearly unequal bargaining power. Mr. Jacobs was in a very unfavourable bargaining position with respect to MindArk who wields almost unlimited power against his interest in his *Project Entropia* account under the EULA.

Second, although not based on any details about the negotiation, this may also be seen as a contract of adhesion given the likely take-it-or-leave-it posture of MindArk. MindArk would have been likely to have a take-it-or-leave it posture, if the issue even came up, considering the fact that they had eight parties display 'serious interest' before the auction even started. Third, a court may find that the terms of the EULA are unfairly harsh and are not necessary for business.

Mr. Jacob's hypothetical parallels *Williams v Walker-Thomas Furniture Co.*, 121 U.S. App. D.C. 315 (D.C. Cir. 1965), where the court held unconscionable a contract entered into by the Williams for the purchase of furniture on credit from Walker-Thomas. The contract allowed Walker-Thomas, upon the Williams' non-payment for a single piece of furniture, to repossess any furniture that the Williams purchased from the company for which there was an outstanding balance. When the Williams missed a payment, Walker-Thomas repossessed multiple pieces of furniture. *Walker-Thomas* parallels the hypothetical in that both purchasers were given take-it-or-leave contracts for purchase. In *Walker-Thomas* the court remanded to the trial court for a determination of whether the furniture company needed to have such unfavourable terms. (Id.)

In this hypothetical, MindArk may argue that it needs to be able to control the use of the virtual property it provides to its users and needs to be able to terminate user accounts for any reason. However, as described earlier, the virtual property theory of bits-in-context may provide a more reasonable distribution of the rights between Mr. Jacobs and MindArk. If this theory, or any theory of virtual property rights, provides a more reasonable distribution of property rights than the one-sided split provided by the EULA, then a court could find that the restrictive virtual property terms of the EULA should be vacated "in the light of the general commercial background and the commercial needs of the particular trade or case." (Id.)

MindArk, of course, has much incentive to avoid destroying virtual property interests. They make all of their revenue from sales of virtual property. If users felt that the company did not protect virtual property interests well, then the users would discontinue buying virtual property from the game makers and MindArk would diminish its only revenue stream.

The law, and not just the economics of game providers, should provide incentives to protect virtual property. If MindArk's economic interests were all that governed the protection of virtual property, then MindArk might encounter situations where they have perverse incentives. Protection of virtual property would not be directly based on the interests of the users, but instead would be based on the self-interested calculus of MindArk, which would balance the gains from 'takings' against the gains from continuing to enforce ephemeral virtual property interests.

Consider, for example, if Mr. Jacobs' character Skalman became unpopular within the game because of a rumour that he is a MindArk employee. Getting rid of an unpopular character may be seen in the virtual society of *Project Entropia* as a net positive action notwithstanding the unpopular player's loss of virtual property. That is, the damage done to MindArk's reputation by destroying virtual property may be outweighed by the benefit afforded to their reputation by excommunicating the unpopular player. The destruction of virtual property in that case may have no negative real-world economic repercussions for MindArk. If this were the case, MindArk would have an incentive to terminate Mr. Jacobs account:

it would get rid of an unpopular avatar, Skalman, and it would allow them to resell the virtual space station, presumably for another $100,000. Virtual property really should be protected by law rather than relying solely on the economic self-interest of the company. (Meehan, 2005)

REFERENCES

Anarchy Online. (n.d.). *Rules of Conduct*. Retrieved from http://anarchy-online.com/content/corporate/rulesofconduct.html

Balkin, J. (2004). Virtual Liberty: Freedom to Design and Freedom to Play in Virtual Worlds. *Va. L. Rev. 90*(2043).

Barlow, J. P. (1994). *The Economy of Ideas: A Framework for Rethinking Patents and Copyrights in the Digital Age*, Wired. BBC News, *Cash Card Taps Virtual Game Funds*, 2006/05/02, available at http://news.bbc.co.uk/go/pr/fr/-/1/hi/technology/4953620.stm

Bartle, R. (2004). *Law Is Code*. Posting to Terra Nova. Retrieved from http://terranova.blogs.com/terr_nova/2004/08/law_is_code.html

Bartle, R. (2004). *Designing Virtual Worlds*. Berkeley, CA: New Riders Publishing.

Bartle, R. (2004). *Virtual Worldliness: What The Imaginary Asks of The Real, 19 N.* Y.L. Sch. R.

BBS. (2005). *The Documentary*. United States: Bovine Ignition Systems.

Bell, A. G. (1972). *Games Playing with Computers*. London: George Allen & Unwin Ltd.

Benkler, Y. (2003). Through the Looking Glass: Alice and the Constitutional Foundations of the Public Domain. *Law & Contemp. Probs. 66*(173).

Benkler, Y. (2003, November 14). *Remarks at State of Play Conference*. Retrieved from http://www.nyls.edu/pages/1430.asp

Berkowitz, S. (1994, July 3). Columbian Player's Death Stuns, Angers World Soccer Community. *Washington Post,* A27.

Berners-Lee, T. (1998 September). *Semantic Web Road Map.* Retrieved from http://www.w3.org/DesignIssues/Semantic.html

Braman, S., & Lynch, S. (2003). Advantage ISP: Terms of Service as Media Law . In *Thinking Rights and Regulations: Institutional Responses to New Communications Technologies.* Cambridge, MA: MIT Press.

Burnstein, M. (2004). Towards a New Standard for First Amendment Review of Structural Media Regulation. *N.Y.U. L. Rev., 79*(1030).

Campbell, J. (1949). *The Hero with a Thousand Faces.* Princeton, NJ: Princeton University Press.

Carter, G. (2002). It's My ['ll Sell It If I Want To. *The Adrenaline Vault.* Retrieved from http://www.avault.com/articles/getarticle.asp?name=mmogsell]. *Time, I.*

Casamiquela, R. (2002). Contractual Assent and Enforceability in Cyberspace. *Berkeley Tech L.J., 17*(475).

Castronova, E. (2002). *On Virtual Economies.* The Gruter Institute of Working Papers on Law, CESifo Working Paper No. 752.

Castronova, E. (2003). *The Price of 'Man' and 'Woman': A Hedonic Pricing Model of Avatar Attributes in a Synthetic World.* CESifo Working Paper Series No. 957

Castronova, E. (2004). The Right to Play. *N.Y.L.Sch. L. Rev. 49*(185).

Cohen, J. (1998). Lochner in Cyberspace: The New Economic Orthodoxy of 'Rights Management.' *Mich. L. Rev. 97*(462).

Craig, K. (2006, May 18). Second Life Land Deal Goes Sour. *Wired News.* Retrieved from http://www.wired.com/news/culture/0,70909-0.html

Dibbell, J. (1998). *My Tiny Life.* New York: Henry Holt & Co.

Dibbell, J. (2003). *OWNED! Intellectual Property in the Age of eBayers, Gold Farmers, and Other Enemies of the Virtual State or, How I Learned To Stop Worrying and Love the End-User License Agreement.* Retrieved from http://www.juliandibbell.com/texts/owned.html

Dreyfus, H. (1992). *What Computers Still Can't Do: A Critique of Artificial Reason.* Cambridge, MA: MIT Press.

Easterbrook, F. (1996). Cyberspace and the Law of the Horse. *U. Chi. Legal F., 207.*

Eisenberg, E. (2005, March 25). Important Changes to Your Citizenship Agreement. *Slate.* Retrieved from http://slate.msn.com/id/2115254

Electronic Privacy Information Center. (1997 December). *Faulty Filters: How Content Filters Block Access to Kid-Friendly Information on the Internet.* Retrieved from http://www2.epic.org/reports/filter-report.html

EverQuest. (n.d.). *Rules of Conduct.* Retrieved from http://eqlive.station.sony.com/support/customer_service/cs_rules_of_conduct.jsp.

EverQuest. (n.d.). *End User License Agreement.* Retrieved from http://everquest.station.sony.com/support/security/eula.jsp

Gartner, J. (2000, January 7). It's the End of TV as We Know It. *Wired News.* Retrieved from http://www.wired.com/news/technology/0,1282,33503,00.html

Gibson, J. (2004). Re-Reifying Data. *Notre Dame L. Rev., 80*(163).

Goldman, E. (2005). Symposium Review: Speech Showdowns at the Virtual Corral. *Santa Clara Comp. & High Tech. L. J., 21*(845).

Gomulkiewicz, R. & Williamson, M. (1996). A Brief Defence of Mass Market Software License Agreements. *Rutgers Computer & Tech. L.J., 22*(335).

Grimes, A. (2005, March 3). Digits. *Wall Street Journal*, B3.

Grimmelmann, J. (2003, December 4). *The State of Play: Free As In Gaming?* LawMeme at http://research.yale.edu/lawmeme/modules.php?name=News&file=article&sid=1290/

Grimmelmann, J. (2005 April 19). *Virtual Power Politics*. Retrieved from http://ssrn.com/abstract=707301

Grimwell, J. (2005, November 28). Sony Station Exchange to Be a Part of All SOE Games. *Gamer-God.com.* Retrieved from http://www.gamergod.com/article.php?article_id=2663

Helbreath, U. S. A. (n.d.). *Conduct Rules*. Retrieved from http://www.helbreathusa.com/rules.php

Herold, C. (2003, February 6). Win Friends, Influence People, or Just Aim and Fire. *N.Y. Times,* G5.

Huizinga, J. (1971). *Homo Ludens: A Study in the Play-Elements in Culture*. Boston, MA: Beacon Press.

Johnson, D.R. & Post, D. (1996). Law and Borders – The Rise of Law in Cyberspace. *Stan L. Rev.* 48(1367).

Johnson, S. (2006). When Virtual Worlds Collide. *Wired*. Retrieved from http://www.wired.com/wired/archive/14.04/collide_pr.html Kim, A. (1998 May). Killers Have More Fun. *Wired.* Retrieved from http://www.wired.com/wired/archive/6.05/ultima.html

Kosak, D. (2002, December 10). Second Life (PC). *GameSpy.Com.* Retrieved from http://archive.gamespy.com/previews/december02/secondlifepc/index.shtml

Kosak, D. (2003, November 13). The Future of Massively Multiplayer Gaming. *GameSpy.com.* Retrieved from http://archive.gamespy.com/amdmmog/week8/index.shtml

Koster, R. (1998, May 11). *The Man Behind the Curtain.* Retrieved from http://www.legendmud.org/raph/gaming/essay5.html

Koster, R. (2005, September 2). Posting to Terra Nova. Retrieved from http://terranova.blogs.com/terra_nova/2005/08/the_golden_1m_w.html

Koster, R. (2006, February 24). *What are the Lessons of MMORPGs Today?* Retrieved from http://www.raphkoster.com/2006/02/24/what-are-the-lessons-ofmmorpgs-today

Koster, R. (n.d.). *The Laws of Online World Design.* Retrieved from http://www.raphkoster.com/gaming/laws.shtml

Koster, R. (n.d.). *Moore's Wall: Technology Advances and Online Game Design.* Retrieved from http://www.raphkoster.com/gaming/moore.shtml

Krotoski, A. (2005, June 16). Online: Virtual Trade Gets Real: Buying Virtual Goods on the Internet is One Thing; Killing for It Is Quite Another. *The Guardian* (London), 23.

Lastowka, F.G. & Hunter, D. (2004). The Laws of the Virtual World. *Calif. L. Rev., 92*(1).

Lastowka, F.G. & Hunter, D. (2004). Virtual Crimes. *N.Y. L. Sch. L. Rev., 49*(293).

Lemley, M. (1995). Intellectual Property and Shrinkwrap Licenses. *S. Cal. L. Rev., 68*(1239).

Lessig, L. (1999). The Law of the Horse: What Cyberlaw Might Teach. *Harv. L. Rev., 113*(501).

Lessig, L. (2000). *Code and Other Laws of Cyberspace*. New York: Basic Books Lienhard, J. (1995). Address Reflections on Information, Biology, and Community. *Hous. L. Rev., 32*(303).

Ma, D. (2000). Delivering Results on the Ground: Improving Service to Citizens in Singapore. *Asian J. Pol. Sci., 8*(137).

MacIntyre, A. (1990). After Virtue . In Solomon, R. C., & Murphy, M. C. (Eds.), *What is Justice? Classic and Contemporary Readings*. Oxford: Oxford University Press.

Mayer-Schönberger, V. (2003). The Shape of Governance: Analyzing the World of Internet Regulation. *Va. J. Int'l L., 43*(605).

Mayer-Schönberger, V. & Crowley, J. (2006). Napster's Second Life? The Regulatory Challenges of Virtual Worlds. *Nw. U. L. Rev., 100*(1775).

McManis, C. (1999). The Privatization (or 'Shrink-Wrapping'). of American Copyright Law. *California Law Review, 87*(173).

Metcalfe, B. (1996, July 15). There Oughta Be a Law. *N.Y. Times,* D7 (Late Ed.).

Milgrom, P., North, D., & Weingast, B. (1990). The Role of Institutions in the Revival of Trade: The Law Merchant, Private Judges, and the Champagne Fairs. *Econ. & Pol. 2*(1). Miller, D. (2003). Determining Ownership in Virtual Worlds: Copyright and License Agreements. *Rev. Litig., 22*(435).

Musgrove, M. (2006, February 2). Sadness in 'Star Wars' World. *Washington Post,* D01.

Nimmer, R., & Krauthaus, P. (1994). Beyond the Internet: Settling the Electronic Frontier. *Stan. L. & Pol'y Rev., 6*(25).

Ondrejka, C. (2004). Escaping the Gilded Cage: User Created Content and Building the Metaverse. *N.Y.L. Sch. L. Rev., 49*(81).

Ondrejka, C. (2005). *Changing Realities: User Creation, Communication, and Innovation in Digital Worlds. Ondrejka, C. (2005, November 27).* Remarks at the Berkman Center Luncheon Series.

Ostrovsky, A. (2005, March 1). Investment Dries Up as Rule of Law Seeps Away in Russia. *Financial Times.* Retrieved from http://news.ft.com/cms/s/02384ae2-89f7-11d9-aa18-00000e2511c8.html

Parloff, R. (2005, November 18). From Megs to Riches. *CnnMoney.com.* Retrieved from http://money.cnn.com/magazines/fortune/fortune_archive/2005/11/28/8361953/index.htm

Pearce, C. (2002). Sims, BattleBots, Cellular Automata God and Go, A Conversation with Will Wright. *International Journal of Computer Game Research*, 2. Retrieved from http://www.gamestudies.org/0202/pearce

Peltz, R. (2002). Use "The Filter You Were Born With": The Constitutionality of Mandatory Internet Filtering for the Adult Patrons of Public Libraries. *Wash. L. Rev., 77*(397).

Playvault.com. (n.d.). Retrieved from http://www.playvault.com

Press Release. (2003 November 14). *Second Life Residents to Own Digital Creations.* Linden Lab. Retrieved from http://lindenlab.com/press/releases/03_11_14

Press Release: Second Life Residents to Own Digital Creations. (n.d.). Retrieved from http://lindenlab.com/press_story_12.php

Press Release, Second Life Residents to Own Digital Creations. (n.d.). Retrieved from http://lindenlab.com/press_story_12.php

Project Entropia. (n.d.a). EULA, Section 5, "Termination." Retrieved from http://www.project-entropia.com/account/Apply.ajp

Project Entropia. (n.d.b). EULA, Section 6, "Ownership and Transactions." Retrieved from http://www.project-entropia.com/account/Apply.ajp

Revesz, R. (1992). Rehabilitating Interstate Competition: Rethinking the "Race-to-the-Bottom" Rationale for Federal Environmental Regulation. *N.Y.U. L. Rev., 67*(1210).

Reynolds, R. (2005, February 24). *Who's Rulz?* Message posted to Terra Nova. Retrieved from http://www.terranova.blogs.com/terra_nova/2005/02/whos_rulz.html

Richards, N. (2005). Reconciling Data Privacy and the First Amendment. *UCLA L. Rev., 52*(1149).

Rickey, D. (2003, November 23). Fascism Is Fun. Message posted to Terra Nova. Retrieved from http://terranova.blogs.com/terra_nova/2003/11/index.html Salem, K., & Zimmerman, E. (2004). *Rules of Play: Game Design Fundamentals.* Cambridge, MA: MIT Press.

Sandoval, G. (2000, April 10). Sony to Ban Sale of Online Characters from its Popular Gaming Sites. *CNET News.com.* Retrieved from http://news.com.com/2100-1017-239052.html?legacy=cnet

Sandoval, G. (2000, April 10). *Sony to Ban Sale of Online Characters from its Popular Gaming Sites.* Retrieved from http://news.com.com/2102-1017-239052.html

Second Life. Terms of Service and End User License Agreement § 5.3, at http://secondlife.com/tos.php

Second Life, Terms of Service at http://secondlife.com/corporate/terms.php.

Shy, O. (2001). *The Economics of Network Industries.* Cambridge, UK: Cambridge University Press.

Smedley, J. (Nov. 9, 2005). President of Sony Online Entertainment, interview at *Sony Online Discusses the MMO Market*, Bus. Wk. Online, http://www.businessweek.com/innovate/content/nov2005/id20051109_602467.htm

Somers, J. (2000). Against Cyberlaw. *Berkeley Tech. L.J., 15*(1145).

Star Wars Galaxies. (n.d.). Policies Index. Retrieved from http://www.starwarsgalaxies.station.sony.com/en_US/players/content.ym?page=Policies%20Index&resource=policies

Terdiman, D. (2004, January 23). Virtual Cash Breeds Real Greed. *Wired News.* Retrieved from http://www.wired.com/news/games/0,61999-0.html

Terdiman, D. (2004, February 13). No Will To Keep Uru Live Alive. *Wired News.* Retrieved from http://www.wired.com/news/games/0,2101,62253.html

Terdiman, D. (2004, July 16). Online Games a Massive Pain. *Wired News.* Retrieved from http://www.wired.com/news/games/0,2101,64153,00.html

Terdiman, D. Virtual Trade Tough Nut to Crack, *Wired*, Dec. 20, 2004, at www.wired.com/news/avantgo/story/0,2278,66074-00.html.

Terdiman, D. (2005, January 22). Dealing with Great Expectations. *Wired News.* Retrieved from http://www.wired.com/news/ebiz/0,1272,66362,00.html

Terdiman, D. (2005, October 29). Making the Virtual World a Better Place. *CNET News.com.* Retrieved from http://news.com.com/2102-1043_3-5920694.html

Terdiman, D. (2005, September 8). 'Second Life' Membership Now Free. *CNET News.com.* Retrieved from http://marketwatch-cnet.com.com/Second+Life+membership+now+free/2100-1043_3-5855481.html Terdiman, D. (2005, November 3). Online Feuds a Big Headache. *Wired.* Retrieved from http://www/wired.com/news/games/0,2101,65562,00.html

Terms of Service and End User License Agreement for Second Life § 5.3. (n.d.). Retrieved from http://secondlife.com/tos.php

The Censorware Project, Blacklisted by Cyber Patrol: From Ada to Yoyo. (1997, December 25). Retrieved from http://censorware.net/reports/cyberpatrol/ada-yoyo.html

There. (n.d.). *Terms of Service (TOS): Behaviour Guidelines.* Retrieved from http://webapps.prod.there.com/login/73.xml Tiebout, C. (1956). A Pure Theory of Local Expenditures. *J. Pol. Econ. 64*(416).

Twist, J. (2005). Picturing Online Gaming's Value. *BBC News.* Retrieved from http://news.bbc.co.uk/go/pr/fr/-/l/hi/technology/4360654.stm

Ultima Online License Agreement. (n.d.). Retrieved from http://www.uo.com/agreement.html

Van Zelfden, N. E. (2005, November 11). MMO Giants Prepare for War. *Business Week Online.* Retrieved from http://www.businessweek.com/innovate/content/nov2005/id20051111_428174.htm

Virtual Game, A Double-edged Sword Hanging Over Real World in China. (2005, June 22). Xinhua Econ. News Service.

Wagner, R.P. (1999). Filters and the First Amendment. *Minn. L. Rev., 83*(755).

Walton, G. (n.d.). *Online Worlds Roundtable #8, Part 1.* Retrieved from http://rpgvault.ign.com/articles/455/455832p2.html

Weinberg, J. (1997). Rating the Net. *Hastings Comm. & Ent. L.J., 19*(453).

White and Williams. LLP, *Virtual Land Lawsuit Reveals Dark Side of Second Life,* Yubanet.com, Oct. 6, 2006, http://www.yubanet.com/cgi-bin/artman/exec/view.cgi/22/43381

World of Warcraft Community Site, *Selling World of Warcraft In-Game Content for Real Money,* at http://www.worldofwarcraft.com/news/announcements.html

Chapter 8

Mischief and Grief:
Virtual Torts or Real Problems?

INTRODUCTION

Perhaps more that any other branch of the law, tort has been the battleground of social theory (Prosser, 1977). According to Black's Law Dictionary (1990), a tort is "a private or civil wrong or injury, including action for bad faith breach of contract, for which the court will provide a remedy in the form of an action for damages (*K Mart Corp v Ponsock*, 732 P.2d 469 (Nev. App.) A violation of a duty imposed by general law or otherwise upon all persons occupying the relation to each other which is involved in a given transaction (*Coleman v California Yearly Meeting of Friends Church*, 81 P.2d 469 (Ca. App.). There must always be a violation of some duty owing to plaintiff (claimant), and generally such duty must arise by operation of law and not be mere agreement of the parties."

Individuals wish to be secure in their person against harm and interference, not only as to their physical integrity, but as to their freedom to move about and their peace of mind. This is important whether they are at home in Bournemouth or at home in a virtual world like Second Life. When an individual is at home in Second Life, they are represented by their avatar. This avatar is the characterisation of them which is valuable and persistent. Avatars embody real people who want food and clothing, homes, goods, money, entertainment, and to be secure and free from disturbance in the right to have these things in their virtual environments. They want to work and deal with others whilst protected against the interference with their private lives, their relationships, and their honour and reputation. In any society, it is inevitable that these interests shall come into conflict.

The gaming community calls people who promote conflict "griefers". Griefers are people who like nothing better than to kill team-mates or obstruct the game's objectives. Griefers scam, cheat and abuse, often victimising the weakest and newest players. In games that attempt to encourage complex and enduring interactions among thousands of players, "griefing" has evolved from being an isolated nuisance to a social disease.

DOI: 10.4018/978-1-61520-795-4.ch008

A. ARE VIRTUAL WORLDS GAMES OR SOCIETIES?

Games are hard to define. Game scholar, Johan Huizinga (1971), identifies them using the notion of irrelevance. Nothing can be a game if it involves moral consequence. Whatever is happening, if it really matters in an ethical or moral sense, cannot be a game. Rather, he believes that games are places where we only **act** as if something matters. Indeed, play-acting seriousness can be one of the most important functions in a given game. According to Huizinga (1971), if some consequence really does matter in the end, the game is over. In fact, the only act of moral consequence that can happen within a game is the act of ending the game, denying its as-if character, spoiling the fantasy, and thereby breaking the collective illusion that the game matters. The collective illusion happens in a specific place, an arena specifically intended to host the game. Games, he says, happen in designated spaces (Id.). This is also known as the magic circle of game play.

With virtual worlds, society seems to have begun an exploration of the dimension of significance that may be attributed to a game. Massively multiplayer online role-playing games (MMOR-PGs) are complex and persistent worlds which are particularly vulnerable to negative behaviour, not only because they offer more rules to break than the average first-person shooter, but also because there is more at stake for players. For every player who is content to view the virtual world as a game, there is another who gleefully buys and sells the game's wands, armour, and gold pieces for U.S. currency on eBay. For every player who does not care if the virtual world is hacked and accounts are robbed, there is another who views the breach as a computer crime of the highest order. For every player who sleeps soundly after being banished from a guild, there is another who thinks about committing suicide (Castronova, 2005)

This broad spectrum of significance and the ensuing emotional reaction that people manifest in virtual worlds provide an incentive for the state to regulate and prosecute virtual torts and crimes. Raph Koster (2000) has drawn up a Declaration of the Rights of Avatar. "Foremost among these rights is the right to be treated as people and not as disembodied, meaningless, soulless puppets. Inherent in this right are therefore the natural and inalienable rights of man. These rights are liberty, property, security, and resistance to oppression." But has something got lost in translation? Perhaps, the status of these places as arenas and the activity taking place within them is a game.

As more companies and groups develop presence in online spaces like Second Life, they are learning that even virtual property is vulnerable to attack and vandalism. Anshe Chung Studios has developed more virtual property than any other Metaverse development company. As such, she is well-liked by many and a wonderful target for others. In December, Anshe was being interviewed by CNET reporter Daniel Terdiman when a group of griefers staged an assault on the proceedings by raining down a torrent of pixelated male genitals (Hutcheon, 2006). Another example of an attack was on John Edwards' virtual campaign headquarters which was plastered with Marxist and Leninist posters and offensive images. Those are just a few recent high-profile attacks by so-called griefers, online game players who set out to disrupt or discomfort others through theft, cheating, harassment, or vandalism (Hoffman, 2007).

B. WHAT IS A TORT?

This chapter will focus on torts. A tort is a legal wrong committed upon the person or property independent of contract. It may be either:

1. a direct invasion of some legal right of the individual
2. the infraction of some public duty by which special damage accrues to the individual

3. the violation of some private obligation by which like damage accrues to the individual (Crowe, 1999)

When a person sustains a harm, the harm may be to his bodily integrity, his property, his wallet, his mental wellbeing, a relational interest, or any combination of these interests (Green, 1927 & 1965) The gaming community would likely to call a tort a grief. Thus, is some particular person, the griefer answerable in tort damages? To answer that question, the injured person, the target user, must satisfy certain inquiries. Did the griefer cause the harm? Did the griefer owe a duty either statutorily or jurisprudentially to the target user? And if so, was the griefer negligent or did he act in an unreasonable manner?

In a virtual world, bodily integrity is unlikely to be at risk as the possibility of 'touch' is not available yet. So when one reads of a virtual rape, for example, Mr. Bungle, the evil protagonist of Julian Dibbell's (1998) famous account, "A Rape in Cyberspace," rejoined the community as Dr. Jest after being 'toaded'-- that is, officially deleted from the servers, it does not matter that it is horribly offensive and morally wrong, there has been no actual contact and therefore does not meet the minimum requirement of any state's laws. There has been no assault or battery. However, it is entirely possible that there has been an intentional infliction of emotional distress or nervous shock which may be actionable.

The gap between virtual worlds and real life is constantly closing, with developers encouraging in-game economies with currencies that translate to real-world pounds and dollars. When someone has sustained a harm to their wallet in a virtual world, there is real world consequence. A player might craft a rare item that can be sold via eBay; if such digital property is stolen, the player is effectively losing real money. Because non-virtual harms can arise in a virtual world, world providers must take steps in order to legally protect themselves and their residents.

1. Causation

The initial inquiry is whether the griefer's affirmative conduct in any way contributed to the target user's harm. Alternately stated, was the griefer a cause of the target user's harm? (Green, 1965). Affirmative conduct as envisioned here encompasses acts of omission as well as commission. One is warned not to seek the cause of the target user's harm. No event results from a single cause; cause and effect are endless and timeless. Second Life is a "free form canvass [where] you can do what you want, and be what you want, and that is what attracts people" (Terdiman, 2006). On the whole, many in-world behaviours mirror the torts that any individual may encounter (Mayer-Schonberger & Crawley, 2006).

Further, one should not, at this stage of the analysis, seek a substantial, legal, or proximate cause (Prosser, 1977). The very term "proximate cause" connotes simultaneous inquiries of factual causation, on the one hand, and morality, culpability, or responsibility on the other hand. One must solve the questions of factual causation first, without any of the entanglements of morality, culpability, or responsibility. After which the problems of morality, culpability, or responsibility can be resolved (Green, 1927). Causation-in-fact generally is a trier-of-fact function. Most of the time, the inquiry into causation-in-fact is not so difficult as we tend to make it. It may be as simple as this: target user avers that griefer harmed him, and griefer answers that he did not. The trier-of-fact then determines which is to be believed (Crowe, 1999).

2. Duty

The second inquiry is whether the target user can articulate some general rule from the terms and conditions of the game or principle of law, contractual, statutory or jurisprudential, which protects his interests. Generally, this inquiry is not a difficult one in the real world. Perhaps, the same could be said in a virtual world. As it may be as uncomplicated as the griefer owes a duty not to create an unreasonable risk of non-game play harm with regard to the target user. The more difficult part of the duty question is the further and bifurcated inquiry as to whether the enunciated rule or principle of law extends to or is intended to protect this target user from this type of harm arising in this manner (See generally Crowe, 1999).

From the beginning Second Life prohibited six categories of activities in its Terms of Service: intolerance, including slurs against individuals or groups; harassment; assault, including using software programmes to attack people's avatars; disclosure of information about other people's real-world lives; indecency, such as sexual behaviour outside areas rated as mature; and disturbing the peace, such as acts that deliberately slow server performance (Clark, 2006; Second Life Community Standards).

Other virtual worlds which have a stronger magic circle to the game are also struggling with the idea of duty to other gamers. As such, even online games based around combat between players (often permitting the winner to take their opponent's possessions) the increasingly high stakes have prompted the gaming community to reassess its ethics, asking whether all strategies are equally permissible simply because they are all possible (Hutcheon, 2006).

For example, Eve Online (in which rival corporations trade and battle across the galaxy) whose selling point has been their potential for ruthless competition, some events have caused gamers to ask what is beyond the pale. One incident entailed the coordination of large numbers of mischief-makers. Calling themselves the Guiding Hand Social Club, they exacted the ruination of a particular player and the corporation she headed, Ubiqua Seraph. Spending more than a year infiltrating Ubiqua Seraph and gaining the trust of its higher members, the Guiding Hand enacted an elaborate heist that resulted in the destruction of the organisation's limited edition flagship and the looting of its considerable funds. The damage translated to thousands of real pounds and years of effort (The Guiding Hand leader's announcement and discussion thread). The scale of the persecution divided the community. Many felt the tactics, while sanctioned by the game's design, were despicable. "People work for months ... to buy things like battleships," said one irate gamer following the Guiding Hand's announcement (Davies, 2006).

The players of World of Warcraft were left with a similar problem, when a group of gamers performed an act whose only purpose was to cause emotional pain. The death of a member of the community inspired her fellow gamers to hold a virtual funeral, which was raided by a malicious mob that made short work of the mourners, all of whom had relinquished their weapons as a sign of respect. Since the funeral was naively held in a zone designed for combat, few could question the legitimacy of the attack within the game's rules. None the less, the mourners were outraged, not at the penalties their characters would have to suffer, but at the brazen attack on their feelings (Id.).

So, how should one generally articulate a rule or principle for the virtual world that Player should not make mischief or grief another player excessively and beyond the realms of fair play? If Player does so and destroys Target User, it may well be that the articulated rule against excessive grief extends to protect the particular target user, for the particular type of harm involved (personal injury or loss), arising in the particular manner (violation of fair play).

However, what should be the result if the target's team sustains loss of consortium with him because of his personal injuries or losses? Does the articulated rule against excessive grief protect this tangential user, from this type of harm (loss of consortium), arising in this manner (target's incapacity to perform his functions as a result of personal injuries sustained)?

a. **Factors of Duty**

It is at this point that courts or world creators, either consciously or subconsciously, resort to the factors of duty, although not always in a clearly articulated fashion. The factors of duty are simply socioeconomic factors of consideration (McDonald, 1970):

1. **Administrative:** When required to determine whether to impose a duty in a given situation, the world creator or the court must be concerned with the administrative factor. Will the imposition of a duty in a given situation open the floodgates to unmanageable complaints or litigation? Usually, both are more concerned with manageability than with flooding. Courts can deal with countless uncontested open account suits on any given day. However, a flood of suits claiming damages for mental distress as a result of having witnessed the assassination of a prominent character could not be handled with the same facility. World creators and courts would rightly be concerned with a significant number of fabricated claims in the area of mental distress because the genuineness of a mental distress claim is often difficult to ascertain.

   For example, Blizzard, the makers of World of Warcraft, reacted to griefing by banning more than 5,400 accounts. This is not a cost-effective way of moderating the world they have created. The act of terminating so many subscriptions and the staff required to man support lines come at huge cost to the developer. Stephen Davis estimates 25% of customer support calls to companies operating online games are a result of griefing: "For a small game, these costs can be the difference between success and failure. For a large game, these costs are a continual drag on the bottom line." (Davies, 2006)

2. **Ease of association:** The ease of association factor is also of overriding importance. Basically: how easily does one associate the target user's complained-of harm with the griefer's conduct? If the griefer lit the target on fire outside the realm of game play, the association is strong and easily ascertained. But if the target user were struck by an ambulance which violated an intersectional traffic control while driven at an excessive speed en route to pick up a woman who had suffered a heart attack as a result of having been informed over the telephone that the griefer had lit her husband on fire for no purpose, the ease of association, if any, approaches the absurd. Although ease of association encompasses the idea of foreseeability, it is not based on foreseeability alone.

   For example, if this were the case in the real world, then all of the well documented case regarding automobiles involved in thousands of deaths annually as well as causing innumerable and horrendous personal injuries, not resulting in death, and staggering losses in property damages, would pose a serious problem. If duty were to be delineated solely by the criterion of foreseeable consequences, automobile manufacturers would be out of business.

3. **Economic:** The economic factor is not simply whether the griefer is or is not better able to bear the loss than the target user, but instead implies broader considerations. If a duty were or were not imposed, what would be the economic impacts upon the target user and persons similarly situated, upon the griefer and persons similarly situated, and upon the local, national, or international economies? Thus, a paper mill which pollutes the air and water in an area where the paper mill is of no great economic significance is likely to be declared a nuisance. However, a similarly offending paper mill in a locality

where ninety percent of the inhabitants are economically dependent upon the paper mill pay roll is less likely to be found a nuisance or, at least, not such a nuisance as to justify injunctive relief completely closing it.

Likewise, in some games, nefarious exploits making unorthodox use of in-game mechanics have been the object of grudging praise. Again, in Eve Online, players role-playing as pirates stole an entire dreadnought warship. The scale of this operation has been compared to purloining the 'Death Star' of *Star Wars* fame, or in real world terms, pilfering an entire aircraft carrier (Wallace, 2005). All virtual warships in Eve Online feature an automatic anti-collision system to prevent them from inflicting damage on each other in congested environments. With the help of a spy, the pirates waited until the target battleship was unoccupied by any enemy personnel. Then pirate ships manoeuvred close enough to the target to bump it out of its dock with their anti-collision shields. Pirates landed their own pilot aboard the ship and proceeded to fly it away. All the while, the pirates had another group staging a diversion to draw attention away from the heist. The dreadnought was worth about two to five million units on in-game currency. The administrators of Eve Online have given their tacit approval by allowing the feat to stand unpunished. The true brilliance of the operation was the bandits' employment of an emergent property of Eve Online, using the anti-collision system in a new and interesting way not contemplated by the designers (Id.).

A further consideration of the economic factor involves a search for a griefer who, if not better able to bear the loss, is in a better position to distribute the risk of loss. This is particularly so in enterprise situations where the loss seems eventually to fall upon the dynamic economic force within a given enterprise.

4. **Moral:** The moral factor is essentially a visceral reaction to what seems right or wrong. Thus, if griefers appear to be villains, world builder and/or courts are innovative in finding ways and means to impose liability upon them. Conversely, if the griefer is viewed as a model citizen, courts seem to create methods for more lenient treatment. Many players now want a say in determining what behaviour is acceptable. Instead of the developer intervening, online gaming is seeing the emergence of systems by which the community can moderate itself. In 2003, eGenesis released *A Tale in the Desert*, which offered players the ability to make laws, determining what actions were permitted and even banning problem players. This experiment paved the way for the transference of some responsibility from developers to gamers. Xbox Live's Gamer Card system indelibly links your actions to your account by allowing other players to rate your behaviour. A low enough reputation will mean few people willing to play with you. Griefing has therefore become a relatively minor support issue for Microsoft (Hoffman, 2007).

5. **Type of activity:** The type of activity factor is simply an inquiry into the nature of the griefer's enterprise. One such inquiry may be whether the griefer's undertaking involves an irreducible risk of harm, such as blasting with dynamite, which justifies the imposition of strict liability. Another inquiry in this area may be whether the griefer's activity is of such importance to society as to warrant the world builder or court's carefully nurturing and safeguarding the activity. Of course, the answers to these inquiries vary in the dimensions of time and space. Thus, industry is not so carefully nurtured by our present courts as it was by the courts of the last century. On the other hand, some who take the virtual plunge are turning to vigilante groups like Anti-Griefer Special Operations (AGSO), a 30-member volunteer

contingent in Second Life. These groups are cropping up to guard against griefers and help victims clean up after an attack. Each member serves a specific role, such as informant, undercover agent, combatant, or officer. Like homeowners who advertise the security company protecting their home, Second Lifers hang posters to show they're protected by AGSO (Id.).

6. **Precedent or historical:** This factor involves not only looking back as a matter of historical curiosity but also looking forward. Frequently, one can or should be able to determine future events by what has occurred in the past. In determining the imposition or not of a duty, courts certainly examine precedent.

   ◦ What has been the rule in the past?
   ◦ Is the reason for the rule still valid, if indeed it was ever valid?
   ◦ In which direction are society and its institutions evolving?

Precedent is important but one can never rely upon it completely and securely. If a rule were established as a precedent over a century ago, and if many exceptions have eroded the rule to an empty and meaningless proposition, one does not have to be a fortune-teller to understand that the last vestiges of the rule are subject to momentary collapse. This type of viewing of the past with an eye to the future is much in accord with the civilian concept of *jurisprudence constante* in theory and with the common law concept of *stare decisis* in practice (Crowe, 1999).

One should always bear in mind that the factors of duty are not capable of precise mathematical application. Five factors may slightly favour the target user in a given situation, and one factor may overwhelmingly favour the griefer. In such a case, the court would likely find no duty. At other times, one or more of the factors may be entirely neutral and, therefore, of no consequence in the finding or not of a duty.

b. Intervening Cause

A last consideration in the general area of the duty inquiry is that of intervening causes (Prosser, 1977) This is closely related to and often may overlap the inquiry of "arising in this manner." There is hardly any harm in which no intervening cause is involved between the griefer's conduct and the target user's harm, even if it be no more than the atmosphere that exists between the griefer's fist and the target user's nose. However, a more clearly delineated intervening cause may be deemed superseding, and if so, such a superseding, intervening cause is assigned full legal responsibility for the target user's harm, thereby relieving the initially scrutinized griefer of any liability.

Thus, if a defendant carelessly leaves gasoline lying about and an intervenor carelessly ignites the gasoline, the intervenor is deemed merely an intervening cause and the defendant remains liable although his liability may now be in solido, or joint and several, with the intervenor. But if the intervenor intentionally ignites the gasoline, he may well be deemed a superseding, intervening cause thereby taking full legal responsibility for any harm occasioned by the ignited gasoline. Of course, intervening causes may have their origin in nature as well as people and similar determinations must be made as to the question of intervening cause as opposed to superseding, intervening cause (Crowe, 1999). A similar scenario could be seen in Second Life. A rogue programme appeared in Second Life called Copybot. This enabled users to quickly replicate in-world objects and characters which, in turn, devalued other players' objects. Linden Lab had originally created the programme for the purpose of finding vulnerabilities in their platform. Intevenors modified the programme to the detriment of other players (Reuters, 2006). Should Linden Lab remain responsible or should the griefers be held liable for the damage they caused?

The problem of intervening cause is essentially a duty-risk matter just as is "proximate cause."

Thus, a court determines, as a matter of law, in the gasoline hypothetical that if the intervenor acted intentionally, the original defendant's duty did not extend to such a risk (Crowe, 1999). Moreover, Linden Lab would not be responsible. Of course, whether the intervenor (griefer) did or did not act intentionally is a matter of fact determination which is a trier-of-fact function.

It is seen then that the inquiry of duty deals not with causation-in-fact, but with legal cause. In other words, of all the causations-in-fact that contribute to any given harm, which one or which ones are to be deemed legal or responsible causes? This inquiry is directed toward duty-risk considerations. Is there a duty, and if so, does it extend to the given risk which is being scrutinized? (Crowe, 1999).

Duty is a legal question. Therefore, in a jury trial, it is a function of the court to instruct the jury as to what the griefer's duty is and, further, as to which target users and which harms, arising in which manners, the duty is to be extended.

c. Duty-Risk vs. Proximate Cause

The duty-risk approach has a more desirable flexibility than any of the various approaches of "proximate cause." A brief examination of some of the approaches to proximate cause will support this view. One of the earlier English cases to consider the area of proximate cause was *In re Polemis*, 3 K.B. 560 (Eng. C.A. 1921), which took the approach that if a defendant is abstractly wrong or negligent, then the defendant is responsible for all harms occurring in the "unbroken chain of causation" emanating from that abstract negligence.

- What is an "unbroken chain"?
- What is abstract negligence?
- How can any defendant be deemed negligent without relating his conduct to a relevant duty?
- If a defendant speeds on a street in Bournemouth at eighty miles per hour,

and miraculously does no harm to person, property, pocketbook, mental wellbeing, or relational interest, is he negligent?

- Insofar as criminal consequences are concerned, perhaps he is, but we are not concerned with criminal consequences. We are concerned with a loss and the person or persons who are to bear that loss.

If there is no loss, considerations of tort law do not come into play with the obvious exception of the area of injunctive relief to prevent a threatened harm. The question of negligence in the abstract is analogous to the question whether there is a sound if a tree falls in a forest where there is no human ear. Is there a sound? Who cares? The English courts eventually retreated from the *Polemis* approach. At the opposite end of the spectrum from *Polemis* is *Wagon Mound #1, Overseas Tankship (U.K.) Ltd. v. Morts Dock & Eng'r Co., (1961) A.C. 388 (P.C.) (Austl.),* which may be read as requiring the foreseeability not only of the exact harm, but also of the manner of the harm coming about in order to establish proximate cause. The English courts retreated from this position in *Wagon Mound #2, Overseas Tankship (U.K.) Ltd. v. Miller Steamship Co.,* (1967) 1 A.C. 617 (P.C.) (Austl.).

A middle ground approach was formulated by an American court in *Kinsman #1, Petition of Kinsman Transit Co.,* 338 F.2d 708 (2d Cir.), cert. denied, 380 U.S. 944 (1964). Here, foreseeability of some harm to a general class of people was sufficient to establish proximate cause, if the actual harm was of the same general nature and affected that same general class of people. The approach of *Kinsman #1,* however, held up no longer than *Kinsman #2* (Id.)

Perhaps the best approach and that most akin to Green's duty-risk analysis can be gleaned from *Palsgraf* (*Palsgraf v. Long Island R.R. Co.,* 248 N.Y. 339 (1928)). There, Justice Cardozo held that a consideration of duty is necessarily antecedent to a consideration of negligence, but that duty is limited to foreseeable risks. Justice Andrews' dissent argued that negligence in the abstract was a viable concept, but that the risks to which such abstract negligence would be extended should be determined by factors of socio-economic considerations. If one rejects Cardozo's "foreseeability" and Andrews' "abstract negligence," and adopts Cardozo's concept of duty and the dissent's approach of factors of socio-economic considerations, then one has reached a valid duty-risk method of analysis (Green, 1965)

If the target user can properly satisfy the initial inquiry dealing with causation-in-fact and the second inquiry concerning duty and the risks encompassed by it, he may proceed to the third inquiry.

3. Violation of Duty

The third inquiry is whether the duty, as delineated by the court, was in fact violated (Green, 1965) In the negligence area, the question is: Was the griefer negligent -- did he act unreasonably? Most definitions of the reasonable man are, in essence, little more than inane statements saying that a reasonable man is a reasonable man. Instead of using this futile and meaningless definition, a more valid analysis involves the application of a consideration of the factors of negligence to any given factual situation (Crowe, 1999). These factors of negligence can be labelled:

1. **Likelihood of the harm** involves nothing more than a consideration of the chances that any given harm might occur. Of course, the chances of a harm occurring must be viewed in the dimensions of time and space in which the griefer acted or failed to act. Certainly in this area, foreseeability plays no mean role (Restatement of Torts § 291).
2. **Gravity of the harm** is simply an inquiry dealing with a determination of how serious the harm would be should it occur (Id §§ 291, 293).
3. **Burden of Prevention** is a consideration of the relative ease or difficulty which would have been encountered by the griefer in taking steps to prevent the harm from occurring (Id § 295) And
4. **Social Utility** of the griefer's conduct is a consideration of the value of the griefer's overall enterprise or activity to society or the community in which it takes place (Id §§ 291-92)

The factors of negligence are no more susceptible of mathematical application than are the factors of duty.

- Thus, if the likelihood of a given harm occurring is great, but the harm which is deemed to be likely is minuscule, the tendency may be toward a finding of no negligence.
- Similarly, if the likelihood and gravity of a given harm are of no particular moment, but the griefer could have, with little or no appreciable effort, avoided the harm, the pendulum may swing back toward a finding of negligence.
- Finally, if all other factors are fairly neutral, but the social utility of the griefer's conduct is deemed of great value, the tendency would be toward a determination of no negligence.

This analysis is not limited in its application to a negligence cause of action; it is equally applicable to an action based on an intentional tort or a strict liability tort. Thus, if a griefer is deemed to be a cause-in-fact of target user's being bombarded with inappropriate objects, and if it is established that the griefer had a duty not to invade the target user's avatar's integrity, it still must be established that the griefer did in fact violate his duty toward this target user. It might seem that, in the intentional tort area, once causation-in-fact is established, violation of duty is simultaneously established. While this will often be true, it is not universally so (Green, 1965).

Just as the parent of the tortfeasor who battered the plaintiff is a cause-in-fact of plaintiff's harm, this does not necessarily mean that such a parent owed the plaintiff any duty or much less that such parent violated any duty. Thus also, if a manufacturer owed a strict liability duty to a given plaintiff not to manufacture a product which was defective so as to be unreasonably dangerous to person or property, it would seem that once causation-in-fact is established, violation of duty is likewise simultaneously established. However, if a plaintiff has been physically injured by a product so defective as to be unreasonably dangerous, the public carrier that transported the product to market is also a cause-in-fact of plaintiff's harm. But again, this does not mean that the public carrier owed a relevant duty to the plaintiff or that the public carrier violated any such duty.

A brief digression here in regard to the concept of fault necessary to support legal responsibility is appropriate. Although few would dispute that both negligent and intentional tort conduct are sound bases for the imposition of legal responsibility, there is less agreement that strict liability conduct is a sound basis for the imposition of such responsibility. Perhaps if more thought were given to a comparison of negligence and strict liability, there would be less opposition to imposing strict liability in tort. Negligence is the failure to abide by the standard of the mythical reasonable man; this is a societal standard which no human can perpetually achieve. Thus, to be culpable of negligence does not necessarily involve a lack of personal morality or integrity. In this sense, negligence approaches strict liability.

Another comparison demonstrates that there is no wide philosophical gap between negligence and strict liability. The four factors of negligence have already been discussed. Yet, the factors for the imposition of strict liability for ultra-hazardous or abnormally dangerous activity are precisely the same four factors of negligence plus two others:

(1) customary usage and (2) abnormality of the activity to the locality (Restatement of Torts, § 520) A further comparison of strict liability can be made in the products liability area, where the basis of liability, inter alia, is a product which is defective so as to be unreasonably dangerous (Id. § 402(a)) If a determination of unreasonableness must be made, it appears necessary to consider the factors of negligence. Once again it appears there is no wide philosophical gap between the concepts of negligence and strict liability.

4. Defences

If the target user can satisfy the trier-of-fact that the griefer has indeed violated the duty owed, he may nevertheless be met with certain affirmative defences (Prosser, 1977). These defences, if validly asserted by griefer, will defeat target user's claim even though target user has satisfactorily established causation-in-fact, a duty owed, and a violation of that duty.

a. Consent and Privileges

- Did the target user consent to the harm sustained? Further, does the law permit the target user to consent? Thus, a woman thirty-five years of age may be permitted to consent to sexual intercourse, whereas a girl thirteen years of age would be deemed incapable of giving such consent.
- An obvious example of an absolute privilege is self-defence, and
- An example of a qualified privilege is defamation of a public official.

b. Contributory Negligence

The negligence of the target user will still bar his recovery in many jurisdictions (Id.). Theoretically, contributory negligence should be determined by the same criteria as negligence. Pragmatically, however, courts and juries frequently do not find contributory negligence when, under the same set of circumstances, if the question of negligence were at issue, a finding of negligence would in all probability be made. This is probably attributable to the harshness of the doctrine. As it is no longer necessary to nurture the nineteenth century industrial revolution, contributory negligence is generally not held in high regard by courts or juries.

However, even if a target user is deemed contributorily negligent, he may avoid being barred from recovery by affirmatively establishing that the griefer had the last clear chance to avoid the incident (Id.) The doctrine of last clear chance does not appear to be consistently applied even within the same jurisdiction, much less from one jurisdiction to another. There are two questions which must be answered when target user asserts last clear chance.

- First, was he in a position of peril from which he could not extricate himself as opposed to his simply being inattentive?
- Second, did the griefer actually discover or, as a reasonable man, should the griefer have discovered the target user's position in peril?

Finally, it is helpful to remember that there need be no consideration of last clear chance unless there has been a determination that the target user was contributorily negligent; similarly, there need be no consideration of target user's contributory negligence unless the griefer is first deemed to be negligent.

c. Assumption of the Risk

Although this defence sometimes overlaps with that of contributory negligence, the two are distinct (Id.). The essence of assumption of the risk is twofold:

1. Knowledge and appreciation of a danger, and
2. A voluntary encountering of it. The essence of contributory negligence is simply carelessness.

One could say that the way to deal with griefers is to avoid virtual worlds altogether. It is sometimes of singular importance to distinguish between the defences of assumption of the risk and contributory negligence. Contributory negligence may be a defence just as is assumption of the risk where the principal action is based upon negligence; it may not be a defence where the principal action is based upon strict liability in the areas of products liability or abnormally dangerous activities, or where the principal action is based upon intentional or wilful, wanton, and reckless tort conduct. Assumption of the risk, on the other hand, may well be a valid defence not only to negligence but also in all of these other areas.

d. Comparative Negligence or Fault

This is not, strictly speaking, an absolute defence, it is nevertheless a partial defence, and therefore mentioned here. Via this doctrine, the target user's total recovery is reduced by that percentage of the total fault which the trier-of-fact determines to be attributable to him. Comparative negligence, a civilian concept, is not yet the majority position in American jurisdictions, but one is hard pressed to deny that it is rapidly gaining ground (Crowe, 1999)

Comparative negligence may be of two applications: pure comparative negligence or modified comparative negligence. The former permits a target user to recover one percent of his damages even though he be deemed to have been ninety-nine percent at fault, a recovery which could be fairly significant if the target user's damages were determined to be of great quantum. In contrast, modified comparative negligence requires that the target user be less than fifty percent at fault, and if not, all recovery is barred.

It is proper to emphasize once again that the determination or not of the violation of a duty is a function of the jury or trier-of-fact. If the target user can establish that the griefer was a cause-in-fact, owed a relevant duty, and violated that duty, and if the griefer is unable to sustain a valid defence, the target user is permitted to move to the fourth and final step of the analysis.

5. Damages

The final step of the analysis is damages (Green, 1965). Damages, in essence, involve nothing more than a mechanical inventory and assessment of the target user's harm or harms -- an enumeration and evaluation. There are three main areas of consideration commonly arising in damages.

Apportionment: As has been noted in the discussion of comparative negligence, the apportionment that is considered in damages is quite distinct from that considered in comparative negligence. The apportionment that takes place here is in regard to the actual harm done and not in regard to the percentage of fault involved (Prosser, 1977).

Contribution: Contribution takes place, if at all, between joint tortfeasors. Joint tortfeasors are those who are jointly and severally, or solidarily, liable to the plaintiff. If allowed, contribution takes effect when one joint tortfeasor has paid more than his pro rata share of damages to the plaintiff. Thus, Defendant One and Defendant Two are joint tortfeasors and therefore liable to plaintiff jointly and severally or in solido. Because of this type of liability, plaintiff can recover the full amount of his damages (e.g., ten thousand dollars) from Defendant One. However, Defendant One can then seek to recover from Defendant Two the excess he paid over his pro rata share (five thousand dollars).

Generally, if there is a more or less reasonable factual basis for apportionment, it will be applicable. Of course, if apportionment is applicable,

contribution among joint tortfeasors will not come into consideration; the tortfeasors in that instance simply are not joint. Finally, regardless of what transactions take place in or out of court, the target user can receive but one satisfaction; there can be no application of any of the rules involved that would permit double recovery by the target user (Id.).

Indemnity: Like contribution, takes place between joint tortfeasors who have solidary or joint and several liability to the plaintiff. Indemnity differs from contribution in that the joint tortfeasor who has satisfied plaintiff's claim seeks to have the other joint tortfeasor pay the entire amount of that claim, and not merely a pro rata share (Id.). There are generally three bases justifying the application of indemnity:

1. a contractual relationship such as a contract of indemnity;
2. other relationships not founded on the basis of a contract of indemnity, such as master/servant; and
3. finally, a group of rather ill-defined cases in which indemnity is allowed seemingly on the basis that there is a "great difference" in the gravity of the fault of the two tortfeasors, which justifies that one should bear the full loss because the extreme degree of his culpability makes it just that he should do so.

The determinations to be made in the area of damages, as with causation-in-fact and violation of duty, are a function for the jury or trier-of-fact, subject to proper instructions from the court (Green, 1965)

C. CONCLUSION

"The most common 'griefer counter-measure' is to put in place a strong community system," says Stephen Davis of IT GlobalSecure, a firm that specialises in developing security technologies for online games. "These community services provide clan features, friends lists, reputation stats, and other features both to tie players more closely to the game and create an environment that reduces anonymity for misbehaving players." (Davies, 2006) Eventually, real-world law will edge into virtual worlds. In the meantime, the solution to griefing is not simply to ban nuisance players, but to encourage the development of virtual societies capable of dealing with their own virtual crimes.

REFERENCES

(1990). *Black's Law Dictionary* (6th ed.). St. Paul, MN: West Publishing.

Castronova, E. (2005). The Right to Play. *N.Y.L.Sch. L. Rev. 49*(185)

Clark, D. (2006). Virtual Vandalism. *The Wall Street Journal Online*. Retrieved from http://online.wsj.com/article

Crowe, L. (1999). The Anatomy of a Tort -- Greenian, as Interpreted by Crowe who has been influenced by Malone -- A Primer. *Loy. L. Rev. 44*(647).

Davies, M. (2006). Gamers don't want any more grief. *The Guardian*. Retrieved from http://www.guardian.co.uk/technology/2006/jun/15/games.guardianweeklytechnologysection2

Dibbell, J. (1998). *My Tiny Life*. New York: Henry Holt & Co.

Green, L. (1927). *Rationale of Proximate Cause*.

Green, L. (1965). The Study and Teaching of Tort Law. In The Litigation Process in Tort Law.

Hoffman, E. C., III. (2007). *Tip Sheet: When Griefers Attack, How to prevent virtual-world vandalism and what to do when your property comes under fire*. Retrieved from http://www.businessweek.com/playbook/07/0416_1.htm

Huizinga, J. (1971). *Homo Ludens: A Study in the Play-Elements in Culture*. Boston, MA: Beacon Press.

Hutcheon, S. (2006, December 21). Good Grief, Bad Vibes. *Sydney Morning Herald*. Retrieved from http://www.smh.com.au/news/web/good-grief-bad-vibes/2006/12/21/1166290662836.html?page=2

Koster, R. (2000). *The Laws of Online World Design*. Retrieved from http://www.raphkoster.com/gaming/laws.shtml

Mayer-Schonberger, V. & Crawley, J. (2006). Napster's Second Life? The Regulatory Challenges of Virtual Worlds. *NW. U. L.Rev., 100*(1775).

McDonald, J. (1970). Comment, Proximate Cause in Louisiana . In Malone, W., & Guerry, L. (Eds.), *Studies in Louisiana Torts Law*.

Prosser, W. (1977). *Law of Torts*. St. Paul, MN: West Publishing.

Second Life Community Standards. (n.d.). Retrieved from http://secondlife.com/coporate/cs.php

Terdiman, D. (2006). Phony Kids, Virtual Sex. *CNET News*. Retrieved from http://news.com.com/Phony+kids+virtual+sex/2100-1043_3-6060132.html

The Guiding Hand. (n.d.). *Leader's announcement and discussion thread*. Retrieved from http://tinyurl.com/8jglz

Wallace, M. (2005). Simply Amazing. *Walkerings*. Retrieved from http://www.walkering.com/walkerings/2005/08/simply_amazing.html

Chapter 9
Beyond Griefing:
Virtual Crime

A. INTRODUCTION

Because there is so much money involved in virtual worlds these days, there has been an increase in criminal activity in these worlds as well. The gaming community calls people who promote conflict "griefers". Griefers are people who like nothing better than to kill team-mates or obstruct the game's objectives. Griefers scam, cheat and abuse. Recently, the have begun to set up Ponzi schemes. In games that attempt to encourage complex and enduring interactions among thousands of players, "griefing" has evolved from being an isolated nuisance to a social disease. Much in the same way crime has become the real world's social disease. Grief is turning into crime.

Some consider virtual worlds to be a game and therefore outside the realms of real law and merely subject to the rules of the game. However, some virtual worlds have become an increasingly important as a method of commerce and means of communication. In most circumstance the law is reluctant to intrude into the rules of the game, but it will do if necessary. (Lastowka & Hunter, 2004) Criminal law applies in virtual worlds as it does in the real world, but not necessarily in the manner that a player would expect or want. The law looks at the real consequences of actions, not the on-screen representations. (Kennedy, 2009)

According to one study, the majority of online crime is theft (73.3%) and fraud (20.2%). The average value of the online gaming loss is about $459 with 34.3% of the criminal loss between $100 and $300. (Chen, 2005) These figures come pre-

DOI: 10.4018/978-1-61520-795-4.ch009

dominantly from Korea and Taiwan as there has been no study elsewhere. However a Newsweek commentator estimates that one million dollars in virtual goods are stolen every year. (Spring, 2006) In fact in the United States, police will not provide any assistance in recovering or investigating virtual theft. Final Fantasy XI player, Geoff Lurrs, brought his case before the Blaine, Minnesota police department after having $4,000 in virtual goods and currency stolen. He was refused any help. (Cavalli, 2008)

Although there are acceptable forms of theft in the rules of game play in most virtual worlds which have a questing theme, this is not the sort of theft which is producing the statistics above. It is important to distinguish between in-game and out-of-game theft. There are ways which a character whose job is thief can steal from other characters within the game. He may 'steal' a valuable object while the owner's attention is diverted. He may 'kill' or 'harm' the other player in battle and take his goods. If this is within the magic circle of game play, then there is no crime. This is part of the risks that a player takes within the game. The courts are unlikely to intervene unless there is actual cheating.

Such as, other in-game scams which may amount to theft or fraud. The most common include: (1) "Trade Window Switch" where the thief attempt to pass a valueless item as valuable only because it is graphically similar to a valuable item; (2) "Anni Scam (muling scam)" which occurs only when the items cannot be traded through a trade window, but instead must be dropped on the ground and left for anyone to pick up; (3) "Guess Who Scam" where the thief pretends to know the player only to ask for an item loan; and (4) "Item Switch Scam" where the player, after a trade, receives an item of less value than anticipated. (Darnoc, 2005)

Then there are out-of-game thefts when a player attempts to obtain access to another player's virtual items through subterfuge, e.g., phishing and hacking. The Council of Europe's Conven-

tion on Cybercrime is the leading international instrument defining computer-related criminal offences of this nature. There are four categories: (1) offences against the confidentiality, integrity, and availability of computer data and systems; (2) computer-related offences; (3) content-related offences; and (4) offences related to infringement of copyrights and related rights. This is an excellent tool for conventional computer crime. But a distinction must be made between hacking and exploiting. Hacking is the equivalent of bending the laws of time and space to acquire someone else's property. Exploiting is finding a flaw in the game and making the most of it. The 'gold dupe' is a classic example. The character finds the gold dupe flaw and duplicates currency to the point of devaluing the currency of the entire world. This is not quite counterfeiting but rather finding an ATM which endlessly provides £100 notes instead of £10 notes. (White, 2008) However, even within the scope of activities permitted in virtual worlds, transactions do go wrong. Some of these 'bad' transactions, in fact, are real world fraud pure and simple.

B. THEFT

Section 1 of the United Kingdom's Theft Act 1968 defines theft: "A person is guilty of theft if he dishonestly appropriates property belonging to another with the intention of permanently depriving the other of it.. ." Section 15(4) of the Theft Act states: "For the purposes of this section 'deception' means any deception (whether deliberate or reckless) by words or conduct as to fact or as to law, including a deception as to the present intentions of the person using the deception or any other person." The U.S. Model Penal Code (MPC) 1962 §223.2(1) theft provisions are divided into an unlawful taking, theft by deception, and embezzlement. A person is guilty of theft by unlawful taking or disposition if "he unlawfully takes, or exercises unlawful control over, movable property of another with purpose to deprive him thereof."

Both acts are similar in that the defendant: 1. property; 2. belonging to another; 3. appropriation; 4. with an intention to permanently deprive; 5. deception.

Theoretically, these definitions could be applied to the theft of virtual goods through phishing scams, where the hacker unlawfully takes or exercises unlawful control over the virtual goods of another with the purpose of depriving the lawful owner of his virtual good. However, in the UK the Computer Misuse Act would be more applicable. Section 1 provides that: "A person is guilty of an offence if – (a) he causes a computer to perform any function with intent to secure access to any program or data held in any computer or to enable any such access to be secured; (b) the access he intends to secure or to enable to be secured, is unauthorised; and (c) he knows at the time when he causes the computer to perform the function that this is the case."

These definitions could also be used to criminalize the actions of a person who uses an unbeatable bot to extract property from others, considering that the person using the bot is unlawfully taking or exercising unlawful control over the virtual goods of another with the purpose of depriving the lawful owner of his virtual good. It might be possible to argue that because force is used in this situation, robbery, instead of theft, has occurred. In *State v. Smalls*, 708 A.2d 737 (N.J. Super. Ct. App. Div. 1998), the court found that the crime of theft becomes robbery, in part, when defendant inflicts bodily injury or uses force upon another in course of committing theft. Section 8 of the Theft Act states that "[A] person is guilty of robbery if he steals, and immediately before or at the time of doing so, and in order to do so, he uses force on any person or puts or seeks to put any person in fear of being then and there subjected to force." The essence of robbery in the United Kingdom has two elements. (1) The defendant must demonstrate both the mens rea

and actus reus of theft. (R v Forrester [1992] Crim LR 793 (CA)) (2) It must then be shown that the defendant has used or threatened to use forceat the time of the theft. (R v Dawson [1976] Crim LR 692 (CA)) However, applying robbery to the bot situation is difficult because the bot applies force to the video game character, rather to than the video game player.

1. Property

Section 4(1) of the U.K. Theft Act defines property as follows: "Property includes money and all other property, real or personal, including things in action and other intangible property." Intangible property includes patents and copyright. (R v Mensah Lartey and Relevey [1996] Cr App R 143 (CA) Confidential information is protected under the Computer Misuse Act 1990. Virtual goods more closely resemble chattels than ideas. (Adrian, 2006) Virtual goods fit the five characteristics of chattel property: the abilities to (1) possess; (2) use; (3) enjoy; (4) transfer; and (5) exclude others (also defined as "rivalrousness"). (Samuelson, 1989) If a player possesses a particular virtual good, a sword of light, other people do not possess that same good, your sword of light. If one person uses or enjoys a virtual good, other players cannot use or enjoy it simultaneously. A person can transfer virtual goods to other players. Finally, a person can exclude others from using her virtual goods. (Adrian, 2006)

Virtual property also resembles chattels more closely than intellectual property on the dimensions of persistence and interconnectivity. Like personal property, virtual goods in MMORPGs are persistent. They "do[] not fade after each use, and [they] do[] not run on one single computer." (Fairfield, 2005) And like chattels, virtual goods in MMORPGs are interconnected, "although one person may control [them], others may experience [them]." (Id.) Virtual goods "share every relevant attribute of physical property, [although] they are not really physical." (Schwartz & Bullis, 2005) Some scholars insist on characterizing virtual goods as intellectual property on the basis of mere intangibility. (Stephens, 2002) Instead, "the same framework that adjudicates the rights of those who want to sell used books, used cars, and used compact discs, [should be] used [for] digital swords." (Reuveni, 2007; Nichols, 2007)

It is important to classify virtual goods as personal property as opposed to intellectual property. Intellectual property, specifically copyright as it would apply to virtual goods, only protects the author's expression of his ideas, because it grants the author specific rights in his expression. (Dunn, 1986) A person who infringes a copyright is not committing a theft. This is because he does not appropriate the copyright; he merely infringes it. The right of possession is not protected through intellectual property. (Green, 2002) Yet the right of possession, as it pertains to virtual goods in MMORPGs, is critical to protect such virtual goods against theft.

What constitutes personal property depends largely on the rights that attach to the item in question. "There are various rights that may be attributed to chattels: (1) right to possess and own; (2) right to use; (3) right to manage how and by whom the property will be used; (4) right to income and profits generated by the property; (5) right to capital--that is, the right to alienate, consume, waste or destroy; (6) right to security--that is, immunity from involuntary transfer and expropriation; (7) right to transfer without limitation; (8) right to no durational limit to interest in property; and (9) right to any residuary interests emerging from the property." (Samuelson, 1989) In contrast, copyright law conveys the rights to: (1) adaptation; (2) distribution; (3) display; (4) reproduction; and (5) performance. (Yu, 2005)

The property rights to possess, use, enjoy, transfer, and exclude are precisely the sorts of protections that virtual world residents need to secure their virtual goods from theft. Yet, intellectual property cannot secure these rights for virtual goods. The Court, in Dowling v. United States,

473 U.S. 207,(1985) rejected the government's theory that equated copyright infringement with the 'theft, conversion, or fraud' element, noting that the interests of those who own physical goods are distinct from the interests of copyright owners." (Byassee, 1995) Instead, theft statutes protect against interferences with use, enjoyment, and possession. Theft statutes are designed to promote security. Once virtual goods are classified as personal property and virtual world inhabitants are granted the right to use, possess, enjoy, and exclude others from the use of such virtual goods, then the current theft statutes will satisfactorily protect virtual world inhabitants from the theft of their virtual goods.

2. Belonging to Another

It is normally straightforward under English law whether the property belongs to another. (R v Sullivan; R v Ballion [2002] Crim LR 758 (CA)) Section 5(1) of the Theft Act states: "Property shall be regarded as belonging to any person having possession or control of it, or having in it any proprietary right or interest (not being an equitable interest arising only from an agreement to transfer or grant an interest)." This means that property does not just belong to the person who owns it, but also to any person who has possession or control of it, or a proprietary interest in it. (R v Woodman (George Eli) [1974] QB 447 (CCA)) This concept is not directly relatable to American law; except in as much that the government cannot deprive a person "of life, liberty, or property, without due process of law". (5th & 14th Amendment, U.S. Constitution) Nor can one individual do as much to another.

In virtual worlds, however, what belongs to who is still a difficult question. Currently, property rights in these virtual worlds are defined by end user license agreements (EULAs) that players agree to when they first log on to the game. Nearly every virtual world has a clause in their EULA requiring that players assign the rights of all property created in-game to the developers of that world. For example, the EULA for World of Warcraft reads: "All title, ownership rights and intellectual property rights in and to the Game and all copies thereof (including without limitation any titles, computer code, themes, objects, characters, character names, stories, dialog, catch phrases, locations, concepts, artwork, character inventories, structural or landscape designs, animations, sounds, musical compositions and recordings, audio-visual effects, storylines, character likenesses, methods of operation, moral rights, and any related documentation) are owned or licensed by Blizzard." (http://www.worldofwarcraft.com/legal/eula.html) While there is the exception of Second Life, the norm is total developer ownership via intellectual property rights of all virtual property created in virtual worlds. The courts have yet to determine if non-intellectual property rights should be available too.

3. Appropriation

Under the Theft Act s3(1) states: "Any assumption by a person of the rights of an owner amounts to an appropriation, and this includes, where he has come by the property (innocently or not) without stealing, any later assumption of a right to it by keeping or dealing with it as owner." There is an appropriation if the defendant has assumed any of the rights of the owner. This means that if the defendant has done something that an owner has the right to do then this is an appropriation. (R v Morris (David Allen); sub nom Anderton v Burnside [1984] AC 320 (HL)) An "unlawful taking" under the MPC §223.2(1) requires that the person actually "takes" or "exercises control" over the stolen good.

A video game player may not physically hold the virtual sword, but his avatar's actions produce the consequences that would be produced by an actual taking: (a) the original owner's avatar no longer can possess or use the virtual sword; and

(b) the thief's avatar now possesses and may use the stolen virtual sword. Although the person controlling the avatar may not have taken the virtual sword per se, the avatar was only able to perform the action per the instruction of his master, making the distinction between the actions of the avatar and those of the thief irrelevant. (Faier, 2004)

The term "exercises unlawful control" over property refers to the moment when the criminal video-game player begins to use the virtual good in a manner beyond his authority. (Green, 2002) This requirement of control may be awkward to prove due to the intangibility of virtual goods. The defendant does not actually exert control over the sword; his avatar merely creates the illusion of control. In reality, the only action that takes place is the transfer from one player account to another of computer code that represents that sword. Moreover, the argument could be made that a person never actually controlled the virtual goods, but instead that the avatar alone performed the act. (Faier, 2004)

U.S. Defence attorneys, however, may question whether thefts of virtual goods constitute an "unlawful taking," because unlawful taking requires the prosecution to prove four elements: stolen thing must have 'value', the person taking it must 'exercise control' over it, the stolen thing must be 'carried away', and 'unlawfully deprive' the victim. (Green, 2002) The first three elements will be compared with UK law here. 'Unlawful deprivation' will be considered later.

First, under the MPC statute, the thing stolen must be something of value. The United Kingdom does not require a thing be of value. There is, in fact, no need to show that the victim's property interest have been adversely interfered with. (R v Morris [1993] 1 All ER 1) In the fact, the consent of the victim does not change the act of appropriation. The victim's state of mind is irrelevant to whether or not there was an appropriation. (R v Gomez [1993] 1 All ER 1) In Hinks [2001] 2 SC 241 (HL), the House of Lords held that even if the property was handed over by the victim to the defendant as a valid gift, this could amount to appropriation.

In the United States, however, the requirement of value could be seen as problematic as virtual goods do not obtain pecuniary value until they are sold through secondary markets, like eBay. If a defendant were caught stealing a good that had never been sold previously in a secondary market (to set a numerical dollar precedent), the prosecutor may have difficulty demonstrating that virtual good's actual value. (Rubenstein, 2004) Fortunately, valuation is a low hurdle for the prosecution. For example, in United States v. Sampson, 6 Computer L. Serv. Rep. 879, 880 (N.D. Cal. 1978), the court found that the time spent using a computer was of value, "sufficient upon which to predicate a legally sufficient indictment" for theft. Time as a commodity is considerably less tangible than virtual goods, yet the court still applies the traditional law of theft to virtual goods. (Olivenbaum, 1997) Moreover, states could use an expert to overcome this hurdle; the expert could use various valuation models to determine the virtual good's value. (Nammacher, 2002)

Second, courts in the United States are divided on the issue of whether "intangibles" may be "taken." While one court has held that "where no tangible objects were ever taken or transported, a court would be hard pressed to conclude that 'goods' had been stolen," (United States v. Bottone, 365 F.2d 389, 393 (2d Cir. 1966), cert. denied, 385 U.S. 974 (1966)) Many courts are willing to accept that a thing has been taken if the rightful owner is denied possession, regardless of tangibility, thus creating the presumption that the other party has asserted control over the good. For example, in People v. Perry, 864 N.E.2d 196, 222 (Ill. 2007), the court held that "the occupancy of a hotel room is 'property within the meaning of section 15-1 of the Criminal Code [of Illinois] and that the taking of such property ... can result in the owner's being permanently deprived of its use or benefit.'" Further in Bridgeport Harbor Place

I, LLC v. Ganim, No. X06CV040184523S, 2006 WL 493352, (Conn. Super. Feb. 16, 2006), the court found that the intangible contractual right to develop property can be taken by theft. In the more technological case of Staton Holdings, Inc. v. First Data Corp., No. Civ.A.3:04-CV-2321-P, 2005 WL 1164179, (N.D. Tex. May 11, 2005), the court decided that a telephone number, though intangible, may be taken, if the rightful owner is deprived of its use.

In the United Kingdom, there is an appropriation if the defendant has assumed any of the rights of the owner. This means that if the defendant has done something that an owner has the right to do then this is an appropriation. It is therefore appropriation to touch someone else's property, offer it for sale, or destroy it. It must be shown that the act is something that only an owner has the right to do.

Third, the MPC statute requires that the virtual good be "carried away". The property was completely moved (however slightly) from the place it was taken. In a virtual setting this seems clear. The sword graphically moves from one avatar to another. However, the data entry for the sword remains physically within the programmer's network server. The only difference is that the sword's computer code is assigned from the rightful owner's account to the thief's account. (Arias, 2008)

Nonetheless, the requirement of "carrying away" may be overcome by the fact that many U.S. courts rely on trespassory taking, which requires mere constructive possession rather than the existence of actual movement. (50 Am. Jur. 2d Larceny § 18 (2007)) For example, one court in the case of United States v. Riggs, 739 F. Supp. 414 (N.D. Ill. 1990), found the act of moving electronic information over a telephone wire to be sufficient to constitute a taking. Tangibility, in this sense, becomes irrelevant--like information transferred over telephone wires, the source code representing the virtual sword has travelled from one video game account to another, and for all purposes of the statute, has been taken. (Franks, 2005)

4. Permanently Depriving

Next, in the United States, the state must prove that the defendant "unlawfully" intended to deprive the defendant of his property, i.e. deprivation without legal right. (MPC § 223.2(1)) "The general rule is that a defendant is not guilty of larceny (or theft) unless he takes another's property with the [specific] intent to deprive the person permanently of that property - an intent referred to at common law as animus furandi (intent to deprive)." (Green, 2002) The intent may be proven by direct or circumstantial evidence. For example, the thief is counting on some "reward" or gain by the sale or return of the property at a minimum, by a substantial risk of permanent loss. Or where the thief plans to eventually return the property, but the risk of permanent loss is present. (Arias, 2008)

This is very similar to English law. Section 6 of the Theft Act states:

1. A person appropriating property belonging to another without meaning the other permanently to lose the thing itself is nevertheless to be regarded as having the intention of permanently depriving the other of it if his intention is to treat the thing as his own to dispose of regardless of the other's rights; and a borrowing or lending of it may amount to so treating it if, but only if, the borrowing or lending is for a period and in circumstances making it equivalent to an outright taking or disposal.

2. Without prejudice to the generality of subsection (1) above, where a person, having possession or control (lawful or not) of property belonging to another, parts with the property under a condition as to its return which he may not be able to perform, this (if done for purpose of his own and without the other's authority) amounts to treating the property as his own to dispose of regardless of the other's rights.

Because most virtual worlds are protected by the magic circle of the game, it may prove hard for the state to demonstrate that the accused actually intended to deprive the rightful owner of his property, unless the accused has sold the virtual good already. Otherwise, the accused could argue that he took the virtual sword in the spirit of role-playing, but that he never intended to permanently deprive the original owner of his sword. Moreover, the accused could, utilizing the claim-of-right defence, assert that he was unaware that the virtual sword was in fact owned by the original owner, because the game does not establish clear ownership rights. (Newton, 1999) The problem with proving intent may demonstrate the limitations of criminal law as a tool to resolve thefts in general, but should not be seen as a barrier to the prosecution of virtual good thefts. Defendants tend to make similar arguments in regular theft cases, and in such cases, juries are given the power to decide the defendant's credibility. (Green, 2002) Thus, current unlawful taking theft statutes could successfully be used to prosecute virtual good theft criminals.

5. Deception

The MPC and the Theft Act could also theoretically address the theft of virtual goods where a party-member, entrusted to hold an item while another player empties his bags, runs off with the item without returning it to the lawful owner. Under s15(4) of the Theft Act, "deception means any deception (whether deliberate or reckless) by words or conduct as to fact or as to law, including a deception as to the present intentions of the person using the deception or any other person. Under the MPC § 223.3(1), a person is guilty of theft by deception if he purposely "creates or reinforces a false impression, including false impressions as to law, value, intention, or other state of mind."

In Commonwealth v. Patterson, 390 A.2d 784 (Pa. Super. Ct. 1978), the court found that if defendant stole a key to a safety deposit box from the owner, or said that he was taking it in order to make a duplicate for the owner's use, and then proceeded to steal a ruby from the box, that act constituted theft by unlawful taking; if, however, defendant told the owner that he wanted to appraise the ruby, or to clean it, and she gave him the key so that he could take possession of the ruby, and defendant sold the ruby and kept the proceeds, then deception by which defendant obtained the key would be related to bringing about a transfer or purported transfer of legal interest in property and theft by deception would be the appropriate charge.

Likewise, in a virtual world, if the defendant stole key to a magical box from the owner, then proceeded to steal the magical ruby from the box, then the act constitutes theft by unlawful taking. On the other hand, if the defendant told the owner that he wanted to use the magical ruby to heal another member of the party. So the owner then gives him the key so that he may possess it; followed by the defendant running off and selling the ruby and keeping the proceeds. Then the deception by which the defendant obtained the key would be related to bringing about a transfer or purported transfer of legal interest in the property and theft by deception would have transpired.

Prosecutors could also use theft-by-deception statutes to prosecute a thief who used one of the aforementioned scams to obtain another player's virtual goods. Prosecuting under the MPC statute, the state would need to prove that (1) the accused obtained control over the property; (2) by means of a false statement or misrepresentation; (3) which deceived the victim; and (4) that the victim in whole or in part relied upon the false statement in relinquishing control of the property to the accused. (State v. Schultz, 850 P.2d 818, 838 (Kan. 1993)) Under the Theft Act s15(4), the prosecutor would need to prove that (1) the statement was untrue; (R v Mandry and Wooster [1973] 1 WLR 1232 (CA)) (2) the victim was deceived; (R v Deller [1952] 36 Cr App R 184) (3) the deception was by means of words or conduct; (R v Barnard [1837] 7 C&P 784) and (4) the deception was either explicit or implicit. (DPP v Ray [1974] AC 370 (HL)) Theft-by-deception may create certain application problems when used in relation to virtual goods. Prosecutors will be able to overcome them in a similar fashion as discussed above.

The first issue is control. Did the thief exert control over the virtual good or merely the illusion of control? As discussed above, prosecutors can prove that a thief exerted control over an intangible good. If a person denies the rightful owner of possession of a virtual good, courts perceive the virtual good as taken and presume the right of control. Thus, the state should be able to show that the virtual good has been taken if the rightful owner no longer possesses the good.

Second is misrepresentation. Did the thief "create or reinforce a false impression" by affirmatively holding on to a virtual good. (MPC § 223.3) Deception is a broad term, requiring merely "the misrepresentation of some existing fact. .. [as to] law, value, or intention. Thus, theft by deception covers almost any type of deceptive practice used to obtain possession of another person's property." (McCullough, 1998) Did the thief behave dishonestly? Section 2 of the Theft Act defines dishonesty in the negative by what stating what is not dishonest first. "A person's appropriation of property belonging to another is not to be regarded as dishonest – (a) if he appropriates the property in the belief that he has in law the right to deprive the other of it, on behalf of himself or a third person; or (b) if he appropriates the property in the belief that he would have the other's consent if the other knew of the appropriation and the circumstances of it; or (c) (except where the property came to him as trustee or personal representative) if he appropriates the property in the belief that the person to whom the property belongs cannot be discovered by taking reasonable steps." So according to s2(2) then, "A person's appropriation of property belonging to another may be dishonest notwithstanding that he is willing to pay for the property."

So, does one need to promise to give the virtual good back? Does tacitly accepting the good automatically create a false impression, even if one does not explicitly promise to give it back? The English courts would follow one more common law test to determine this. In Pattni, Dhunna, Soni and Poopalarajah [2001] Crim LR 570, the court considered two further questions: "Was what the defendant did dishonest according to the standards of reasonable and honest people? And would the defendant realize that reasonable and honest people would regard what he did as dishonest?" If the answer to both these questions is 'yes' then the defendant is dishonest. If the answer to either question is 'no' then the defendant is not dishonest.

In reality, the virtual world thief or his avatar may not have to say anything at all. "Various forms of misleading nonverbal conduct" can be sufficient to constitute deceit. (R v Barnard [1837] 7 C&P 784; Green, 2001) Thus, circumstantial evidence should be sufficient to prove that a "false impression" was created or reinforced. (DPP v Ray [1974] AC 370 (HL); State v. Hogrefe, 557 N.W.2d 871 (Iowa 1996); Martinez v. State, 198 S.W.3d 36 (Tex. App. 1996); Griffin v. State, 614 S.W.2d 155 (Tex. Crim. App. 1981)) Thus, current theft-by-deception laws could be used to prosecute virtual criminals, but only in limited situations and with discovery-related difficulties. (Arias, 2008) These laws, however, should prove useful to prosecute thieves who use scams to obtain virtual goods.

Embezzlement is another tool U.S. prosecutors may use. To prove embezzlement under state penal statutes, prosecutors must show that there was a knowing conversion of property by one lawfully entrusted with its possession. Conversion, within the meaning of embezzlement statutes, is the "fraudulent appropriation of a thing to one's own use and beneficial enjoyment." (29A

C.J.S. Embezzlement § 16 (2007) citing State v. Pietranton, 84 S.E.2d 774 (W. Va. 1954)). However, appropriation here means something more than mere possession of the property. (State v. Barbossa, 384 A.2d 523 (N.J. Super. Ct. App. Div. 1976)). "Embezzlement statutes protect against knowing conversion of specific items or services which are in the possession of another occupying a designated fiduciary relation ... [and require] the prosecution [to] prove that an ownership interest is in someone other than the accused, and that there has been a conversion of the property with fraudulent intent." (Jorgensen, 1987)

Embezzlement statutes do not present the possession and control problems typically associated with the application of the other suggested laws in relation to virtual goods because the courts recognize that embezzlement statutes may be properly applied to intangibles, even those that cannot be physically possessed. For example, electricity: People v. Menagas, 11 N.E.2d 403 (Ill. 1937) holding that larceny includes the taking of electricity; Ferens v O'Brien [1883] 11 QBD 21 also holding theft of electricity to be an offense. In such cases, the analysis turns on whether "the victim's interest in the subject matter is sufficiently important that defendant's interference with it should be penalized." (Comment, 1960) Thus, if the state is able to demonstrate that the victim's interest is sufficiently important and that actual conversion, as opposed to mere possession, has taken place, then the state should be able to use embezzlement statutes to successfully prosecute certain virtual good thefts. (Arias, 2008)

C. EVE INTERGALACTIC BANK

EVE Online is a science-fiction-based massively multiplayer online game set in an outer space persistent world. Players take the role of spaceship pilots seeking fame, fortune, and adventure in a huge, exciting, and sometimes hostile galaxy. (EVE FAQ) Unlike other virtual worlds with a wild-west-style space opera theme, the world of EVE Online is unique in two ways. First, unlike most virtual worlds, EVE Online does not "shard," that is, all players in the entire universe exist on the same server, and all players of the game exist in the same world. A shard is an instance of a world, realm, or playground in some massively multiplayer online games. In MMOGs, the term shard is often associated with Ultima Online and Silkroad Online. Other MMOGs call them servers instead, although their function is the same. The usage originated with the Ultima Online story, where each of the game's servers were said to be different images of the world, trapped in the shattered shards of a mystic gem. (Wikipedia) The lack of sharding in EVE Online is important, as a scam of the magnitude to be described would be extremely difficult to attempt if it were necessary to create an individual bank for every instance of the server. Another significant point is that this makes EVE Online larger than games with more total players. It also means that every player of EVE Online is able to interact with every other player. (Glushko, 2007)

The second distinction of EVE Online is that the interaction amongst players is more hostile and competitive than other relationship-oriented games like Second Life. Relationships in EVE Online can be cooperative, such as in trading resources or building ships, or hostile, such as pirating other players' resources, cheating them in business deals, or destroying their ships and bases in combat. The basic role-playing and space simulation aspects of EVE are really just the tip of the iceberg. When players amalgamate to form factions and alliances, the game evolves to grand-scale strategic level. Political intrigue, corporate espionage and the very essence of Darwinism bring dimension and depth to the game as the struggle for fame and fortune ebbs and flows with each new day in EVE. (EVE FAQ)

Players form alliances, or corporations, and pool their resources. (EVE Corporation Guide) These corporations often have significant assets, with large amounts of virtual property. While player groups or guilds are common in many online games, the scope of EVE Online is massive, with over one hundred thousand players potentially online at any given time. (EVE Press Release, 2006) The size of the virtual world makes it important for players to band together to avoid being overpowered by more powerful players. Furthermore, since EVE Online attracts a sophisticated player base, the level of competition can be higher than in virtual worlds targeted at younger audiences. Games which primarily emphasize personal interaction tend to draw older audiences than games which focus on the acquiring of property and experience through accomplishing tasks, generally hunting monsters. Also, players tend to react negatively to having their property taken or their character killed by another human, as opposed to the game itself. (Glushko, 2007)

Real world corporations sell stock in speculative business ventures to players in the game. (Wallace, 2006) It was within this setting that a player, whose avatar went by the name of Cally, created the Eve Investment Bank, a corporation that took deposits of players' in-game money for safekeeping. A safe place to keep money was very attractive to those inhabiting such a dangerous place. For half a year, Cally had accepted in-game transfers of Inter Stellar Kredits ("ISK") and paid interest on those deposits. (Stefanescu, 2006) EVE Online Insider Forums suggested that some players appeared to be converting dollars to ISK through online currency traders just to earn a greater return than would be available in real-world dollars because the interest rates were so high. For example, large-scale investors were guaranteed nearly a nine percent return on their money. During the nine months it was operating, the bank took in hundreds of billions of ISK, or nearly $125,000. Cally's avatar then absconded into the uncharted in-game space with the depositors' money.

With so much capital removed from circulation all at once, shockwaves permeated the virtual economy and threw the EVE Online community into chaos. As Peter Pollack (2006) commented, "it might have been a scene out of some movie about the Great Depression; hundreds of frantic people tearing their hair out as they mob the doors to a bank, only to realize that the bank's owners, along with their money, had vanished into thin air." In the following weeks, the outcry prompted Crowd Control Productions ("CCP"), the makers of Eve Online, to release a statement in a virtual press conference, saying that while they recognized that the money stolen represented a huge investment in players' time and money; however, they would not delete Cally's account. (Husemann, 2006) Although CCP implied that they would be closely watching the account to ensure that the ISK would not be converted to real-world currency. (Id.) This is not particularly useful as there are billions of ISK for sale through online currency traders, indicating that it is possible to sell ISK on the black market. This merely creates an incentive for similar scams.

However, in the case of Cally's EIB scam, there are sufficient anecdotal facts to support each element of theft, though perhaps not beyond a preponderance of the evidence, let alone a reasonable doubt.

First, the prosecutor will need to convince the court that property has been lost. This has been demonstrated above. Next to be proved is that the property belongs to another.

Cally enticed potential investors in EVE Online to deposit approximately 790 billion in in-game currency to the EIB. (McCarthy, 2006) The creation and marketing of the EIB convinced investors to turn over billions of in-game currency to Cally. He clearly appropriated what they would conceivably still possess of these funds. Based on both Dentara Rast's (aka Cally) message-board and video confession, the representation of the EIB as a legitimate investment was made falsely with Cally knowing of the falsity of the scheme, as evidenced by Cally's statements that "[t]he only person involved was me. 1 Person. And that one

character I used was Cally .... I fooled everyone. I win EVE." (Cally Confession) Cally clearly intended others to rely on the false representation, for what is a bank, or a Ponzi scheme for that matter, without depositors.

The prosecutor will also be able to demonstrate that he had every intention of permanently denying his depositors their funds. At the time of this writing, Cally's location is unknown. Presumably the avatar and the money he stole are off in some unknown area of EVE Online, or more likely, merely inactive. He was frank in his closing statements: he was a pirate, and everyone foolish enough to trust him with their money got "owned." (Cally Confession) The term "owned" is used by gamers to "acknowledge a form of superiority through the downfall of another entity, be it another gaming clan, or a single user. This can be in the context of winning an online game, a debate on a forum, or attaining a successful hacking ...." (Wikipedia)

The next element is deception. Within EVE Online, the game's creators have implicitly tried to establish what passes for "justifiable" reliance: "[a] scam is the act of obtaining goods from other players through misinformation, confusion, pressure or by taking advantage of basic trust. Players enter into business dealings with others at their own risk and are strongly urged to exercise good judgment and common sense when trading." (EVE FAQ) In attempting to contractually define what passes for fraud, the game's creators take for granted too much. For example, a real-world store owner may post a sign warning "all sales final" or "buyer beware", it would be up to the fact-finder in adjudication to determine whether, and how much, that warning could impact some finding of reasonableness (or justifiability) on the part of the hearer. (White, 2008) Further, the definition of a scam in EVE Online does not say a scam is legal or authorized, only that a player should be on the lookout for such behaviour. In the MMOG context, the level of reliance on the representation that was justifiable would need to be examined on the basis of a plaintiff's specific facts, and perhaps due to embarrassment, no users taken by the EIB scheme have come forward with details of their reliance. (Id.)

The EVE Online community was upset by CCP's response. Even though most players understood that the game incorporated elements of deception and theft, the EVE Investment Bank scam went far beyond any previous scam and at least some players felt that CCP should intervene. (Murdoch, 2006) It is likely that some players had acquired ISK through online currency traders to invest in the EVE Online Bank. Until the scam, CCP had turned a blind eye to many violations of their restrictions on purchasing or selling ISK online, and this complacency contributed to the size of the players' loss. The company's laissez-faire attitude towards the EVE Investment Bank scandal does not reflect the rules set out in its terms of service ("ToS"). (EVE ToS) The EULA bans many types of fraudulent behaviour, including impersonating CCP staff, soliciting for "pyramid schemes and chain letters," and "violating any local, state, national, or international laws or regulations." This is an interesting element, as the EVE Investment Bank was a classic pyramid scheme. Given their comments about the nature of EVE Online, perhaps CCP means this solely in a physical world context.

CCP retains an extensive right to control the importation of physical world material into the virtual world, and has wide latitude to take action against players in the virtual world, such as suspending service, confiscating property, or terminating accounts. CCP reserves the right to "close, temporarily or permanently, any user's account without advance notice" and "to delete all user accounts or inventory of characters as warranted." (EVE ToS) Although it seems clear that CCP could take action in this case, return the stolen ISK to its owners, and hopefully deter future scams of this type, the ToS does not state that CCP will (or must) regulate such behaviour.

The EVE Online banking scandal demonstrates the limitations that arise from governing virtual worlds through an agreement that can only be enforced by the game developer. Unfortunately for the players, the terms of the EVE Online EULA do not require game developers to assist players, and the game developers have incentives not to get involved in disputes among players. Any such involvement would only have increased CCP's workload or potential for liability. The inability of players to enforce property rights in their virtual property is a key failing of the EULA as a tool to govern virtual worlds as they continue to grow.

D. CONCLUSION

If in the real world, a swindled investor can resort to the courts, in most case, to recover their principal and punish the offender, why should a player in a virtual world not seek a similar right? According to the gaming companies, the "gods" of these worlds, there are only two ways to deal with these situations. The first, a hard-line approach taken in the above example, refuses to recognize any player's right to in-game property and maintains all property rights are held by the company itself. (EVE EULA) This approach seems to deny a cause of action. If an in-game fraud is alleged, the game company typically deletes the offending accounts for violating the company's terms of use.

On the other hand, the company ignores the problem and allows the players to work it out amongst themselves. This approach is less drastic but still gives the player no real recourse. Even if a fraud is alleged, the company will do nothing. This approach is demonstrated by CCP Games' reaction to a massive fraud perpetrated in EVE Online, where a CCP Games executive stated that "[t]he behaviour of [the perpetrator] and his [scheme] is despicable, but allowed. As long as he kept all of his work within the boundaries of the EULA, there's nothing CCP Games will do to touch him." (McCarthy, 2006) Because the in-game currency worth real-world dollars was fraudulently obtained by Cally during the EIB scam, there is a possibility of criminal charges. The scheme to defraud money would seem to fall under the theft statutes of both various states of the United States and the United Kingdom. Further, there is the possibility of U.S. federal criminal charges for wire fraud, as well as the associated Racketeer Influenced and Corrupt Organizations (RICO) statutes. See 18 U.S.C.A § 1343 stating "Whoever ... for obtaining money or property by means of false or fraudulent pretenses, representations, or promises, transmits or causes to be transmitted by means of wire ... shall be [penalized.]" As well as 18 U.S.C.A. §1961(1)(B) which states that "'racketeering activity' means ... any act which is indictable under any of the following provisions ... section 1343 (relating to wire fraud)"

Participants in virtual worlds should not be left without legal recourse for the simple fact that the real world result cannot be reconciled with the persistent world result. In both instances, real time and money are at stake. Therefore, when money disappears through a fraudulent investment scheme, in both instances, the victim should be able to turn to the courts for remedy.

REFERENCES

Adrian, A. (2006). Intellectual Property v. Intangible Chattel. *Journal of International Commercial Law and Technology (JICLT), 1*(2).

Arias, A. (2008). Life, Liberty, and the Pursuit of Swords and Armour: Regulating the Theft of Virtual Goods. *Emory L.J., 57*(1301).

Byassee, W. (1995). Jurisdiction of Cyberspace: Applying Real World Precedent to the Virtual Community. *Wake Forest L. Rev., 30*(197).

Cally. (n.d.). *"Confession" Video*. Retrieved from http://dl.qj.net/Cally-s-EVE-Online-Confession-Video-Movie-PC-Gaming-MMORPG-Other-Games/pg/12/fid/9542/catid/476

Cavalli, E. (2008). Police Refuse to Aid in Virtual Theft Case. *Wired*. Retrieved from http://blog.wired.com/games/2008/police-refuse-t.html

Chen, Y. (2005). An Analysis of Online Gaming Crime Characteristics. *Internet Research, 15*(246).

Darnoc Postings. (2005). Retrieved from http://forums.diabloii.net/showthread.php

Dunn, S. (1986) Defining the Scope of Copyright Protection for Computer Software. *Stan. L. Rev., 38*(497).

Faier, A. (2004). Digital Slaves of the Render Farms?: Virtual Actors and Intellectual Property Rights. U. Ill. J.L. Tech. & Pol'y 321.

Fairfield, J. (2005). Virtual Property. *B.U. L. Rev. 85*(1047)

Franks, C. (2005). Comment, Analyzing the Urge to Merge: Conversion of Intangible Property and the Merger Doctrine in the Wake of Kremen v. Cohen. *Hous. L. Rev., 42*(489).

Glusko, B. (2007). Tales of the (Virtual) City: Governing Property Disputes in Virtual Worlds. *Berkeley Tech. L. J., 22*(507).

Green, S. (2001). Lying, Misleading, and Falsely Denying: How Moral Concepts Inform the Law of Perjury, Fraud, and False Statements. *Hastings L.J., 53*(157).

Green, S. (2002). Plagiarism, Norms, and the Limits of Theft Law: Some Observations on the Use of Criminal Sanctions in Enforcing Intellectual Property Rights. *Hastings L.J., 54*(167).

Husemann, C. (2006). All about the ISK. *Gaming Nexus*. Retrieved from http://www.gamingnexus.com/Default.aspx?Section =Article&I=1181

Jorgensen, P. (1987). Embezzlement. *Am. Crim. L. Rev., 24*(513).

Kennedy, R. (2009). Law in Virtual Worlds. *No. 10 J. Internet L., 12*(3).

Lastowka, G., & Hunter, D. (2004) Virtual Crimes. *N.Y.L. Sch. L. Rev., 49*(293).

McCarthy, C. (2006). Cons in the Virtual Gaming World. *CNET News.com*. Retrieved from http://news.com.com/Cons+in+the+virtual+gaming+world/2100-1043_3-6111089.html

McCullough, T. (1998). Note, United States v. O'Hagan: Defining the Limits of Fraud and Deceptive Pretext Under Rule 10b-5. *Seattle U. L. Rev., 22*(311).

Murdoch, J. (2006). 612 Lawns. *Gamers With Jobs*. Retrieved from http://www.gamerswithjobs.com/node/26703

Nammacher, S. (2002). Financial Valuations for the Practicing Attorney. *Practicing L. Inst., 1325*(647).

Newton, D. (1999). Comment, What's Right with a Claim-of-Right. *U.S.F. L. Rev., 33*(673).

Nichols, W.J. (2007). Painting Through Pixels: The Case for a Copyright in Videogame Play. *Colum. J.L. & Arts, 30*(101).

Olivenbaum, J. (1997). <Ctrl><Alt><Del>: Rethinking Federal Computer Crime Legislation. *Seton Hall L. Rev., 27*(574).

Online, E. V. E. Press Release. (2006). *EVE Online Reaches the 100,000 Subscriber Mark*. Retrieved from http://www.gamespot.com/pc/rpg/evethesecondgenesis/news.html?sid=6143803

Online, E. V. E. *Corporation Guide*. (n.d.). Retrieved from http://www.eve-online.com/guide/en/g12.asp

Online, E. V. E. *End User License Agreement*. (n.d.). Retrieved from http://www.eve-online.com/pnp/eula.asp

Online, E. V. E. *EVE Insider Forums*. (n.d.). Retrieved from http://myeve.eve-online.com/ingameboard.asp?a=topic&threadID=347657

Online, E. V. E. *Frequently Asked Questions*. (n.d.). Retrieved from http://www.eve-online.com/faq/faq_01.asp

Online, E. V. E. *Terms of Service*. (n.d.). Retrieved from http://www.eve-online.com/pnp/terms.asp

Pollack, P. (2006). Online 'banker' runs off with cash, avatars cry foul. *Ars Technica*. Retrieved from http://arstechnica.com/news.ars/post/20060828-7605.html

Reuveni, E. (2007). On Virtual Worlds: Copyright and Contract Law at the Dawn of the Virtual Age. *Ind. L.J., 82*(261).

Rubenstein, D. (2004). eBay: The Cyber Swap Meet. *U. Miami Bus. L. Rev., 13*(1).

Samuelson, P. (1989). Information as Property: Do Ruckelshaus and Carpenter Signal a Changing Direction in Intellectual Property Law? *Cath. U. L. Rev., 38*(365).

Schwarz, A., & Bullis, R. (2005). Rivalrous Consumption and the Boundaries of Copyright Law: Intellectual Property Lessons from Online Games. *Intell. Prop. L. Bull., 10*(13).

Spring, S. (2006). Games: Virtual Thievery. *Newsweek*, 10.

Stefanescu, T. (2006). EVE Online Economy Suffers 700 Billion ISK Scam. *Softpedia*. Retrieved from http://news.softpedia.com/news/Eve-Online-Economy-Suffers-700-billion-ISK-Scam-33737.shtml

Stephens, M. (2002). Note, Sales of In-Game Assets: An Illustration of the Continuing Failure of Intellectual Property Law to Protect Digital-Content Creators. *Tex. L. Rev., 80*(1513).

Wallace, M. (2006). EVE Online Mega-Corporation Goes Public. *3pointD.com*. Retrieved from http://www.3pointd.com/20061214/eve-online-mega-corporation-goes-public/#more-962

Wikipedia.org. (n.d.). *Owned*. Retrieved from http://en.wikipedia.org/wiki/Owned

Wikipedia.org. (n.d.). *Shard*. Retrieved from http://en.wikipedia.org/wiki/Shard

Yu, P. (2005). Intellectual Property and the Information Ecosystem. Mich. St. L. Rev 1.

Chapter 10

Why Virtual Worlds Matter

"Existence, faculties, assimilation - in other words, personality, liberty, property - that is what man is.

Of these three things one may say, without any demagogic quibbling, that they are anterior and superior to all human legislation.

It is not because men have passed laws that personality, liberty, and property exist.

On the contrary, it is because personality, liberty, and property already exist that men make laws."

Frederic Bastiat (1993 trans.)

INTRODUCTION

To return to the quote which began this book, what is man? He has existence. He uses his faculties to improve his existence. He assimilates the world around him. Bastiat labelled these personality, liberty and property. What is an avatar but a mani-

festation of self beyond the realm of the physical? He has existence in a virtual world. He has a distinct personality. The avatar must use his faculties to improve his existence. He must level himself into a more powerful character to survive in his virtual world. He must have the liberty to become what he wants or needs to become. The avatar assimilates the world around him. By questing and click slavery, an avatar can acquire property. Personality, liberty and property are intrinsic traits of avatars as well as men. And they exist whether laws have been passed by governments or game companies. If there is a world to exist in, then these traits exist and men will want to set limits on them.

Gaming identities are becoming indistinguishable from 'real' identities – just as e-commerce has become indistinguishable from 'commerce'. Control over these online avatar identities has real-world consequences. As soon as something is valuable and persistent, people seek to associate rights and duties with it. The questions posed in this book revolved around the ideas of personality (personhood, identity), liberty (freedom v servitude), and property (copyright and intangible property).

DOI: 10.4018/978-1-61520-795-4.ch010

People in the gaming community already focus on their real, rich identities online from a human perspective, and who is in charge of it. Online identities are emergent. Identity is by definition a group project. It is created by the context in which the identified operates. Identity is not a matter of 'rights' in the abstract or in advance. Thus, having some centralized one-size-fits-all 'law of identity' (and associated rights) does not make sense. The context for identities does not arrive before us fully formed, and different groups have and will continue to have different ways for dealing with identity-removal questions in virtual worlds. (Crawford, 2005)

However, just as the thought of contextual yet customized online avatar identities shaped by its chosen group becomes a norm, it is alarming to learn that the online intermediaries have 'ownership' of these online identities. They also have hooks which allow them to remove identities they do not like, as seen in *Bragg v Linden Lab*. In other words, the 'gods' or 'wizards' of the virtual worlds are formulating all the rules (or laws) about identity. But because there is no norm of transparency with respect to these laws -- no way for an individual to understand or predict how his/her identity will be treated by the intermediary -- accountability is difficult. The question "who is in charge of who I am?" is not a usual question to pose. Often we prefer to think of ourselves as fully formed by our own actions within our chosen environment. Or, if we think of ourselves as having various role-playing identities, we imagine ourselves to be voluntarily, purposefully role-playing. These assumptions are only partial. In fact, we are constantly bumping up against and watching and learning from everyone around us. Everyone who makes up our 'group' has a hand in our identity. We emerge over and over again changed by the interactions we have with that group (or those groups). The duet played by groups and individuals is constant, seamless and endlessly productive of identity.

Identity is not just credit card data or click-stream information or address details. In *The Presentation of Self in Everyday Life*, Erving Goffman (1959) suggested the notion of identity as a series of performances, where we use 'impression management' to portray ourselves appropriately in different environments. Some part of identity is controlled by the individual, but most of identity is created by the world in which that individual operates. Identity then is a streaming picture of a life within a particular context. Each of us has multiple identities. (Clarke, 1994) "Identity is used to mean 'the condition of being a specified person', or 'the condition of being oneself ... and not another'. It clusters with the terms 'personality', 'individuality' and 'individualism', and, less fashionably, 'soul'. It implies the existence for each person of private space or personal lebensraum, in which one's attitudes and actions can define one's self ... The dictionary definitions miss a vital aspect. The origin of the term implies equality or 'one-ness', but identities are no longer rationed to one per physiological specimen. A person may adopt different identities at various times during a life-span, and some individuals maintain several at once. Nor are such multiple roles illegal or even used primarily for illegal purposes. Typical instances include women working in the professions, artists and novelists, and people working in positions which involve security exposure (such as prison wardens and psychiatric superintendents.)" (Id.) The role of groups in shaping 'real life' identities is implicit, as is the multiplicity of 'real life' identity. What is interesting and new about virtual worlds is that they make this group-shaping explicit and multiplicity of identity actionable.

Indeed, as Richard Bartle (2004) puts it, "the celebration of identity is the fundamental, critical, absolutely core point of virtual worlds." The combination of interactions with fellow players and code-driven constraints produces a 'stream of challenges' that shapes the identities of virtual world inhabitants in an explicit way over a compressed period of time. (Id.) It may be that people now go to virtual worlds at least in part because of this compressed, playful, group-based identity-creation experience.

Once it is acknowledged that identity is a group project, the tension produced by the physics of virtual worlds is obvious. The 'gods' of the online world -- the people writing the code that makes the world run -- can have a conclusive effect on identity. They can remove all traces of anyone and anything. Indeed, the 'gods' may see themselves as shaping identity; their shaping is done through code rather than hints, actions, and conversations. What happens when emergent, group-shaped identity is threatened with erasure?

Who owns identity? Who owns reputation? From the game companies' perspective, software creates rules that control what social context can be moved elsewhere. An avatar's identity is 'really' a database entry, and the game company can argue that the avatar's identity is their intellectual property, not the game player's. The game player may attach great importance to it, but this identity (and its reputation) will not, as a practical matter, survive outside the world in which it was formed. Virtual world designers have incentives to raise switching costs and capture all the value of this reputation. As Raph Koster (2003) puts it, "Make sure that players have a reasonable expectation of future interaction. This means persistence of identity and limited mobility." But players may defect from environments that attempt to constrain them in how persistent their reputations and identities are. The difficult task for developers and intermediaries is how much freedom to give their users. This takes us from the realm of risks to the realm of opportunities.

Hegel's conception of property as an extension of personality has been discussed as well as related modern theories. (Waldron, 1988; Radin, 1993) In essence, these theorists argue that property rights are related - either as necessary conditions for, or as connected to - human rights such as liberty,

identity, and privacy. The theory of personality would weigh in favour of recognizing property rights, in order for the self to be realized or other human needs secured.

This theory works in the virtual world in an interesting way. First, there is no distinction between the accumulation of real-world chattels or land and its virtual analogues. To the extent that personality theory justifies private property in land or goods, it justifies property in virtual land or goods. The theory is predicated on the effect of the property interest on human needs like liberty and identity, and these are presumably not different just because the property at issue is virtual. More importantly, when it comes to avatars, personality theory would seem to be strongly in favour of granting property rights. As discussed, people feel connected to their avatar, not as a thing but as a projection of their self. If, as personality theory would have it, property might be justified by reference to the effect on the self, it would seem that there is a normative basis for claiming property in virtual realty, virtual chattels, and, a fortiori, avatars.

Locke's (1690) central property proposal was that "whatsoever [man] removes out of the state that nature hath provided and left it in, he hath mixed his labour with, and joined to it something that is his own, and thereby makes it his property." This theory is a theory of dessert from labour. The person who expended labour to render the 'thing in nature' into valuable form deserves to reap its value. (Munzer, 1990; Radin, 1993) Players and avatars will have a property claim in their virtual-world assets based on the Lockean labour-dessert theory. These assets become apparent from the time and effort of the players. Depending on the theory one adopts, the limitations on rights in virtual property may be uncertain. Nonetheless, there seems to be no reason under traditional theories of property to exclude virtual properties from legal protection. Further, based on the earlier discussion, there is no descriptive disconnection between the real-world property system and virtual assets. Owners of virtual assets do, or should, possess property rights.

These theories of property provide strong grounds for recognizing that property rights should inhere in virtual assets, whether chattels, realty, or avatars. Intellectual property rights, specifically copyright as it would apply to virtual goods, protect the author's expression of his ideas, because it grants the author specific rights in his expression. (Dunn, 1986) As such, copyright law has been the first line of defense for the games companies, but the protection afforded to the games companies can be equally applied to the games users. The question remains who is creating what? The games company provides the backdrop and venue or the players who provide the dialogue, action, and plot. The structure and building-blocks are the legal property of the creator-company; however, each character is the embodiment of a player's story. Fair use will be a defense in the future. As has been previously illustrated, the fair use doctrine creates a "breathing space" for certain subsidiary or derivative uses of a work by declining to recognize the copyright holder's entitlement to control (or exploit) the markets for these uses. In determining which of these uses fall into this breathing space, the courts will use a sliding scale.

While property rights may exist in virtual assets, the allocation of those rights will depend largely on the End-User License Agreements that define the terms of access to the virtual world. Since the EULAs are written by the game companies, their terms inevitably grant all rights to the owner of the virtual world. This practice would give the impression of making the resolution of property disputes simple. The game companies get everything and the subscribers get nothing. Virtual worlds and their inhabitant are increasingly challenging the strength of EULA-based property demarcations. Courts may be likely to reject EULAs to the extent that they place excessive restrictions on the economic interests of users as they did in

Specht v Netscape Communications Corp., 150 F. Supp. 2d 585, 595 (S.D.N.Y. 2001). As there is already so much money and property at stake in these worlds, expect more lawsuits rooted in these property-rights disputes. Players will likely raise arguments that attempt to circumvent or attack EULA restrictions. So far, most courts have been sceptical of such arguments. See *DeJohn v The .TV Corp. Int'l*, 245 F. Supp. 2d 913 (C.D. Ill. 2003); *Forrest v Verizon Communications, Inc.*, 805 A.2d 1007 (D.C. 2002); *I. Lan Sys. v Netscout Serv. Level Corp.*, 183 F. Supp. 2d 328 (D. Mass. 2002) However, as more people live out more of their lives in these worlds, any simple resolution of the property rights issues will become more difficult.

REFERENCES

Bartle, R. (2004). *Designing Virtual Worlds*. Berkeley, CA: New Riders Publishing.

Bastiat, F. (1993). *The Law* (Russell, D., Trans.). New York: The Foundation for Economic Education.

Clarke, R. (1994). Human Identification in Information Systems: Management Challenges and Public Policy Issues. *Information Tech. & People, 4*(7). Retrieved from http://www.anu.edu.au/people/Roger.Clarke/DV/HumanID.html

Crawford, S. (2005). Who is in Charge of Who I Am? Identity and Law Online. *N.Y.L. Sch. L. Rev., 49*(211).

Dunn, S. (1986). Defining the Scope of Copyright Protection for Computer Software. *Stan. L. Rev., 38*(497).

Goffman, E. (1959). *The Presentation of Self in Everyday Life*. New York: Basic Books.

Koster, R. (2003). Small Worlds, Competitive and Cooperative Structures in Online Worlds. In *Proceedings of Computer Game Developers' Conference*. Retrieved from http://www.legendmud. org/raph/gaming/smallworldsfiles/frame.htm

Locke, J. (1967). *Two Treatises of Government, Second Treatise* (Laslett, P., Ed.). 2nd ed.). Cambridge, UK: Cambridge University Press.

Munzer, S. (1990). *A Theory of Property*. Cambridge, UK: Cambridge University Press.

Radin, M. J. (1993). *Reinterpreting Property*. Chicago, IL: University of Chicago Press.

Waldron, J. (1988). *The Right to Private Property*. New York: Clarendon Paperbacks.

Compilation of References

Ackerman, B. (1989). Constitutional Politics/Constitutional Law. *Yale L.J., 99(453).*

Adrian, A. (2006). Intellectual Property v. Intangible Chattel. *Journal of International Commercial Law and Technology (JICLT), 1*(2).

Alter, A. (2007). Is This Man Cheating on His Wife? *The Wall Street Journal. Allakhazam's Magical Realm* (n.d.). Retrieved from http://links.allakhazam.com/EverQuest/Guilds

Anarchy Online. (n.d.). *Rules of Conduct.* Retrieved from http://anarchy-online.com/content/corporate/rulesofconduct.html

Andersen, H. C. (1984). *The Complete Hans Christian Andersen Fairy Tales.* London: Landoll.

Aoki, K. (1993). Adrift in the Intertext: Authorship and Audience Recording Rights. *Chi.-Kent L. Rev., 68*(805).

Appelcline, S. (n.d.). *A Brief History of Role Playing.* Retrieved from http://www.skotos.net/articles/TTnT_134.phtml

Arias, A. (2008). Life, Liberty, and the Pursuit of Swords and Armour: Regulating the Theft of Virtual Goods. *Emory L.J., 57*(1301).

Axelrod, R (1984). *The Evolution of Cooperation.*

Baage, J. (2006, December 21). Five Questions with Philip Rosedale, Founder and CEO of Linden Lab, Creator of Second Life. *DIGITAL MEDIA WIRE.* Retrieved from http://www.dmwmedia.com/news/2006/12/21/five-questions-with-philip-rosedale-founder-and-ceo-of-linden-lab-creator-of-second-life

Baker, J. H. (1990). *An Introduction to English Legal History* (3rd ed.). London: Butterworths.

Baldrica, J. (2007). Mod as Heck: Frameworks for Examining Ownership Rights in User Contributed Content to Videogames, and a More Principled Evaluation of Expressive Appropriation in User Modified Videogame Projects. *Minn. J. L. Sci. & Tech., 8*(681).

Balkin, J. (2003). The Proliferation of Legal Truth. *Harv. J. L. & Pub. Pol'y, 26*(5).

Balkin, J. (2004). Virtual Liberty: Freedom to Design and Freedom to Play in Virtual Worlds. *Va. L. Rev. 90*(2043).

Balkin, J. (2005). Law and Liberty in Virtual Worlds. *N.Y.L. Sch. L. Rev., 49*(63).

Balkin, J. (2008). Digital Speech and Democratic Culture: Theory of Freedom of Expression for the Information Society.

Barboza, D. (2005, December 9). Ogre to Slay? Outsource It To The Chinese. *N.Y. Times,* A1. Retrieved from http://www.iht.com/articles/2005/12/08/business/gaming.php

Barlow, J. P. (1994). *The Economy of Ideas: A Framework for Rethinking Patents and Copyrights in the Digital Age,* Wired. BBC News, *Cash Card Taps Virtual Game Funds,* 2006/05/02, available at http://news.bbc.co.uk/go/pr/fr/-/1/hi/technology/4953620.stm

Barlow, J. P. (2004). *Selling Wine without Bottles: the Economy of Mind on the Global Net.* Retrieved from http://www.eff.org/Misc/Publications/John_Perry_Barlow/HTML/idea_economy

Barr, W.P. (2005). The Gild That is Killing the Lily: How Confusion Over Regulatory Takings Doctrine is Undermining the Core Protections of the Takings Clause. *Geo. Wash. L. Rev., 73*(429).

Bartholomew, M. (2001). Protecting the Performers: Setting a New Standard for Character Copyrightability. *Santa Clara L. Rev., 41*(341).

Bartle, R. (1990, November 15). *Early MUD History*. Retrieved from http://www.mud.co.uk/richard/mudhist.htm

Bartle, R. (1996). Hearts, Clubs, Diamonds, Spade: Players who suit MUDs. *Journal of MUD Research, 1*(1). Retrieved from http://www.mud.co.uk/richard/hcds.htm.

Bartle, R. (2004). *Designing Virtual Worlds*. Berkeley, CA: New Riders Publishing.

Bartle, R. (2004). *Law Is Code*. Posting to Terra Nova. Retrieved from http://terranova.blogs.com/terr_nova/2004/08/law_is_code.html

Bartle, R. (2004). *Virtual Worldliness: What The Imaginary Asks of The Real, 19 N.* Y.L. Sch. R.

Barzel, Y. (1997). *Economic Analysis of Property Rights* (2nd ed.). Cambridge, UK: Cambridge University Press. doi:10.1017/CBO9780511609398

Bastiat, F. (1993). *The Law* (Russell, D., Trans.). New York: The Foundation for Economic Education.

BBS. (2005). *The Documentary*. United States: Bovine Ignition Systems.

Beier, K. P. (n.d.). *Virtual Reality: A Short Introduction*. Retrieved from http://www-vrl.umich.edu/intro/index.html.

Bell, A. G. (1972). *Games Playing with Computers*. London: George Allen & Unwin Ltd.

Benkler, Y. (2003). Through the Looking Glass: Alice and the Constitutional Foundations of the Public Domain. *Law & Contemp. Probs. 66*(173).

Benkler, Y. (2003, November 14). *Remarks at State of Play Conference*. Retrieved from http://www.nyls.edu/pages/1430.asp

Bentham, J. (1931). *The Theory of Legislation*. Amsterdam: Thoemmes Cortinuum.

Beren, K., & Howard, G. (2001). *The Rough Guide to Videogaming*. London: Rough Guides.

Berkowitz, S. (1994, July 3). Columbian Player's Death Stuns, Angers World Soccer Community. *Washington Post,* A27.

Berman, L. (1995). An Artist Destroys His Work: Comments on Creativity and Destructiveness. In Panter, (Eds.), *Creativity and Madness: Psychological Studies in Art and Artists*. New York: AIMED.

Berners-Lee, T. (1998 September). *Semantic Web Road Map*. Retrieved from http://www.w3.org/DesignIssues/Semantic.html

Beverley-Smith, H. (2002). *The Commercial Appropriation of Personality*. Cambridge, UK: Cambridge University Press. doi:10.1017/CBO9780511495229

Bhagwati, J. (2004). *In Defense of Globalization*. Oxford: Oxford University Press.

BinaryBonsai.com. (2004). *Being Foxed*. Retrieved from http://binarybonsai.com/archives/2004/07/20/cease-and-desist/

Birks, P. (1986). *The Roman Law Concept of Dominium and the Idea of Absolute Ownership. Acta Juridica 1. Black's Law Dictionary. (1990)*. St. Paul, MN: West Publishing.

Black's Law Dictionary (6th ed.). (1990). St. Paul, MN: West Publishing.

Blackstone, W. (n.d.). *Commentaries on the Laws of England* (Vol. 2).

Bleich, D. (1978). Subjective Criticism. [National Council of Teachers.]. *Urbana (Caracas, Venezuela)*, IL.

Bolter, J. D. (1984). *Turing's Man: Western Culture in the Computer Age*. Chapel Hill, NC: University of North Carolina Press.

Bolter, J. D., & Grusin, R. (2000). *Remediation: Understanding New Media*. Cambridge, MA: MIT Press.

Boone, M.S. (2008). *Ubiquitous Computing, Virtual Worlds, and the Displacement of Property Rights.* 4 I/S: J. L., & Pol'y for Info. Soc'y 91.

Bordwell, D., & Thompson, K. (2001). *Film Art* (6th ed.). New York: McGraw-Hill.

Boyle, J. (1988). The Search for an Author: Shakespeare and the Framers. *Am. U. L. Rev., 37*(625).

Boyle, J. (1996). *Shamans, Software, and Spleens: Law and the Construction of the Information Society.* Boston, MA: Harvard University Press.

Bradley, C., & Froomkin, M. (2005). Virtual Worlds, Real Rules. *N.Y. L. Sch. L. Rev. 49*(103).

Braman, S., & Lynch, S. (2003). Advantage ISP: Terms of Service as Media Law. In *Thinking Rights and Regulations: Institutional Responses to New Communications Technologies.* Cambridge, MA: MIT Press.

Bukatman, S. (1993). *Terminal Identity: The Virtual Subject in Post-Modern Science Fiction.* Durham, NC: Duke University Press.

Bulkley, K. (2007). Today Second Life, tomorrow the world. *The Guardian.*

Burns, R.P. (1985). Blackstone's Theory of the Absolute Rights of Property. *Cin. L. Rev., 54*(67).

Burnstein, M. (2004). Towards a New Standard for First Amendment Review of Structural Media Regulation. *N.Y.U. L. Rev., 79*(1030).

Byassee, W.S. (1995). *Jurisdiction of Cyberspace: Applying Real World Precedent to the Virtual Community.* 30 Wake Forest L. Rev. 197.

Caillois, R. (2001). *Man, Play, and Games* (Barash, M., Trans.). Urbana, IL: University of Illinois Press.

Cally. (n.d.). *"Confession" Video.* Retrieved from http://dl.qj.net/Cally-s-EVE-Online-Confession-Video-Movie-PC-Gaming-MMORPG-Other-Games/pg/12/fid/9542/catid/476

Campbell, J. (1972). *The Hero with a Thousand Faces.* Princeton, NJ: Princeton University Press.

Carter, G. (2002). It's My ['ll Sell It If I Want To. *The Adrenaline Vault.* Retrieved from http://www.avault.com/articles/getarticle.asp?name=mmogsell]. *Time, I.*

Casamiquela, R. (2002). Contractual Assent and Enforceability in Cyberspace. *Berkeley Tech L.J., 17*(475).

Castaneda, H. (1975). *Thinking and Doing.* New York: Springer Publishing.

Castells, M. (1996). *The Rise of the Network Society.* London: Blackwell Publishing Professional.

Castronova, E. (2001 December). *Virtual Worlds: A First-Hand Account of Market and Society on the Cyberian Frontier.* CESifo Working Paper Series No. 618.

Castronova, E. (2002). *On Virtual Economies.* The Gruter Institute of Working Papers on Law, CESifo Working Paper No. 752.

Castronova, E. (2003). *The Price of 'Man' and 'Woman': A Hedonic Pricing Model of Avatar Attributes in a Synthetic World.* CESifo Working Paper Series No. 957

Castronova, E. (2003). *Theory of the Avatar.* CESifo Working Paper Series No. 863.

Castronova, E. (2004). The Right to Play. *N.Y.L.Sch. L. Rev. 49*(185).

Castronova, E. (2006 April). Geekonomics. *Wired Magazine.*

Cavalli, E. (2008). Police Refuse to Aid in Virtual Theft Case. *Wired.* Retrieved from http://blog.wired.com/games/2008/police-refuse-t.html

Cervantes, M. (1605). *Don Quixote de la Mancha (W. Starkie, trans.).* London: MacMillan & Co.

Chein, A. (2006) *A Practical Look at Virtual Property.* 80 St. John's L. Rev. 1059.

Chen, Y. (2005). An Analysis of Online Gaming Crime Characteristics. *Internet Research, 15*(246).

Clark, D. (2006). Virtual Vandalism. *The Wall Street Journal Online.* Retrieved from http://online.wsj.com/article

Clarke, R. (1994). Human Identification in Information Systems: Management Challenges and Public Policy Issues. *Information Tech. & People, 4*(7). Retrieved from http://www.anu.edu.au/people/Roger.Clarke/DV/HumanID.html

Coase, R. H. (1960). The Problem of Social Cost. *The Journal of Law & Economics, 3*(1). doi:10.1086/466560

Cobley, P. (Ed.). (2004). *Routledge Introductions to Media and Communications.* Abingdon, UK: Routledge.

Cohen, J. (1998). Lochner in Cyberspace: The New Economic Orthodoxy of 'Rights Management.' *Mich. L. Rev. 97*(462).

Cornish, W. (1999). *Intellectual Property -- Patents, Copyright, Trade Marks and Allied Rights* (4th ed.). London: Sweet & Maxwell.

Craig, K. (2006, May 18). Second Life Land Deal Goes Sour. *Wired News*. Retrieved from http://www.wired.com/news/culture/0,70909-0.html

Crawford, S. (2005). Who is in Charge of Who I Am? Identity and Law Online. *N.Y.L. Sch. L. Rev., 49*(211).

Crowe, L. (1999). The Anatomy of a Tort -- Greenian, as Interpreted by Crowe who has been influenced by Malone -- A Primer. *Loy. L. Rev. 44*(647).

Csikszentmihaly, M. (1994). *The Evolving Self.* New York: Perennial.

Cunningham, R., Stoebuck, W., & Whitman, D. (1993). *The Law of Property* (2nd ed.). New York: LexisNexis Publishing.

Cyberspace, Virtuality, and the Text. (1999). In Ryan, M.-L. (Ed.), *Cyberspace Textuality: Computer Technology and Literary Theory*. Southbend, IN: Indiana University Press.

Daily, C. (2003, November 20). *Lawsuit Fires Up in Cases of Vanishing Virtual Weapons.* Retrieved from http://www.chinadaily.com.cn/en/doc/2003-11/20/content_283094.htm

Daix, P. (1993). *Picasso Life and Art* (Emmett, O., Trans.). New York: Harper Collins.

Damer, B. (1998). *Avatars!* Berkeley, CA: Peachpit Press.

Damgaard, I. (2002). *Legal Implications of the Project Entropia: Conducting Business in Virtual Worlds.* Juridiska Institutionen Handelshögskolan vid Göteborgs Universtiet. Retrieved from http://www.handels.gu.se/epc/archive/00003250/

Darnoc Postings. (2005). Retrieved from http://forums.diabloii.net/showthread.php

David, P. A.(20005). From Keeping 'Nature's Secrets' to the Institutionalization of 'Open Science. In Ghosh, R. A. (Ed.), *CODE: Collaborative Ownership and the Digital Economy.*

Davies, E. (2002). Synthetic Mediations: Cogito in the Matrix. In Toffts, D., Jonson, A. M., & Cavallaro, A. (Eds.), *Prefiguring Cyberculture: An Intellectual History.* Cambridge, MA: MIT Press.

Davies, M. (2006). Gamers don't want any more grief. *The Guardian*. Retrieved from http://www.guardian.co.uk/technology/2006/jun/15/games.guardianweekly-technologysection2

Davies, M., & Naffine, N. (2001). *Are Persons Property? Legal Debates about Property and Personality.* Dartmouth, MA: Ashgate.

Delwiche, A. (2004). *Massively Multiplayer Online Games in the College Classroom,* N.Y. L. Sch. L. Rev. (online publication) at http://www.nyls.edu/lawreview

Demsetz, H. (1967). Toward a Theory of Property Rights. *The American Economic Review, 57*(347).

Demsetz, H. (1970). *The Private Production of Public Goods.* 13 J.L., &. *De Economía*, 293.

Demsetz, H. (1988). *Ownership, Control, and the Firm: The Organization of Economic Activity.* London: Blackwell.

Denicola, R.C. (1981). Copyright in Collections of Facts: A Theory for the Protection of Nonfiction Literary Works. *Colum. L. Rev., 81*(516).

Dewey, J. (1980). *Art as Experience.* New York: Perigee Books.

Dibbell, J. (1998). *My Tiny Life*. New York: Henry Holt & Co.

Dibbell, J. (2003 January). The Unreal Estate Boom: 79th Richest Nation on Earth Doesn't Exist. *Wired Magazine*.

Dibbell, J. (2003 March). Your Next Customer is Virtual, But his Money is Real. *Business 2.0*. Retrieved from http://www.business2.com.articles/mag/0,1640,47157,00.html

Dibbell, J. (2003) Serfing the Web: Blacksnow Interactive and the World's First Virtual Sweat Shop. *Wired Magazine*. Retrieved from http://www.juliandibbell.com/texts/blacksnow.html

Dibbell, J. (2003). *OWNED! Intellectual Property in the Age of eBayers, Gold Farmers, and Other Enemies of the Virtual State or, How I Learned To Stop Worrying and Love the End-User License Agreement*. Retrieved from http://www.juliandibbell.com/texts/owned.html

Dibbell, J. (2003). The Unreal Estate Boom: 79th Richest Nation on Earth Doesn't Exist. *Wired Magazine*. eBay (n.d.). *Listings, Internet Games*. Retrieved from http://listings.ebay.com/pool2/listings/list/all/category4596/index.html

Dick, P. (1969). *Ubik*.

Doctorow, C. (2006 April). The Massively Multiplayer Magic Kingdom: Theme Park Imaginer Danny Hillis on the Wonderful Virtual World of Disney. *Wired Magazine*.

Drabble, M. (Ed.). (1985). *The Oxford Companion to English Literature* (5th ed.). Oxford: Oxford University Press.

Drahos, P. (1996). A Philosophy of Intellectual Property. Ch 4 'Hegel: The Spirit of Intellectual Property' citing Hegel, Philosophy of Right s. 39, Dartmouth, MA: Aldershot.

Dreyfus, H. (1992). *What Computers Still Can't Do: A Critique of Artificial Reason*. Cambridge, MA: MIT Press.

Duffy, J., & Carless, S. (March 2007). For the People, By the People, Game Developer. *Entropia Universe*. Retrieved from http://www.entropiauniverse.com

Dunn, S. (1986) Defining the Scope of Copyright Protection for Computer Software. *Stan. L. Rev., 38*(497).

Easterbrook, F. (1996). Cyberspace and the Law of the Horse. *U. Chi. Legal F., 207*.

Edwards, E. (2003). Plug (the Product) and Play; Advertisers Use Online Games to Entice Customers. *Washington Post*, A1.

Eisenberg, E. (2005, March 25). Important Changes to Your Citizenship Agreement. *Slate*. Retrieved from http://slate.msn.com/id/2115254

Electronic Privacy Information Center. (1997 December). *Faulty Filters: How Content Filters Block Access to Kid-Friendly Information on the Internet*. Retrieved from http://www2.epic.org/reports/filter-report.html

Elins, M. (2006 April). Dream Machines: Will Wright Explains How Games Are Unleashing the Human Imagination. *Wired*.

Ellickson, R.C. (1993). Property in Land. *Yale L.J., 102*(1315).

Entertainment Software Association Press Release. (2005, January 26). *Computer and Video Game Software Sales Reach Record $7.3 Billion in 2004*. Retrieved from http://wwwtheesa.com/archives/2005/02/computer_and_vi.php

Everquest User Agreement and Software License. (n.d.). Retrieved from http://eqlive.station.sony.com/support/customer_service/cs_EULA.jsp

EverQuest. (n.d.). *End User License Agreement*. Retrieved from http://everquest.station.sony.com/support/security/eula.jsp

EverQuest. (n.d.). *Rules of Conduct*. Retrieved from http://eqlive.station.sony.com/support/customer_service/cs_rules_of_conduct.jsp.

Faier, A. (2004). Digital Slaves of the Render Farms?: Virtual Actors and Intellectual Property Rights. U. Ill. J.L. Tech. & Pol'y 321.

Fairfield, J. (2005). *Virtual Property*. Indiana University School of Law – Bloomington, Legal Studies Research Paper Series, Research Paper Number 35

Filiciak, M. (2003). *Hyperidentities – Post-modern Identity Patterns in Massively Multiplayer Online Role-Playing Games in Mark J.P. Wolf & Bernard Perron edited 'The Video Game Theory Reader*. London: Routledge.

Fisher, C. (2004). Interview. *Star Wars Trilogy* [Motion Picture]. Bonus Materials. United States: LucasFilm.

Fitch, C. (2004). *Cyberspace in the 21ˢᵗ Century: Mapping the Future of Massive Multiplayer Games*. Retrieved from http://www.gamasutra.com/features/20000120/fitch_04.htm

Foucault, M. (1980). *Power/Knowledge: Selected Interviews and Other Writings 1972-1977* (Gordon, C., Ed.). London: Harvester.

Fouts, J. (2005, June). *Internationalism: Worlds at Play*. Paper presented at the International DiGRA Conference, Vancouver, British Columbia, Canada.

Franks, C. (2005). Comment, Analyzing the Urge to Merge: Conversion of Intangible Property and the Merger Doctrine in the Wake of Kremen v. Cohen. *Hous. L. Rev., 42*(489).

Frasca, G. (2001). *Videogames of the Oppressed: Videogames as a Means for Critical Thinking and Debate*. Georgia Institute of Technology Masters Thesis. Retrieved from http://www.jacaranda.org/frasca/thesis

Freedberg, D. (1989). *The Power of Images: Studies in the History and Theory of Response*. Chicago, IL: University of Chicago Press.

Garnett, K., James, J. R., & Davies, G. (1999). *Copinger and Skone James -- On Copyright* (14th ed.). London: Sweet & Maxwell.

Gartner, Inc. (2007). *Gartner Says 80% of Active Internet Users will have a Second Life in the Virtual World by the End of 2011*. Gartner Symposium/ITXpo. Retrieved from http://www.gartner.com/it/page.jsp?id=503861

Gartner, J. (2000, January 7). It's the End of TV as We Know It. *Wired News*. Retrieved from http://www.wired.com/news/technology/0,1282,33503,00.html

Gaudiosi, J. (2006 April). Product Placement to Die For: The Rise of In-game Advertising. *Wired Magazine*.

Gauntlett, D. (2002). Anthony Giddens: The Theory of Structuration. In *Media, Gender, and Identity: An Introduction*. London, New York: Routledge. doi:10.4324/9780203360798

Gauthier, D. (1986). *Morals by Agreement*. Oxford: Oxford University Press.

Geist, M. (2003). Cyberlaw 2.0. *B.C. L. Rev. 44*(323).

Gibbons, L.J. (1997). *No Regulation, Government Regulation, or Self-Regulation: Social Enforcement or Social Contracting for Governance in Cyberspace*. 6 Cornell J.L., & Pub. Pol'y 475.

Gibson, J. (2004). Re-Reifying Data. *Notre Dame L. Rev., 80*(163).

Gibson, W. (1984). *Neuromancer*. London: HaperCollins Publishers.

Giradin, F., & Nova, N. (2006). Getting Real with Ubiquitous Computing: The Impact of Discrepancies on Collaboration. *eMinds: Int'l J. on Human-Computer Interaction, 60*.

Glare, P. G. W. (Ed.). (1982). *Oxford Latin Dictionary*. Oxford: Oxford University Press.

Glasser, D. (2001). Copyrights in computer-generated works: Whom, if anyone do, we reward? *Duke Law & Technology Review, 24*.

Glassman, A. (1994). *Visions of Light*. Retrieved from http://www.imdb.com

Glusko, B. (2007). Tales of the (Virtual) City: Governing Property Disputes in Virtual Worlds. *Berkeley Tech. L. J., 22*(507).

Goffman, E. (1959). *The Presentation of Self in Everyday Life*. New York: Basic Books.

Goldman, E. (2005). Symposium Review: Speech Showdowns at the Virtual Corral. *Santa Clara Comp. & High Tech. L. J., 21*(845).

Goldschmidt, E. P. (1969). *Medieval Texts and their First Appearance in Print*. Cheshire, CT: Biblo-Moser.

Goldsmith, J.L. (1998). Against Cyberanarchy. *U. Chi. L. Rev., 65*(1199).

Goldstein, P. (1994). *Copyright's Highway: Gutenberg to the Celestial Jukebox*. New York: Hill and Wang.

Gombrich, E. H. (1984). *The Story of Art* (14th ed.). Boston, MA: Phaidon Press.

Gomulkiewicz, R. & Williamson, M. (1996). A Brief Defence of Mass Market Software License Agreements. *Rutgers Computer & Tech. L.J., 22*(335).

Gordon, W. (1990). Toward a Jurisprudence of Benefits: The Norms of Copyright and the Problem of Private Censorship. *U. Chi. L. Rev., 57*(1009).

Gordon, W. (1993). A Property Right in Self-expression: Equality and Individualism in the Natural Law of Intellectual Property. *Yale L.J., 102*(1533).

Gourvitz, E. (2006). Virtual Gaming Worlds Test Boundaries of Intellectual Property Law, Panellists Say. *Electronic Comm. & L. Rep. (BNA), 11*(143)

Graham, J. (2002). Preserving the Aftermarket in Copyrighted Works: Adapting the First Sale Doctrine to the Emerging Technological Landscape. *Stan. Tech. L. Rev.* (1).

Grant, D.L. (1995). Western Water Rights and the Public Trust Doctrine: Some Realism About the Takings Issue. *Ariz. St. L. J., 27*(423).

Grau, O. (2003). *Virtual Art: From Illusion to Immersion*. Cambridge, MA: The MIT Press.

Green, L. (1927). *Rationale of Proximate Cause*.

Green, L. (1965). The Study and Teaching of Tort Law. In The Litigation Process in Tort Law.

Green, S. (2001). Lying, Misleading, and Falsely Denying: How Moral Concepts Inform the Law of Perjury, Fraud, and False Statements. *Hastings L.J., 53*(157).

Green, S. (2002). Plagiarism, Norms, and the Limits of Theft Law: Some Observations on the Use of Criminal Sanctions in Enforcing Intellectual Property Rights. *Hastings L.J., 54*(167).

Greene, K. J. (2004). Abusive Trademark Litigation and The Incredible Shrinking Confusion Doctrine – Trademark Abuse in The Context of Entertainment Media and Cyberspace. *Harv. J. L. & Pub. Pol'y, 27*(609).

Greenfield, A. (2006). *Everyware: The Dawn of Ubiquitous Computing*.

Grimes, A. (2005, March 3). Digits. *Wall Street Journal*, B3.

Grimmelmann, J. (2003, December 4). *The State of Play: Free As In Gaming?* LawMeme at http://research.yale.edu/lawmeme/modules.php?name=News&file=article&sid=1290/

Grimmelmann, J. (2004). Virtual Worlds As Comparative Law. *N.Y. L. Sch. L. Rev. 49*(147).

Grimmelmann, J. (2005 April 19). *Virtual Power Politics*. Retrieved from http://ssrn.com/abstract=707301

Grimmelmann, J. (2005). *Virtual Borders: The Interdependence of Real and Virtual Worlds*. Yale Law School Information Society Project.

Grimwell, J. (2005, November 28). Sony Station Exchange to Be a Part of All SOE Games. *GamerGod.com*. Retrieved from http://www.gamergod.com/article.php?article_id=2663

Grodal, T. (2003). Stories for Eye, Ear, and Muscles: Video Games, Media, and Embodied Experiences. In Wolf, M. J. P., & Perron, B. (Eds.), *The Video Game Theory Reader*. London: Routledge.

Gupte, E. (2008). Register your IP rights at the SLPTO. *Managing IP*. January

Halewood, P. (2008). On Commodification and Self-Ownership. *Yale J.L. & Human., 20*(131).

Hardin, G. (1968). The Tragedy of the Commons. In Ackerman, B. (Ed.), *Economic Foundations of Property Law*. New York: Aspen Publishing.

Harkin, J. (2006, November 17). Get a (second) life. *Financial Times*.

Harris, C.I. (1993). Whiteness as Property. *Harv. L. Rev. 106*(1709).

Hebert, J. (Oct. 9, 2005). Online Gamer? Buy Your Way to the Top. *San Diego Union-Tribune*, F-3.

Hegel, G. W. F. (1952). *Philosophy of Right* (Knox, T. M., Trans.). Oxford: Oxford University Press.

Helbreath, U. S. A. (n.d.). *Conduct Rules*. Retrieved from http://www.helbreathusa.com/rules.php

Helfand, M. (1992). Note, When Mickey Mouse is as Strong as Superman: The Convergence of Intellectual Property Law to Protect Fictional Literary and Pictorial Characters. *Stan. L. Rev., 44*(623).

Helfgott, S. (1992). Claim Practice Around the World: A Comparison of How Inventions Are Claimed. *J. Proprietary Rts, 4*(9).

Herold, C. (2003, February 6). Win Friends, Influence People, or Just Aim and Fire. *N.Y. Times,* G5.

Herz, J. C. (1997). *Joystick Nation: How Video Games Ate Our Quarters, Won Our Hearts and Rewired Our Minds*. Boston, MA: Little, Brown, and Company.

Herz, J.C. (June 2002). 50,000,000 Star Warriors Can't Be Wrong, *Wired Magazine*

Hettinger, E.C. (1989). Justifying Intellectual Property. *Phil., & Pub. Aff., 18*(31).

Heylighen, F. (1994, October 17). *Cyberspace*. Retrieved from http://pespmc1.vub.ac.be/CYBSPACE.html

Hoffman, E. C., III. (2007). *Tip Sheet: When Griefers Attack, How to prevent virtual-world vandalism and what to do when your property comes under fire*. Retrieved from http://www.businessweek.com/playbook/07/0416_1.htm

Hoffman, H. (2004). Virtual Reality Therapy. *Scientific American, 291,* 58–65.doi:10.1038/scientificamerican0804-58

Hohfeld, W.N. (1917). Fundamental Legal Conceptions as Applied in Judicial Reasoning. *Yale L.J. 26*(710).

Honore, A. M. (1961). Ownership. In Guest, A. G. (Ed.), *Oxford Essays in Jurisprudence* (1st ed.). Oxford: Oxford University Press.

Howland, G. (1998). *Game Design: the Essence of Computer Games*. Retrieved from http://www.lupinegames.com/articles/essgames.htm

Hughes, J. (1998). The Personality Interest of Artists and Inventors in Intellectual Property. *Cardozo Arts & Ent L. J., 16*(81).

Huhtamo, E. (1995). Encapsulated Bodies in Motion: Simulators and the Quest for Total Immersion. In Penny, S. (Ed.), *Critical Issues in Electronic Media*. Albany, NY: State University of New York Press.

Huizinga, J. (1971). *Homo Ludens: A Study in the Play-Elements in Culture*. Boston, MA: Beacon Press.

Hunt, K. (2007). This Land is not Your Land: Second Life, Copybot, and the Looming Question of Virtual Property Rights. *Tex. Rev. Ent. & Sports L. 9*(141).

Husemann, C. (2006). All about the ISK. *Gaming Nexus*. Retrieved from http://www.gamingnexus.com/Default.aspx?Section =Article&I=1181

Hutcheon, S. (2006, December 21). Good Grief, Bad Vibes. *Sydney Morning Herald*. Retrieved from http://www.smh.com.au/news/web/good-grief-bad-vibes/2006/12/21/1166290662836.html?page=2

IBM Virtual World Guidelines (n.d.). Retrieved from http://domino.research.ibm.com/comm/research_projects.nsf/pages/virtualworlds.IBMVirtualWorldGuidelines.html

Imparato, N. (Ed.). (1999). *Capital for Our Time: The Economic, Legal, and Management Challenges of Intellectual Capital*. Stanford, CA: Hoover Institution Press.

Information Slurp. (n.d.). Retrieved from http://www.informationslurp.com/Film/Special_effect.html

Iser, W. (1978). *The Act of Reading: A Theory of Aesthetic Response*. Baltimore, MD: John Hopkins University Press.

Iser, W. (1989). *Prospecting: From Reader Response to Literary Anthropology*. Baltimore, MD: John Hopkins University Press.

Jaszi, P. (1991). Toward a Theory of Copyright: The Metamorphoses of Authorship. *Duke L.J., 41*(455).

Jaszi, P. (1992). On the Author Effect: Contemporary Copyright and Collective Creativity. *Cardozo Arts & Ent. L. J., 10*(293).

Jefferson, T. (1813). A Letter to Isaac McPherson. *The Founders' Constitution, 3*(1), Section 8, Clause 8, Document 12. Retrieved from http://press-pubs.uchicago.edu/founders/documents/a1_8_8s12.html

Jenkins, H., & Squire, K. (2002). The Art of Contested Spaces. In King, L. (Ed.), *Game On: The History and Culture of Video Games*. New York: Universe.

Johnson, D.R., & Post, D. (1996). *Law and Borders – The Rise of Law in Cyberspace*. 48 Stan L. Rev. 1367.

Johnson, S. (1997). *Interface Culture: How New Technology Transforms the Way We Create and Communicate*. San Francisco, CA: Harper Edge.

Johnson, S. (2006). When Virtual Worlds Collide. *Wired*. Retrieved from http://www.wired.com/wired/archive/14.04/collide_pr.html Kim, A. (1998 May). Killers Have More Fun. *Wired*. Retrieved from http://www.wired.com/wired/archive/6.05/ultima.html

Johnson-Eilola, J. (1998). Living on the surface: learning in the age of global communications networks. In Snyder, I. (Ed.), *Page to Screen: Taking Literacy into the Electronic Era*. London: Routledge. doi:10.4324/9780203201220_chapter_9

Jorgensen, P. (1987). Embezzlement. *Am. Crim. L. Rev., 24*(513).

Joyce, J. (1939). *Finnegan's Wake*. New York: Viking Press, Inc.

Jung, C. (1959). *The Undiscovered Self*. New York: Signet Books.

Kant, I. (1930). *Lectures on Ethics* (Infield, L., Trans.). London: Methuen and Co.

Kapstein, E. B. (1994). *Governing the Global Economy: International Finance and the State*. New York: McGraw Hill.

Kennedy, D. (1979). The Structure of Blackstone's Commentaries. *Buff. L. Rev., 28*(205).

Kennedy, D. (2001). *Key Legal Concerns in E-commerce: The Law comes to the New Frontier*.18 T.M. Cooley L. Rev. 17.

Kennedy, R. (2009). *Law in Virtual Worlds*. 12 No. 10 J. *Internet, L*, 2.

Kimbrell, A. (1995). *Life for Sale*. Utne Reader.

Kines, M. (2001). *Planning and Directing Motion Capture for Games*. Retrieved from http://www.gamasutra.com/features/20000119/kines_01.htm

King, B. (2001) *Making Those Games Sound Right*. Retrieved from http://www.wired.com/news/games/0,2101,53156,00.html

King, B. (n.d.). *Star Wars Fans Strike Back*. Retrieved from http://www.wired.com/news/digiwood/0,1412,52561,00.html

King, B. (n.d.). *World Creators: We Got Game*. Retrieved from http://www.wired.com/news/culture/0,1284,42381,00.html

Kline, S., Dyer-Witheford, N., & de Peuter, G. (2003). *Digital Play: The Interaction of Technology, Culture, and Marketing*. Montreal, Canada: McGill-Queen's University Press.

Kosak, D. (2002, December 10). Second Life (PC). *GameSpy.Com*. Retrieved from http://archive.gamespy.com/previews/december02/secondlifepc/index.shtml

Kosak, D. (2003, November 13). The Future of Massively Multiplayer Gaming. *GameSpy.com*. Retrieved from http://archive.gamespy.com/amdmmog/week8/index.shtml

Koster, R. (1998, May 11). *The Man Behind the Curtain*. Retrieved from http://www.legendmud.org/raph/gaming/essay5.html

Koster, R. (2000). *A Declaration of the Rights of Avatars*. Retrieved from http://raphkoster.com/gaming/player-rights.shtml

Koster, R. (2000). *The Laws of Online World Design*. Retrieved from http://www.raphkoster.com/gaming/laws.shtml

Koster, R. (2003). Small Worlds, Competitive and Co-operative Structures in Online Worlds. In *Proceedings of Computer Game Developers' Conference*. Retrieved from http://www.legendmud.org/raph/gaming/small-worldsfiles/frame.htm

Koster, R. (2005, September 2). Posting to Terra Nova. Retrieved from http://terranova.blogs.com/terra_nova/2005/08/the_golden_ 1m_w.html

Koster, R. (2006, February 24). *What are the Lessons of MMORPGs Today?* Retrieved from http://www.raphkoster.com/2006/02/24/what-are-the-lessons-ofmmorpgs-today

Koster, R. (n.d.). *Moore's Wall: Technology Advances and Online Game Design*. Retrieved from http://www.raphkoster.com/gaming/moore.shtml

Koster, R. (n.d.). *The Laws of Online World Design*. Retrieved from http://www.raphkoster.com/gaming/laws.shtml

Krotoski, A. (2005, June 16). Online: Virtual Trade Gets Real: Buying Virtual Goods on the Internet is One Thing; Killing for It Is Quite Another. *The Guardian* (London), 23.

Kushner, D. (2003). It's a Mod, Mod World: For Computer Game Developers, Encouraging Users to Modify Copyrighted Material is Good for Business. *Spectrum Online*. Retrieved from http://www.spectrum.ieee.org/careers/careerstemplate.jsp?_ArticleId=i020203

Lahti, M. (2003). As We Become Machines – Corporealized Pleasures in Video Games. In Wolf, M. J. P., & Perron, B. (Eds.), *The Video Game Theory Reader*. London: Routledge.

Lape, L. (1997, Fall). A Narrow View of Creative Co-operation: The Current State of Joint Work Doctrine. *Albany Law Review*.

Lastowka, F.G. & Hunter, D. (2004). The Laws of the Virtual World. *Calif. L. Rev., 92*(1).

Lastowka, G., & Hunter, D. (2004) Virtual Crimes. *N.Y.L. Sch. L. Rev., 49*(293).

Lastowka, G., & Hunter, D. (2004). *The Laws of the Virtual World*. 92 Calif. L. Rev. 1.

Latour, B., & Woolgar, S. (1986). *Laboratory Life: The Construction of Scientific Facts*. Princeton, NJ: Princeton University Press.

Lehdonvirta, V. (2008) *Real Money Trade of Virtual Assets: New Strategies for Virtual World Operators*. Helsinki Institute for Information Technology (HIIT). Retrieved from http://www.hiit.fi/u/vlehdonvirta

Lehdonvirta, V. (n.d.). *Real Money Trade of Virtual Assets: New Strategies for Virtual World Operators*. Helsinki Institute for Information Technology (HIIT). Retrieved from http://www.hiit.fi/u/vlehdonvirta

Lemley, M. (1995). Convergence in the Law of Software Copyright? *High Technology Law Journal, 10*(1).

Lemley, M. (1995). Intellectual Property and Shrinkwrap Licenses. *S. Cal. L. Rev., 68*(1239).

Lessig, L. (1999). The Law of the Horse: What Cyberlaw Might Teach. *Harv. L. Rev., 113*(501).

Lessig, L. (2000). *Code and Other Laws of Cyberspace*. New York: Basic Books Lienhard, J. (1995). Address Reflections on Information, Biology, and Community. *Hous. L. Rev., 32*(303).

Leupold, T. (2005, May 6). Virtual Economies Break Out of Cyberspace. *Gamespot*. Retrieved from http://www.gamespot.com/news/2005/05/06/news_6123701.html

Leval, P. (1990) Toward a Fair Use Standard. *Harv, L. Rev., 103*(1105).

Levy, S. (1984). *Hackers: Heroes of the Computer Revolution*. New York: Anchor.

Life, S. *Create Anything*. (2008). Retrieved from http://secondlife.com/whatis/create.php.

Linden Scripting Language Wiki. (n.d.). Retrieved from http://secondlife.com/badgeo/wakka.php?wakka=prim

Linden, P. (n.d.). *Second Life Official Blog*. Retrieved from http://blog.secondlife.com/2006/10/18/when-precisely-did-we-hit-1-million-residents/

Lineage User Agreement. (n.d.). Retrieved from http://www.lineage.com/support/terms.html

Litman, J. (1990). The Public Domain. *Emory L.J., 39*(965).

Liu, J. (2001). Owning Digital Copies: Copyright Law and The Incidents of Copy Ownership. W&M L. Rev., 4.

Livingstone, S. (2002). *Young People and New Media: Childhood and the Changing Media Environment.* London: Sage.

Locke, J. (1689). *Two Treatise of Civil Government and A Letter Concerning Toleration* (Shapiro, I., Ed.). New Haven, CT: Yale University Press.

Locke, J. (1690). *Two Treatises of Government, Second Treatise* (Laslett, P., Ed.). 2nd ed.). Cambridge, UK: Cambridge University Press.

Loren, L.P. (2004). Slaying the Leather-Winged Demons in the Night: Reforming Copyright Owner Contracting with Click Wrap Misuse. *Ohio N. U. L. Rev., 30*(495).

Lucas, G. (2004). Interview. *Star Wars Trilogy* [Motion Picture]. Bonus Materials. United States: LucasFilm.

Ma, D. (2000). Delivering Results on the Ground: Improving Service to Citizens in Singapore. *Asian J. Pol. Sci., 8*(137).

Machiavelli, N. (1992). *The Prince* (2nd ed.). London: W.W. Norton.

MacIntyre, A. (1990). After Virtue. In Solomon, R. C., & Murphy, M. C. (Eds.), *What is Justice? Classic and Contemporary Readings.* Oxford: Oxford University Press.

Malkan, J. (1997). Stolen Photographs: Personality, Publicity, and Privacy. *Tex. L. Rev., 75*(779).

Marcus, T. D. (2008). Fostering Creativity in Virtual Worlds: Easing the Restrictiveness of Copyright for User-Created Content. *J. Copyright Soc'y U.S.A, 55*(469).

Market Wire. (2005, November 8). *Press Release, Virtual Island Purchase of $26,500 Recoups Investment in First Year With Room for Ongoing Profit.* Retrieved from http://www.marketwire.com/mw/release_html_bl?release_id=100596

Marks, R. B. (2003). *EverQuest Companion: The Inside Lore of a Gameworld.* Berkeley, CA: New Riders Publishing.

Martens, C. (2007). WORLDBEAT: ID malleability creates virtual-world issues. *IDG News Service.* Retrieved from http://www.itworld.com/Net/2614/070627id/

Massive Multiplayer Online: Clans and Guilds, Open Directory Project. Retrieved from http://dmoz.org/Games/Video_Games/Roleplaying/Massive_Multiplayer_Online/Clans_and_Guilds

Mayer-Schönberger, V. & Crowley, J. (2006). Napster's Second Life? The Regulatory Challenges of Virtual Worlds. *Nw. U. L. Rev., 100*(1775).

Mayer-Schönberger, V. (2003). The Shape of Governance: Analyzing the World of Internet Regulation. *Va. J. Int'l L., 43*(605).

McCarthy, C. (2006). Cons in the Virtual Gaming World. *CNET News.com.* Retrieved from http://news.com.com/Cons+in+the+virtual+gaming+world/2100-1043_3-6111089.html

McCullough, T. (1998). Note, United States v. O'Hagan: Defining the Limits of Fraud and Deceptive Pretext Under Rule 10b-5. *Seattle U. L. Rev., 22*(311).

McDonald, J. (1970). Comment, Proximate Cause in Louisiana. In Malone, W., & Guerry, L. (Eds.), *Studies in Louisiana Torts Law.*

McMahan, A. (2003). Immersion, Engagement, and Presence: A Method for Analyzing 3-D Video Games. In Wolf, M. J. P., & Perron, B. (Eds.), *The Video Game Theory Reader.* London: Routledge.

McManis, C. (1999). The Privatization (or 'Shrink-Wrapping'). of American Copyright Law. *California Law Review, 87*(173).

McMurdo, G. (1995). *Netiquette for Networkers.* 21 J. Info. Science 305.

Meehan, M. (2005). *Virtual Property: Protecting Bits in Context.* Stanford Law School's Legal Studies Workshop. Retrieved from http://lasso.textdriven.com/blog/lsw/2005/12/06/bits-in-context

Meikle, E. (2002, October 21). Barbie Goes to Court. *Brand Channel.com*. Retrieved from http://www.brand-channel.com/features_effects.asp?pf_id=127

Merrill, T.W. (1998). Property and the Right to Exclude. *Neb. L. Rev., 77*(730).

Merrill, T.W., & Smith, H.E. (2001). The Property/Contract Interface. *Colum. L. Rev., 101*(773).

Merrill, T.W., & Smith, H.E. (2001b). What Happened to Property in Law and Economics? *Yale L.J., 111*(357).

Metcalfe, B. (1996, July 15). There Oughta Be a Law. *N.Y. Times,* D7 (Late Ed.).

Metz, C. (1982). *The Imaginary Signifier: Psychoanalysis and the Cinema* (Britton, C., Trans.). Bloomington, IN: Indiana University Press.

Milgrom, P., North, D., & Weingast, B. (1990). The Role of Institutions in the Revival of Trade: The Law Merchant, Private Judges, and the Champagne Fairs. *Econ. & Pol. 2*(1). Miller, D. (2003). Determining Ownership in Virtual Worlds: Copyright and License Agreements. *Rev. Litig., 22*(435).

Millard, C. (2002). Copyright. In Reed, C., & Angel, J. (Eds.), *Computer Law*. Oxford: Oxford University Press.

Mnookin, J. (1996). Virtual(ly) Law: The Emergence of Law in LambdaMOO. *Journal of Computer-Mediated Communication, 2*(1).

Mogul. (2004). Interview with John Diamond, Founder of COR Entertainment. *Planetquake.gamespy.com*. Retrieved from http://planetquake.gamespy.com/View.php?view=Articles.Detail&id=346

Moringiello, J.M (2005). Signals, Assent, and Internet Contracting. *Rutgers L. Rev., 57*(1307).

Morningstar, C., & Farmer, F. R. (1991). *The Lessons of LucasFilm's Habitat, in Cyberspace: First Steps*. Retrieved from http://www.fudco.com/chip/lessons.html

Morong, C. (1994 Winter). Mythology, Joseph Campbell, and the Socio-Economic Conflict. *The Journal of Socio-Economics.*

Morse, M. (1994). What do cyborgs eat? Oral Logic in an Information Society. In Bender, G., & Duckrey, T. (Eds.), *Culture on the Brink: Ideologies of Technology*. Seattle, WA: Bay Press.

Mortinger, S. A. (1990). Comment: Spleen for Sale, Moore v Regents of the University of California and the Right to Sell Parts of Your Body. *Ohio St. L. J., 51*(499).

Mossoff, A. (2003). What Is Property? Putting The Pieces Back Together. *Ariz. L. Rev., 45*(371).

Munzer, S. (1990). *A Theory of Property*. Cambridge, UK: Cambridge University Press.

Munzer, S. (1990). *A Theory of Property*. Cambridge, UK: Cambridge University Press.

Murdoch, J. (2006). 612 Lawns. *Gamers With Jobs.* Retrieved from http://www.gamerswithjobs.com/node/26703

Murray, J. (1997). *Hamlet on the Holodeck: The Future of Narrative in Cyberspace*. Cambridge, MA: The MIT Press.

Musgrove, M. (2006, February 2). Sadness in 'Star Wars' World. *Washington Post,* D01.

Nammacher, S. (2002). Financial Valuations for the Practicing Attorney. *Practicing L. Inst., 1325*(647).

Negroponte, N. (1996). *Being Digital*. London: Hodder and Stoughton.

New World Notes. (2006, November 15). Retrieved from http://nwn.blogs.com/nwn/2006/11/second_life_clo.html

Newman, J. (2004). *Videogames*. Abingdon, UK: Routledge.

News, B. B. C. (2005, November 9). *Virtual Property Market Booming*. Retrieved from http://news.bbc.co.uk/go/pr/fr/-/1/hi/technology/4421496.stm

Newton, D. (1999). Comment, What's Right with a Claim-of-Right. *U.S.F. L. Rev., 33*(673).

Nichols, W.J. (2007). Painting Through Pixels: The Case for a Copyright in Videogame Play. *Colum. J.L. & Arts, 30*(101).

Nimmer, M., & Nimmer, D. (2008). *Nimmer on Copyright*. New York: Westlaw.

Nimmer, R., & Krauthaus, P. (1994). Beyond the Internet: Settling the Electronic Frontier. *Stan. L. & Pol'y Rev., 6*(25).

Noveck, B. S. (2005). Trademark Law and The Social Construction of Trust: Creating The Legal Framework for Online Identity. Wash. U. L. Q., 83(1733).

Nozick, R. (1974). *Anarchy, State, and Utopia*. Chicago, IL: Basic Books.

Nozick, R. (1989). *The Examined Life*. New York: Simon & Schuster.

O'Donovan, K. (1997). With Sense, Consent, or Just a Con? Legal Subjects in the Discourses of Autonomy. In Naffine, N., & Owens, R. (Eds.), *Sexing the Subject of Law*. Sydney, Australia: Law Book Company.

O'Rourke, M. A. (2001). Property Rights and Competition on the Internet: In Search of an Appropriate Analogy. *Berkeley Tech. L.J., 16*(561).

O'Rourke, M.A. (1997). Legislative Inaction of the Information Superhighway: Bargaining in the Shadow of Copyright Law. *B.U. J. Sci. & Tech. L. 3*(193).

Olivecrona, K. (1974). Appropriation in the State of Nature: Locke on the Origin of Property. *Journal of the History of Ideas, 35*(211).

Olivenbaum, J. (1997). <Ctrl><Alt><Del>: Rethinking Federal Computer Crime Legislation. *Seton Hall L. Rev., 27*(574).

Olson, D.P. (1983). Copyright Originality. *Mo. L. Rev., 48*(29).

Ondrejka, C. (2004). Escaping the Gilded Cage: User Created Content and Building the Metaverse. *N.Y.L. Sch. L. Rev., 49*(81).

Ondrejka, C. (2005). *Changing Realities: User Creation, Communication, and Innovation in Digital Worlds*. Retrieved from http://www.themis-group.com/uploads/Changing% 20Realities.pdf

Ondrejka, C. (2005, May 7). A \$200 Million Market? *Terra Nova*. Retrieved from http://terranova.blogs.com/terra_nova/2005/05/a_200m_market.html

Ondrejka, C. (2005, November 27). *CTO, Linden Lab, Remarks at the Berkman Center Luncheon Series*.

Online, E. V. E. *Corporation Guide*. (n.d.). Retrieved from http://www.eve-online.com/guide/en/g12.asp

Online, E. V. E. *End User License Agreement*. (n.d.). Retrieved from http://www.eve-online.com/pnp/eula.asp

Online, E. V. E. *EVE Insider Forums*. (n.d.). Retrieved from http://myeve.eve-online.com/ingameboard.asp?a=topic&threadID=347657

Online, E. V. E. *Frequently Asked Questions*. (n.d.). Retrieved from http://www.eve-online.com/faq/faq_01.asp

Online, E. V. E. Press Release. (2006). *EVE Online Reaches the 100,000 Subscriber Mark*. Retrieved from http://www.gamespot.com/pc/rpg/evethesecondgenesis/news.html?sid=6143803

Online, E. V. E. *Terms of Service*. (n.d.). Retrieved from http://www.eve-online.com/pnp/terms.asp

Online, X. (2003, December 19). *Online Game Player Wins 1st Virtual Properties Dispute*. Retrieved from http://news.xinhuanet.com/english/2003-12/19/content_1240226.htm

Ostrovsky, A. (2005, March 1). Investment Dries Up as Rule of Law Seeps Away in Russia. *Financial Times*. Retrieved from http://news.ft.com/cms/s/02384ae2-89f7-11d9-aa18-00000e2511c8.html

Pagliassotti, D. (n.d.). What is Role-playing? *The Harrow: The RPG Collection*. Retrieved from http://www.theharrow.com/rpg/whatisroleplaying.html

Pareles, J. (1997, February 9). Searching for a Sound to Bridge the Decades. *N.Y. Times*, B34.

Parker, S. (2003, June 23). Second Life goes live. *Yahoo! Games*. Retrieved from http://videogames.yahoo.com/newsarticle?eid=434909&page=0

Parloff, R. (2005, November 18). From Megs to Riches. *CnnMoney.com*. Retrieved from http://money.cnn.com/magazines/fortune/fortune_archive/2005/11/28/8361953/index.htm

Pearce, C. (2002). Sims, BattleBots, Cellular Automata God and Go, A Conversation with Will Wright. *International Journal of Computer Game Research, 2*. Retrieved from http://www.gamestudies.org/0202/pearce

Peltz, R. (2002). Use "The Filter You Were Born With": The Constitutionality of Mandatory Internet Filtering for the Adult Patrons of Public Libraries. *Wash. L. Rev., 77*(397).

Penner, J.E. (1996). The Bundle of Rights Picture of Property. *UCLA L. Rev., 43*(711).

Planet Modz Gaming Network. (n.d.). Retrieved from http://www.planetmodz.com/index.php

Playvault.com. (n.d.). Retrieved from http://www.playvault.com

The Pocket Oxford Dictionary. (1975). Oxford: Clarendon Press.

Pollack, P. (2006). Online 'banker' runs off with cash, avatars cry foul. *ArsTechnica*. Retrieved from http://arstechnica.com/news.ars/post/20060828-7605.html

Poole, S. (2000). *Trigger Happy: The Inner Life of Videogames*. London: Arcade.

Posner, R. (2000) *Antitrust in the New Economy*. U. Chicago, John M. Olin Law and Economics Working Paper No. 106.

Poster, M. (1999). Theorizing Virtual Reality. In Ryan, M.-L. (Ed.), *Cyberspace Textuality: Computer Technology and Literary Theory*. Southbend, IN: Indiana University Press.

Poster, M. (1999). Theorizing Virtual Reality. In Ryan, M.-L. (Ed.), *Cyberspace Textuality: Computer Technology and Literary Theory*. Southbend, IN: Indiana University Press.

Poulet, G. (1980). Criticism and the Experience of Interioricity. In Tompkins, J. P. (Ed.), *Reader Response Criticism:*

From Formalism to Post-Structuralism. Baltimore, MD: John Hopkins University Press.

Powell, J.A. (1990). New Property Disaggregated: A Model to Address Employment Discrimination. *U. S.F. L. Rev. 24*(363).

Press Release. (2003 November 14). *Second Life Residents to Own Digital Creations*. Linden Lab. Retrieved from http://lindenlab.com/press/releases/03_11_14

Press Release: Blacksnow Interactive Sues Mythic in Federal Court for MMORG Player's Rights. (n.d.). Retrieved from http://www.kanga.nu/archives/MUD-Dev-L/2002Q1/msg00363.php

Press Release: Second Life Residents to Own Digital Creations. (n.d.). Retrieved from http://lindenlab.com/press_story_12.php

Project Entropia. (n.d.a). EULA, Section 5, "Termination." Retrieved from http://www.project-entropia.com/account/Apply.ajp

Project Entropia. (n.d.b). EULA, Section 6, "Ownership and Transactions." Retrieved from http://www.project-entropia.com/account/Apply.ajp

Prosser, W. (1977). *Law of Torts*. St. Paul, MN: West Publishing.

Provenzo, E. (1991). *Video Kids: Making Sense of Nintendo*. Boston, MA: Harvard University Press.

Radin, M. (1938). A Restatement of Hohfeld. *Harv. L. Rev., 51*(1141).

Radin, M. J. (1993). *Reinterpreting Property*. Chicago, IL: University of Chicago Press.

Radin, M. J. (1996). *Contested Commodities*. Chicago, IL: University of Chicago Press.

Radin, M.J. (1982). Property and Personhood. *Stan. L. Rev., 34*(957).

Ragaini, T. (2002). *Post Mortem: Turbine Entertainment's Asheron's Call*. Retrieved from http://www.gamasutra.com/features/2 0000525/ragaini_02.htm

Rao, R. (2007). Genes and Spleens: Property, Contract or Privacy Rights in the Human Body? *The Journal of Law, Medicine & Ethics, 35*(371).

Rawls, J. (1971). *A Theory of Justice.* Boston, MA: Bellnap Press.

Raysman, R., & Brown, P. (2005, August). Computer Law (virtual property law). *New York Law Journal.*

Read, H. (1974). *A Concise History of Modern Painting.* London: Thames and Hudson.

Reese, R.A. (2001). Copyright and Internet Music Transmissions: Existing Law, Major Controversies, Possible Solutions. *U. Miami L. Rev. 55*(237).

Reese, R.A. (2003). The First Sale Doctrine in the Era of Digital Networks. *B.C. L. Rev. 44*(577).

Reese, R.A. (2008). Transformativeness and the Derivative Work Right, *Colum. J.L. & Arts, 31*(467).

Rehak, B. (2003). Playing at Being: Psychoanalysis and the Avatar. In Wolf, M. J. P., & Perron, B. (Eds.), *The Video Game Theory Reader.* London: Routledge.

Reich, C. (1964). The New Property. *Yale L.J., 73*(733).

Reid, C. (2009). Fair Game: The Application of Fair Use Doctrine to Machinima, *Fordham Intell. Prop. Media & Ent. L.J., 19*(831).

Reid, E. (n.d.). *Text-based Virtual Realities: Identity and the Cyborg Body.* Retrieved from http://www.rochester. edu/College/FS/Publications/ReidIdentity.html

Reputation Guide (n.d.). Retrieved from http://www. worldofwar.net/guides/reputation/

Resnick, P., Zeckhauser, R., Swanson, J., & Lockwood, K. (2006). The Value of Reputation on eBay: A Controlled Experiment. *Experimental Economics, 9*(2). doi:10.1007/ s10683-006-4309-2

Reuveni, E. (2007). On Virtual Worlds: Copyright and Contract Law at the Dawn of the Virtual Age. Ind. L.J., 82(261).

Revesz, R. (1992). Rehabilitating Interstate Competition: Rethinking the "Race-to-the-Bottom" Rationale for Federal Environmental Regulation. *N.Y.U. L. Rev., 67*(1210).

Reynolds, R. (2003). *IPR, Ownership and Freedom in Virtual Worlds.* Retrieved from http://www.ren-reynolds. com/downloads/RReynolds-IPR-CRIC-2003.doc

Reynolds, R. (2005, February 24). *Who's Rulz?* Message posted to Terra Nova. Retrieved from http://www.ter-ranova.blogs.com/terra_nova/2005/02/whos_rulz.html

Richards, N. (2005). Reconciling Data Privacy and the First Amendment. *UCLA L. Rev., 52*(1149).

Richtel, M. (Nov. 28, 2002). *Big Mac Is Virtual, But Critics Are Real,* N.Y. Times, at G8.

Rickey, D. (2003, November 23). Fascism Is Fun. Message posted to Terra Nova. Retrieved from http://terranova. blogs.com/terra_nova/2003/11/index.html Salem, K., & Zimmerman, E. (2004). *Rules of Play: Game Design Fundamentals.* Cambridge, MA: MIT Press.

Riddell, R. (1997). Doom Goes to War: The Marines are Looking for a Few Good Games. *Wired.* Retrieved from http://www.wired.com/wired/archive/5.04/ ff_doom_pr.html

Rollings, A., & Morris, D. (2000). *Game Architecture and Design.* Scottsdale, AZ: Coriolis.

Rooster Teeth. (2007) *Red v Blue.* Retrieved from http:// rvb.roosterteeth.com/home.php

Rose, C.M. (1998). Canon's of Property Talk, or Blackstone's Anxiety. *Yale L.J., 108*(601).

Rouse, R. (2001). *Game Design Theory and Practice.* Plano, TX: Wordware Publishing.

Rubenstein, D. (2004). eBay: The Cyber Swap Meet. *U. Miami Bus. L. Rev., 13*(1).

Rushkoff, D. (1994). *Cyberia: Life in the Trenches of Hyperspace.* New York hypertext Ed. Retrieved from http://www.rushkoff.com/cyberia/

Salem, K., & Zimmerman, E. (2004). *Rules of Play: Game Design Fundamentals.* Cambridge, MA: MIT Press.

Sam Francis Exhibition. (1996 January) Jeu de Paume Museum, Paris.

Samuelson, P. (1989). Information as Property: Do Ruckelshaus and Carpenter Signal a Changing Direction in Intellectual Property Law? *Cath. U. L. Rev., 38*(365).

Samuelson, P. (1994). A Manifesto Concerning the Legal Protection of Computer Programs. *Columbia Law Review, 94*(2308).

Sanders, A. J. (2009). Case Comment: J. K. Rowling and the Lexicon. *E.I.P.R., 45.*

Sandoval, G. (2000, April 10). *Sony to Ban Sale of Online Characters from its Popular Gaming Sites*. Retrieved from http://news.com.com/2102-1017-239052.html

Sax, J. L. (1980). Liberating the Public Trust Doctrine from Its Historical Shackles. *U.C. Davis L. Rev., 14*(185).

Schwartz, A.D. & Bullis, R. (2005). Rivalrous Consumption and the Boundaries of Copyright Law: Property Lessons from Online Games. *Intell. Prop. L. Bull., 10*(13).

Scott, R. (1981). *The Body as Property*. London: A. Lane.

Scott, R. (2003). *Contract Law and Theory* (3rd ed.). New York: LexisNexis Publishing.

Second Life Community Standards. (n.d.). Retrieved from http://secondlife.com/coporate/cs.php

Second Life Wiki. *GJSL*. (n.d.). Retrieved from http://secondlife.com/tiki/tiki-index.php?page=GJSL.

Second Life. Terms of Service and End User License Agreement § 5.3, at http://secondlife.com/tos.php

Second Life--Land. *Islands*. (n.d.). Retrieved from http://secondlife.com/community/land-islands.php

Second Life--Terms of Service. (n.d.). Retrieved from http://secondlife.com/corporate/tos.php

Sellers, M. (2006, January 9). *The Numbers Game*. Retrieved from http://terranova.blogs.com/terra_nova/2006/01/index.html

Sherry, J., Lucas, K., Rechtsteiner, S., Brooks, C., & Wilson, B. (2001). *Videogame Uses and Gratifications as Predictors of Use and Game Preference*. ICA Convention Video Game Research Agenda Theme Session

Panel. Retrieved from http://www.icdweb/cc/purdue.edu/~sherry/videogames/VGUG.pdf

Shy, O. (2001). *The Economics of Network Industries*. Cambridge, UK: Cambridge University Press.

Simpson, Z. B. (1999). *The In-game Economics of Ultima Online*. Retrieved from http://www.mine-control.com/zack/uoecon/uoecon.html

Singer, J.W. (1992). Re-reading Property. *New Eng. L. Rev. 27*(711).

Sipress, A. (2006, December 26). Where Real Money Meets Virtual Reality, the Jury is Still Out. *The Washington Post*. Retrieved from http://www.washingtonpost.com/wp-dyn/content/article/2006/23/25/AR2006122500635.html

Smed (John Smedley President, Sony Online Entertainment). (n.d.). Message posted to Everquest II Official Forums. Retrieved from http://eqiiforums.station.sony.com/eq2/board/message?board.id=stex&message

Smedley, J. (Nov. 9, 2005). President of Sony Online Entertainment, interview at *Sony Online Discusses the MMO Market*, Bus. Wk. Online, http://www.businessweek.com/innovate/content/nov2005/id20051109_602467.htm

Smith, A. (2001, February 12). 3D Realms Fences in Foxing Fans. *The Register*. Retrieved from http://www.theregister.co.uk/2001/02/12/3d_realms_fencing_in_foxing/

Smith, A. (2001, January 25). Everquest Class Action Threat Over Auction Spat. *The Register*. Retrieved from http://www.theregister.co.uk/2001/01/25/everquest_class_action_threat_over/

Snider, M. (2003, June 24). When Multiplayer Worlds Collide. *USA Today*,1D.

Sommer, J.H. (2000). Against Cyberlaw. *Berkeley Tech. L.J., 15*(1145).

Spring, S. (2006). Games: Virtual Thievery. *Newsweek,* 10.

Star Wars Galaxies. (n.d.). Policies Index. Retrieved from http://www.starwarsgalaxies.station.sony.com/en_US/players/content.ym?page=Policies%20Index&resource=policies

Star Wars Galaxies. (n.d.). Retrieved from http://starwarsgalaxies.station.sony.com/features/faq_pages/faq_2.jsp#201

Stefanescu, T. (2006). EVE Online Economy Suffers 700 Billion ISK Scam. *Softpedia.* Retrieved from http://news.softpedia.com/news/Eve-Online-Economy-Suffers-700-billion-ISK-Scam-33737.shtml

Stephens, M. (2002). Note, Sales of In-Game Assets: An Illustration of the Continuing Failure of Intellectual Property Law to Protect Digital-Content Creators. *Tex. L. Rev., 80*(1513).

Sterling, J. A. L. (1998). Creators' Rights and the Bridge Between Authors' Rights and Copyright. In INTERGU (Ed.), Shutz von Kulture und geistigen Eigentum in der Informationsgesellschaft. Amsterdam: Nomos Verlag.

Steuer, J. (1992). Defining Virtual Reality: Dimensions Determining Telepresence. *The Journal of Communication, 42*(4). doi:10.1111/j.1460-2466.1992.tb00812.x

Stewart, T. A. (1997). *Intellectual Capital: The New Wealth of Organizations.* New York: Currency.

Stock, G. (2002). *Redesigning Humans: Our Inevitable Genetic Future.*

Stokes, S. (2001). *Art and Copyright.* Oxford: Hart Publishing.

Strickler, J. (2002, May 19). Skywalker Ranch: George Lucas creates a magic world in real life found. *Star Tribune.* Retrieved from http://www.startribune.com/stories/411/2839700.html

Suler, J. (2002). Identity Management in Cyberspace. *Journal of Applied Psychoanalytic Studies, 4*(455).

Taylor, C. (1989). *Sources of the Self: The Making of Modern Identity.* Cambridge, UK: Cambridge University Press.

TechTarget. (n.d.). *MP3.* Whatis.com definition. Retrieved from http://whatis.techtarget.com/definition/0,sid9_gci212600,00.html

Terdiman, D. (2004 February). When Play Money becomes Real. *Wired Magazine.*

Terdiman, D. (2004, February 13). No Will To Keep Uru Live Alive. *Wired News.* Retrieved from http://www.wired.com/news/games/0,2101,62253.html

Terdiman, D. (2004, January 23). Virtual Cash turns into Real Greed. *Wired Magazine.*

Terdiman, D. (2004, July 16). Online Games a Massive Pain. *Wired News.* Retrieved from http://www.wired.com/news/games/0,2101,64153,00.html

Terdiman, D. (2005, January 22). Dealing with Great Expectations. *Wired News.* Retrieved from http://www.wired.com/news/ebiz/0,1272,66362,00.html

Terdiman, D. (2005, October 29). Making the Virtual World a Better Place. *CNET News.com.* Retrieved from http://news.com.com/2102-1043_3-5920694.html

Terdiman, D. (2005, September 8). 'Second Life' Membership Now Free. *CNET News.com.* Retrieved from http://marketwatch-cnet.com.com/Second+Life+membership+now+free/2100-1043_3-5855481.html Terdiman, D. (2005, November 3). Online Feuds a Big Headache. *Wired.* Retrieved from http://www/wired.com/news/games/0,2101,65562,00.html

Terdiman, D. (2006). Phony Kids, Virtual Sex. *CNET News.* Retrieved from http://news.com.com/Phony+kids+virtual+sex/2100-1043_3-6060132.html

Terdiman, D. (2006, December 14). 'Second Life' hits second million in eight weeks. *Cnet News.* Retrieved from http://news.com.com/2061-10797_3-6143909.html?part=rss&tag=2547-1_3-0-5&subj=news

Terdiman, D. (May 8, 2004). *Fun in Following the Money,* Wired Magazine.

Terdiman, D. Virtual Trade Tough Nut to Crack, *Wired,* Dec. 20, 2004, at www.wired.com/news/avantgo/story/0,2278,66074-00.html.

Terms of Service and End User License Agreement for Second Life § 5.3. (n.d.). Retrieved from http://secondlife.com/tos.php

Terra Nova Blogs. (2008). Retrieved from http://www.terranova.blogs.com.

Terrett, A., & Monaghan, I. (2000). The Internet – An Introduction for Lawyers. In Edwards, L., & Waelde, C. (Eds.), *Law & the Internet: a framework for electronic commerce*. Oxford, UK: Hart Publishing.

The Censorware Project, Blacklisted by Cyber Patrol: From Ada to Yoyo. (1997, December 25). Retrieved from http://censorware.net/reports/cyberpatrol/ada-yoyo.html

The Guiding Hand. (n.d.). *Leader's announcement and discussion thread*. Retrieved from http://tinyurl.com/8jglz

The Unknown Player. (2003, June 5). *Have you Guys missed Me? Blacksnow sure has.* Retrieved from http://www.unknownplayer.com/modules.php?op=modload&name=News&file=article&sid=1517

There. (n.d.). *Terms of Service (TOS): Behaviour Guidelines*. Retrieved from http://webapps.prod.there.com/login/73.xml Tiebout, C. (1956). A Pure Theory of Local Expenditures. *J. Pol. Econ. 64*(416).

Todorov, T. (1980). Reading as Construction. In Suleiman, S. R., & Crosman, I. (Eds.), *The Reader in The Text*. Princeton, NJ: Princeton University Press.

Totilo, S. (2004, November 11). Do-It-Yourselfers Buy Into This Virtual World. *N.Y. Times,* G5.

Turkle, S. (1995). *Life on the Screen: Identity in the Age of the Internet*. New York: Simon & Schuster.

Turner, M. (1995). Do the Old Legal Categories Fit the New Multimedia Products? A Multimedia CD-Rom as a Film. *E.I.P.R., 3*(107).

Twist, J. (2005). Picturing Online Gaming's Value. *BBC News*. Retrieved from http://news.bbc.co.uk/go/pr/fr/-/l/hi/technology/4360654.stm

Ultima Online License Agreement. (n.d.). Retrieved from http://www.uo.com/agreement.html

Ultima Online Renaissance Playguide. (2000). Retrieved from http://www.uo.com/guide/renaissance.pdf

Ultima Online Visitor's Center. *What is a Virtual World?*(n.d.). Retrieved from http://www.uo.com/visitor/whatisvw.html

Ultima Online. (n.d.). *New Player Guide*. Retrieved from http://www.uo.com/newplayer/newplay_0.html

Ultima, O. R. P. (2000). Retrieved from http://www.uo.com/guide/renaissance.pdf

Underkuffler, L.S. (1990). On Property: An Essay. *Yale L.J., 100*(127).

United States Copyright Office. (2001). *DMCA Section 104 Report*. Retrieved from http://www.copyright.gov/reports/studies/dmca/sec-104-report-vol-1.pdf

United States Copyright Office. (2001). *Executive Summary Digital Millennium Copyright Act, Section 104 Report*. Retrieved from http://www.copyright.gov/reports/studies/dmca/dmca_executive.html

United States Copyright Office. (2001a). *DMCA Section 104 Report*. Retrieved from http://www.copyright.gov/reports/studies/dmca/sec-104-report-vol-1.pdf

Van Alstyne, W. (1977). Cracks in The New Property: Adjudicative Due Process and the Administrative State. *Cornell L. Rev., 62*(445).

Van Zelfden, N. E. (2005, November 11). MMO Giants Prepare for War. *Business Week Online*. Retrieved from http://www.businessweek.com/innovate/content/nov2005/id20051111_428174.htm

VerSteeg, R. (1993). Rethinking Originality. *Wm., & Mary L. Rev., 34*(801).

VerSteeg, R. (1996). Defining 'Author' for Purposes of Copyright. *Am. U.L. Rev., 45*(1323).

Virtual Game, A Double-edged Sword Hanging Over Real World in China. (2005, June 22). Xinhua Econ. News Service.

Virtual Words Review. (2008). *Index*. Retrieved from http://www.virtualworldsreview.com/index.shtml

Wagner, R.P. (1999). Filters and the First Amendment. *Minn. L. Rev., 83*(755).

Waldron, J. (1988). *The Right to Private Property*. New York: Clarendon Paperbacks.

Wallace, M. (2005). Simply Amazing. *Walkerings.* Retrieved from http://www.walkering.com/walkerings/2005/08/simply_amazing.html

Wallace, M. (2006). EVE Online Mega-Corporation Goes Public. *3pointD.com.* Retrieved from http://www.3pointd.com/20061214/eve-online-mega-corporation-goes-public/#more-962

Walsh, M. (2004). *I, Product.* Wired Magazine.

Walton, G. (n.d.). *Online Worlds Roundtable #8, Part 1.* Retrieved from http://rpgvault.ign.com/articles/455/455832p2.html

Weinberg, J. (1997). Rating the Net. *Hastings Comm. & Ent. L.J., 19*(453).

Weisberg, R. (1993). *Creativity: Beyond the Myth of Genius.* New York: W.H. Freeman & Company.

Weiser, M. (1991, Sept.). The Computer for the 21st Century. *Scientific American,* 94. doi:10.1038/scientificamerican0991-94

Weiser, M., & Brown, J. S. (1996). *The Coming Age of Calm Technology.* XeroxPARC. Retrieved from http://www.ubiq.com/hypertext/weiser/acmfuture2endnote.htm

Wellner, P. Mackay, W. & Gold, R. (1993). Computer-Augmented Environments: Back to the Real World. *Commc'ns of the ACM, 36*(24).

Westbrook, T. J. (2006). Comment, Owned: Finding a Place for Virtual World Property Rights. *Mich. St. L. Rev., 2006*(779). Wikipedia, Mod (Computer Gaming), http://en.wikipedia.org/wiki/Mod_(computer_gaming).

White and Williams. LLP, *Virtual Land Lawsuit Reveals Dark Side of Second Life,* Yubanet.com, Oct. 6, 2006, http://www.yubanet.com/cgi-bin/artman/exec/view.cgi/22/43381

Wikipedia, Virtual World, http://en.wikipedia.org/wiki/Virtual_world

Wikipedia.org. (n.d.). *Owned.* Retrieved from http://en.wikipedia.org/wiki/Owned

Wikipedia.org. (n.d.). *Shard.* Retrieved from http://en.wikipedia.org/wiki/Shard

Wiley, Jr., J.S. (1991). Copyright at the School of Patent. *U. Chi. L. Rev., 58*(119).

Williams, A., Callow, D., & Lee, A. (1996). *Multimedia: Contracts, Rights, and Licensing.* London: FT Tax & Law.

Wolf, M. J. P., & Perron, B. (Eds.). (2003). *The Video Game Theory Reader.* London: Routledge.

Woodcock, B. S. (2008). *An Analysis of MMOG Subscription Growth.* Retrieved from http://www.mmogchart/com

Woodcock, B. S. (2008). *An Analysis of MMOG Subscription Growth.* Retrieved from http://www.mmogchart/com

World of Warcraft Community Site, *Selling World of Warcraft In-Game Content for Real Money,* at http://www.worldofwarcraft.com/news/announcements.html

World of Warcraft: Terms of Use Agreement. (2009). Retrieved from http://www.worldofwarcraft.com/legal/termsofuse.html

Wright, R. (2001). *Nonzero: The Logic of Human Destiny.* New York: Vintage.

Wu, T. (2000). When Law & the Internet First Met. *Green Bag, 3*(171).

Yee, N. (2004). The Daedalus Project. Retrieved from http://www.nickyee.com/daedalus

Yee, N. (n.d.). *The Norrathian Scrolls: Real-Life Demographics.* Retrieved from http://nickyee.com/eqt/demographics.html

Yen, A. C. (2002). Western Frontier or Feudal Society?: Metaphors and Perceptions of Cyberspace. *Berkeley Tech. L.J., 17*(1207).

Yi, M. (2003, June 23). Online Game Bets on Self-Expression: Linden Lab's Second Life Premieres Today. *S.F. The Chronicle,* E1.

Yu, P. (2005). Intellectual Property and the Information Ecosystem. Mich. St. L. Rev 1.

Zemer, L. (2006). The Making of a New Copyright Lockean. *Harvard Journal of Law & Public Policy, 29*(3), 891.

Zimmer, L. (2000). *Identity versus Reputation: Wandering and Wondering in Virtual Spaces*. Retrieved from http://freshtakes.typepad.com/sl_communicators/2007/05/identity_versus.html

Zjawinski, S. (2006 April). The Players. *Wired Magazine.*

About the Author

Angela Adrian started her career in business after acquiring a Masters degree from Schiller International University in London. After working for a number of years, she decided to focus on law. She received her Juris Doctorate from Loyola University, New Orleans. She then became a qualified attorney in Louisiana. After practising for a few years, she specialised in Commercial Law and gained an LLM with distinction from the University of Aberdeen. Concurrently, she became a solicitor in England and Wales. Ms. Adrian practiced for a while before becoming an academic. She then pursued a PhD in which she explored the nature of law in virtual worlds. This book reflects that research. Ms. Adrian remains in the academic world where she teaches Intellectual Property Law, Commercial Law, Contract Law, and International Trade Law. Her research interests are intellectual property, virtual reality, money laundering, commercial law, international trade law, oil and gas law, and entertainment law.

Index